CONSTANT MINDS:
POLITICAL VIRTUE AND THE LIPSIAN PARADIGM
IN ENGLAND, 1584–1650

# THE MENTAL AND CULTURAL WORLD OF TUDOR AND STUART ENGLAND

Editors

Paul Christianson
Camille Slights
D.R. Woolf

ADRIANA McCREA

# Constant Minds: Political Virtue and the Lipsian Paradigm in England, 1584–1650

UNIVERSITY OF TORONTO PRESS
Toronto Buffalo London

© University of Toronto Press Incorporated 1997
Toronto Buffalo London
Printed in Canada

ISBN 0-8020-0666-3

∞

Printed on acid-free paper

B
785
.L4
M33
1998

---

**Canadian Cataloguing in Publication Data**

McCrea, Adriana Alice Norma, 1951–
 Constant minds : political virtue and the Lipsian
paradigm in England, 1584–1650

(The mental and cultural world of Tudor and Stuart England)
Includes bibliographical references and index.
ISBN 0-8020-0666-3

1. Lipsius, Justus, 1547–1606 – Influence.  2. Political
science – England – History – 16th century.  3. Political
science – England – History – 17th century.  4. Humanists
– England.  I. Title.  II. Series.

JC145.L8M23 1997    320'.0942'09032    C97-930192-0

---

University of Toronto Press acknowledges the financial assistance to its
publishing program of the Canada Council and the Ontario Arts Council.

This book has been published with the help of a grant from the
Humanities and Social Sciences Federation of Canada, using funds
provided by the Social Sciences and Humanities Research Council of
Canada.

*Dedicado a mi mamá
y
a la memoria de mi querido papá*

# Contents

LIST OF FIGURES   ix
ACKNOWLEDGMENTS   xi
A NOTE ON TEXTS, SOURCES, TRANSLATIONS, AND CONVENTIONS   xv
PROLOGUE: RECOVERING THE LIPSIAN PARADIGM   xix

**Introduction: Justus Lipsius and the Doctrine of Constancy**   3
   Seneca, Tacitus, and the Moral Universe of Neostoicism   5
   The Linguistic Universe of Neostoicism   11
   The Politics of Neostoicism   16
   Doctrine: The Method of Constancy   21
   Neostoicism in France   26
   Lipsius and English Humanism   31

**Chapter 1   The Constant Courtier: Sir Walter Ralegh in Jacobean England**   40
   Ralegh and the *vita activa*   41
   Ralegh on Seneca and Tacitus   48
   Ralegh and Political Prudence   55
   Ralegh's Legacy   65

**Chapter 2   Francis Bacon and the Advancement of Constancy**   71
   Bacon and the Crisis in Learning   72
   Bacon and the Crisis in Humanism   75
   The *Advancement of Learning* as Apologia for Tacitism   79

viii  Contents

    Bacon and the Stoics   87
    Bacon on Fortune, Virtue, and Prudence   90
    Bacon and the *vita contemplativa*   96

**Chapter 3   The Constant Friend: Fulke Greville's Life after Sidney**   102
    Greville and the *vita activa*   106
    Right Reason and Grevillean Constancy   113
    Greville, Knowledge, and Prudence   120
    Greville, Virtue, and Counsel   128
    Greville, Authority, and Obedience   133

**Chapter 4   A Neostoic Scout: Ben Jonson and the Poetics of Constancy**   138
    Life and Circle   139
    Learning, Humanism, and Religion: Jonson's Road to
      Constancy   145
    Politics and the Poetry of Constancy   155

**Chapter 5   Joseph Hall and 'That Proud Inconstant Lipsius': The English Face of Neostoicism?**   171
    The Making of 'our English Seneca'   172
    Competing Moral Paradigms: Hall versus Bacon   184
    Hall and Theophrastus versus Tacitus   191
    Hall, Obedience, and Authority   196

EPILOGUE: CONSTANCY IN THE ENGLISH REVOLUTION   206
NOTES   213
BIBLIOGRAPHY   295
INDEX   331

# List of Figures

1 Portrait of Lipsius in *Iusti Lipsi Opera Omnia*   xxi
2 Frontispiece, *Iusti Lipsi Opera Omnia*   25
3 Frontispiece, Pierre Charron, *Of Wisdome*, trans. S. Lennard   28
4 Frontispiece and Jonson's 'The Minde of the Front' from Walter Ralegh, *History of the World*   68–9
5 *Impresa* of the Plantin Press from C. Cornelius Tacitus, *Opera quae extant.*   142
6 Jonson's autographed motto on his copy of Lipsius, *De Militia Romana*   156
7 Parody of Lipsius in *Mundus Alter et Idem* (1643 edition; first published 1605)   176
8 Portrait of Lipsius, frontispiece to his edition of Seneca's *Opera Omnia*   177
9 Frontispiece, Joseph Hall, *The Shaking of the Olive-Tree*   181
10 Title-page, R. Fletcher, *Mercurius Heliconicus* (Numb. 2)   210

# Acknowledgments

*Constant Minds* has evolved from my PhD thesis, entitled 'Neostoicism in England: The Impact of Justus Lipsius' Neostoic Synthesis in England, 1584–1650,' defended at Queen's University at Kingston, Ontario, in September 1991. My supervisor, Paul K. Christianson, critically encouraged my enterprise in those days as he still does, and my board of examiners included Ian Gentles, Bert Hamilton, James Stayer, and the late George Rawlyk. I owe each of these individuals a great debt in helping me refine my ideas, bringing the thesis closer to its present shape. Daniel Woolf, Tom Mayer, Ernest Sprott, and F.J. Levy (as well as a number of anonymous readers) read later drafts of the work and I have benefitted from their critical insights. To them I extend my gratitude for their time and interest, and if my conclusions differ from the suggestions they have offered it is not for their lack of good counsel but my own determination to establish the flexibility of an ideological approach to society best exemplified by Lipsius and to show how English thinkers of the period were of a mind-set similar to that of the Fleming. Thus I hope to overcome modern preconceptions and also show the close intellectual affinities between English and Continental thinkers in the period in question.

This book would never have been begun, much less brought to a conclusion, without much other generous support and encouragement. I am grateful to the Social Sciences and Humanities Research Council of Canada for two years of post-doctoral funding which gave me time to pursue work on a related topic; this in turn helped me refine ideas for the subject of this book. Long ago, two teachers at Trent University inspired my studies and encouraged my endeavours: Elizabeth M. Orsten of the English Department, and David Page of the Classical

Studies Department. To them I offer heartfelt and continuing thanks. I must also draw attention to the inspiration of my first teacher in early modern British and European political thought, David Wootton, whose own work and teaching methods have been a model I only wish I could emulate. My labours in my present area of study have been eased by Ernest Sprott, who generously loaned me his copy of the 1675 edition of Lipsius's *Opera Omnia* from which two illustrations are reproduced in this book. And besides sharing the fruits of his own research with me, Daniel Woolf not only helped me procure documents from afar but also alerted me to the resources available to an early modern scholar right here in Nova Scotia. In this respect I offer thanks to Mark Bartlett, of TUNS in Halifax, for his gift of a copy of the catalog *Pre-1701 Imprints in Nova Scotia* (Halifax, 1994); and also to Drake Petersen, Patricia Chalmers, and other members of the staff at The Library, University of King's College, and to Karen Smith and the staff at Special Collections, Killam Library, Dalhousie University, for their good spirits in meeting my numerous requests for rare books; thanks, too, to Findlay Muir, of Instructional Media Service, Dalhousie University, who kindly slotted my request for photographs into his own busy schedule. I am also grateful to Richard Childs, County Archivist at the West Sussex Records Office, for his speedy response to a query; and to Walter Hannam, Classics Department, Dalhousie University, for responding to a last-minute question on Latin.

The extent of intellectual debts I have incurred in producing the main arguments of this book will be apparent from my notes, but I must single out the help of Mark Morford, not only for his inspiring work but for his prompt response to an urgent last-minute request on the location of documents. And for seeing the book from manuscript through to print, I extend my gratitude to the editorial staff at the University of Toronto Press. The questions put to me by Dr Mirian Skey have helped refine my prose; and I am most grateful to Suzanne Rancourt and Barb Porter for extending me patience and support when their production schedule was interrupted by eventualities at my end. *Constant Minds* has survived fire and flood; in the end and thanks to my own recent experience, some of the morals mapped out in this book (perseverence and adaptability to circumstances) have had application in seeing it through to print. Of course, notwithstanding all the support and help of which I may boast, it remains true that any flaws remaining in the book – any deficiency of argument or infelicity of language, prose, or style – are my own responsibility.

*Constant Minds* asserts that the main priority in the lives of the subjects it discusses was the *vita activa*, derived from the application of learning to action. In my own case, learning is a way of life, but life itself gains importance from other quarters – from those whom I love. I last saw my father, George McCrea, as I set off to begin PhD studies at Kingston in September 1986; he died suddenly a month later. He was confident my studies would be productive; I only wish he could be here to share these their first fruits. I dedicate the book to his memory and to my mother, Ana, who has supported me financially and emotionally through many rough times. My brother David and his family are also always on call for support; and I owe a special debt to my brother George, who provides me with bed, board, and recreation whenever research takes me to London. More recently, George did me an invaluable service by helping me acquire some much needed material from London before setting off himself for India. My children, Lola and Beau, have kept me in tune with contemporary forms of discourses; they bring laughter and joy into our world. Lastly, this book would never have reached this stage were it not for Aleksander Simonič, my husband. Alex has shared his precious work station with me, allowing *Constant Minds* to intrude into the time and energy he has needed for completing *WinEdt*. Beyond that, he has given over his own expertise in preparing the final version of the manuscript for submission to the Press, as well as providing me with much needed intellectual and spiritual stimulation. Alex and I are both indebted to Sir Walter Ralegh for the sustenance provided by tobacco (and we are both convinced Ralegh was not the traitor the recent find suggests), but it is to Alex that I owe more than can be expressed in a preface to a scholarly study.

# A Note on Texts, Sources, Translations, and Conventions

A full list of the texts consulted (and others pertaining to the subject) appears in the Bibliography at the end of the book. I supply full bibliographic identification the first time a work is mentioned in each chapter. In quoting from any source I have tried to maintain fidelity to it; thus spelling and punctuation are reproduced as encountered, and any departure from that rule is signalled by the use of square brackets. I have also opted to follow the growing convention among historians (in America if not the United Kingdom) to spell Sir Walter Ralegh's surname without an 'i.'

In my use of primary sources, I have preferred standard, printed editions where possible but have also leaned heavily on original publications, as mediated through microfilm and either the *Short-Title Catalogue of Books Printed ... 1475–1641* (*STC*) or the *Short-Title Catalogue of Books Printed ... 1641–1700* (*STC* [ed. Wing]). Thus I have consulted and quoted from the standard editions of the writings of Bacon, Greville, and Jonson, while relying, for Ralegh and Hall, on the original publications. I have used the modern editions of Tacitus, though for Seneca I rely throughout on the seventeenth-century translation of his work by Thomas Lodge. In all cases, the first reference to an early-modern publication in any given chapter will include its *STC* number.

I have been rather more eclectic in dealing with the writings of Lipsius. As scholars in the field know only too well, the sheer volume of his writings (compounded by the multiplicity of editions and his own editorial habits) makes the task of studying him that much more difficult. I have had access to a copy of the 1584 edition of *De Constantia*; otherwise I've had to rely on those works of his published in London, the 1675 edition of his *Opera Omnia*, and, as well as the contemporary

English translations, the scholarship of others. In the belief that we inhabit a modern commonwealth of letters, I have taken full advantage of this scholarship, freely borrowing text quotations, source citations and, on a number of occasions, translations. Similar problems of accessibility to the writings of Guillaume du Vair, Jean Duvergier, Isaac Casaubon, and others who make a brief appearance in *Constant Minds*, also led me to rely on the work of others. All such debts are acknowledged in the notes.

Each chapter, save the introduction, opens with one or more epigraphs. I have elected to fully identify these when the occasion requires – that is, when an allusion or reference in the text of the chapter makes it necessary. Throughout the book I use the term 'neostoicism' as a shorthand for 'the Lipsian paradigm,' preferring the latter when possible but not hesitating to use the former, according, that is, to the definition given in the Prologue and Introduction. As well, 'constancy' is sometimes set, as here, within quotation marks, a form adopted to stress its Lipsian connotations and draw attention to the ambiguity of its use, as particular contexts will suggest. I have tried to keep in mind present-day sensibilities and limit my use of the word 'man,' opting instead for the generic 'individual.' It bears emphasizing, nevertheless, that the issues discussed in *Constant Minds* revolve around *political* individuals. The early-modern mind would not question that such entities referred to very gendered, distinguished, elite, and cultured males. On the other hand, it is true that, as modern parlance would have it, I am dealing throughout the book with a number of 'dead, white dudes.'

The fact that they are dead has played a different sort of function in the organization of this book. Had I been guided by dates of compositions or publications, or by particular themes common to various authors, chapters 1 to 5 might easily have been reversed. I have chosen instead to order them according to the chronology of their authors' deaths. Thus Ralegh (d. 1618) is followed by Bacon (d. 1626), then Greville (d. 1628), Jonson (d. 1633), and finally Hall (d. 1656). It also happens that Lipsius grows in importance as the book proceeds. While with Ralegh and Bacon the neostoic writings of the Fleming serve mainly as illustration, with Greville, Jonson, and Hall they present firmer measures of comparison and, at times, form a clear parallel. It might be objected that this book could have been written differently, without giving such prominence to individuals and adopting a scheme that smacks of old-fashioned liberalism. To have organized *Constant Minds* according to themes, however, would have altered the book substantially, suggesting the existence of a system of ideas without allowing for the extent of difference within that system. It would also have resulted in the neglect of due emphasis on the circumstances that informed those ideas, contexts that made them relevant, and assumptions that underlay them – not to mention the difference of personality among the individuals expressing them. While the present organization has necessitated a certain amount of repetition, it projects, I hope, a unique historical appreciation of its several subjects and allows the contingency of their lives – and the 'constant minds' they presented – to be made evident.

# Prologue

# Recovering the Lipsian Paradigm

> My figure and face are not unpleasing. ... I have an honest appearance, I am modest in spirit, with a docile nature, and apt in most things, excepting music. Besides clear and direct judgement, I have a memory which, even in my youth, astonished my teachers, and which now, although weaker, has not forsaken me. In public, I speak with facility and not without grace; in private company, I am more restrained and less pleasant. Style and ideas come easy to me. ... My dress is as simple as my demeanour and my conversation, and there have been many times when strangers, on seeing me, have asked where is Lipsius. For the rest, I have loved good things and also good people, who have, in turn, loved me. I have cultivated knowledge, even more wisdom; I have avoided quarrels and shunned honours.
>
> (Justus Lipsius, self-portrait, 1600)

This book is an exercise in the history of ideas, revisiting the thought of five Englishmen of some stature: Sir Walter Ralegh, Francis Bacon, Fulke Greville, Ben Jonson, and Bishop Joseph Hall. All are well known to students of early modern English history, literature, and political thought, though each is usually studied according to now specialized concerns, methods, and assumptions within particular disciplines. In my representation of their thinking, I have attempted to reintegrate both modern trends in scholarship and the various components in the ideas of my subjects. Thus I have sought to recapture the contemporary direction and relevance of their thought.

In consequence, Ralegh, Bacon, Greville, Jonson, and Hall become the 'constant minds' of my title. This descriptive term refers to the philosophy of 'constancy' which I argue lies at the heart of much political discussion in England during the period covered by this book. My study focuses on a complex of preoccupations on the part of these (and many

xx  Prologue

other) early modern Englishmen – preoccupations with political participation, virtue, the disjuncture between private and public virtue, and the lessons of history. The reference point for elucidating the thought of Ralegh et al is a European world in which such preoccupations were most fully addressed by the Flemish philologist, Justus Lipsius, who lived from 1547 to 1606. The writings of Lipsius (Joest Lips, in the Flemish vernacular), I suggest, offer a 'paradigm' against which to situate the writings of the English humanists and politicians studied here.[1] Such a paradigm, however, should be understood less as a tightly integrated system of discourse than as exemplum. Yet, by adapting the Kuhnian idea of paradigm and applying it as an *interpretative tool*, Lipsius also presents *us* with a model against which to gauge the writings of others, while his own writings simultaneously offer a framework against which we can discern the expansion and development of such a model.[2]

In examining the consitituent elements of such a Lipsian paradigm, we begin by entering an international (European) community in which no strict line of demarcation distinguished scholars as a race apart, when learning enfolded within its ranks not only academics, but statesmen, churchmen, and amateur literati to boot.[3] Lipsius belonged to this community, providing it with editions of the works of Tacitus and Seneca that remained authoritative for centuries, and composing for it a number of writings based on his scholarship that became immensely popular and widely acclaimed. His particular originality – and thus his contribution to the contemporary literary-political culture – lay in his construction of 'neostoicism,' which taught 'prudence' as an approach to political issues and promoted 'constancy' as a justification for political engagement. *De constantia libri duo* (1584), and *Politicorum sive civilis doctrinae libri sex* (1589), exemplified, even as they articulated, a 'modern' philosophy of neostoicism, which, as the following introductory chapter will reveal, was as much a method as a set of political prescriptions. Lipsius believed that these two works, written in the language of the diplomacy and scholarship of the day, would last as long as Latin letters.[4] They did.

Even as Lipsius wrote, however, the ascendancy of Latin was being challenged, reflected in the very fact that, popular as the original editions of his writings were, translations into 'the principal languages of Europe' quickly followed.[5] In view of this assault, well might the champion of the Latin tongue himself have asked, 'Where is Lipsius?' (see figure 1).[6] Nowadays, his name is virtually unknown outside academic circles, his thought still fully unexplored, and his relevance remains

1 Portrait of Lipsius in *Iusti Lipsi Opera Omnia* (Wesel 1675). Reproduced with permission from S.E. Sprott.

underestimated. For example, in Quentin Skinner's important study, *Foundations of Modern Political Thought*, 2 vols. (Cambridge, 1978), Lipsius is viewed as an apostle of resignation, a transitory figure in a period which culminated with the philosophy of political obedience adumbrated by Thomas Hobbes, as Skinner argues that neostoicism articulated a cardinal obligation 'to submit to the existing order of things, never resisting the prevailing government but accepting and where necessary enduring it with fortitude' (II, p. 279).

True, Lipsius said as much in *De constantia* – but not in a wholly resigned tone and only after promoting a revised version of the well-known virtue of 'constancy.' Moreover, he was deeply concerned with the idea of the moral validity of political action, and if *De constantia* was an exercise in spelling out how the individual might attain the Lipsian sense of constancy and persevere in a political society bursting at the seams, the *Politica* sought to establish the grounds of moral governance in the context of a bellicose Reformation Europe. As fundamental to understanding Lipsian neostoicism as *De constantia*, the *Politica* is virtually ignored as Skinner presents his analysis, placing Lipsius beside Montaigne in articulating a philosophy of political submission.[7]

In a series of related articles and studies, Richard Tuck has in many ways broadened Skinner's version of early modern political thought while accepting and developing what is seen as the transitional role played by Lipsius in the intellectual history of the period. In *Hobbes* (Oxford, 1989), Tuck argues that Lipsius was as crucial as Montaigne in anticipating Hobbes's claim of self-preservation as a principle defining human nature and conduct. According to Tuck, 'what for Lipsius and Montaigne had been an ineluctable and natural principle of human conduct, namely self-preservation, becomes in Hobbes the fundamental *right* upon which a new kind of ethics can be constructed' (p. 11).[8] Recently revising his Skinnerian approach in *Philosophy and Government 1572–1651* (Cambridge, 1993), Tuck delineates the emergence of a 'new humanism' in the late sixteenth and early seventeenth centuries and draws on Lipsius's uses of Tacitus to acknowledge his role in the formation of a *prudential* approach to politics. Though still operating to elucidate the background to the later and more formally 'natural rights' theorists like Selden, Grotius, and, of course, Hobbes, this new humanism was characterized by its uses of Tacitism, the dynamic element in its formation and expression. Thus if neostoicism taught political disengagement in response to the dilemmas provoked by the European Wars of Religion, Tacitism, itself a technique adopted by Lipsius as a means of understanding the dilemmas provoked by those wars, offered a way to transcend them.

A number of other scholars have noted the emergence in the 1590s of what they might rather label a 'Lipsian moment.' According to Gerhard Oestreich, and following him, I.A.A. Thompson and J.H. Elliott, such a phenomenon can be identified as Lipsius harnessed classical learning and passed on to contemporaries and following generations the 'value to be attached to the Roman virtues of discipline, command and obedience.'[9] Oestreich also contends that the Lipsian emphasis on discipline was adopted in German lands, leading to the rise of the modern military state. Indeed, commanders in the Austrian Hapsburg army, and many others, studied Lipsius who, following Machiavelli, produced commentaries on Polybius and a famous military treatise, *De Militia Romana* (1595). Machiavelli's particular dynamism, however, is a feature entirely absent in Lipsian writings, even though Lipsius admired and respected his predecessor's political insight, openly stating that admiration in a Preface of his *Politica*, having in that work transformed the Machiavellian idea of *virtù* into the Lipsian precept of *prudentia mixta*.[10]

Important distinctions between Machiavelli and Lipsius emerge from the ways in which Lipsius privileged the wisdom of the past while Machiavelli merely sought to utilize it for present purposes (a point that is fully analysed in the introductory chapter). But the role of scholarship and language for Lipsius and subsequent humanists is as much unexplored by Tuck as it is by Robert Bireley in his study, *The Counter-Reformation Prince: Anti-Machiavellianism or Catholic Statecraft in Early Modern Europe* (Chapel Hill and London, 1990). Seemingly oblivious to Lipsius's rhetorical sleights of hand and philological goals, Bireley portrays him as a founder of the anti-Machiavellian tradition of the seventeenth century. Rather than accepting this verdict, I shall argue that Lipsius was about as much an anti-Machiavellian as the English clergyman Joseph Hall an anti-Lipsian. Although there was a real animosity behind his challenge to Lipsius, Hall was keenly involved in tapping into the heritage so fruitfully exploited by Lipsius. Yet if Lipsius's role as the *éminence grise* of an approach to political society is to help in elucidating an important strain in English political thinking, that approach itself needs further clarification, such as I present in the Introduction.

The Lipsian paradigm explored here is associated with the neostoicism constructed by Lipsius. It was a pattern of scholarship as well as a crystallization of a number of political ideas. It is the latter that lures modern-day scholars, who obviously do not quite agree on its impact among contemporaries. And if Gerhard Oestreich's views contrast with those of Skinner, J.H.M. Salmon has recently challenged Oestreich's argument to contend that – in England, at least – neostoicism was less a call to action than a lament for lost virtue. Instead of providing a source for creating a modern state, Professor Salmon insists, it was harnessed by Englishmen to express their discontent with the Jacobean government.[11] While part of this argument can be validated, its main weakness, I would suggest, derives from the confusion that surrounds our use and conception of the word 'neostoicism.'

Indeed, in contemporary intellectual history it is usually taken to cover a broad, amorphous system of thought – mainly centring around the revival of stoic ethics and their application to the Christianized world of early modern Europe, including England.[12] Like the term Puritanism, neostoicism has become something of a reification, gaining greater coherence than it either enjoyed at the time or assumed. The problem is compounded by the fact that stoicism itself has associations with a specific moral and ethical system (one relating to a long-gone age although widespread in early modern Europe), and its derivatives have come to be used mainly as descriptions of responses to situations, of attitudes adopted after the fact, of traits of character and personality. Lipsius's formulation, however, was quite eclectic – not least in his use of Tacitus – and it differed radically from the 'neo-stoicism' that had been adopted in Europe in the Middle Ages and was still pervasive in the fifteenth and sixteenth centuries.[13] Consequently, although Bishop Hall might in all sincerity declare 'stoicism' to be wanting, he would have some difficulty in disassociating himself from the tradition in which he participated – and to which the diplomat Sir Henry Wotton alluded in his ironic reference to 'our spiritual Seneca.'[14]

Does that mean that all who participated in this tradition can be implicated in creating 'the early modern state' described by Oestreich? In my introductory chapter, I concentrate on analysing the elements and functions of the Lipsian paradigm rather than being overtly concerned with the consequences of neostoicism – a study of which might lead rather into an explanation of 'unintended consequences'.[15] And I shall make much of the fact that Lipsius composed his neostoic treatises amidst the very concrete and devastating circumstances of the Wars of Religion: they threatened life in the most blatant way and a way of life no less obviously. The unity of Christendom might have been something ephemeral, but in terms of scholarship and the commonwealth of letters, it was tangible enough. In defence of life and, importantly, way of life,

Lipsius turned to the past to extract lessons for application in his society, which was hanging together precariously as the engines of war marched roughshod over it. His own practice was to make manifest his teachings – he changed his religious confession repeatedly, when the situation so required. For such outward *in*constancy he provoked relentless criticism, dooming his reputation among many of his contemporaries as well as subsequent generations of scholars who have been uncomfortable with, if not downright hostile to, the chameleon-like behaviour he manifested and seemingly endorsed.[16] Lipsius's critics did not see what was perhaps, in Lipsius's own view, the most important aspect of his political argument – his use of the past and the rhetorical strategies he developed in discussing political behaviour. Moreover, like Montaigne he was a master of self-effacement, a technique that is prominent in his autobiographical letter of 1600, excerpted above, and which might seem only apropos in light of the contemporary anxieties about and animosities of late sixteenth-century life. This was the situation in which Lipsius discussed 'constantia' and 'prudentia mixta.' By these, he sought to preserve the humanist tradition to which he belonged; he was concerned, that is, to maintain its validity for a society that was suffering the threat of dissolution in the face of internecine war.

The precise nature of that humanist tradition remains a controversial issue. Of the two main interpretive models that currently vie for authority, the Kristeller paradigm, which holds that the tradition was one of academic scholarship, discussion, and tutelage, is still ascendant. Not yet to be dismissed, however, is the perspective which affirms that an ideological current underpinned the humanism practised during the Renaissance and early modern period – whether in the republican emphasis insisted on by Hans Baron or in a spiritual, pious mode as argued by William Bouwsma. Daniel Javitch's concept of 'courtly humanism' and F.J. Levy's 'political humanism' are further derivatives that assume an activist and utilitarian concept of study deriving from Cicero and the Stoics.[17] The term 'humanism' itself, however, remains problematic. Introduced into modern vocabulary by the early nineteenth-century German pedagogue F.J. Niethammer, the term is on the verge of being dismissed by a number of scholars as less than useful as an analytical tool. Alistair Fox, for instance, has recently insisted that humanism can hardly be described as a unified movement, at least in England. He complains that the term has been much abused in current scholarship.[18]

As if oblivious to such trenchant criticism, two collections of essays have recently appeared – *The Impact of Humanism on Western Europe* (ed.

Goodman and MacKay [1990]) and *The Renaissance in National Context* (ed. Porter and Teich [1992]). Although directed to a wide audience, they reflect recent debates on the word 'humanism'; and while caveats pervade the studies that comprise the first, the second deftly dodges the issue, in both title and individual essays, by addressing the broader concept – 'the renaissance' – out of which humanists if not 'humanism' emerged. Both collections attempt to define new approaches to the subject, and at the forefront of both lies the vexing issue of pointing up the terminal dates of the Renaissance phenomenon.[19] David Starkey's account of the Renaissance in England ends by insinuating the openness of the English experience and indicating the links between the Whig aristocracy and their intellectual ancestors in Tudor times.[20]

Overviews such as these contrast sharply with what is frequently presented as an open-and-shut case of finding in humanism the seeds of its own demise. This is the view of Victoria Kahn in her study *Rhetoric, Prudence, and Skepticism in the Renaissance* (Ithaca and London, 1985) and David Quint in *Origin and Originality in Renaissance Literature* (New Haven and London, 1983). From a less literary perpective, James D. Tracy has expressed the view that as an historical movement, and as its curriculum became widespread and its influence all-pervasive, humanism disappeared amidst its very success. 'At some point, perhaps with the generation of Lipsius and Scaliger,' Tracy suggests, 'one should speak rather of "classical scholars"' than of humanists.[21] Still, as James K. Cameron insists, Lipsius was an outstanding representative of 'a late yet magnificent flowering of humanism in the Netherlands ... the embodiment of Renaissance humanism ... one of the great internationals of the age and ambassador of humanism.'[22] The tag of humanism in these instances is clearly modern terminology; the spirit and sense of Cameron's assessment of Lipsius in the 1580s, I will argue, is historically valid.

Identifying Lipsius as a humanist, however, is not to say that all humanists were neostoics; rather, the reverse. As well, it is not to claim humanism as a monolith but to stress that the humanism that undergirded the writings of both Lipsius and the English authors examined here does present itself as an ideology. For a central guiding motif in their writings was a fundamental assumption about the role of scholarship in society. For example, while Bacon lived and wrote, the humanism he expressed *was*, contrary to Fox's assertions, 'a dye with which men were indelibly stained for life', it *was not* (or was not allowed to become) 'a practice and set of assumptions that could be repudiated at will.'[23]

This view of humanism gains force when examined, in the words of Andrew Lockyer, as 'an historical subject [with] an identity which endures through change.'[24] Again, this is not to say that humanism transmutes into neostoicism. It is to claim that the Lipsian paradigm emerged from the humanist belief in learning in service of the *vita activa*.[25] In response to the perceived threats to this ideal Lipsius took a number of key humanist concepts – 'constantia,' 'prudentia,' and 'similitudo temporum' (the likeness between an age past and the present) – infused them with new meaning, and re-presented them as tools with which to confront the contemporary situation. According to J.H. Elliott, Lipsius was the 'supreme evangelist of the gospel of prudence in the late sixteenth century,' insofar as he laid out certain terms to express this so-called 'gospel of prudence,' Lipsius became something of 'an innovative speaker,' as J.G.A. Pocock might put it, and neostoicism a political and humanist 'sub-language,' which, in Pocock's terms, comprises its own special way of talking about politics, with 'its own vocabulary, rules, preconditions and implications, tone and style.'[26] Such a sub-language, we shall see, was frequently echoed if not sometimes adopted, and was sometimes defended though often contested in England – not least by the five important thinkers studied here.

Sir Walter Ralegh, Sir Francis Bacon, Sir Fulke Greville, Ben Jonson, and Joseph Hall (after 1627, a bishop) are considered in terms of the Lipsian paradigm. Placing their writings within this context illustrates how individual authors promoted distinctive versions of political virtue that are best illustrated with reference to a Lipsian paradigm.[27] To this end, language or the context of a 'tradition' made relevant (or provocative) by Lipsius forms an important methodological approach in this study. In following the transformation of humanist into neostoic political concepts, neostoic political concepts into statist precepts, and a prudential vocabulary into various English manifestations of it, the language framework I adopt resists rigidity, particularly since one of the very attributes of the Lipsian synthesis – and neostoicism – was flexibility.[28] Meaning might thus seem ultimately unstable in the linguistic world of neostoicism, but the point about the fundamental slipperiness of such prudential language was the possiblities presented thereby. Transformations of Lipsian terms and ideas by Guillaume du Vair and Pierre Charron in France neatly establish the point, as I illustrate in a latter section of the Introduction.

The major thrust of this book, however, lies less in charting the shifting emphasis of a specific language and set of precepts than in exploring why such shifts occurred. I argue that the concern with prudential politics and 'constancy' in England was wholly tied up with the political situation confronting the English in the closing years of Elizabeth's reign, a situation which persisted after the coming of the Stuarts. Put most simply, this was the 'crisis of counsel,' a crisis perceived not so much on the part of successive monarchs as in the estimation of those who expected but were thwarted in their quest for office.[29] In this context it is useful to cite Kenneth Burke, who has written that all 'critical and imaginative works are answers to questions posed by the situation in which they arose. They are not merely answers, they are *strategic* answers, *stylized* answers.'[30] In Burkean terms, the task of this book becomes threefold: first, to discuss particular situations and the questions they posed to the individual authors studied here – while probing to discover what further questions underlay the problem of political virtue for them; second, to expose the strategies the authors used in framing answers to those questions and discuss the purpose of such strategies; and third, to examine the style of the answers to discover what style reveals about author, strategy, and answer.

Thus *Constant Minds* also submits to becoming an investigation into the intentions and motives of the authors under scrutiny – a task as crucial to this venture into the history of ideas as the attempt to establish any intellectual position *vis-à-vis* the Lipsian paradigm.[31] Quentin Skinner's adaptation of the concepts of convention and speech-acts are useful methodological tools for extracting authorial intentions; but while most historians and many literary critics frown upon attempts to apply motives to their subjects, I exercise the principle of rational reconstruction in combining a close reading of texts with a number of insights derived from texts, correspondence, intellectual circles, and the actual dealings and behaviour of the individual writers, in the hope, as it were, of getting under the author's skin. If I have thus adopted a *Sitz-im-Leben* approach, I have also aspired to provide a 'developmental narrative' on the question of political virtue, to recover the extent of the dialogue over 'constancy,' and always with an eye to exploring contexts other than the linguistic, for what they reveal about assumptions not so readily discernable through language.[32]

That is not to say that the task of retrieving historical subjects – whether a mind, a personality, or an idea – is not fraught with dangers. Anachronism always beckons; and literary scholars continue to warn about the potential folly of relating 'extrinsic' events to the 'intrinsic' character of 'literature.'[33] In some quarters a 'life and works' approach is decried even louder, although at issue in both these cases is less the early modern approach to either politics or the species of the written word than the modernist and post-modernist concerns over, primarily, aesthetics.[34] In keeping with current hermeneutical concerns, Harold Bloom has avowed that 'there are no texts, but only interpretations.' By contrast, in speaking of his *Commedia*, Dante allowed that its meaning 'is not of one kind only; rather the work may be described as "polysemous," that is, having several meanings.' These two statements might act as a guide for what follows. This study, describing a variety of 'constant minds' – a number of alternatives produced between the years 1584 and 1650, though each denoting 'constancy' as the prime political virtue – is, in Bloom's terms, an interpretation. It is also a book that privileges one set of meanings from writings and lives that can be regarded as 'polysemous' – according, that is, to the nature of the questions being posed.[35]

The questions I ask of Ralegh, Bacon, Greville, Jonson, and Hall yield answers that result, I hope, in adding a new perspective to our understanding of these authors and to the prominent cultural practice taking shape in the England of their day. Kevin Sharpe and Peter Lake have recently asserted that the hermeneutics of the period were based on a range of communications and that the linguistic, or literary 'language,' was by no means the primary medium in the 'multi-media society' that was early modern England.[36] One of my main contentions, however, lies in my argument about the role of the written word among English humanists, for whom 'culture' and learning were inextricably associated with politics and action. If I thus take issue with some important contemporary historians, I also hope to undermine certain orthodoxies that, over the years, have been constructed around the individuals I treat.

In this regard I should reiterate that I deliberately adopt a narrower (perhaps less cautious) than usual approach to the concept of paradigm for elucidating neostoic writings in England. For instance, in dealing with 'classical republicanism' in the thought of Algernon Sidney, Jonathan Scott speaks of 'a *paradigm* of thought which derives principally from classical Greek and Roman, and Italian Renaissance sources, combining Aristotelian political forms with the Polybian idea of balance between them, and the republicanism of Machiavelli's *Discourses*.'[37] With a slight alteration towards the end of this definition Lipsius himself can be seen participating in a structure of discourse greater than the one he developed, and I certainly agree that he did. Likewise with the Englishmen treated here, and by no means were they limited to a rigid Lipsian framework; nor were they rigidly following or indebted to Lipsius, except in a number of important respects, as I will show. Still, my concern has been to illuminate a pattern of thinking and writing about politics which is best illustrated in Lipsian writings, themselves profitably offering a standard for comparison with the English thinkers at the heart of this study. In this context, therefore, 'paradigm' has been rendered 'exemplum'.

In chapter 1 I argue that Ralegh was more adaptable than has been generally recognized. An implicit challenge is laid out to the very recent 'gallant traitor' thesis suggested by the recovery of Thomas Egerton's papers on Ralegh's role in treason against the newly installed James I.[38] For my part, I will insist that as a soldier and courtier, Ralegh would fain have served the first Stuart monarch as he did the last Tudor queen but that he became bound to a stoic rather than a neostoic, or Lipsian, form of constancy. Yet his compositions while a prisoner in the Tower reveal his affinity with a number of elements in the Lipsian paradigm; they also indicate the extent to which his earlier rivalry with the Earl of Essex coloured his strictures on political virtue. A would-be counsellor to Prince Henry, Ralegh's discussions of political prudence betray his growing participation in the language of neostoicism.

In chapter 2 Bacon emerges as less the proto-modernist or prophet of modernity depicted by Whiggish scholarship than the avid political animal he undoubtedly was. Recent scholarship has made many in-roads in correcting whig approaches to Bacon, but the key factor in his career and much of his writing, I suggest, was his so-called betrayal of Essex, in 1601. Subsequently, the problem of loyalty stalked him (despite his eventual climb to the pinnacle of office). His concern with political virtue, I argue, was closely tied to his efforts to restore his reputation and win him advancement in home politics, while he also hoped to enhance his standing with scholars, intellectuals, and politicians at home and abroad. Bacon's was a prime instance of a peculiar form of English humanism, whose terms are set in sharp relief by resort to the Lipsian paradigm.

Fulke Greville, often considered a morose religious poet, is the subject of chapter 3. The disclosure of the language of constancy within the predominant Calvinism with which he is associated is indicative of the hypocrisy with which he was charged by some of his contemporaries. To fall for appearances, however, is to miss the relation of his writings to the Lipsian paradigm, as well as to that paradigm as a valid and informing approach to politics. In particular, it is to miss the depth of Greville's ongoing mourning for the friend of his youth. Sir Philip Sidney's death in 1586 haunted him for the close to half a century that Greville outlived him – and throughout which he continued to aspire towards political service.

Sidney also lurks in the background of Ben Jonson's poetics of constancy, the subject of chapter 4. This court poet challenged Sidney's concept of humanism, promoting the poet as the leader and guide of society in terms quite distinct from those championed by Sidney. Jonson's personal circumstances had much to do with the tenor of his professional stance, but a key feature in much of his verse was his attempt to create political relationships based upon a classicism derived from his Lipsian leanings.

Chapter 5 discusses Joseph Hall and his largely successful attempt to replace Lipsian tenets with his own. Hall's challenge struck close to home as well, I argue, as he sought to countervail ideas advocated by Bacon and others. His concern with obedience to legitimate authority, however, brought him closer to his arch-foe Lipsius than he acknowledged. It was largely because of the particular character of the Interregnum in England that he was able to remain constant in a way that Lipsius had not. The study closes with a brief overview of the terms by which 'constancy' was invoked during the great crisis that shook England at mid-century, when the political community reeled under the effects of the abolition of monarchy and the establishment of the Commonwealth. It was at this critical juncture that the legacy of the debate over political virtue proved applicable to the English state. Appeals to Tacitus justified the execution of the king; and as 'constancy' and mixed prudence were promoted as the means to enable many to make their peace with a new and unprecedented regime, the terms of the Lipsian paradigm became virtually naturalized in England, allowing Interregnum (and later, Restoration) authors to exploit or abuse or develop the language of prudence for purposes of their own.[39]

# CONSTANT MINDS

# Introduction

# Justus Lipsius and the Doctrine of Constancy

Justus Lipsius was already renowned as the editor and interpreter of Tacitus when he responded to the crisis provoked by religious wars in the Netherlands by composing a short dialogue entitled, *De constantia*. Appearing in 1584, the work became an international best-seller, and five years later, amidst the ongoing ravages of war, a companion volume, the *Politica*, appeared, to enjoy equal popularity. Lipsius would go on to provide an authoritative edition of the writings of Seneca and compile a number of treatises on classical Roman traditions and institutions, as well as other works, but together the two pieces of the 1580s contain all the elements of the political philosophy of neostoicism.[1] Consisting of a call for 'constancy,' achieved in practice by the application of 'mixed prudence,' neostoicism was predicated on Lipsius's assertion of the value of learning and demonstrated by recourse to classical texts.

On the face of it there was nothing new in the Lipsian venture. An appeal to antiquity was standard in humanist writings, and principles of 'constancy' and 'prudence' had long been topics of discussion in the Renaissance.[2] Indeed, in creating his particular synthesis Lipsius counted upon a certain familiarity with its central concerns. His teachings contained recognizable aspects of the Christian stoicism which, deriving principally from the mediations of the fifth-century Christian Boethius, had been prevalent since the Middle Ages and remained popular in the sixteenth and seventeenth centuries.[3] In his *Consolatio Philosophiae* Boethius had delineated a philosophy of fortitude and solace: in the midst of the calamities imposed by unstable circumstances of life people were urged to focus inwardly, to cultivate perseverance and faith, and to trust that the world turned under the benevolent overlordship of God. The stoic creed in this, its simple form, offered comfort to the defeated and the condemned; it stressed that virtue was an attribute of the mind, to be pursued without reference to outward circumstances.

Lipsius argued otherwise in *De constantia*, declaring that virtue – or constancy – should be pursued through active engagement in public life precisely *because* of the instability of outward circumstances. But while he thus challenged the legacy of a Christian stoicism that promoted introspection as a refuge from the hostility of the world, the broad stoic tradition from which it emerged could yield other lessons.[4] The writings of Seneca provided the key. In his epistles and treatises this first-century Roman stoic taught moderation and a constant alertness to the folly of passion, maintaining all the while that 'Man is a sociable creature, and is made for the common good of others ... men of the best iudgement doe think that that which concerneth the commonwealth is of greater importance than that which toucheth their owne particular.'[5] Any stoical retreat advocated by Seneca in Neronian Rome was one that arose only after public activity had merited it; he insisted on the moral reformation of society as well as individual moral reform.

Senecan stoicism, combining a stress on reason with an insistence on its practical application, had been compatible with the aims of humanist reformers in the early sixteenth century. The most acclaimed of these, Erasmus of Rotterdam, compiled new and complete editions of Seneca's writings; published in 1515 and 1529, they gained a broad audience by being incorporated into university curricula. The coming of the Reformation, however, jeopardized much of the Erasmian endeavour and brought into sharp relief the requirement for a stringent reassessment of Erasmus's optimistic and universalist view of society.[6] His fundamental aim had been the promotion of a true Christian commonwealth.[7] To that end he had borrowed heavily from classical writers but he was also selective, finding Seneca, for instance, particularly useful due to the affinity of his ethics with the practical Christianity he commended. Erasmianism, in other words, was more concerned with contemporary issues than with the offerings of antiquity, a priority which (as we shall see) Lipsius deftly reversed.[8] When Christianity became an issue of bloody contention others were left to reassess the goals of the humanist endeavour. Among these was Lipsius. Perhaps more than any other, he captured the anxious and uncertain mood of the day by adopting a particular style of writing and by incorporating into his brand of stoicism Tacitus, the hard-headed and disenchanted historian of early imperial Rome. Tacitus was the surprise ingredient in what can thus be called *neo*stoicism; by linking together Seneca and Tacitus, Lipsius promoted a distinctive approach to society, privileging the role of ancient wisdom as the means to understand the demands of the contemporary world.

## Seneca, Tacitus, and the Moral Universe of Neostoicism

*De constantia* treated the problem of the individual confronting civil and religious chaos. The piece was composed in the form of a dialogue, and Lipsius announced that in both 'matter' and 'method' *De constantia* presented a novel approach to attaining that 'one Hauen of a peaceable and quiet mind.'[9] The method of both *De constantia* and the *Politica* is a crucial aspect of the Lipsian paradigm, but how far the 'matter' of Lipsius's argument departed from prevailing convention should first be considered, for it provides the key to his method.

In the dialogue, a youthful Lipsius is distraught by the war which is tearing his native Belgica apart and is contemplating escape to more peaceful climes. The wise (and older) Langius uses the Socratic method to get to the heart of the problem that confronts the troubled youth. Lipsius learns that his own understanding holds the key to his distress. In the midst of worldly conflict and unrest, Lipsius is urged to pursue 'constancy,' a frame of mind where 'right reason,' 'strength,' and 'patience' govern and triumph over the influences of the 'passion' which derives from 'opinion.' The ancient and widely established practice of separating the sources of the human faculties is followed as Langius argues that opinion – that which often precipitates rash action and brings with it such inner turmoil – responds to the body and emerges from the outward circumstancesthat inform the body. Reason, on the other hand, pertains to the mind, and what sets it apart is that it 'hath her offspring from heaven, yea from God.'[10] The troubled young Lipsius of the story is exposed to the peculiarly stoical interpretation of reason, according to which, reason, lodged in the soul, contains that spark of divinity common to all men, but which is trained to prevail in few.[11] Urged to retrieve that spark by pursuing *right* reason, described as 'a true sense and judgement of thinges humane and divine' and achieved by distinguishing the goods and evils of the mind from those of external circumstance, Lipsius learns that the mind is the true battlefield in which opinion contends with reason for supremacy. Once 'right reason' triumphs he will be prepared for any experience life might offer, for his 'constancy' will guide him. And constancy is that state 'where vertue keepeth the meane, not suffering any excesse or defect in her actions, because it weigheth all things in the ballance of Reason' (I, iiii, p. 9).

*De constantia* is thus in large part a treatise on the priority of reason as taught by the stoics, by which Lipsius countered a number of challenges provoked by the circumstances reigning in late-sixteenth-century Europe. Battle raged, ostensibly at least, because of disagreement over Christianity; and in the Low Countries, as elsewhere, the issue of religion compounded a patriotic call that justified rebellions against despotism and a distant and foreign emperor.[12] Lipsius had things to say about patriotism as well as suggestions to make about Christianity, even as Langius informed his young listener that 'we must be good commonwealths-men,' by which we are obliged 'to loue, to defend, and to die' for our country. Yet this country, Langius went on, is merely a temporary habitat and is distinguished from 'heaven[,] our true and rightful countrey' (I, xi, p. 28). Social duties are therefore offset by the call of a higher 'nature' that derived from God and was universal. 'Constancy' turned on – as the dialogue turned to – discovering the means by which these two callings were interwoven, all the while remaining separate aspects in the human sojourn through life.

*De constantia* demonstrated how the philosophy of the stoics, which taught the very distinctions and duties described above, could be reconciled to the tenets of Christianity.[13] Lipsius had no quarrel with the existence of either religion in general or Christianity in particular. Indeed, he fully accepted its relevance and in *De constantia* established the fundamental claim of religion on individuals by the same distinction he set up between the temporal and the eternal. In the *Politica*, Lipsius's advice-book for princes, the first part of the virtue that he demanded in a prince, was 'a right beleefe in God,' the 'true light' of which, he noted, 'is to be seene in holy Scriptures, albeit certaine sparkles lye scattered here and there in prophane authors.'[14] *De constantia* was vitally important here, because it ascertained those 'certaine sparkles' and established the 'prophane authors' who diffused them. But this in the face of Christianity's distrust of human reliance on the power of human reason: although many Christian thinkers argued the reconcilability of classical thought and the tenets of the Church, orthodoxy conceded little space for the 'heretical' doctrine of self-sufficiency that was fundamental to classical stoicism; then had come Martin Luther, whose 'sola fides' issued the most damaging critique of any claim for the superiority of human reason (not to mention its relation to the divine).[15] One task taken up by Lipsius in *De constantia* was the dismissal of that which was most offensive – but not just in pagan philosophy.

He began with an adaptation of the doctrine of providence.[16] The given in any Christian interpretation of the world and a precept to be inferred from many of the stoics' utterances, the first cause of the world's turning was acknowledged to be God. The major stoical precepts of 'fate' and 'destiny' were then made subservient to the power of providence and amenable to the doctrine of free will – itself, of course, an issue full of controversy in Lipsius's day.[17] But while battle raged on behalf of the contest for the true doctrine by which the Christian message should be understood, Lipsius refrained from engaging in the confessional dispute.[18] He leans, it is true, to the view argued by Erasmus in his debate with Luther. Marjorie Boyle has discussed this debate in terms of the rhetoric of the sceptical debater (Erasmus) versus that of the stoic dogmatist (Luther), in which, moreover, Erasmus used the strategies of 'invert nature' to foil Lutheran assertions. Thus he played the old fool to a Luther full of brash confidence in his own knowledge; thus he also purported to be a puny fly to Luther's gigantic and ostensibly majestic elephant.[19]

Lipsius had no need for such literary ironies, natural inversions, or classical allusions – although, to be sure, Langius's garden and porch are the important places from which the world can be viewed with a clear perspective.[20] His approach to the issue of human freedom, however, follows from a demonstration of the undogmatic character of stoic doctrines together with an implicit critique of the notion of certain theological knowledge. This is accomplished in three ways. First, it is what men have said about God that is emphasized throughout *De constantia*, where Christian authorities are minimal, consisting of the odd invocation of Saint Augustine and a few excerpts from the Old Testament. Second, it is classical poets like Homer, Euripides, Pindarus, and above all the Roman authors Seneca and Tacitus, who provide the the case for the providential governance of creation. And third, it is the voice of Languis that argues persuasively for both the ruling power of Providence and the important role played by humans in the working out of providential design. This strategy distinguished Lipsius from predecessors (as well as contemporaries) who flirted with or borrowed stoic ideas. For instance, John Calvin had been attracted to Seneca, and in 1532 published his commentary on the stoical *De clementia*. Yet Calvin shared with Erasmus the same misgivings about Seneca, considering him much too secular in his philosophy and neglectful of giving due place to God. In the 1539 edition of *Institutes*, Calvin repudiated 'new Stoickes' of his own time.[21] Later Calvinists used stoicism and any other classical authorities to specific purpose, and as secondary to Christian teachings.[22] By contrast,

Lipsius emphasized the wisdom that persisted independently of Christian teachings yet, as he clearly showed, also supported them.

Langius is the father-figure leading a timid student in this exercise; he is also a doctor of knowledge, and the medical analogy, much favoured by Lipsius, permeates the dialogue.[23] The temporary retreat into Langius's abode affords the naïve Lipsius of the dialogue an opportunity to mature. As he explores his own mind he comes to an understanding of the operations of the human mind itself, and as he does so no irony punctuates the uncertainty, trepidation, and doubts he (publicly) displays. The character is so well portrayed that it is hard to ascertain whether it is deliberately autobiographical or whether Lipsius thereafter adopted such a persona for himself.[24] Either, indeed, might be the case since Lipsius probably belonged to the Family of Love.[25] Founded in the 1540s under the leadership of Hendrik Niclaes of Westphalia, the Family's main tenet was: 'If any man be a Christian let him then also have a Christian nature and stand under the obedience of the love of Jesus Christ.' In response to the extremities that had come to pass in Münster, Niclaes insisted that 'in the House of Love men do not curse nor swear; they do not destroy or kill any ... They seek to destroy no flesh of men.' Familists concerned themselves with individual redemption and came together for the singular purpose of engaging in the 'fight of the cross and patience to the subduing of sin.'[26] Against but not contrary to this spiritual aim, Niclaes enjoined external observance of the rules of the Church into which individuals were born or under which they lived. He thereby recognized (and we shall see that Lipsius fully accepted) the validity of the formula which had come into existence as a consequence of the Reformation, *cuius regio, eius religio*.[27] The Family's irenic and spiritualist goals were, nevertheless, provocative and so much against the grain of orthodox Christianity that secrecy became a hallmark of Familist practice.[28] And indeed, the application of a rhetoric of diffidence in *De constantia* operates to conceal rather than reveal what may well have been the author's confessional beliefs. Yet that rhetoric of diffidence will finally enable the young Lipsius of the dialogue to learn – as the only sure rule in the midst of the uncertainty of the world – the validity of the principle of 'constancy,' that 'right and immoueable strength of the minde, neither lifted up, nor pressed downe with externall or casuall accidentes' (I, iiii, p. 9).

Constancy, then, the fundamental precept of Lipsian neostoicism, was argued primarily in stoical terms and was conditioned by a broad Christian perspective of God's governance of the world. *De constantia* stressed that it was folly to attempt to second-guess the inscrutable wisdom of the Almighty, but the existence of a moral order was 'proved' when, in Book II, by recourse to history (in particular the histories of Tacitus), Lipsius illustrated the operations of a providential justice which was ascertainable only by learning (or the application of reason in the study of history), and only after the fact. Two issues were at stake here. First, the notion of human freedom was reiterated when, in light of this 'unknowing' of God's mind and plans, the young Lipsius of the dialogue was urged to pursue 'constancy' and thus maintain his position in the world, not seek to escape it. Langius insists that not only should his student 'yeeld to God,' but that he 'give place to the time.' An adjustment of perspective – not neglect of his duty or the needs of society – was recommended.[29] Second, in this scheme 'right reason' was hardly devoted, as it had been from the time of Boethius onwards, to discovering the unchanging inroads of the universe. Courtesy of Lipsius's use of history as illustration, it became a technique by which to read the flux of mundane experience, dictating an adjustment of behaviour according to reigning circumstances. Both 'right reason' and 'constancy' thus underwent a radical shift in meaning, ceasing to be either quite Christian or quite stoic.

In this respect it should be stressed that neostoicism thereby hardly translated into a secular approach to survival based on principles of self-interest. Fifty years after the appearance of *De constantia*, the Italian Virgilio Malvezzi maintained that 'whoever does not refer to God to explain political events is a bad Christian.'[30] Lipsian neostoicism was founded on that first principle – putting it to the test of reason even while refusing to engage in debate over dogma. Indeed, one of Lipsius's goals was to divest religion of any ideological force. In the face of the pernicious effects of religious militancy he rejected claims to any infallible truth other than the existence of a providential God and sought to limit human inquiry to the realm of shared human experience.[31] By the same token, Lipsius's strictures implied that he had little patience with appeals for the religious toleration advocated by many of his contemporaries.[32] He seems to have well understood (as modern commentators are beginning to realize) that claims for toleration by the Reformers usually entailed an ongoing commitment to the ideal of uniformity of religion within a state, in which the toleration demanded by unorthodox groups was to serve as a temporary measure during which the rest were to be persuaded of the veracity of their beliefs; alternatively, such appeals betrayed a predilection for the laxity or 'libertinism' that characterized the pre-Reformation approach to the enforcement of doctrine, particularly in the Netherlands.[33] Lipsius did not object to the idea that individuals should follow the tenets of their own faith – even if these diverged from those sanctioned by the state. Privacy and quietude were essential in this case, however, and he strongly objected to any religion which challenged the established order. Pluralism, he believed, was viable only when the state could not enforce uniformity; otherwise, as a mere look around Europe and the Netherlands showed, division and warfare ensued.[34] It was in this context that the Lipsian version of 'constancy' became crucial. Reflecting Familist teachings on the necessity of outward conformity, *De constantia* established the moral basis for the individual to subsume his private beliefs for public duty's sake. 'Right reason,' guided as it was by history, taught the validity of such a lesson.

Together with the appeal to reason, then, the examples to be gleaned from history demonstrated that an overriding providence governed the world. As the marriage between 'reason' and 'history' was effected, Lipsius responded to religious dogmatists who insisted that their version of the Christian truth was authoritative and enforceable. As mentioned above, this had been, as well, the opportunity to introduce Tacitus, who furnished the view that contemporary times were not unique in their suffering. Thereby Lipsius reiterated that humanity only has the power to trust God, and cannot presume to fully understand Him.[35] Moreover, the crucial question of how individuals might remain politically engaged and morally virtuous in an age in which politics had become unstable and violent, at times treacherous, and at others, morally debased, now had its full neostoic expression. Neostoic 'constancy' provided the moral anchor in the Lipsian scheme; within this scheme, Tacitus yielded the disenchanted view of political realities required for effective engagement in the present.

In a critique of contemporary dogmatism and religious fanaticism, it was of little consequence that Tacitus himself had not been a stoic.[36] Besides, he was an important source for the stoicism that persisted in Neronian Rome and later, with things to say on Seneca and stoic martyrs like Clodius Thrasea Paetus.[37] More to the point, there was an underlying moral scheme to his portrait of the Roman world of the first century, and Lipsius insisted that the decline of Rome witnessed by Tacitus resembled and was as good a metaphor as any for the turbulent Europe of the late 1500s. Tacitus also provided lessons on political behaviour and approaches to governance that emerged not in any straightforward prose but from his labyrinthine form of expression – that is, when Tacitus himself was not cutting through the labyrinth of language.[38] While Lipsius was only one of a number who came to practise Tacitean stylistics, *De constantia* stood as a model of Tacitean discourse in which the medium, as much as the message, conveyed a morality deriving less from stoicism proper than a broader concept of antiquity. As a philologist, Lipsius naturally championed the classicizing of literature; yet as he founded his system on the authority and style of classical authors, so the paradigm he constructed was devoted to a revision of political relationships in the present. The application of language, or style, was the crucial component of Lipsius's entire endeavour.

**The Linguistic Universe of Neostoicism**

In the forewords to his publications, Lipsius insisted upon the *usefulness* of his compositions and mode of instruction. According to his own example, scholarship did not entail disengagement from the world.[39] Lipsius's brand, in fact, demanded application and was informed by the practical end of inspiring its readers to action.

To this end, rhetoric played a key role, and neostoicism thus formed part of a broad general revival of 'Senecan' forms and style, a movement in which language was mobilized to combat the florid and embellished Ciceronian prose style of the period.[40] This campaign went back to the days of Machiavelli and Erasmus but by the 1580s participants in the anti-Ciceronian school included Lipsius and Montaigne, whose own homeland, France, was as embroiled as the Netherlands in civil and religious disorder. Following Erasmus, they rejected ornate Ciceronianism for its propensity to flow into abstractions. 'Fie unto that eloquence,' decried Montaigne, 'which makes us in love with itself, and not with the thing.' The hallmark of anti-Ciceronians was their interest in 'the thing' – be it a physical, social, or political question. Learning was 'distempered,' Francis Bacon would later pronounce, 'when words are valued more than matter.'[41] In the eyes of these critics, Ciceronianism was tightly bound to the evils of the day.

In a seminal study, Morris Croll argued that 'the central idea of the anti-Ciceronian movement ... was that style should be adapted to the differences of men and times.'[42] Ben Jonson, in the early 1600s, would censure the verses of Drummond of Hawthornden on the basis that 'they smelled too much of the Schools, and were not after the fashion of the time.' Jonson held that 'nothing is more ridiculous than to make an author a dictator, as the Schools have done Aristotle.' He saw much to be commended in the legacies of Aristotle and Cicero, but their wholesale adoption by men of his own time was something to be scorned as 'sluttish or foolish.'[43]

Lipsius, too, continued to admire Cicero, and prefiguring both Bacon and Jonson, was an important antecedent to these later 'anti-Ciceronians.'[44] For stylistic expression he favoured 'brevity,' the grammatically short period or phrase, which resulted in the expression of what Croll has described as 'a progress of imaginative apprehension, a revolving and upward motion of the mind as it rises in energy, and views the same point from new levels.'[45] Croll also distinguished two forms of brevity: a 'curt' and a 'loose' form. In its curt form the focus fell on the thought being pursued. Noting this as the style favoured by Lipsius, Gerhard Oestreich has argued that *De constantia* is carefully constructed on the basis of an extended military metaphor, by which means Lipsius (or rather Langius) continually outflanks the forces of despair and retreat. 'Form, language and content,' Oestreich concludes, 'attain perfect unity in the *Constantia*.' Whether, as Oestreich also suggests, this feature was designed to induce the discipline that eventually enabled the formation of the Prussian military state, is another question entirely.[46] In this respect it is useful to compare Lipsius with Montaigne.

In the hands of Montaigne, brevity was used in a 'loose' way, setting the pattern for what has been called the 'libertine' mode, where the object of any given exercise entailed the free experimentation with thoughts.[47] Principles of punctuation took the place of grammatical explications, but in its libertine manifestation, and as Montaigne's *Essais* still demonstrate, the end result diverged radically from the optimistic stress on reason sounded by Lipsius. Lipsius argued that stability could be retrieved only with the triumph of reason – at once a universal concept and an attribute of the mind which the individual could train to conquer the passions, thence to accommodate himself to the inconstancy of the world. Stability was thus an internal affair, created by the individual through his power of reason. By contrast, Montaigne's 'thoughts' on the subject led him to deny any conclusion about the universality of the power of reason, except to insist on its difference from individual to individual.[48] In response to the crisis created by the onset of religious warfare, however, Montaigne could agree with Lipsius that the religion of any state should be unanimously upheld by all its citizens and that outward conformity need not impose on the subject's conscience. He also held that the ruler's task was to ensure unity and to provide for the security of his subjects, and that it was incumbent on subjects, therefore, to obey the command of their prince. 'I have found no one in Europe,' wrote Lipsius, 'whose sense of these matters agrees more with my own.'[49]

Still, Montaigne's irenicism was expressed in a unique and individualistic form – the *essai*; Lipsius's writing, on the other hand, was informed by a corporate sense of individualism, reflected in his adoption of the well-tried and tested form of the dialogue. (We shall see that while he altered its technique, he affirmed its value as a teaching tool.) The greatest difference between them, however, was the language in which they chose to write. Where Montaigne took to the vernacular in his *Essais*, Lipsius composed in Latin. This brought him much closer to Erasmus than to Montaigne, as his services were devoted to preserving a heritage – in Lipsius's case the classical legacy and the language in which it was expressed. Lipsius refused to participate in the shift to the vernacular, writing: 'What should I be but the laughing stock of sailors and inn-keepers? Like Icarus who fell in his flight because he rose on deceptive wings.'[50] Lipsius's reverence for the classical language, indeed for antiquity, bespoke a traditionalism wholly absent in Montaigne, whose sceptical musings operated to provoke further thought on the issues he raised.

By contrast, Lipsius's great concern with finding an end to tumultuous warfare in Europe by reference to the past led him to appeal to ancient models in reconstructing the present. To that end, he mobilized 'brevity,' then focused on the use of disjunction. In *De constantia*, particularly when discussing the idea of patriotism, disjunctive phrases predominated. The result was that patriotism was rendered less a thing to command followers than a word that inflamed passions, a word, moreover, that, as he illustrated, tended to serve the vested interests of only those few – the wealthy and the nobility of any area – who had most to lose but also all to gain from a 'patriotic' cause.[51]

Lipsius's use of disjunction earned him some opprobrium. In England John Earle disparaged 'Lipsius his hopping style,' and John Milton would later refer to him as 'the tormentor of semi-colons.'[52] The same feature, however, ensured the approbation of others. But Lipsius did not invent it. A dedication he composed in 1581 and included in his 1585 edition of Tacitus offered a prime example of the succinct prose which derived from Tacitus himself:

Tacitus doesn't present you with showy wars or triumphs, which serve no purpose except the reader's pleasure; with rebellions or speeches of the tribunes, with agrarian or frumentary laws, which are quite irrelevant to our time. Behold instead kings and rulers and, so to speak, a theatre of our modern life. I see a ruler rising up against the laws in one passage, subjects rising up against a ruler elsewhere. I find the devices which make the destruction of liberty possible and the unsuccessful effort to regain it. I read of tyrants overthrown in their turn, and of power, ever unfaithful to those who abuse it. And there are also the evils that accompany liberty regained: chaos, rivalry between equals, greed, looting, wealth pursued from, not on behalf of, the community. Good God, he is a great and useful writer! And those who govern should certainly have him at hand at all times.[53]

Here, in 1581, and later in *De constantia* and the *Politica*, Lipsius hailed Tacitus as the premier voice from the past, and one who spoke a decisively 'modern' language. Tacitus had been known since his rediscovery during the Italian Renaissance, but through the new and up-to-date editions of his writings by Lipsius and the pride of place accorded him in neostoicism his work was exposed to and captured the contemporary European imagination on a scale previously unknown.[54] Thus 'Tacitism' reached its heyday. Peter Burke has recently noted that between 1580 and 1700 more than one hundred authors wrote commentaries on Tacitus; and in an earlier study, Burke distinguished four aspects in Tacitus which appealed to the age of Lipsius. There was Tacitus the stylist, Tacitus the historian, Tacitus the moralist, and Tacitus the master of politics.[55] The lessons to be gleaned from Tacitus could be ambiguous; long before Lipsius was born Guicciardini had written that 'Cornelius Tacitus teaches those who live under tyrants how to live and act prudently, just as he teaches tyrants how to establish tyranny.'[56] 'As a result of his ambiguity,' writes Peter Burke, 'he could be claimed by both the opponents and supporters of monarchy in early modern Europe, the "red" and the "black" Tacitists, as they were called in an essay published in Italy not long after the First World War.'[57] Yet a closer contemporary to Lipsius, Francis Bacon, lauded the Tacitean neat but 'dark' lines, writing that Tacitus 'utters the very morals of life itself.' As Kenneth Schellhase has noted: 'Whether for political maxims or for historical information, and whether for moralisms or stylistic examples, Bacon seems to have used Tacitus as a kind of commonplace book of neat lines.'[58]

In his reverence for Tacitus Bacon belongs to the tradition mapped out by Lipsius; it was not one particular aspect of 'Tacitism' that Lipsius highlighted but its unity, compressed within Tacitean language itself, and typified, in the words of Einar Lofstedt, by 'its concentrated form, its sombre seriousness, and its lofty movement.' 'Brevity in Tacitus,' B. Walker has noted, 'means not so much the writing of curt, bare sentences as the condensation of complex ones by the omission of all insignificant repetitions and unimportant words.' 'His principle devices,' writes Sir Ronald Syme, 'are structure, digression, comment, and speeches. And not least, omission – which more recent exponents of imperial Rome have seldom skill or courage to emulate.'[59] Not so with Lipsius, who was fearless in this regard. Seneca, too, manifested the same devices. Thomas Lodge, who made great use of Lipsius's 1605 edition of Seneca in producing his own English translation of the Roman moralist, rendered Seneca's verdict on brevity as 'abrupt sentences and suspicious, in which more is to be understood than heard.'[60] *Obscura brevitas*, as contemporaries understood this feature, was the distinctive rhetorical element common to both Seneca and Tacitus; it was also the single, most important feature in the Lipsian paradigm, which translators and many others rushed to adopt.[61]

Neostoicism was thus a language, and the universe of neostoicism was linguistic, culled from the wise sayings of the ancients. Lipsius exemplified this technique in both *De constantia* and the *Politica*, although what precisely he was up to in the latter has tended to elude later scholars as much as those critics of his own time, many of whom, like Dirck Coornhert, disliked what they read. Coornhert objected to Lipsius' views on uniformity and especially the proposal that a ruler reject clemency in dealing with disturbers of religious peace. 'Burne, sawe asunder, for it is better that one member be cast away, than that the whole body runne to ruine,' Lipsius had proclaimed. Coornhert called this a barbarous teaching, to which Lipsius responded, to little avail, that his language was taken from medicine and that this surgical metaphor had been popular among the ancients, and was also used by Cicero.[62] Indeed, from this perspective 'the body' was the state, and according to both ancient and early modern (not to mention modern) medical practice, it was better to sever a limb than have the entire body infected by a disease that would overwhelm it. Lipsius's frequent invocations of the medical analogy are noteworthy. In *De constantia*, Langius's teachings on constancy were promoted as a medicine and Langius was the doctor who healed his patient by razor and fire, cutting into the affections to root out false opinions, and then applying fire to burn them away. There, too, God was invoked as the great doctor, who intermittently purges and cleanses his creation.[63] But, as Lipsius insisted, while doctors often used drastic methods, they also had alternatives. In 1586 he wrote to Sir Philip

Sidney (recently come from England to take up his post under the command of his uncle Leicester, commander-in-chief of the defence of the Netherlands) to complain of the harsh treatment being meted out to critics of Leicester's policies. 'These rapid torrents,' wrote Lipsius referring to those who fled in the face of Leicester's activities, 'are leading us to internal strife ... That you will have a free and firm use of the the reigns of government, that I do approve of and recommend; but only if it is done with moderation and with a certain ease. In so sick a body, will you cure everything in a few months? A diet is required.'[64] 'Even in corporeall diseases,' he wrote in the *Politica*, 'nothing is more dangerous than unseasonable Phisicke.' Lipsius's 'prince' was to be a doctor, knowing when to purge and when to abstain from using 'untimely remedies.'[65] 'Opus est diaetae' was Lipsius's ultimate stricture in dealing with 'disease' in the body politic. In other words, the medical analogy served as an organizing principle in neostoicism, in which individuals, society, and the state were reconstructed both linguistically and metaphorically.

## The Politics of Neostoicism

Yet if first and foremost a language, neostoicism was also a political philosophy which had its fullest expression in the *Politica*. And whereas *De constantia* yielded lessons for those under governance, the *Politica* concerned governance itself. The key to its argument emerged in Book IV, where Lipsius turned to examine 'Proper Prudence, to wit, that which is requisite to be in a Prince.' The longest of the 'Six Bookes,' Book IV was devoted to explicating this 'proper prudence,' which Lipsius considered the least acknowledged aspect of princely virtue, and which, he claimed, was usually erroneously set against the dictum, 'nothing is permitted to him which commandeth, but that onely which is honest.' Stressing the role of contingencies in political life, he insisted on the practice of *prudentia mixta*, by which 'the Prince in desperat matters, should alwaies follow that which were most necessarie to be effective, not that which is honest in speech.'[66] Invoking the examples of the Holy Roman Emperors Sigismund (1368–1437) and Frederick (1415–93), he proclaimed the worthy lineage and validity of the axiom, 'qui nescit dissimulare, nescit regnare.' And with the added example of Tacitus's description of Tiberius, Lipsius insisted, 'They shall neuer gouerne well, who know not how to couer well.'[67]

Contemporaries recognized this aspect of the *Politica* as 'Machiavellian,' and it clearly was, especially when Lipsius proclaimed, 'Where we cannot preuaile by the Lions skinne, we must put on the Foxes,' an idea notoriously associated with Machiavelli and believed to result in acts of barbarity like the Saint Bartholomew Day massacre of 1572.[68] Before discussing the three forms of deceit contained within *prudentia mixta*, Lipsius defended Machiavelli, 'who poore soule,' he lamented, 'is layde at of all hands.'[69] He then went on to speak of 'light' and 'middle' deceit, necessary in governors because of the very fact of vice in the world. Consequently, he insisted, mistrust and dissimulation were virtuous in a prince; and although bribery and deceit were less virtuous, they, too, were indispensable. The third type, 'great deceit' – involving the breaking of oaths – was to be at all times shunned, Lipsius declared. Quoting Tacitus again, deceit and dissimulation were rendered 'virtuous,' being declared necessary in procuring the common good. At the same time, something of an *apologia* was set forth for Machiavelli.

Three issues need to be highlighted in regard to Lipsius's controversial prescriptions on 'prudentia mixta.' The first has less to do with any debt to Machiavelli than with the view of those scholars who argue that Lipsius favoured Tacitus because of the resemblance between his discussion of dissimulation and Machiavelli's concept of *virtù* – which Lipsius translated as *prudentia mixta*. According to these commentators, Lipsius's Tacitean stance fell somewhat short of Machiavelli's morality. Thus Felix Raab: 'To Machiavelli, as firmly as to the theologians whom he ignored, good was good and evil was evil. It was the *ragione di stato* school, coming after Machiavelli, who invented a moral scale for statesmen.' Against this view, Robert Bireley has recently argued that Lipsius is a prime exponent of 'reason of state,' in fact providing a moral order for Machiavellism and in the process becoming himself an 'anti-Machiavellian.' The most concise expression of the same fundamental view is given by J.H. Elliott. He notes that neostoicism, with its stress on Tacitus, 'possessed all the practical advantages associated with the teachings of Machiavelli without the obliquy attached to his name.'[70]

To see the issue like this, with a dissembling Lipsius presenting Machiavellism beneath the blanket of Tacitism, is to ignore the power of the text – be it a Tacitean or a Machiavellian one, in terms of authorship – in Lipsius's thinking. And this brings us to the second point – the area in which Lipsius actually diverged not only from Machiavelli but from most of his own contemporaries who were engaged in the same problems. Robert Hariman has recently argued that the authority of the text was a thing that Machiavelli set out to undermine, opposing the rhetoric of virtue (that informed the genre of *speculum principis*) to the reality of the world of action (that he portrayed in the *Prince*). Thereby language, Hariman insists, became 'extrinsic to reality'; by denying all the characteristics conveyed in other species of the genre Machiavelli averred that 'the world of texts is not the world of princes,' which for him was concerned less with textual authority than 'unencumbered experience.'[71]

If Machiavelli thereby repudiated humanism, that he even set out a body of teachings for princes remains a measure of his humanist assumptions.[72] But it is true that in method and goals Machiavelli and Lipsius were somewhat at odds. Lipsius did not use classical sources merely as a starting point for commentary; he sought to recapture and revive the wisdom of 'the dead,' that is, 'good authors, and such other monuments, who ... [not] keeping anything secret, do lay open the pure and simple troth.'[73] The *Politica* belongs to the same genre as Machiavelli's *Prince*, but it consisted of little more than a prudently arranged compilation of quotations 'gathered' from the works of antiquity, 'amongst the which,' as William Jones faithfully translated, 'Cornelius Tacitus hath the preheminence, being recited extraordinarily, because he alone affordeth more matter, then all the rest.'[74]

This emphasis on textual authority signals a crucial distinction between Lipsius and Machiavelli, as well as between Lipsius and contemporaries like Giovanni Botero and Scipione Ammirato, who are renowned for their contribution to the philosophy of *raison d'état*.[75] According to Machiavelli, politics was the art of the possible and thus he set forth the 'arts' that hardly received the time of day from many of his contemporaries. For Lipsius, prudence, the main topic of the *Politica*, had two important parents – 'use, and Memorie of things.' 'Use' was what Machiavelli hailed as experience and action. But 'memory' was by far the all-important rule for Lipsius. Memory, he wrote, 'agreeth with all men, and fitteth all times, and seasons. And whereas the iourney we make by our owne experience is long and dangerous, this way is more safe, and assured, & therefore more plaine and beaten.' Citing Tacitus, he underlined the point: 'They are not fewe in number who are instructed by the euents and examples of others, and that is by history, which [now invoking Cicero] is no other thing than the soule and life of memorie.'[76] Lipsian 'textualism' was such that it illustrates his adherence to that which Machiavelli denied – an ontology of the written word.

But in the third place, Lipsius sought to give priority to two specific issues. Much like Machiavelli, he wanted to highlight the role of contingencies in human experience and thus assert the existence of evil in the world. Hence he could confirm the need for the practice of *prudentia mixta*. But if an echo of Machiavelli, this aspect of virtue was also the political equivalent of constancy, established by the association he set out in Book III of the *Politica*. Discussing the various duties of a prince, Lipsius devoted a chapter to the choice of counsellors to avow that 'he ought not be accused of inconstancie, who like unto a shipman, doth moderate his opinion, in the rough tempest of a Commonwealth. For he is truly prouident and wise, that keepeth not alwayes to the same pase, but the same way.' He quoted Cicero to insist that such a man 'is not therefore to be esteemed variable, but rather applyable, and fitting things to the purpose'; and maintaining the nautical metaphor, he concluded by affirming that a servant of the state must not hold 'one and the same course, though he tend to one and the same hauen.'[77] 'Constancy,' as it had been re-defined in *De constantia*, was based on the fact of the existence of 'publick ills,' or evil. The politicization of the concept occurred as Lipsius affirmed its value in princes and counsellors. In this respect, however, it became not so much the existence of evil in the world that preoccupied Lipsius as the problem of language. As he introduced his discussion of the concept of *prudentia mixta* the problem of language was brought into stark relief:

It seemeth vnto me, that I haue freely enough, and as they say with a full hand, offered thee of the best and purest wine which I could drawe out of the double spring of prudence. May it be lawfull for me to mingle lightly and ioyne with it some dregs of deceipt? I iudge it may: Howsoeuer these Zenoes doe not think it good who doe onely approue the path which by vertue leadeth vnto honor: who do not beleeue that it is lawfull that the reason which we haue receaued of God, to giue vs good counsell, ought to be imployed to deceiue, and do a mischief, whome truly in other matters I will most willingly belieue: but herein how can I? They seeme not to knowe this age, and the men that liue therein, and do giue their opinion, as if they liued in the commonwealth of Plato, and not in dregs of the state of Romulus.[78]

With this comment he launched into his discussion of the three types of deceit, after which he reiterated that that which was to be effective should take precedence over that which 'is honest in speech.'

A fundamental concern in neostoicism, therefore, was the meaning attached to language; in other words, the rhetoric of political behaviour. Rhetoric as politics had come into its own during the Roman Republic, when the capacity to move an audience had had its greatest exemplar in Cicero.[79] Tacitus and Seneca, statesmen and philosophers of the early

Empire, rejected Ciceronian rhetoric and introduced 'Silver Latin' prose in expressing the new experience of Julio-Claudian governance, or 'absolute monarchy.' Their rhetorical strategies revealed the means by which emperors, councillors, and citizens operated in the service of a different, imperial Rome. Orthodox virtues, inherited from the Greeks, continued to be bandied about. But Seneca and Tacitus, in their different ways, examined them – honesty, fellowship, generosity –in light of current practice. Quentin Skinner, in charting the history of this trend in rhetoric, has identified the phenomenon as an ongoing examination of the rhetorical figure of *'paradiastole.'* For the humanists of the sixteenth century, Skinner argues, 'the precise purpose' of the figure 'was to show that any given action can always be redescribed in such a way as to suggest that its moral character may be open to some measure of doubt.'[80]

Tacitus was an examplar here. In the *Agricola*, Tacitus has the rebel Calgacus declare, 'To robbery, slaughter, plunder, they give the lying name of empire; they make a solitude and call it a peace.'[81] Calgacus then leads his warriors into battle against the Romans, led by Agricola. Tacitus showed, however, how when words were perverted, one man, Agricola in this case, continued to serve his country 'neither by a perverse obstinacy nor an idle parade of freedom,' but through 'moderation and prudence ... obedience and submission.'[82] Tacitus hailed the prudential as the secret of life and public service in the *Agricola*; in the *Annals* and *Histories* he demonstrated how certain emperors, particularly Tiberius, had raised it to the status of an art (albeit not always commendable in accordance with his application of *paradistole*).

Lipsius manifested both aspects of Tacitus's approach to *paradiastole*. In *De constantia*, patriotism was deconstructed according to the paradiastolic figure, but 'constancy' was re-constructed. In the *Politica*, 'prudence' was given a treatment similar to 'constancy.' In this venture, Lipsius resembled Machiavelli, who, as both Skinner and Eugene Garver have argued, was engaged in the problem of the relation of rhetoric to political action.[83]

But for Lipsius, political philosophy could not consist, as it did for Machiavelli, of mere prudential action. As he indicated in his distinction between 'use' and 'memory,' it derived above all from history and was nothing other than his own *métier*, philology, the study of language.[84] Through an astute application of 'memory' Lipsius developed and contoured neostoicism, basing his teachings on a classical authority that Machiavelli would never acknowledge. From Lipsius's perspective, reality was indeed textual, with knowledge and living wholly enclosed within, as Hariman puts it, a 'metaphysic of textuality.'[85] Some time ago, Morris Croll discerned that in Lipsius 'the art of writing and the art of managing one's life are one and the same thing.'[86] So, too, was the art of governing of a state.

**Doctrine: The Method of Constancy**

Still, like Machiavelli, Lipsius showed little patience for principles of what he termed 'vain philosophy,' fit for what he dismissed as relevant only to Platos's commonwealth. By them, he wrote, quoting Seneca, 'we learn not how to live, but how to dispute.'[87] This observation was the starting point for his task in the *Politica*, where he noted, 'It is not sufficient for vs to obtaine wisdome onely, but we must likewise use it, and profite thereby.' He went on, 'Not he that knoweth many things, but he that understandeth those things which are necessarie and profitable, is right wise.' He cited the example of (Tacitus's) Agricola, who 'kept backe and restrained his mind set on fire with a desire for learning, knowing it to be a very hard thing to hold a meane in wisdome.'[88] Wisdom was prudence for Lipsius, and the cultivation of wisdom entailed the cultivation of prudence.

Lipsius derived this view from the authority of Tacitus, of ancient stoics like Zeno, and of middle stoics like Cicero and Seneca.[89] But by promoting wisdom as prudence, Lipsius signalled his place in the age-old battle between rhetoric and philosphy, setting his standard firmly in the camp of rhetoric.[90] Not that from his perspective the two were antithetical. The goal of rhetoric, Melanchthon had written, was to transfer 'philosophy aptly to use and common life,' a sentiment which Lipsius endorsed.[91] In the *Politica*, however, he confronted 'vain philosophy' and declared that 'learning' itself did not confer virtue. Instead, he argued the relevance of the latinate 'doctrine' (*doctrina*), which, he considered, 'prepareth our mindes to embrace' wisdom. 'Doctrine then is diligently to be sought for,' he averred, but to the end 'that we may put [learning] into practice.'[92] Promoting prudence as the premier virtue – making it the key to politics, peace, and prosperity in the *Politica*, and in *De constantia* the guide for life and action – was at bottom a method.[93] Neostoic doctrine as method was first rehearsed in *De constantia*.

As noted earlier, Lipsius pronounced that the novelty of his work lay in both the 'matter' and the 'method' of his dialogue. The key feature of his method emerged when, by invoking Tacitus as the authority providing examples of the tyranny endured under the Roman empire, he furnished the proof that contemporary times were not unique in their dealings of suffering.[94] In using this technique he was, on the one hand, merely indulging in the appeal to *similitudo temporum*, a characteristic of humanist scholarship, and the principle was applied as an important means by which to procure 'constancy.'[95] On the other hand, in his particular usage, Lipsius departed from the usual method of the humanist dialogue. This was the requirement to argue, or debate, the two contrary aspects of a given question – to argue *in utramque partem* – thus to introduce antitheses or contradictions to provide food for thought (and at the same time display the ingenuity of the author).[96] Book II of *De constantia* was not at all concerned with discovering the flip-side of any argument for 'right reason' or 'constancy.' Rather, it was constructed to enhance the argument of Book I by establishing that humanity continually faced and endured woes like those confronting the generation of Lipsius.

In his insistence that history revealed not difference but similarity, a point that was shorn up by a maverick combination of commentary and quotation, Lipsius dispensed with the required 'openness' of the dialogue form.[97] He concluded that such openness was less than useful, inviting uncertainty and endless discussion about matters which, in this case, had no certain resolution. His display of learning and knowledge of the classics easily identified Lipsius as a humanist. But he repudiated the key humanist concern for persuasion through deliberative and argumentative techniques. Turning to Tacitus, Lipsius substituted forensic knowledge. And using *similitudo temporum* for closure, neostoicism became an answer not only to dogmatists in religion, but to humanists attached more to forms and modes of argumentation than to providing sure guidance when society was confronted with so many 'publick ills' and dilemmas.

Method and matter came together in a unity that was highlighted by an infusion of not just historical, but Tacitean, authority, teaching constancy. Tacitus was not just someone who provided *exempla*, or a model of any sort; as Lipsius insisted in his 1581 'Dedication' to the States of Holland of his 'Commentaries' on the *Annals*, the Tacitean portrait of the Roman world of the first century was *theatrum hodiernae vitae*. Read in light of the Spanish sack of Antwerp in 1576, or under the shadows of the political manoeuverings of the Duke of Alba's governorship of the Netherlands, Tacitus's Rome looked, indeed, all too familiar. In calling this portrait 'a theatre of our modern life,' Lipsius invoked two literary principles that were familiar in humanist exercises. One was the idea of 'theatrum mundi,' an important Stoic concept by which the duty one owed to society was taught, and Lipsius not only affirmed it as a literary trope but set it in a political framework; the other was that humanist favourite, *similitudo temporum*.[98] Yet this affirmation should be set against not only humanism's usual concern for the openness of rhetorical argumentation, but also its careful distinction between past and present. Erasmus had indulged as much (if not more) in distinguishing the past as in praising it, while in his humanist phase Calvin had done the same. In Lipsius's own day, his contemporary Montaigne went so far as to totally undermine the value of history and classical learning in his challenge to the concept of absolute knowledge. Another recent challenge was presented in the work of Jean Bodin. Like Montaigne, Bodin was deeply involved in developing a means by which to escape the dilemmas provoked by the civil wars in France; he developed a methodological approach to classical learning whereby contemporaries were called upon to critically appraise the past, learn the relevance of contextual analysis, and, before assessing its value for the present, view any period of the past on terms which were uniquely its own.[99] In answer to all these challenges, Lipsius responded by *applying* the wisdom of the past to present issues.

Lipsius thus rejected humanism as a mere tradition of argumentation. Yet he continued to adhere to what Andrew Lockyer has defined as 'an ideological tradition,' one embodying 'a set of beliefs and values' comprising the idea of the utility of learning and the belief in its application to society.[100] Lipsius fits that description of humanism provided by Guiseppe Toffanin, for whom the universality of the movement was its outstanding feature and the Latin language the cement that held it together.[101] This was the heritage that Lipsius sought to re-validate, in response to what he saw as the crisis in humanism, the crisis in politics, and the crisis of religion. Rhetoric had the power to convince, he believed; the wisdom of the past the power to teach. His was indeed an ontology of the text. He was no 'poetical' dreamer in this regard – even as he enjoined that philosophy must meet up with oratory and poetry in order to have the desired effect on an audience.[102] This was only applying the prudential to rhetoric, in promotion of which he had clear targets – those whose teachings he openly contested, and the way of life and society that he strove, through his teachings, to preserve.

Lipsius's category of 'memory' was a tool geared less towards correcting Machiavelli than the much closer target of argumentative humanists whom he dismissed as 'Zenoes.'[103] Hence the relevance of Lipsian 'doctrine.' Employing the notion of *similitudo temporum*, Lipsius revised its status as a principle in learning and action. His definitive editions of Seneca and Tacitus were imperative here, too, for if from one perspective they were Lipsius's lasting contribution to humanist scholarship, from another they were nothing less than the necessary complement to his own neostoic writings. The twin pillars representing Seneca and Tacitus, as the design by Rubens well illustrated, held up the neostoic edifice which Lipsius created.[104] Anthony Grafton has remarked that, courtesy of Lipsius, humanism was transformed 'from a device for criticizing the world as it is by comparing it to an ideal past into a device for leaving the world unchanged while learning from the past how to cope with its defects.'[105] Grafton's insight implies the censure of Lipsius and underestimates his goal of relating language to political action, which started with the realization that society resembled less Plato's commonwealth than the 'dregs of the state of Romulus.'[106]

Moreover, his motto had been *Moribus Antiquis*, 'for the morality of antiquity,' and as a teacher his goal was to revive classical attitudes and behaviours. He met with some success; his presence first at Lutheran Jena, and then at the University of Leiden – the Calvinist centre where he spent thirteen years and composed both *De constantia* and the *Politica* – were occasions for an influx of students and visiting dignitaries seeking to hear his lectures and learn from them. His return to Catholic Louvain in 1592 did little to dampen the enthusiasm of audiences, even though traversing confessional boundaries to take up a professorship entailed a public declaration of faith.[107] As Lipsius dutifully conformed, his apostasies earned him criticism, first in Protestant Frankfurt, where the Wechel family suspended publication of his works.[108] Then there was the reaction of James VI of Scotland, soon to become James I of England, who dubbed the Fleming 'that proud inconstant LIPSIVS.'[109] At Louvain, nevertheless, students such as Johannes Woverius and Philip Rubens faithfully adopted the morality which Lipsius himself strove to embody.[110]

Later in life, looking back over his career, he hailed *De constantia* and the *Politica* as the measure of his achievement, claiming that he was actually the first 'or the only one' of his own time to 'convert learning into Wisdom.' *Ego e Philologia Philosophiam feci*, he said; 'I turned Philology into Philosophy.'[111] His were bold claims, deriving from his unshakeable belief in the ontology of the written word. Seneca had bemoaned that (in Imperial Rome) the study of philosophy had degenerated into the study of words.[112] Lipsius was addressing Seneca as much his own contemporaries when he took this complaint and set out to redress matters.

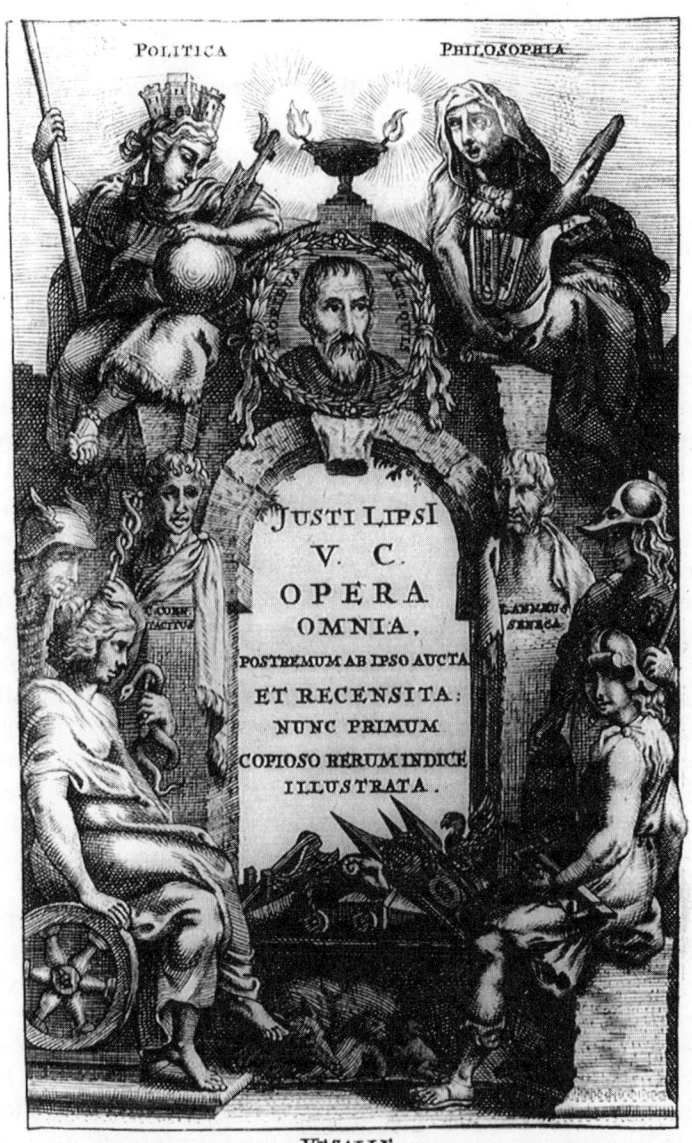

2 Frontispiece, *Iusti Lipsi Opera Omnia* (Wesel, 1675). Reproduced with permission from S.E. Sprott.

## Neostoicism in France

What he created was versatile in the extreme. Following in his wake, scholars throughout Europe began to examine Roman political and military institutions with an eye to contemporary problems; and as the secrets of Roman imperial counsellors and armies were laid bare, and as such lessons were applied to the European political scenario, conscious emulation of Roman examples began to take place.[113] Rival European states saw themselves as heirs to ancient Rome's legacy of greatness; wars of religion were transformed into wars of imperial aggression.[114] A cult of Lipsius arose in Spain, inspiring the statecraft of subsequent generations.[115] And in France neostoicism was quickly appropriated, reformulated to incorporate other strains of thought, and given a distinctly 'nationalist' flavour. As noted earlier, the French political context resembled the Flemish one of the1580s, though in France dynastic rivalries intensified the confessional divide, and the memory of the massacre of the Huguenots on the eve of St Bartholomew's Day, 1572, and the murderous contest for the crown in 1588–9 left an indelible impression of instability and treachery upon contemporaries. In consequence, political thinking was undergoing a major shift that would result in the emergence of statism. Richard Tuck has recently described the complexity of late sixteenth-century French political culture, with its strong Italianate strain, its familiarity with Tacitism, and its engagement with Machiavellism.[116] Lipsius was not the only theorist from whom statism emerged; nor did his influence – nor, for that matter, that of Montaigne – predominate in the rich theoretical environment of the French. Yet that same context was particularly conducive to the reworking of a number of Lipsian ideas.

Moreover, French *politiques*, a group which included Montaigne and whose most renowned member was the king, Henry IV, admired Lipsius's work. Henry sought several times to attract Lipsius to France, and while Lipsius declined the invitations, his works were warmly received. *De constantia* appeared in French in the same year as the Latin original and went through twelve printings in the next fifteen years; the *Politica* was translated into French in 1590 and by 1613 it had been printed five times in its Latin version and thirteen in the French translation.[117] Lipsius's twin guides of prudence and virtue based on right reason accorded with the *politiques'* political prescriptions, manifested in 1593 when the king concluded that Paris was worth a mass and abandoned his own confessional leanings to create the grounds for peace.[118] Several authors sought to convince the French reading public to accept the king's settlement. To this end, two immensely influential French works appeared, derivatives of Lipsian neostoicism – Guillaume du Vair's *Traité de la constance* (1594) and Pierre Charron's *De la sagesse* (1601). Both du Vair and Charron exploited the neostoic concept of constancy, revising it for specifically French purposes.

Du Vair rechannelled Lipsius's 'universalist' perspective into a patriotic framework, as love of the *patrie* took du Vair from the realm of the universal to that of the particular – in his case, France. He had once celebrated the life of contemplation in retirement from public duties, but after the murder of Henry III in 1588 and the subsequent renewal of civil war, he abandoned the stance of the isolated and contemplative stoic to call for the active participation of citizens in procuring peace. In his *Traité de la constance*, and then the *Exhortation à la vie civile*, he advocated 'the use of our right reason, that is, virtue, the firm disposition of our will,' to bring an end to the horrors that only succeeded in decimating his beloved land.[119] In both *De la Constance* and the *Exhortation* du Vair highlighted what he had incorporated only in passing in an earlier piece, *La Philosophie Morale des Stoïques* (c. 1585): 'I beseech you therefore to haue more care of your countrie, then of all the world besides, and neuer preferre your particular profit before the good thereof.'[120] In his numerous restatements of the Senecan call to action, du Vair came to insist that the first call of duty had to be towards France.

While du Vair focused on 'nationalizing' neostoicism, Charron, by making ample use of Bodin and Montaigne as well as Lipsius, secularized the basis of its political precepts. But his immensely successful *De la sagesse* was more than a mélange of absolutist doctrine, scepticism, and neostoicism. His synthetic approach took him, rather, to break with the humanist endeavour and provide a basis for the development of a political ethic independent of the teachings of the past, and based more purely on a neutral interpretation of nature.[121] Charron made it abundantly clear that his brand of 'wisdom' came not from the gleanings of the accumulated wisdom of the past (the existence of which he would dispute); following Montaigne, he argued that, rather, it derived from 'the study and knowledge of ourselves.'[122]

*De la sagesse* is marked by its tripartite, Aristotelian divisions. Charron's 'three books' – by which he approached 'wisdom' – examine the three types of human existence, the 'interior or private,' the domestic, and the public, and then recommends the corresponding forms of wisdom. Prudence is the foremost moral virtue for Charron, and as far as all

3 Frontispiece, Pierre Charron, *Of Wisdome*, trans. S. Lennard (London, 1640). Courtesy of Special Collections, Dalhousie University Libraries.

three spheres of life concern the private individual, his recipe for prudence differs little from that recommended by Lipsius:

> He then is wise who mainteining himselfe truly free and noble, is directed in all things according to nature, accommodating his owne proper and particular to the vniuersall, which is God, liuing and carying himselfe before God, with all, and in all affaires, vpright, constant, cheerfull, content, and assured, attending with one and the same foote, all things that may happen, and lastly death itselfe.[123]

Where Lipsius might have stressed right reason, Charron bows to nature. Yet the neostoic strain of *De la sagesse* is very much to the fore when Charron promotes his concept of the sage. This is one who maintains 'a liuely vertue, resolution, and constancie of the mind, whereby a man seeth and confronteth all accidents without trouble, he wrestleth and entreth into combat with them.'[124] Charron also calls for the practice of prudence in governance. He repeats the three Lipsian types of deceit that the ruler might have recourse to; and the wise man of Charron's mould will, like Lipsius' governor, recognize that prudence is like 'a sea without either bottome or brinke,' it 'cannot be limited and prescribed by precepts and aduisements. It doth but compasse things and goeth about them, like a darke cloude, many times vaine and friuolous.'[125] Politics, however, is a distinct sphere for Charron, and is justified neither by virtue of the existence of evil nor by any problem with the rhetoric of political behaviour but by the one precept allowed as a political guide: *salus populi suprema lex esto*. In implementing the public good the state is charged with maintaining safety and security; it is granted autonomy of action and excused from the normal codes of behaviour limiting society at large. For Charron much more than for Lipsius, the state enjoyed a morality independent from that of citizens.[126]

This view of political prudence had important repercussions for the sage whom Charron wished to enlighten. Obedience is incumbent on all subjects protected by the actions of the state. While the sage might distinguish himself from the masses who must be awed and made to live peaceably together by all the force and artifice the state deems fit to employ, he must also recognize that the established laws and customs, if falling far from representing any ideal, do reflect the practical operations of society in its quest for survival. The sage must learn to live with the discrepancies in the public realm. Charron's concept of wisdom results in what Nannerl O. Keohane describes as 'the vision of the schizophrenic sage who finds appropriate composition of his character in a strict separation of his internal and external life, who walks through the world with equanimity but as an alien.'[127]

Charron's sage was thus something other than the neostoic depicted by Lipsius, who put constancy into action and recognized the need for political prudence. Furthermore, Charron's strict dichotomy between the private realm and the public was one that Lipsius had striven to avoid and, through his privileging of language and scholarship, managed to do so. It also ran counter to du Vair. Yet while both these Frenchmen engaged in exploiting Lipsian ideas, their work demonstrated the inherent flexibility of neostoicism. *De la sagesse*, moreover, was particularly welcomed by those who, following du Vair in his rallying call to the *patrie*, discovered that the elements of the tripartite division of human duties could lead to the elevation of the state in a way quite beyond Charron's construction. In 1609 the young Jean Duvergier, subsequently the Abbé de Saint-Cyran and a founder of Jansenism, sought to answer the question posed by the king, who asked whether a subject was bound to give his life, if required, for his monarch. Duvergier responded by calling upon the Charronian distinctions of self, family, and state, each enjoying a corresponding set of laws, duties, and ethics. Insisting that the highest duty was owed to the state, not the self, he avowed that a citizen ought willingly to sacrifice individual existence for the good of the greater whole. Accordingly, the state was the highest form of community – the 'brotherhood of the dying.' As a participant in this most 'austere religion,' as Duvergier called it, an individual might be called upon to 'give up his life for his Prince, to immerse himself in the love and memory of his fellow citizens by a generous death, in order not to engage himself in the ruin of his country.' The stoics' concept of suicide, sidestepped by Lipsius and du Vair, was revived by Duvergier, who lauded the example of Socrates. Needless to say, this response proved gratifying to Henry IV; to Duvergier's apparent surprise, it was also popular with the book-buying public.[128]

Thus Charron was not to have it all his own way. His treatise on wisdom offered consolation to many who disdained the methods of government, enjoying a wide readership in England, yet it also provided fodder for other interpretations. The same might be said for his view of learning. *De la sagesse* represented a turning away from humanism; by its cleavage of the public and the private realms, it promoted study and enquiries of the past only insofar as they benefited the private individual. Learning was limited to the pursuit of individual *sapientia*; its role as *scientia*, or as Lipsius would have put it, *doctrina*, was wholly undermined. One consequence of this renewed sceptical assault was that history again ceased to have a public function. Any critical insights of the sage were to be applied only to the self and only in his inner and domestic capacities.

Henry IV and his successors in power seem to have preferred the Lipsian affirmation of the study of history, however.[129] As J.H. Elliott has noted, Richelieu owned the complete works of Lipsius, whose influence infused the Cardinal's own *Testament Politique*.[130] Under royal auspices, scholars, jurists, and historians searched the past for examples of French greatness and lessons for present political uses. Tacitus played a key role here, for his *Agricola* and *Germania*, depicting the northern Europeans of classical times in a favourable light, made him an important source for that period among later students.[131] Scholarship became, according to William H. Church, 'a vehicle of orthodoxy, a source of moral teachings and lessons by examples.'[132] The function of history thus mutated once again. In the Lipsian paradigm, history taught constancy and was invoked to secure the wisdom required by the circumstances of the times; as the seventeenth century progressed, it became a means of indoctrination as the nation was inundated with the philosophy of reason of state.[133]

## Lipsius and English Humanism

Sketching one direction in which the Lipsian paradigm was developed does not mean that everywhere it followed the same route. Lipsius had critics as well as admirers, and as the sixteenth century wore into the seventeenth, Lipsius could be invoked as much in derision as in admiration, and was, particularly across the Channel. As noted earlier, James Stuart, while yet king of Scotland, set an important precedent by dismissing him as 'proud' and 'inconstant.' Whereas the remark initially pertained to Lipsius's religious peregrinations, neither James nor, later, his churchmen admired Lipsian political teachings, even though they set out an explanatory scheme for the actions of the very king who abhorred them.[134] In a sermon preached before the Parliament of 1621, William Loe lamented that too many Englishmen 'studie Bodines Commentaries, Lipsius Pollitiques, and Machiuells Prince ..., more than the holy Scriptures.'[135] If in France, then, Lipsian thought could be turned into a prop for absolutism, in England there was no guarantee the same would follow.

That is not to say that initially Lipsius was not admired. The intellectual community that claimed Lipsius as a distinguished member also included the young Elizabethan courtier, Sir Philip Sidney. In 1577 Sidney had visited Louvain, where audiences of dignitaries thronged to listen to Lipsius's lectures on Tacitus.[136] Little evidence survives to indicate whether Sidney and Lipsius actually met at this juncture, but soon thereafter Sidney wrote to his younger brother, Robert, recommending a number of authors for study, and isolating Tacitus as superior among the ancients and inestimable in the study of politics, 'in the pithy opening the venom of wickedness.'[137] Robert duly took Philip's advice, acquiring Lipsius's 1585 edition of Tacitus and filling its margins with annotations on the parallelisms between Tacitus's Rome and the England of his day. As well, he entered into correspondence with the Flemish scholar, whom his brother had hoped to entice to England.[138] In September 1586, Philip wrote to Lipsius assuring him that his invitation to bring him to England looked about to win royal favour: 'I know,' wrote Sidney, 'that you would be most welcome to our Queen and to many others, yea all others.'[139] Sidney thus wrote not just to the foremost authority on Tacitus; by this date a keen friendship had grown between them, based upon a number of mutual concerns, not least their common assumptions about humanism. And although Sidney's chief concern was the *vita activa* and Lipsius's the life of scholarship, differences in vocation are more apparent than real when we take into account their shared belief in the relationship between living and learning. Humanism as the application of study to life had been a lesson upon which Sidney's mentor, Hubert Languet, had never failed to insist.[140] Harsh experience, however, prepared Sidney for a role that he could hardly have foreseen in the Lipsian paradigm.

Sidney encountered troubles enough in attempting to realize a life of action. In 1579, after criticizing the marriage negotiations between Elizabeth and the Duke of Alençon, he was virtually banished from court and never again entirely trusted by the Queen.[141] She relented somewhat in 1585; as a result of the assassination of William of Orange, the gaining foothold of the Spaniards in the Netherlands, and the growing fear of Spanish intentions against England, the Earl of Leicester was finally dispatched to lead an alliance of Protestant forces and Sidney was allowed to accompany him. After a five-year hiatus in his career, Sidney's talents were finally employed. In the interim he had turned to writing.

In his *Defense of Poesie*, Sidney articulated a theory of poetry as the highest form of instruction; subsequently he composed the *Arcadia*, which was largely an exercise in the practical application of his theory.[142] Through the form and language of allegory, Sidney touched upon questions bearing on England's refusal to become a major partner in the Protestant cause on the continent and the Queen's policy of maintaining her knights at the tilt instead of charging them with true battle.[143] Mingling the chivalric and pastoral traditions, Sidney called the *Arcadia* a 'toy' and his friend Fulke Greville later spoke of it as a 'dainty work,' but through the vehicle of imaginative literature Sidney explored the realm of politics to suggest the likely consequences for the state when monarchs abdicated their responsibilities.[144] The *Arcadia* was closely affiliated with the literature of instruction – the mirror for princes genre – though also a testament to Sidney's personal frustration in face of Elizabethan policies and the Queen's reticence in employing him.[145] In these circumstances, writing was action by other means; Fulke Greville later insisted that Sidney's 'end was not in writing, even while he wrote; nor his knowledge moulded for the tables or schools, but both his wit and understanding bent upon his heart to make himself and others, not in words and opinion, but in life and action, good and great.'[146] Sidney, as indeed Greville, would have preferred to apply learning to deeds; instead it permeated their literature of complaint.

Sidney had not been alone in his frustration. It was shared by advocates of a strong Protestant alliance both at home and on the Continent. Sidney represented the future leadership of England to many Continentals, as well as the most likely candidate to lead an alliance against the forces of Hapsburg Spain.[147] In the *Politica* (1589), Lipsius would advocate the adoption of Roman techniques of warfare and mobilization, stressing the need for preparedness in the face of aggressive neighbours; although by that time he was also considering the advantages of Spanish sovereignty in the Netherlands, earlier, in 1585, he too had been convinced that the restoration of peace in Europe depended upon a strong military alliance against Spain. Moreover, in *De constantia* (1584), he had spoken of the rise of England as successor to Rome (a prognosis that, in the 1650s, would be eagerly appropriated by English republicans).[148] Familist teachings on the role of prophecy as spiritual engagement probably informed Lipsius's own prediction of English triumph, since the prophetic and *similitudo temporum* intermeshed in his writings. With his belief in the utility of knowledge and scholarship, and his concept of the vitality of the written word, Lipsius must have expected his words to materialize into reality, as they did among some of his students. And as his acquaintance with Sidney grew, he became assured that Roman virtue had not disappeared from the world and that Sidney's triumph might perhaps herald the *pax britannica* evoked in *De constantia*. The death of Sidney and Leicester's mismanagement of the Netherlands ultimately led him to repose his trust in the power of Spain and migrate back to Louvain.[149] But this turn of events was by no means a foregone conclusion in 1586.

Rather, in that year London seemed his likely destination. The possibility was enhanced not only by Sidney's efforts on his behalf but by Lipsius's belief that Sidney represented the hope of the West. Dedicating to him his dialogue on correct Latin pronounciation, Lipsius called Sidney the 'bright star of Britannia'; and with reference to Sidney he remarked to a friend, 'Blessed is England in this, that its nobility is truly noble, educated as it is in studies of *virtus* and *doctrina*.'[150] Neostoicism as 'doctrine,' we will remember, was what Lipsius defined in the *Politica*, where he invoked the example of Roman commander Agricola. A measure of his reverence for the classical past, the reference masked any contemporary parallel he had in mind, leaving it open for readers to decide for themselves. His letter of 1585 suggests, however, that his own concept of 'doctrine' had taken firmer shape according to the pattern he saw manifested in Sidney, and it was subsequent to his friendship with Sidney that he set out to define and validate it.[151] In the end Lipsius never did migrate to England. Instead something of the reverse occurred. If in his own writings, Sidney harked to prevailing English courtly and Italianate models, Lipsius, in devising neostoicism, identified the model of virtue represented by Sidney, appropriated it, and applied it in both *De constantia* and the *Politica*.

Yet if Sidney embodied *virtus* and *doctrina* for Lipsius, all was far from well among the English nobility. Humanism as a system of education was certainly thriving, but the principle of application left many – as it had Sidney – frustrated in view of the inadequate employment afforded by the state. In this sense, humanism did not so much need rescuing as it did leeway to accommodate its devotees, a task which engaged many who were associated with one of the central figures of the 1590s, Robert Devereux, Earl of Essex – Sidney's designated heir and, after the deaths of Leicester and Walsingham, the would-be leader of the anti-Spanish faction at the Elizabethan court. In the heady days of Essex's rise, scholars supported by Essex inquired into the powers and privileges of an earl in England, thus to establish Essex as preeminent in the social and political spheres.[152] Implicit in this approach was the subtle circumvention of the idea of the monarch as the fountain of all honour, an aspect of

English politics which Essex resented in view of the favour Elizabeth could show a 'knave' like Sir Walter Ralegh, who shared Essex's militant anti-Spanish stance but owed his rise to the Queen's whim (as Essex saw it) and little to noble birth (which indeed Ralegh lacked).[153] The rivalry between Essex and Ralegh dated to the days of Leicester, who had sought to counterpose Ralegh's growing influence with the Queen by promoting Essex as successor to his office of Master of the Horse. With the death of Leicester, however, it was less any anti-Spanish faction which came to predominate at court than the cautious advice of Lord Burghley. Contemporaries soon noticed that Burghley was grooming as *his* successor his son, Sir Robert Cecil; this at the expense of others, themselves able and worthy, to whom Burghley offered only 'fair words, with no real show of kindness' or advancement.[154]

In this context of court rivalries and diminishing opportunities, Essex's circle grew. Fulke Greville, lifelong friend and long-term mourner of Sidney, eventually took up quarters at Essex House in London, joining others who, like Greville, felt totally at home in its intellectually stimulating atmosphere. Learning – comprising both reading and writing – was an important occupation in Essex's household, and the Earl's political and intellectual interests were reflected in the cosmopolitanism and talents of those he recruited into his service.[155] Henry Cuffe, the Oxford Tacitean, was one of Essex's principal secretaries and advisors, and Henry Savile, who in 1591 produced the first English translation of Tacitus, won the provostry of Eton in 1595 through Essex's efforts on his behalf. Eventually (in 1623) Savile would be succeeded at Eton by Henry Wotton, whose own diplomatic career under James I culminated in that academic office but had its beginnings in the service of Essex. Antonio Perez, the Spanish exile with a penchant for Lipsian ideas, and Anthony Bacon, elder brother of the more famous Sir Francis, were also members of the Essex household.[156] During a long stay in France, Anthony Bacon had befriended Montaigne; John Aubrey later wrote that Anthony 'was a very great states-man, and much beyond his brother for the Politiques.' Bacon, himself in Essex's service, wrote of his brother as 'a gentleman whose ability the world taketh knowledge of for matters of state, especially foreign.'[157] Whatever their specific areas of expertise, Essex's clients and secretaries were all proponents of the conjuction of learning and action. And by virtue of their expertise, 'politic history,' as F.J. Levy has called it, in close relationship with Tacitism, emerged onto the English political scene.[158]

Essex himself, if we can believe Ben Jonson's later remark, composed the Preface to Savile's translation of Tacitus' *Histories*, signing himself 'A.B.'[159] Here, readers were informed that 'there is no learning so proper for the direction of the life of a man as Historie; there is no historie (I speake onelie of prophane) so well woorth the reading as Tacitus.' Tacitus was also recommended for two other special qualities. On the one hand, he 'hath writen the most matter with best conceyt in fewest wordes of anie Historiographer ancient or moderne. But he is harde. *Difficilia quae pulchra*: the second reading ouer will please thee more then the first, and the third then the second.' On the other hand, Tacitus taught 'all the miseries of a torne and declining state: The Empire vsurped; the Princes murthered; the people wauering; the soldiers tumultuous; nothing vnlawful to him that hath power, and nothing so vnsafe as to bee securely innocent.' Concluding with a discreet hymn of praise to Elizabeth, 'A.B.' reminded each reader to 'be thankfull for thine owne peace,' to 'acknowledge our owne happie gouernement,' and 'to thanke god for her vnder whom England enioyes as manie benefites, as euer Rome did suffer miseries vnder the greatest Tyrant.'[160]

Caveats nothwithstanding, the emphasis on what Lipsius had defined as 'doctrine,' with its important parent 'memory,' pervade the tenor of this preface. According to Lipsius, the 'apparent Similitude that is betwixt those times and ours' made Tacitus deeply relevant to late sixteenth-century European contexts; it also made him not only valuable in Essex's estimation but of ultimate political point. The particular Tacitean compositions chosen by Savile for translation – the *Histories*, which opens with Julius Vindex's rebellion against the tryant Nero, and the *Agricola*, the biography of Tacitus's father-in-law set against the machinations of Vespesian's Rome – bespeak much of Essex's political agenda. On the one hand, they depict the sordid world of Imperial Roman politics and illustrate the cunning required for political survival. On the other, while highlighting the corrupt nature of politics, they hail the martial spirit of certain Roman generals. As Malcolm Smuts has remarked, 'Savile bracketed Tacitus' narrative of civil wars with stories of two noble and patriotic soldiers, who emerge as virtually the only admirable characters in the volume.'[161] Tacitus could be read as an authority on political and courtly behaviour, and Tacitus – together with Lipsius, who helped revive the interest in Roman military imperialism – paid great attention to the military techniques by which Rome achieved its victories, which Henry Savile studied in preparation for his own treatises on Roman warfare.[162] Agricola, we will remember, exemplified virtue for Tacitus, just as Philip Sidney did for Lipsius; Essex strove to fill

Sidney's (and Leicester's) place, aspiring to emerge the premier general in England. The emulation of Roman warfare and the relationship of war to court politics were central to the role he saw for himself in the English state; his secretaries, advisors, and clients busied themselves in uncovering ancient wisdom for contemporary application.

But Essex could not escape the growing conviction that he bore the brunt of all that was wrong in a political system that was dominated by court faction.[163] By 1599 Robert Cecil had gained the Queen's confidence, although his triumph over Essex was as yet incomplete. Essex gambled that his preeminence could be achieved through an expedition to Ireland, recently risen in rebellion against the English. Francis Bacon advised him not to imperil his reputation by either staking it on dangerous quicksands (which Ireland usually proved to be) or leaving the home field (the English court) in the hands of his enemies.[164] Essex ignored this advice, just as earlier he ignored the advice of Thomas Egerton. After a controversial disagreement with the Cecils at court – which led to the famous scene in which Elizabeth boxed the earl's ears and he responded by making to draw his sword – Essex had sullenly withdrawn from the court. Subsequently, Egerton wrote begging Essex to conquer his pride and return to actively serve his queen and country. Alluding to the authority wielded at court by the Cecils, he urged Essex to submit to political reality. To drive home his point, Egerton invoked the Senecan dictum on the necessity of yielding unto fortune: 'cedendu est fortunae.' Essex replied: '... you say I must give way to time. So I do, for now that I see the storm come, I have put myself into harbour. Seneca saith, we must give way to Fortune: I know that Fortune is both blind and strong, and therefore I go as far as I can out of the way.'[165] If Tacitus had offered useful parallels for Essex's position, Seneca, too, was thus harnessed by him. But it was a somewhat disingenuous use of Seneca; Essex also hoped that force of personality – and his activities in Ireland – would alter his fortune. They didn't. As one of his earliest biographers, his own one-time secretary Sir Henry Wotton, noted, the fault for his failures lay fundamentally with Essex himself. Comparing Essex with a later favourite (of King James), the Duke of Buckingham, Wotton remarked that 'the Earl was the worst Philosopher, being a great Resenter and a weak Dissembler of the least disgrace: And herein likewise, as in the rest, no good pupill of my Lord of Leicester, who was wont to put all his passions in his pocket.'[166] Disregarding Leicester's example, the fundamental lessons on political prudence taught by Tacitus, Seneca, Lipsius, and others also went unlearnt.

Not two years later, moreover, the force of his personality, combined with his use of learning and the past, passed the point of no return. In a final mad bid for the Queen's ear, Essex endorsed a staging of *Richard II*, a history which, earlier, had provoked some concern among the authorities. That Yorkist king had been as much the subject of a *Life* of Henry IV (1599), by John Hayward, as the title character, and on the *Life*'s first appearance, Hayward was summoned to court to answer for a history in which 'a kinge is taxed for misgovernm[en]t, his councell for corrupt and covetous for their private [ends], the king censured for conferring benefits of hatefull parasites and fauorites, the nobles discontented, the commons groning vnder continuall taxation, herevpon the king is deposed, [and] by an erle and in the end murdres [murthered].'[167] Essex himself was implicated in two ways. First, the *Life* was dedicated to him, and in the dedication Hayward likened him to the Bolingbroke of his history, silently suggesting that Essex was the virtuous commander who would ultimately triumph in contemporary England. Second, Essex's disaffection with the court was too well known, and Hayward's history depicted, in the words of F.J. Levy, 'a reign whose troubles were all too similar to those of late Elizabethan England.'[168]

The consequences of that episode turned out to be minimal for Essex. His sponsorship of *Richard II*, however, brought Elizabeth and her council face to face with the now undisguised implications of *similitudo temporum* as a tool in literature. She who had previously been depicted as 'Cynthia' and other allegorical characters, now found herself openly associated with real and historical characters – characters, moreover, whose reputations were tarnished and whose overthrow was praised. As she told the antiquary William Lambarde, 'I am Richard II. Know ye not that?'[169] And she was right; the play had been staged to arouse popular support for Essex's cause and *her* suspicions about textual ontology were awakened. The consequences of Essex's misplaced assumptions were far-ranging.

Essex had finally come to sponsor learning not only as a justification for action but as the prelude to rebellion. Neither amounted to much; history did not repeat itself. Essex was tried and executed for treason; and for providing 'expositions' on ancient texts, Cuffe the Tacitean was accused of having moved Essex to commit the 'perfidiousness' of rebellion.[170] Cuffe paid for his labours with his life; others, like the more fortunate Savile, found themselves briefly imprisoned.[171] But not only did Essex's aims and ambitions collapse as a result of his failure; the relationship between learning and politics was brought to a new crisis point.

Force of circumstances, intellectual preferences, and personality had coalesced in bringing Essex – and with him English humanism – to this point. The shift away from allegory and courtly styles to historical and realistic ones had made an impact on politics; and whether as rival, patron, or problematic *exemplum*, Essex would remain of major significance to those overwhelmingly concerned with the *vita activa*. Ralegh, his old nemesis, and Bacon and Greville, his one-time clients, outlived Essex and were left to grapple anew with the problems facing English humanism. In these twilight years of Elizabeth's reign, and in the next decade when they sought to participate in the Jacobean public sphere, one certainty presented itself to them – political virtue perforce had to be redefined.

# 1

# The Constant Courtier: Sir Walter Ralegh in Jacobean England

I beleve it that sorrows are dangerus companions, converting badd into yevill and yevill into worse, and do no other service than multeply harms. They ar the treasures of weak harts and of the foolishe. The minde that entertayneth them is as the yearth and dust wheron sorrows and adversetes of the world do, as the beasts of the field, tread, trample, and defile. The minde of man is that part of God which is in us, which, by how mich it is subject to passion, by so mich it is farther from Hyme that gave it us.    (Ralegh to Cecil, 1597)

[T]he same iust God who liueth and gouerneth all things for euer, doeth in these our times giue victorie, courage, and discourage, raise, and throw downe Kinges, Estates, Cities, and Nations, for the same offenses which were committed of old, and are committed in the present: for which reason, in these and other the afflictions of Israel, alwaies the causes are set downe, that they might bee as precedents to succeeding ages.   (*The History of the World*, II, xix, 3)

Let thy love, therefore, be to the best so long as they do well, but take heed that thou love God, thy country, thy prince, and thine own estate before all others, for the fancies of men change, and he that loves today hateth tomorrow. But let reason be thy schoolmistress, which shall ever guide thee aright.
            (Ralegh's *Instructions to His Son*)

Sir Walter Ralegh is popularly remembered as a gallant Elizabethan courtier, the raider of the Spanish Main, founder of Virginia, and the introducer of tobacco to England. Scholars, of course, know that he was the great rival of that other dashing Elizabethan, the Earl of Essex, surviving him only to become a long-term political prisoner, ultimately meeting his end in 1618, a martyr to Jacobean pro-Spanish policies. In the seventeenth century, much of Ralegh's fame was due to the manner in which he faced death. Some fifty years after his execution John Aubrey remarked that Ralegh had 'many things to be commended in his life, but none more than his *constancy* at his death'; in 1618, King James himself had agreed that Ralegh met his death 'with a great deal of courage and *constancy*.'[1]

Expressed thus, prevailing English notions of 'constancy' appear unrelated to ideas about political participation, pertaining more to outward comportment – the conventional, Boethian sense, evoking steadfastness, dignity, even resigned obedience to dictates from above. How far Ralegh would have agreed is suggested from the epigraphs above and is the subject of this chapter. For his engagement with the idea of political virtue was lifelong, preoccupying him right up until his death on the block. It led him to pursue questions troubling others of his generation who outlived the Virgin Queen, simultaneously drawing him into the European arena of political discussion. Ralegh borrowed heavily from Seneca, Tacitus, and other authors of the classical world in his Jacobean writings, and, as we shall see, the ideas he expressed on political virtue in those years were shaped in light of English uses of both Tacitus and Lipsius. Joining the dialogue over (what is narrowly termed) Tacitism, he responded with political prescriptions geared towards gaining him service under the Stuarts. In this respect, Ralegh was a *constant* courtier, constant in a Lipsian sense as he wrote to demonstrate his talents as an advisor to a king who was of a different political stripe from Elizabeth. If posterity has dubbed him 'the last Elizabethan,' he perhaps deserves better to be remembered as a would-be but frustrated Jacobean. Moreover, by virtue of his reputation among contemporaries and posterity alike, such 'constancy' as he invoked, and even (as we shall see) the neostoicism he adopted, can stand as a measure of approaches to political virtue on the part of those contemporaries of his whom we shall meet in subsequent chapters.

**Ralegh and the *Vita Activa***

An analysis of Ralegh's attitude towards political virtue may begin with a sketch of his career, which divides, quite neatly, into two phases.[2] Under Elizabeth, he rose from virtual obscurity to become a prominent courtier; for twenty years he arduously combined service to the state with personal advance. Five years of disgrace intervened when he married without the Queen's consent, but he was soon restored to favour.

Under James, he lost everything, spending the majority of the years left to him after 1603 in the Tower condemned as a traitor. He kept his life only by the grace of a king who stayed the execution of the death sentence against him for fifteen years.

The vacillations of his fortunes under Elizabeth, and the long years of imprisonment which culminated in his execution under James, certainly suggest the 'absolute' nature of the monarchy in early modern England, although Ralegh's career was clearly subject to the changing nature of international relations.[3] In the 1580s and 1590s, while Spain presented a real military threat to England, Ralegh's star rose; in the years after the arrival of the first Stuart to the English throne, Spain was placated and Ralegh's anti-Spanish reputation turned him into a liability. King James did find one occasion to call upon Ralegh's military and naval talents. In 1616, the condemned traitor was released from the Tower and 'commissioned' to seek out the wealth of Guiana to help restore the ailing royal coffers. The expedition proved a miserable failure that culminated in an engagment with the Spaniards. On his return, the Spanish ambassador in England demanded Ralegh's head; the English king complied. His execution was witnessed by both John Eliot and John Pym – future critics of Charles I. And since his admirers included the revolutionaries of the subsequent generation, Oliver Cromwell and John Milton, some scholars have tended to view the beheading of King Charles in 1649, and the abolition of the English monarchy in the same year, as Ralegh's ultimate exoneration. 'The ghost of Ralegh,' concluded G.M. Trevelyan, 'pursued the House of Stuart to the scaffold.'[4] Strictly speaking, however, there was little irony in the occasion; Ralegh, who had risen to prominence by virtue of his military and naval exploits, finally went to the block precisely because he failed to make good his reputation on behalf of the monarch.

International diplomacy – compounded by military failure – was only one factor at play in determining Ralegh's fate. Court intrigue was another. His Elizabethan career epitomizes the politics of courtiership, but in serving Elizabeth as he did he had made few friends and many enemies at court.[5] In the wake of the new king's arrival he was promptly accused of complicity in the two early conspiracies against James. The Bye Plot, by which James was to be abducted, and the Main Plot, by which he was to be replaced by Lady Arabella Stuart, were uncovered before they had any chance of realization, and Ralegh's involvement was largely a matter of the prosecution's invention. 'Thou hast a Spanish heart, and thyself art a spider of hell,' pronounced

Attorney-General Edward Coke, whose case consisted of attempting to establish the validity of these allegations.[6] The idea that Ralegh was supporting any Spanish claim to the throne of England was indeed a travesty. As he wrote in a letter to Sir Robert Cecil begging his intercession, it was a 'hevy burden of God to be in danger of perishinge for a Prince [the king of Spain] which I have so longe hated ...'[7] Ralegh conducted his own defence, maintained his innocence, and questioned both the procedure of the court and the substance of the charges. Coke and his colleagues were able to sway the jury to bring in a guilty verdict against Ralegh; but others were not so sure. One Scottish observer related that 'whereas when he saw [Ralegh] first, he was so led with the common hatred that he would have gone a hundred miles to have seen him hanged, he would, ere he parted, have gone a thousand to have saved his life.' Ralegh's self-defence had been so impressive that the ever alert Dudley Carleton noted that 'in the opinion of all men he had been acquitted.'[8]

Ben Jonson's Tacitean play, *Sejanus*, with its plots and subterfuges, and with its depiction of the manipulations of power on the part of Roman Emperor Tiberius's favourite, evoked the travesty of Ralegh's trial; for his pains, Jonson had to answer to the king's Council.[9] All men, indeed, were as nothing before the court which had found Ralegh guilty; nor could he expect much clemency from the king, his dealings with James having suffered from the start. Ignoring James while he had been merely king of Scotland, Ralegh had held fast to his support of the queen on the question of the succession – an issue that punctuated politics during Elizabeth's reign but which, had it been settled in her lifetime, would have threatened the opening of a reversionary interest at best, and, at worst, the prospect of the queen's removal.[10] Elizabeth's determination to avoid naming her successor disturbed many of her courtiers, but to a large extent it kept them faithful to her.

This issue, which only troubled the Queen, proved lethal to Ralegh, who, unlike Essex in the late 1590s, abstained from making overtures to James. Moreover, after the death of Essex, Robert Cecil (who was a councillor) and Henry Howard (a one-time client of Essex who aspired to royal service) shared none of Ralegh's inhibitions.[11] These English suitors assured James of their support and, seeking to prepare for a smooth transition, they also hoped to establish themselves as candidates for his future English government. They thus sought to discredit potential rivals. Cecil, a sometime ally of Ralegh, did not hesitate to warn the Scottish king against him:

Let me, therefore, presume thus far upon your Majesty's favour that, whatsoever he [Ralegh] shall take upon him to say for me, upon any new humour of kindness – whereof sometimes he will be replete, upon the receipt of private benefit – you will no more believe it ... be it never so much in my commendation ... Would God I were as free from offence towards God in seeking, for private affection, to support a person whom most religious men do hold anathema.[12]

Cecil, it has been noted, had the 'sense to abandon a friend who was obviously bound for trouble.'[13] And indeed, James's accession augured trouble for Ralegh – more than Ralegh could have foreseen. By calling into doubt not only Ralegh's political integrity but his entire character, Cecil was probably instrumental in subverting Ralegh's hopes to make a good, if late, impression on James.

Any further chance was eroded by Henry Howard, whose indictment of Ralegh was both more damning than Cecil's and less discreet. He labelled Ralegh and two others (Ralegh's friends, Lord Cobham and the Earl of Northumberland) a 'diabolical triplicity' which James should do well to avoid.[14] Even before the death of Elizabeth, Howard had expressed his hatred for Ralegh, confiding, in a letter to Cecil, his hope that Ralegh would incur Elizabeth's displeasure: 'by how much this man wanteth better helps by nature, art, or industry, to countenance a pride above the greatest Lucifer that hath ever lived in our age, by so much shall he sooner run himself on the ground in rage and make the queen more sensitive in scorning so great sauciness in so great infirmity.'[15] To Howard, Ralegh stood as one 'that in pride exceedeth all men alive.' Almost every word he expressed about Ralegh gave testimony to John Aubrey's observation that Ralegh was widely hated because 'he was so damnably proud.'[16]

Of this pride, which coloured the impressions of so many contemporaries including, presumably, James VI of Scotland, there can be little doubt. Elevated by Elizabeth from virtual obscurity, Ralegh rose to dizzying heights, wearing, in the words of Steven May, 'his newly acquired wealth and status with a haughty swagger that infuriated his fellow-courtiers and lesser countrymen alike.'[17] In 1587 he was described as 'the best hated man of the world, in Court, city, and country.'[18] Ralegh never repented of the outward carriage which gave rise to such vehement condemnation – nor even openly acknowledged it as the source of his troubles. Rather, his raw experiences during the transitional year in which James VI of Scotland became king of England drove home for him the lesson that a certain amount of deceit was vital for political survival.

We shall see that Ralegh approached what Lipsius had called *prudentia mixta* in something of a Lipsian way, focusing on language and inspecting its application in society. There was also a hard-hearted realism to his advice on political survival – as the last epigraph at the opening of this chapter indicates. And he noted, 'great men forget such as have done them service when they have obtained what they would, and will rather hate thee for *saying* thou hast been a mean of their advancement than acknowledge it.'[19] With reference to his own experience, such advice suggests that Ralegh was well aware of the tenor of Cecil's disavowal of him.[20] He would also have known that Howard's animosity towards him was perhaps exacerbated by his own demeanour but sprang from another quarter.

For as Ralegh rose in the queen's estimation, Howard, a nobleman and kinsman to the queen, struggled, in his own words, 'below the compass of my birth.'[21] And as Ralegh prospered, Howard lay under a cloud of suspicion for his support of Mary Queen of Scots's claim for the succession of the English throne. Many of Elizabeth's leading councillors, including Ralegh, considered him a natural enemy. After 1587, however, Ralegh jostled with Essex for Elizabeth's undivided favour, and in the 1590s Howard became closely associated with Essex, whose views of nobility matched Howard's own. But Ralegh and Essex both faced Cecil's growing supremacy at court. As events aligned themselves for the fiasco of the Essex rebellion, Howard played safe. A court-watcher described him as 'a neuter,' cautioning his correspondant, Ralegh's close friend Sir Robert Sidney, to 'take heed of him, be not too bold to trust him.'[22] Howard survived the crisis bought about by Essex's rising, but at Essex's trial, Ralegh had been called to testify against him and Essex derided Ralegh, asking, 'What booteth it to swear this fox?'[23] Notably, however, he called for reconciliation with Ralegh before his execution, in his last minutes declaring that Ralegh was among the 'true servants' of the queen. Yet Essex's final exoneration of Ralegh meant little to Howard, who in the aftermath of the rebellion became the chief mediator for the transmission of the English crown to James VI of Scotland. Any promise Ralegh might have had to establish his credentials with James was instantly diminished. Ralegh referred to Howard as 'my heavy enemy'; but James valued Howard's assessments above all others.[24] Indeed, Howard had proved his worth on at least two counts. He had always championed the claims of the House of Stuart; and (despite his fence-sitting at the end) he had been a trusted advisor of Essex, the instigator of the Scottish correspondence. James wrote Cecil with a commendation of Howard, calling him 'his long approved and trusty 3' – which was the code ascribed to Howard. The secret letter went on, 'since long before this time 3 dealt very earnestly with 30 [James] to take good conceit of 10 [Cecil], offering himself to be a dealer betwixt them, whereupon 30 was contented 3 should deal betwixt Essex and 10 ... for the well [sic] of 30.'[25] Howard gauged events well. When James succeeded to the English throne his star was to rise as Ralegh's correspondingly plummetted. Ralegh was not to taste freedom under the Stuart monarchy until Howard, after 1603 the Earl of Northampton, was dead.

Ralegh was imprisoned, but the route of the written word remained open. From the Tower, Ralegh maintained many friendships: with Sir Robert Sidney, brother of the long dead Sir Philip and himself a friend and correspondant of Lipsius; with Sir Robert Cotton, whose collection of manuscripts and books was the envy of the political nation; and, among others, with Jonson, the playwright and poet.[26] With the help of such friends he wrote the incomplete but still monumental *History of the World*. First published in 1614, it was immediately recalled by James I 'for divers exceptions, but specially for being too sawcie in censuring princes.'[27] Appearing with the censors' approval in 1616, it went on to enjoy numerous reprintings during the seventeenth century. Ralegh also devoted considerable time to furnishing testaments of his political views in tracts such as *Instructions to his Son* and *The Prerogative of Parliaments*. Nor did he ever give up hope for his release. Letters requesting pardon went out to the king and Cecil (after 1605, the Earl of Salisbury), and he developed schemes for exploration and colonization in the hope that these might furnish the grounds for his release.[28] While they had little effect on the king, his words and plight struck home with Queen Anne and the young Prince of Wales.

Henry was particularly interested in Ralegh's views on the threatening power of Spain.[29] Ralegh urged the seizing of every initiative against the Spaniards, maintaining that Spain 'is to be feared' and warning that 'neutrality is always a thing dangerous and disallowable' – ideas subsequently rendered virtually synonymous with Ralegh's name.[30] Proponents of an aggressive anti-Spanish policy in the 1620s would call upon 'Ralegh's Ghost' to resurrect his calls for military preparedness and engagement.[31] Posterity has tended to view Ralegh's intellectual importance in the same light. Christopher Hill, for instance, while hailing Ralegh as one of the thinkers most 'relevant for the pre-revolutionary age' (which was the first quarter of the seventeenth century), considers that, with his practical concerns with expansion, empire-building, and naval reform, Ralegh was instrumental in laying the foundations for the growth of the concept of English empire in the later seventeenth century.[32] Richard Tuck, however, has recently drawn attention to the Tacitean overtones of Ralegh's expansionist strain of thought, which Tuck associates with Richelieu's vision of 'French universalism,' itself drawn from what Tuck calls the 'new humanism' developed by Lipsius, Botero, Ammirato, and others in the 1590s.[33] Tacitus, as we saw in the Introduction, depicted an imperialism that was scrutinized by Lipsius and his scholarly contemporaries, adopted in both Spain in the early 1600s and France slightly later, and, indeed, was advocated by Ralegh in his Jacobean writings.

For Ralegh, the quest for empire and expansion loomed large, but that quest formed only one aspect of his political thinking; it represented, moreover, a consequence or outcome of political virtue as he defined it. For he also took it upon himself to impart to Henry lessons of politics and proper rule. *The Cabinet-Council* and *The Prince, or Maxims of State* were compilations made for Henry's instruction. Once accepted as original Ralegh compositions, their authorship now appears in question; Ernest A. Strathmann has argued that the former was written not by Ralegh but a certain 'T.B.' (probably Thomas Bedingfield, the English translator of Machiavelli's *History of Florence*); of the latter, Pierre Lefranc concedes that Ralegh probably had some role in compiling it but suggests that it be dismissed from the Ralegh canon on the grounds that it is inconsistent both in style and tenor with what he considers the authoritative Ralegh writings.[34] Yet those same tracts reflect views which Ralegh made the basis of the *History of the World*. And if indeed his, they were likely compiled, as the *History* itself was composed, in response to other 'mirror for princes' pieces addressed to the prince (as we shall see in a subsequent section). Ralegh's writings had the desired effect on the prince. 'Only my father,' Henry is reported to have complained, 'could keep such a bird in a cage.'[35] The alternative court of the precocious prince looked as if it might provide political pressure enough to bring an end to Ralegh's imprisonment. In 1612 Dudley Carleton wrote to tell John Chamberlain that Henry had convinced the king to release Ralegh in time for Christmas. But then Henry died; thus, Carleton noted, Ralegh 'hath lost his greatest hope.'[36]

With the death of Prince Henry, Ralegh's term as princely councillor came to an end. It was a post he had sought under Elizabeth but never quite attained in full, and when won – in a very unofficial capacity – proved to be of short duration. Henry's death also signalled the end of the project to examine the course of world history within three volumes for the instruction of the prince. Only one volume was written, and the *History of the World*, begun with the Creation, terminated with the rise of Rome in 130 B.C., an apostrophe to death, and a powerful lament on the loss of the work's dedicatee.[37]

Ralegh was never one to despair for long, however. He continued to ply his scheme for the exploitation of Guiana, and in 1616, with Salisbury and Northampton no longer alive to provide obstacles, his release loomed close. His freedom, it turned out, was both temporary and conditional; in 1618 he finally confronted the long delayed death penalty. On receiving his sentence, Ralegh defiantly told the chief justice: 'I take God to be my judge, before whom I shall shortly appear, I was never disloyal to His Majesty; which I shall justify where I shall not fear the face of any king on earth.'[38] Then, he faced death with no outward sign of either fear or regret. It was reported that 'smiling, [he] spake unto M. Sheriffe saying, this is a sharpe medecine, but it is a physician that will cure all diseases.'[39] Treason was certainly not the disease to which he had been susceptible; nor infirmity or old age, which certainly did stalk him. The real disease from which he suffered was the quest for a life in service of his monarch.

**Ralegh on Seneca and Tacitus**

Commitment to the *vita activa* was thus the guiding principle of Ralegh's life. Denied for the most part the opportunity to serve the king, in his long-term experience as a prisoner in the Tower he never veered from his goal of royal service. It underlay his discussion of the rise and fall of ancient civilizations in the *History of the World*, where Ralegh framed his argument with reference to the stoics. His debt to ancient stoicism is the first pointer towards his engagement with neostoicism, both as it had taken shape in Europe and was being shaped in England.

The stoical element of Ralegh's thought goes unremarked among current scholarship even though it is often dominant in his work.[40] He cited the authors of classical stoicism throughout the *History*, where even in its darkest passages, and especially in the closing peroration on death, stoical teachings prevail. Ralegh put much stock in the manner of a person's death; in the *History*, it is not the activities of conquering monarchs that stand out, but the lives and deaths of dedicated servants such as the fourth-century B.C. Theban general Epaminondas, and Alexander the Great's subjects Philotas and Parmenio.[41] Many of Ralegh's portraits evoke Seneca: 'It skils not whether a man die sooner or later,' wrote Seneca in one of his *epistles*, 'to die either well or ill, that importeth much.' In another, he avowed that 'he that hath learned to die hath forgotten to serve, it is all above power, undoubtedly beyond all. What careth he for prisons, holds or restraints? He hath alwayes free passage.'[42]

Ralegh's English contemporaries were particularly critical of this Senecan attitude. Francis Bacon, though himself variously indebted to Seneca, held that 'the Stoics bestowed too much cost upon death, and by their great preparations made it appear more fearful.'[43] And for his part, Joseph Hall commended the philosophy of the stoics but expressed misgivings about the absence of Christian teachings among them, writing that he had 'followed Seneca, and gone beyond him: followed him as a philosopher, and gone beyond him as a Christian.'[44] By contrast, the saving grace of Christianity was given only lip-service by Ralegh, whose morality was characterized by a providentialism secular in tone and infused with stoical teachings.[45]

Moreover, in the *History*, pride of place – if the number of such citations can be used as a gauge – go to the utterances of Seneca. Axioms on the upright conscience, on approaches to adversity, on the folly of passion, on the misjudgments that arise from the mere appearance of things, and on the judgments of kings, were all Senecan borrowings.[46] Boethius, the early synthesizer of stoicism and Christianity, and Charron, the more recent commentator who, as we have seen in the previous chapter, was one among many altering the tenor of neostoicism in France, were also invoked in the *History*, and they reinforced the distinction Ralegh offered on the fallibility of human knowledge with respect to the purposes of providence.[47] Noting the providentialism that pervades the *History*, some Ralegh scholars have argued that his historical and political ideas were 'largely traditional and solidly Elizabethan.'[48] Thus he is considered 'representative of the cross currents of the time' and the 'culmination' of English Renaissance traditions; consequently, though, he manifested 'a view that was already passing.'[49]

It is important to stress, therefore, that the issues of the day (rather than the trajectory of intellectual history) occupied much of his time.[50] And though the power of providence was certainly upheld by Ralegh, the value of history was never denied. Moreover, insofar as Charron and others repudiated the value of history in any quest for wisdom while Ralegh (emulating the Lipsian scheme of *De constantia*) validated it (and with a vengeance, proposing to chart the experience of monarchs and kingdoms since the beginning of time), the *History* is very much a rejoinder to Charron. In 1608 the English translation of *De la Sagesse* appeared, dedicated to Prince Henry; Ralegh's counter, with its emphasis on the role of history as a guide to the operations of providence, was thus timely and, in light of his view of the educational requirements of a future king of England, necessary.[51] But before considering the extent of Ralegh's challenge to Charron and, by extension, his alternative rendition of 'constancy,' we must pause to note how one particular court rivalry affected the lessons he would convey, particularly to kings.

Thus we must briefly return to the late Elizabethan period and make note of his dealings with Essex, who, as we have seen, finally applied Tacitism not just as political criticism but as a prelude to rebellion. Ralegh owned the English translations of Tacitus; perusing them in the Tower he must have discerned the various lessons by which his friend Sir Robert Sidney could justify a position of alienation from the Stuart court.[52] But Ralegh was already keenly aware of how a certain Tacitean reading of events could encourage disservice to the monarch.

He even witnessed at first hand the performance which eventually inspired Essex to opt for rebellion as a way of enforcing his will on the queen. In 1597, as guests of Cecil, Essex and Ralegh had attended a production of *Richard II*. Ralegh wrote to Cecil noting that Essex was 'wonderfull merry att your consait' of the play – which suggests that it was Cecil who first planted in Essex's mind the idea of similitude between the last years of Richard and those of Elizabeth.[53] The evening had been planned in token of a pact of cooperation among the three, who, separately, had vied for ascendancy over the others. As Ralegh jostled with Essex for the queen's favour, Lord Burghley, who enjoyed her full confidence, was grooming his own son, Cecil, to succeed him in office. In 1597 Cecil was made a royal secretary, Ralegh regained the favour of the queen, and Essex made his peace with both. 'None but Cecil and Ralegh,' it was remarked, 'enjoy the Earl of Essex; they carry him away as they list.'[54]

Such new-found amicability was short-lived. Essex and Ralegh clashed over the operation known as the Islands voyage, in which Essex, as commander-in-chief, and Ralegh, as rear-admiral, set off to pre-empt an anticipated naval attack by the Spaniards in the summer of 1597. The entire venture was marked by the inability of the erstwhile colleagues to cooperate. Essex's volatile personality matched Ralegh's own, but for Ralegh, Essex had the unforgiveable tendency to give full vent to his rages. Essex's own close associates worried about his temper; when he was put under house arrest after his unauthorized return from Ireland in

1599, Sir John Harington complained that Essex's 'speeches of the Queen become no man who hath *mens sana corpore sano.*'[55] Ralegh's alienation from Essex became complete. Early in 1600 he wrote to Cecil: 'I am not wize enough to geve yow advise; butt if yow take it for a good councell to relent towards this tirant, yow will repent it when it shalbe too late. His mallice is fixt, and will not evaporate by any your mild courses.'[56] Thereafter Ralegh never veered from this opinion of Essex, whom he considered wanting in duty to his sovereign, not to mention indiscreet and lacking in political acumen.

Much later, in his *Prerogative of Parliaments,* he wrote that 'undutiful wordes of a subiect do often take deeper roote then the memory of ill deedes do ... The late Earle of Essex told Queene Elizabeth that her conditions were as crooked as her carkasse; but it cost him his head, which his insurrection had not cost him, but for that speech.'[57] He, by contrast, was ever mindful to be dutiful and respectful towards his sovereign – in words if not deeds. His marriage to Elizabeth Throckmorton in 1592 without the queen's permission had earned him his banishment from court; his hasty return from Guiana in 1595 reignited Elizabeth's displeasure and prolonged his punishment. In the interim, however, he compensated with words, writing justifications for his missions, a defence of the royal position on the succession, and a series of poems – from the 'Ocean' (Ralegh) to 'Synthia' (the queen) – to elicit forgiveness. In one poetic endeavour, he pronounced his unswerving loyalty as Elizabeth shifted her focus towards Essex:

> Fortune hath taken thee away, my Love,
> My live's Joy and my sowle's heaven above;
> Fortune hath taken thee away my princess,
> My world's delight and my true fancy's mistris ...
>
> With wisdome's eyes had but blind fortune seen,
> Then had my love my love for ever bin;
> But Love farewell, though fortune conquer thee,
> No fortune base shall ever alter me.

Elizabeth responded with some lines that began, 'Mourne not my Wat, nor be thou so dismaid.'[58] Ultimately, she forgave his several misdeeds.

Throughout his life, and in contrast to Essex, Ralegh addressed his monarch in a befitting manner. Circumstances dictated that he was continually asking forgiveness – from Elizabeth for his personal misdemeanours, and later from James for a wronged reputation. As Leonard Tennenhouse has noted, Ralegh always framed his words to appeal to his monarch's particular literary predilections – for romantic verse steeped in courtly conventions, in the case of Elizabeth; for learned prose discourses, in the case of James.[59] And although *The History of the World* was written for Prince Henry, it also seems designed to encourage James – through Henry – to release Ralegh from the Tower.[60] Insofar as James would consider Ralegh 'too sawcie' in his criticisms of monarchs, freedom became something of a forlorn expectation. Still, as Tennenhouse has remarked, 'the preferred literary style for patronage with the new monarch was drawn from the texts he wrote and those he promoted.'[61]

Ralegh clearly appealed to James' love of learning, constructing his own work as an exercise in it. Then, in several places, James himself was cited as a reputable authority. Ralegh invoked James' *Trew Law of Free Monarchies* late in the *History* in support of the argument that God punished tyrants; although Ralegh's use of the argument hardly conformed to that of the king, James had been cited with less ambivalence earlier. In Book I, Ralegh entered into a discussion on magic and approvingly alluded to the king's work on the subject.[62] James, in the words of Tennenhouse, 'responded favourably to lavish praise of his intellectual abilities.'[63] From this perspective, the *History* was nothing if not a prudential appeal to the king. Ralegh's willingness to please may have extended so far as to omit authors of whom James disapproved. While still king only of Scotland, James had expressed scorn for 'that proud inconstant LIPSIVS,' and in later editions of *Basilikon Doron* James continued to inveigh against false constancy and dissimulation, evoking Lipsius, whose name, however, was dropped.[64] For one so keenly aware, as was Ralegh, of a monarch's preferences and animosities, there was good reason to include a Charron, a Seneca, a Boethius, in a work that addressed a continental debate but maintained a guarded silence on one of the key members of that debate. Self-censorship, which Ralegh noticed did not prevail in Essex, was one of his own cultivated talents, permeating his indirect address to the king in the *History*.

A more direct appeal to the king was made in the *Prerogative of Parliaments*, written in 1615, in the aftermath of the dissolution of the 'Addled Parliament,' so called for its failure to resolve any of the issues for which it had been summoned, in particular the king's need for financial solvency. This too was a learned document, framed in the form of a dialogue between a justice of the peace and a privy councillor, where

Ralegh, in the words of Steven May, 'takes it upon himself to become the good advisor James lacks.'[65] Ralegh gambled somewhat in dedicating the work to the king, if only because the *History* had just been banned from publication. Quick on the heels of its suppression Ralegh purported to give advice where it was least wanted. The *Prerogative*, however, was hardly a straightforward defence of any 'prerogative' of parliaments. J.P. Sommerville has noted the 'absolutist' strain in the *Prerogative*, arguing that 'Raleigh provides a persuasive instance of a man who subscribed to absolutist notions while opposing royal policies.'[66] This is a succinct reading, but it overlooks the nature of Ralegh's own 'absolutist' frame of mind, which was wholly informed by the moral obligations under which, in his view, sovereigns laboured. The *Prerogative of Parliaments* was a call for co-operation within the body politic.[67] As a dialogue, moreover, it was quite unconcerned with any argument *in utramque partem*. Two points of view are certainly represented – one by the privy councillor, who undermines both himself and his cause; the other by the justice of the peace, who appeals for a parliament and calls for the king's co-operation. Thus schematically, the *Prerogative* is dominated by a (Lipsian) concern for closure. The scheme of the dialogue also provided Ralegh with an opportunity to draw attention to two particular details. Both related to the topic of rebellion and both reflect the contrast he would establish between himself and Essex as moral agents and as crown servants.

The first is to be seen in his reference to Essex's 'undutiful words,' in which Ralegh implicitly compared his situation under James to that of Essex in the last years of Elizabeth. Essex's angry words against the queen overshadowed any good deeds he had ever performed and shone a dark light over the particular deed for which he was condemned. By contrast, the treason charges against Ralegh – his so-called 'misdeeds' – overshadowed his many and repeated loyal words directed towards James. Essex had been blatantly 'undutiful' while Ralegh's dutiful subjection kept him incarcerated in the Tower. He complained, it is true, but always decorously and through the proper channels. Ralegh never made his cause a public one, nor, as Essex had done, a focus for rallying support against his monarch. Invoking duty and Essex together in the same context, Ralegh held himself up for contrast to the Essex whom James had befriended and whose fate James and his early councillors had lain at the feet of Ralegh.

The second point further develops the contrast with Essex and occurs when Ralegh invokes Richard II as an example of a king whose passion overtook his judgment and whose reign ended in rebellion. If the 'concait' of Richard II had struck deep with Essex, who organized a production of the play to precipitate his abortive rebellion against Elizabeth in 1601, the same parallel could be used by Ralegh to underline the conflict between reason and passion in rulers, as well as to emphasize that a king's paramount responsibility was the protection of his people. In dedicating the *Prerogative* to the king Ralegh asserted that 'the bonds of Subiects to their Kings should always be wrought out of Iron, the bonds of Kings unto Subiects but with Cobwebs.'[68] The analogy suggests that while subjects owed unswerving allegiance to their monarch, kings had a more delicate and complex relationship to maintain with their subjects. The dialogue went on to assert that the king's absolute power gave the law a force without which the kingdom could not be ruled effectively but that it was incumbent on the king to heed the complaints of his subjects. 'Shall the head yeeld to the feet?' Ralegh asked in the dedication; 'certainly it ought, when they are grieued ..., seeing if the feet lye in fetters, the head cannot be freed, and where the feet feele but their own paines, the head doth not only suffer by participation, but withall by consideration of the evil.'[69]

Richard II provided a striking illustration of one 'head' being made to yield to the 'feet.' Richard was a monarch whose passion overcame his judgment, and who, 'had he delivered up to Iustice but three or four [of his minions], he had still held the loue of the people, and thereby his life and estate.'[70] Parliament thus served an inestimable purpose in Ralegh's argument about the folly of Richard, where it operated as a corrective to abuses and an embodiment of the conscience of the land. According to Ralegh, conscience was sorely lacking in Richard, who brought his very position into question. '[W]hen a King will suffer himselfe to be eaten up by a company of pretty fellowes, by himselfe raised, therein both his judgment and courage is disputed.'[71] A contemporary parallel was implied, for such a generalization evoked the widespread complaint against James' own liberality towards favourites.[72] As in the many examples cited by Ralegh in the *History*, however, Richard II provided a model which kings should avoid emulating. Thus in contrast to Essex's use of the parallel of the reign of Richard II as a means to incite rebellion, Ralegh's purpose was to teach the king a valuable lesson on statesmanship. Where Essex had identified tyranny and then proceeded to counter it head-on, Ralegh identified misrule and went on to urge correction from within. He recommended virtue and conscience as the indispensable guides in sovereignty; under no circumstances did he condone insurrection as a response to tyrannical government. Exposure and the means to correct tyranny were one thing, incitement to rebellion another entirely. Thus Ralegh's reading of Richard II's reign clearly repudiated Essex's a decade earlier, showing, at the same time, that a Tacitist critique of princes and personalities need not result in personal alienation from the court (which was how a number of contemporaries were applying Tacitus to current affairs).

Yet there is a curious twist in Ralegh's assessment of Essex. Essex uttered 'undutiful words,' was himself a rebel, and thus provided a valuable contrast to Ralegh in his conduct towards his successive sovereigns. But the criticism of Essex tends also to exonerate him, as the blame for his demise is cast upon those among whom words, to use Bacon's phrase, are valued more than matter. Essex insulted the queen; this, posits Ralegh, was of far greater consequence than his actual insurrection. An implicit criticism is extended to a society whose mode of judgment is based upon the superficiality of words and manners. Was Ralegh pandering to the well-known sympathy of the king for Essex, whose death, fourteen years earlier, was considered by James a martyrdom to his cause during the succession crisis of Elizabeth's last years?[73] Clearly, Ralegh struggled to emerge from under the shadow cast upon him by Essex. Was there then an inconsistency between this oblique apologia for Essex and his repudiation of Essex's rebellion and the Tacitist means by which Essex had sought to galvanize support for it? The answer is contained in Ralegh's response to contemporary discussions about political dissimulation in England.

### Ralegh and Political Prudence

Most scholars agree that the primary English interest in Lipsius centred on his moral justifications of dissimulation in statecraft.[74] A late adaptation of the Lipsian formula of *prudentia mixta* was found in Robert Dallington's *Aphorismes Civill and Militarie*:

All morallists hold nothing profitable that is not honest. Some politicks have inverted this order and perverted the sense, by transposing the tearmes of the proposition, holding nothing honest that is not profitable. Howsoever those former may seeme too streight laced, these [latter] surely are too loose. For there is a middle way betweene both which a right Statesman must take.[75]

Modelled on Guicciardini, the *Aphorismes* presented a series of such snippets, touching on all aspects of governance. And for Dallington *prudentia mixta* was *the* indispensible political virtue that should be cultivated by governors. He cited in abundance the authority of Tacitus, Lipsius, and others who discussed the operations of *prudentia mixta*, dedicating the fruits of his labour to Prince Henry.[76]

Dallington's perspective, however, did not go unchallenged. Ralegh was concerned by it, and his response went in tandem with his approach to the king's repudiation of Tacitism as a form of political criticism. James was ever vigilant towards intellectual innovation, and 'Of Tacitus, James said [in conversation with Isaac Casaubon] they were wrong, who thought him the one historian, who was a master of political wisdom.'[77] The Jacobean court's misgivings about modern uses of Tacitus were apparent even before 1610, when this conversation between the king and Casaubon took place. Playwrights had brought the issue into sharp relief. Jonson's play *Sejanus* (as we saw) and Samuel Daniel's tragedy *Philotas* (1605) were Tacitist pieces which exposed the hypocrisy and corruption that followed in the train of tyrannical emperors. For their audacity, and to discover the extent of their intentions, the authors, in their respective turns, were summoned to answer to the Privy Council. Each managed to convince the judges that no aspersions on contemporary figures were intended; although thus vindicated it was plain for all who cared to see that the court disliked this form of literary endeavour.[78] Alan T. Bradford has argued that James instigated an anti-Tacitist 'reaction' which became fully expressed in Edmund Bolton's *Nero Caesar, or Monarchie Depraved*. Despite its title, this work served to show, and in words quite like those of James himself, that 'No Prince is so bad as not to make monarckie seeme the best forme of government.'[79]

Ralegh, who was among the most sensitive and responsive to royal literary tastes, joined this discussion. In the *History of the World* he noted that monarchy was relative as far as governments went; but echoing James (and indeed many others, including Lipsius), he remarked that it was 'the best Regiment, which resembleth the sovereign Government of God himself.'[80] Thus Ralegh's overall approach to monarchy largely complemented the tenor of official Jacobean rhetoric, hardly deviating from the general assumptions informing his contemporaries.[81] But it did not wholly conform to the views of James. Ralegh contested the king's assertion that kings were answerable only to God.[82] This implied a restriction on society which Ralegh countered was neither merited nor moral. The monarch was certainly peerless in honour and authority in Ralegh's view; but Ralegh also insisted that he live up to a stringent moral code, exemplifying virtue and setting a model for society at large. James I himself in writings affirmed such principles (though in life they were not always in view).[83]

Ralegh thus required a transparency in governors which his king could not quite manifest in actions, and which 'Lipsians' like Dallington – and even Lipsius himself – held to be folly but without which Ralegh considered government to be lacking in sanction. In his tracts addressed to Prince Henry, Ralegh stressed the moral factor in politics, in contrast to the greater tendency on the part of other writers in Henry's entourage to proclaim the realm of statescraft as one conditioned by criteria unique to itself. Such was the advice of Dallington, who posited that those in public employment

> must of necessity wear vizards, and change them in every scene. Because, the generall good and safetie of a State is the Center in which all their actions, and counsailes must meete: To which men cannot alwaies arrive by plaine pathes, and beaten waies. Wherefore a prince may ... sometimes leave the common high way, and take down an un-used bypath, in the lesser of dangers, so he be sure to recompence it in the greater of safetie.[84]

The problem with Dallington's advice, as Ralegh would have seen it, was that his axiomatic approach to politics opened the gate for injustices to be done and resembled, rather than any recipe for good governance, what Ralegh called the 'sophisms of tyrants.' These, he advised Prince Henry, were to be known, but not practised.[85] In both the *Maxims of State* and the *History of the World*, Ralegh stressed the sharp divide between the exercise of rule among just monarchs and tyrants, a divide which, in view of the popularity of a number of recent authors, had become fuzzy and indistinct. Among these, Lipsius had upheld the occasional use of 'immoral' acts – which he sought to define and limit, basing their sanction on the fact that contemporary language hardly conformed to the needs of a world collapsed into the 'dregs of the state of Romulus.' Charron, however, had given grounds for distinguishing between the public and the private spheres. Ralegh deferred to Charron's concept of 'wisdom' insofar as it provided insights into character, cautioned against rash judgments, and underlined the folly of opinion. By contrast, Charron's political strictures were embraced in their entirety by many surviving members of Essex's literary retinue, who in the early 1600s sought the patronage of Prince Henry.[86] Charronian assumptions also underlay the advice imparted by Dallington to the prince. Ralegh engaged in the same dialogue to urge restraint against the growing acceptance, among Henry's circle, of the use of deception as a matter of policy. In the *History of the World* he pointed towards events that had lately taken place in France and pronounced:

> It was reason of state that perswaded the last famous French King Henrie the fourth to change his religion, yet the Protestants whom hee forsooke obeyed him, but some of the Papists whom hee followed murdered him. So strongly doth the painted vizzor of wise proceeding delude euen those that know the foule face of impietie lurking vnder it and behold the wretched endes that haue euer followed it.[87]

Ralegh repeatedly condemned dissimulation in state affairs as a 'false doctrine' associated with the name of 'Machiavel.'[88] He joined in the chorus that condemned this aspect of Machiavelli but was concerned, as Lipsius, Botero, and others on the Continent had been, to redefine the parameters of political virtue in light of contemporary conditions. These had gone too far in the direction of amorality in Ralegh's estimation. He held it 'lamentable ... that the taking of oathes now-a-daies is rather made a matter of custome than of conscience.'[89] And that lying was tolerated as a rule for governors he held to be perfidious: 'when Power, which is a Character of the Almightie, shall be made the supporter of vntruth, the falshood is most abhominable.'[90] Ralegh noted that practitioners of political dissimulation ended by falling prey to their own subterfuge. And apart from being a travesty, dissimulation rested on the false premise that power grew from the ability to control and impose fear upon subjects; the love of the people far more than their fear, posited Ralegh, ensured both the success of the prince and the security of the realm.[91]

Ralegh thus took issue with the movement towards statism, in which the safety of the state was the be-all and end-all of political practice, dictating an ethics separate from private morality. Yet side by side with his vociferous condemnation of any regal practice of dissimulation, he could not help but notice that unbridled ambition prevailed and that hypocrisy characterized most social and political relationships. 'Wee professe that wee know GOD, but by workes we deny him,' he complained. 'Wee are all (in effect) become Comaedians in religion: and while we act in gesture and voice, diuine vertues, in all the course of our liues wee renounce our Persons, and the parts wee play.'[92] This evocation of life as drama and the lives of men as performances is a measure of Ralegh's 'stoical' leanings, and as a feature in his writings has won some deserved attention.[93] Ralegh was not unique in this regard, however; set in its political context, his invocation of the metaphor stands in direct contrast to its use by Dallington and others, who recommended the use of 'vizards' as a necessity in statecraft. It has also been argued that the acting analogy conveyed the pessimism that intermittently characterizes Ralegh's writings.[94] The actuality of worldly dealings, however, could provoke undisguised and aggressive complaint. Ralegh's approach to deceit as a way of life at court was captured in the Elizabethan poem 'The Lie':

> Go, soul, the body's guest,
> Upon a thankless arrant.
> Fear not to touch the best;
> The truth shall be thy warrant.
> Go, since I needs must die,
> And give the world the lie.
>
> Say to the court, it glows
> And shines like rotten wood;
> Say to the church, it shows
> What's good, and doth no good.
> If the court and church reply,
> Then give them both the lie.
>
> Tell potentates, they live
> Acting by others' action,
> Not loved unless they give,
> Nor strong but by affection.
> If potentates reply,
> Give potentates the lie.
>
> Tell men of high condition
> That manage the estate,
> Their purpose is ambition,
> Their practice only hate.
> And if they once reply,
> Then give them all the lie. [...][95]

'The Lie' is a long and consistent complaint against the barely covert corruption which for Ralegh characterized the public domain. The poem was probably composed in 1595 – a year filled with tribulation and dismay – and it expressed in no uncertain terms the hypocrisy he beheld at the highest levels of society. He laid down a literary gauntlet to all such practices. The outright challenging tone in this verse would give way to a more detached point of view in later prose writings. He also came to accept that – to a certain degree – the circumstances of society necessitated the use of some deceit. His stance came to resemble that adopted by Robert Sidney, though Ralegh demonstrated great reticence in promoting any version of *prudentia mixta*.[96] There were only two circumstances in which Ralegh could hold it really warrantable. One related to international affairs of state which we will turn to examine in due course. The other concerned the usefulness of deceit as a corrective to vice and deserves extended analysis for elucidating Ralegh's position *vis à vis* Essex and King James. Ralegh's clearest articulation of the legitimacy of the practice of such mixed prudence is found in his *Instructions to his Son*.[97]

Composed in the early years of his imprisonment in the Tower, the *Instructions* is both a testament to Ralegh's concept of political virtue and a manual on political survival. Much like 'The Lie,' it portrays a society composed of predatory members, and its primary lessons are the need for self-suffiency and prudence. Ralegh urged his son to follow reason and to love God, his country, his prince, and 'his estate.'[98] These were to be his priorities in life. Young Wat was also advised to cultivate the friendship of his social superiors, but to do so cautiously and never entirely trustingly. Ralegh's own late experiences in a treason trial, and as a once influential courtier abandoned by his political allies, doubtlessly underlay these observations. Prudence and caution were the key attitudes he advised his son to cultivate in all civil and political dealings.

The *Instructions* thus considered the route to political success. But as Ernest Strathmann has rightly observed, 'in this hardheaded treatise ..., the pragmatic wisdom neither neglects nor obscures ethical considerations, and the advice to his son ends with an emphatic admonition to serve God first.'[99] Indeed, Ralegh's first priority was to pass on the strong moral grounds upon which his son should base his social and political relations. One imperative went thus:

as there is nothing more shameful and dishonest than to do wrong, so truth itself cutteth his throat that carrieth her publicly in every place. Remember the divine saying, 'He that keepeth his mouth closed, keepeth his life.' Do, therefore, right to all men where it may profit them and thou shalt thereby get much love, and forbear to speak evil things of men though it be true (if thou be not constrained) and therby thou shalt avoid malice and revenge. Do not accuse any man of any crime if it be not to save thyself, thy prince, or country, for there is nothing more dishonourable, next to treason itself, than to be an accuser.[100]

In this 'instruction,' Ralegh implied that truth and language were not always compatible – that language pertains to the realm of the mutable, where truth becomes relative to the profit it brings. What is more, Ralegh condones the deliberate suppression of the truth unless the security of self, prince, or country necessitates its disclosure. Survival and success appear to be the only and ruling criteria by which Ralegh would have his son live. Yet he qualified these remarks by recommending that his son act to protect his reputation, that he avoid public disgrace, and that he rather die than live a coward. The point of these observations were that they emphasized, as they simultaneously provided a barrier against, the inconstancy of a world in which 'the fancies of men change and he that loves today hateth tomorrow.'[101]

And so practices of dissimulation became essential to the 'constancy' required in a society populated, in Ralegh's view, by some 'wise and sober men' but mostly 'with ignorant persons.'[102] They were a means of self-censorship, whereby the individual learned to protect himself and prepared to countermine the widespread practices of society which, in this treatise, were too ingrained to correct. Here a first priority was to guard one's tongue. In a passage that prefigured his later commentary on Essex, Ralegh explained to his son that 'in all that ever I observed in the course of worldly things, I ever found that men's fortunes are oftener made by their tongues than by their virtues and more men's fortunes overthrown thereby also than by their vices.'[103] To be sure, Wat was encouraged to renounce vice; failing that, he should at least make every attempt not to display it in public. He conveyed to his son the wisdom of Solomon apropos speech: 'The mouth of a wise man is in his heart; the heart of a fool is in his mouth, because what he knoweth or thinketh, he uttereth, and by thy words and discourses men will judge thee.' He then invoked Socrates to drive home the message that 'Such as thy words are, such will thy affections be esteemed, and such will thy deeds as thy affections, and such thy life as thy deeds.'[104] His advice also resembles the 'strange course' advocated by Lipsius in *De constantia*, as he wrote, the 'tongue alone is bridled, not [the] mind.'[105]

Ralegh's *Instructions* thus bears on the growing contemporary debate over textual authority and the relationship between language and action. Ralegh's position in this debate is elucidated by recourse to the role of language in the Lipsian paradigm. Like Lipsius, Ralegh demanded that one's speech and comportment be guided by the requirement to maintain one's position in society. But unlike Lipsius, Ralegh then suggested that words in fact suggested matter since they could be held to account for the reliability (or unreliability, if that were the case) of one's commitment to society. If private vices were concealed, Ralegh's argument went on, they proved to be only temporary aberrations; consequently, no real dissimulation took place at all. There was a difference between the pretence of virtue and the concealment of vice (or truth) by omission. The world of 'The Lie' revealed the predominance of the former; that of the *Instructions*, which portrayed the same context of widely practiced subterfuge, taught a response according to the latter. Where virtue was totally ineffectual in the first case, it emerged triumphant in the second.

Hence, for Ralegh, language was not merely an instrument to be manipulated to serve either private or public ends or to fool fools; it had to be a trusted guide for public use and a means to indicate character and worthiness for public service. His strictures on discourse harked to the common enterprise which had engaged Lipsius and Montaigne in the 1580s, and then Charron, and which, finally, continued to preoccupy contemporaries. For Ralegh, as for those who insisted on its dual nature, virtue remained an internal affair. But Ralegh insisted that language must act as the handmaiden of virtue, leading the private into the public domain. Thus personal prudence was inseparable from public virtue. On the whole, he had little patience for the idea of Charronian dichotomies.

Ralegh's idea of 'constancy' thus hinged on this association between language and action. Yet he realized that there was one flaw in his advocacy of language as a true gauge of virtue. The prevalence of flattery revealed both the vulnerability of language and the danger which flatterers posed. 'Flatterers are the worst kind of traitors,' Ralegh cautioned his son, 'for they will strengthen thy imperfections, encourage thee in all evils, correct thee in nothing, but so shadow and paint all thy vices and follies as thou shalt never by their will discern evil from good or vice from virtue.'[106] Ralegh's conjunction of the verisimilitude of language and the dangers of flattery provide an interesting contrast, shedding light on his response to the two issues, raised earlier, involving his reactions to Essex and Tacitism. First, his Socratic outlook helps clarify his position *vis à vis* his old political nemesis, the Earl of Essex. If words reflect character, Essex had indeed sinned, and doubly so. His 'unflattering words' were a linguistic prefiguring of his treasonous intent towards his queen – his private outburts a sign of his public affections (better, disaffections); his deeds a consequence of those affections. Secondly, applying his argument on language to both the intent of the *Prerogative of Parliaments* and, simultaneously, to the nature of his response to Tacitism, one feature stands out. Ralegh isolated 'flattery' as a vicious and harmful perversion of language. For all the repercussions that had followed in the train of the transference of Tacitist history onto the stage ten years before he composed his own treatise and dedicated it to the king, Ralegh chose to echo Daniel and Jonson and expose the evils of flattery in a kingdom – purportedly the England of Richard II. Thus, he called into question the judgment of kings who succumbed to flattery and heeded its unworthy purveyors, asserting in the dialogue of the *Prerogative* that 'when a king will suffer himself to be eaten up by a company of pretty fellows, by himself raised, therein both his judgement and his courage is disputed.' This verdict on the folly of Richard, as we noted earlier (p. 54), could have been as applicable to James in the present; but it also cast a shadow back on James as a hopeful successor to Elizabeth in the 1590s. For with its finger pointing to the earlier parallel of Richard II, along with the knowledge of Essex's connection with that parallel, it suggested that as far back as those last days of Elizabeth, the king, by trusting Essex, displayed early his lack of judgment. It was not, then, the polity which had condemned and executed Essex that was at fault. Rather, Essex got his just desserts when he went to the block, and it was the contemporary polity, Ralegh suggested, which was guilty of falling prey to the malpractice of language.

The *Prerogative of Parliaments* thus operated as Ralegh's post-mortem of events that took place in 1601 (the year of Essex's trial and conviction for treason) and 1603 (the year of Ralegh's own treason trial) and much more besides. And most damaging for the king was the fact that Ralegh's parallel of Richard, combined with his criticism of flattery, reflected a very current issue. The year in which the *Prerogative* was written was also the year that saw the disgrace of James's one-time favourite, Robert Carr, the Earl of Somerset. Another year would elapse before the charges of his having plotted the death of Sir Thomas Overbury would result in Somerset's conviction for murder. In the meantime, a race had begun to promote a new favourite for the king. Whoever won, it was clear the result would be the arrival of a new '*primum mobile* ... by whose motion all the other spheres must move, or else stand still.'[107] Against such courtly manoeverings, the relevance of Ralegh's parallel became more pointed. His dialogue advised the king to desist from raising favourites and to rely instead on his parliaments.

Ralegh, then, actually presented a Tacitist critique of tyranny. John Milton thus acted with some justification in later promoting *The Cabinet-Council* as an authentic Ralegh composition.[108] A digest of political axioms distilled from numerous relevant political works, this tract might well have been a direct copy of a compilation made, as Ernest Strathmann has suggested, by Thomas Bedingfield. The important point about Milton's ascription of it, however, is that it shows that Ralegh's near contemporaries recognized his position in the heated dialogue over political virtue. Milton clearly discerned his relevance as political moralist and would-be counsellor to the Stuarts, appreciating Ralegh's concern with manifestations of tyranny in order to draw awareness to and correct them – a plight with which Milton himself was closely identified in the chaotic last months of the Commonwealth, when the spectre of Restoration loomed ahead.[109]

And Milton would also have recognized and approved the one area in which the idea of dissimulation was not only accepted by Ralegh but considered crucial as a political tool. This was in the realm of international relations. Ralegh's strictures here provide a neat contrast to the ethical priorities he demanded in normal princely dealings with subjects. Distrust and cunning were rejected as deceitful in most situations, but they were hailed as essential in foreign affairs, especially in circumstances of war. Commending the pretences by which Hannibal, a Carthagian commander, managed to entrap a Spanish army in the second century B.C., he wrote:

Hee that makes himself a bodie of Crystall, that all men may looke through him, and discerne all the parts of his disposition; makes himselfe (withall) an Asse: and thereby teacheth others, either how to ride, or driue him. Wise men, though they haue single hearts in all that is iust or vertuous; yet they are like coffers with double bottomes: which when others looke into, being opened, they see not all that they hold, on the sudden, and at once.[110]

In contrast to the transparency of virtue which was preferred in (what Bacon would call) 'civil' situations, in the realm of foreign relations and the specific circumstances of war a whole new strategy was promoted. Here cunning and dissimulation were not only accepted; they were the necessary aspects if not the manifestation of virtue.

The lessons of experience and past history became the touchstone for what Ralegh (quoting Bacon) called this 'sinister kinde of wisedome.'[111] In admitting it as legitimate behaviour, he pointed back to the frequent bad faith displayed between states. Treaties, he maintained, were continually dishonoured; using examples drawn from the European experience during the previous one hundred years, he argued that 'all the bonds, eyther by the bed or by the booke, eyther by weddings, or Sacramentall Oathes, had neither faithfull purpose nor performance.'[112] The *History of the World* gave repeated instances of the double-dealings engaged by neighbouring states. What this double-dealing showed, Ralegh reiterated, was the perpetual nature of the human lust for power and glory.

This did not necessarily imply a pessimistic attitude on Ralegh's part, for he argued that this lust for power and glory was the prime characteristic of an aggressive Spain, which threatened the peace and security of the rest of Europe, most especially England. Officially, a policy of peace and friendship existed between England and Spain, the result of the treaty signed in 1604. But as Ralegh noted in the *History*, when it came to international diplomacy, only 'the rustie sword and the emptie purse ... pleade performance of couenants.'[113] This was a blatant reversal of his stated view that the breaking of oaths was 'odious and contrary to God,' and shows that when he argued for the security of England, even solemnly given promises were there to be contravened and repudiated.[114] He insisted that the Spaniards 'haue made many attempts to make themselues Masters of all Europe.'[115] With this specific circumstance in mind, he upheld an extreme usage of the practice of mixed prudence, going on, in the *History*, to map out how England might contest the power of Spain. He declared that with a budget devoted to war, Spain, in the space of 'two yeares or three at the most ..., may not only be perswaded to liue in peace, but all their swelling and ouerflowing streames may be brought backe into their naturall channels and old bankes.'[116] Ralegh's successive and repeated excursions into the area of war and the necessity for dissimulation therefore had point; they provided the means and the justification by which he sounded a clarion call for preparedness to challenge the power of Spain.

## Ralegh's Legacy

Ralegh's writings provided a number of important lessons for readers. Not least among these was the demand for a high standard of kingship.

Essentially, Ralegh's 'sawciness' knew no bounds, for through the *History* he also became the most public protagonist for an aggressive policy against Spain. His method, however, as the means by which he fashioned his endeavour, ensured that the *History* was something more than a disengaged discourse while less than a blatant condemnation of royal policy.

More to the point, Ralegh's adoption of techniques that Lipsius had called 'doctrine' were the means by which he sought to heal the rupture that had occurred in defining the nature of political virtue. Ralegh took issue with Charron and his suggestion that politics was like 'a sea without either bottom or brink.'[117] For Charron, this meant that virtue had to be seen as a dichotomous thing. Not so, countered Ralegh, although a caveat was allowed in the extraordinary conditions imposed by war. As with Charron, so with a number of English authors, whom Ralegh challenged in their instruction of Prince Henry. As we trace, in subsequent chapters, the variety of attitudes towards political participation in England, we will see more clearly how Ralegh's reaffirmation of the unity of virtue formed a part of the ongoing dialogue over how far private virtue should underlie political activities.

Ralegh's strictures on virtue were also a response to those adumbrated by Francis Bacon, the subject of the next chapter. Bacon's ideas had been largely defined and were available to Ralegh before he composed many of the works examined here. Moreover, Bacon's later attempt at history writing offsets certain aspects in Ralegh's *History of the World*. Where Bacon looked at the reign of one king as a study in politics and psychology, Ralegh adhered to terms identifiable through the Lipsian paradigm, taking the entirety of history under his compass to find relevant lessons on virtue and warfare scattered throughout the magnitude of time. Thereby Ralegh contoured a peculiarly 'Raleghean paradigm,' which fit a specifically English context.

Nor was Ralegh content merely to draw historical parallels and leave the matter at that. Buried in his account in the *History* lay a distinct political agenda. It alternated with a gloomy millenarian view of the approaching day of the world's end, but to stress the optimism of the former would not be amiss, since it was a dynamic factor impelling the *History* onwards.[118] Contemporaries were probably struck by the promise proclaimed in the work, a promise that, side by side with the moral admonitions which operated to give it greater force, implied God's favour was now to be felt among the English. This promise was contained in Ralegh's portrait of the English, and followed after his discussion of the Romans under the command of Julius Caesar. The Roman's were incomparable in time, he declared – until, that is, the advent of the English.[119] He then hailed the English not only as the proper heirs of Roman greatness, but suggested that in valour and virtue they had the potential to supersede the Roman achievement. Against the victories achieved by the Romans under Caesar, Ralegh declared that the 'noble acts of our Nation in warre' were by far the more worthy, 'performed by no aduantage of weapon; against no sauage or vnmanlie people; the enemie being farre superiour vnto vs in numbers, and all needfull provisions, yea as well trained as we, or commonly better, in the exercise of warre.'[120] Classical precedent, which he repeatedly found praiseworthy, had been overtaken by modern experience. In order to take advantage of this situation, however, Ralegh maintained that virtue had to prevail, 'for it is by men armed with fortitude of minde,' he asserted, 'that enemies are beaten.'[121] Thence, 'by Gods blessing ..., the enemie that shall dare to trie our forces, will finde cause to wish, that auoiding vs, hee had rather encountered as great a puissance, as that of the Roman Empire.'[122]

The stress on 'fortitude of mind' defines the basically stoical aspect of Ralegh's teachings – his acclamation of the potential of the English, the particular force of his strictures on virtue, and, by extension, his contribution to English neostoicism. Ultimately, Ralegh proffered a vision of a strong and virtuous king who would lead a strong and virtuous nation to perform the moral task of halting the evil ambitions of a foreign power – a task not unlike that which had occupied Lipsius in the *Politica*. That Ralegh's vision parted ways with affairs as they actually existed could not, in the end, be avoided, emerging in the Preface to the *History* and in its conclusion. As he acknowledged, after the death of Prince Henry his *History* was left 'without a Maister.'[123] Still, his faith in his work was expressed in the *History*'s frontispiece, which depicted the world turning, and history unfolding, under the ever-watchful providential eye of God. The classicism of Ralegh's endeavour was established by this emblem, which was described in words by Ben Jonson. He wrote the accompanying verse in honour of 'grave Historie,' who,

> ... chearefully supporteth what shee reares;
> Assisted by no strengths, but are her owne,
> Some note of which each varied Pillar beares,
> By which, as proper Titles, shee is knowne,
>
> Times Witnesse, Herald of Antiquitie,
> The Light of Truth, and Life of Memorie.

4 Frontispiece (above) and Ben Jonson's 'The Minde of the Front' (opposite) from Walter Ralegh, *History of the World* (London, 1628). This engraved title-page keeps the first date, 1614, until 1652. Courtesy of The Library, University of King's College, Halifax, Nova Scotia. Photography by Findlay Muir, Instructional Media Services, Dalhousie University.

# THE MINDE OF
## THE FRONT.

From Death, and darke Obliuion (neere the same)
The Mistresse of Mans life, graue HISTORIE,
Raising the World to good, or euill FAME,
Doth vindicate it to ETERNITIE.

High PROVIDENCE would so: that nor the Good
Might be defrauded, nor the Great secur'd,
But both might know their waies are vnderstood,
And the reward and punishment assur'd.

This makes, that lighted by the beamie hand
Of TRVTH, which searcheth the most hidden springs,
And guided by EXPERIENCE, whose straight Wand,
Doth mete, whose Line doth sound the depth of things;

Shee cheerefully supporteth what she reares:
Assisted by no strengths, but are her owne.
Some note of which each varied Pillar beares,
By which, as proper Titles, she is knowne,

Times Witnesse, Herald of Antiquitie,
The Light of Truth, and Life of Memorie.

This English adaptation of a Ciceronian theme came from a poet who advocated 'constancy' to a courtier who remained constant in both his commitment to political service and his attempt to procure political virtue by appeals to the past.[124] In a later chapter we shall see that Jonson's views on politics and virtue differed in tenor from those advocated by Ralegh, but in terms of the value of history they agreed. According to Ralegh, 'we reade Histories to informe our vnderstanding by the examples therein found.'[125] These he gave aplenty in the effort to instruct a king and fulfil the role he held out for the English. Oliver Cromwell was only one among countless Englishmen who were suitably impressed by Ralegh's endeavour. He advised his son to 'Recreate yourself with Sir Walter Raughleye's History: it's a body of history, and will add much more to your understanding than fragments of story.'[126] And Ralegh, while aspiring to teach a royal master, had found instances enough to show that 'The infinite wisedome of God doth not worke alwaies by one and the same way, but very often in the alteration of Kingdomes and Estates.'[127] Ralegh's providential acclamations struck home with Cromwell. And while Ralegh was mainly thwarted in the hope that his writings might provide the key to unlock his prison doors, their effect, to gauge from the responses of Cromwell and Milton, was to encourage an independent and critical approach to all political questions, not least the activities of a king who was judged to have deserted his charge, betrayed his duty, and thus merited the death penalty. Ralegh had argued convincingly that God acted through secondary causes and that manifestations of His judgments sometimes took the form of political unrest. Cromwell came to see himself as a vessel of God's judgment, going on, in the circumstances of 1649, to carry out that judgment against King Charles.

# 2

# Francis Bacon and the Advancement of Constancy

But men must know, that in this theatre of man's life it is reserved only for God and Angels to be lookers on. (*Advancement of Learning*)

Believing that I was born for the service of mankind, and regarding the care of the commonwealth as a kind of common property which like the air and the water belongs to everybody, I set myself to consider in what way mankind might best be served, and what best service I was myself best fitted by nature to perform. (*Of the Interpretation of Nature*)

I find the wisdom of the ancients to be like grapes ill-trodden: something is squeezed out, but the best parts are left behind and passed over.
(*De Sapientia Veterum*)

I cannot but be raised to this persuasion, that this third period of time will far surpass that of the Graecian and Roman learning: only if men will know their own strength and their own weakness both; and take one from the other light of invention, and not fire of contradiction; and esteem of the inquisition of truth as of an enterprise, and not as of a quality or ornament; and employ wit and magnificence to things of worth and excellency, and not to things vulgar and of popular estimation. (*Advancement of Learning*)

Francis Bacon aspired to both literary and political greatness. In his *Advancement of Learning* (1605), he set down the principles for a brand of political virtue that he had modelled out of his experience, and his concern with virtue as political service was developed in other compositions, notably the later editions of the *Essayes* (1612, 1625), and his *De Sapientia Veterum* (1609).[1] Composed and published in Latin, *De Sapien-*

*tia* was soon translated into English; along with the *Essayes* it remained the most popular of Bacon's works during his lifetime. The appeal of his writings stretched to France, where he was admired by Cardinal Richelieu, among others, and Italy, where eager audiences demanded fresh translations of his work into their own vernacular.[2] If such widespread popularity also signals a general acceptance of his political ideas, Bacon succeeded in producing a formula of virtue that rivalled the endeavours of contemporary Europeans, including the famed classicist, Lipsius.

Bacon's role as a champion of 'political virtue,' however, has been overshadowed by posterity's greater interest in his place in the development of a 'modern' theory of experimental science.[3] Yet while he accorded that 'science' needed to be purged of various errors, in Bacon's vocabulary the word was synonymous with the broader concept of 'knowledge.' As he informed Lord Burghley, 'I have taken all knowledge to be my province.'[4] Accordingly, he would have been amply rewarded to have known the praise that was to be lavished on him by Samuel Taylor Coleridge, for whom Bacon was not only 'the Athenian Verulam and the British Plato,' but above all 'our philosophical Samson' – analogies resplendent in the optimism of early nineteenth-century England, but matching, as well, the faith that Bacon himself conveyed for his program for the reform of learning, expressed in the last epigraph quoted at our opening.[5]

Bacon wrote copiously, always suggesting that his motives for desiring the advancement of learning were, if not entirely altruistic, for the common good. Jonathan Marwil has demonstrated the unique lengths to which Bacon would go to defend his particular view of society and justify the special place he should occupy in it.[6] This belief sprang from the fact that, like so many others of his generation, he was raised in the humanist tradition of preparation for state service; the son of Sir Nicholas Bacon, Elizabeth's Lord Keeper, the *vita activa* was his main vindication for existing. If political engagement was his one abiding principle, however, he quickly learned that to live by it he had to be prepared to serve the monarch in whatever capacity he might be called upon to fulfil. Justifying this very personal position underlay a political philosophy highly evocative of neostoicism, and, as we shall see, at times pointedly engaging with the terms of the Lipsian paradigm. It began, however, with Bacon's claim to reform the state of learning.

**Bacon and the Crisis in Learning**

Bacon's program was set against the background of what he called 'the times.' He argued that three features in the contemporary European experience were responsible for the shortcomings in contemporary learning: the growing pattern of civil war, the greater manifestation of religious division and dispute, and 'those compendious artifices and devices which have crept into the place of solid erudition.'[7] Bacon offered to reform the world of such ills, beginning with the fundamental repair to learning. In its current form learning threatened to sink, claimed Bacon, and in his view that was not an altogether bad turn of affairs. He condemned the preponderance of what he called 'fair-weathered learning,' 'nursed by leisure,' which 'blossom[ed] under reward and praise,' but which omitted 'that knowledge whose dignity is maintained by works of utility and power.'[8]

Before he addressed the problem of how to 'advance' learning in his *Advancement*, however, Bacon took some time to reiterate his complaints against its current state. He isolated three faults that corresponded to the influence of three groups of 'detractors,' as he called them: the 'divines,' who viewed the pursuit of knowledge as either evil or vain; the 'politiques,' who also denigrated learning and put knowledge based on experience over knowledge acquired from study; and the 'learned' themselves, with their claims for study as a scholarly exercise requiring the life of contemplation and their view of study as an automous mode of life.[9] The divines were informed, with due respect, that learning was a means to study nature; it was an activity not only proper to man but respectful towards God.[10] It was less the divines, though, than the other two groups whom Bacon conceived as enemies to his brand of humanism. He castigated the politiques for refuting bookly learning, which Bacon considered as tantamount to myopia; he then charged the learned with neglecting the real aim of learning and for causing the divorce between learning and activity. Bacon's famed repudiation of the reigning Ciceronian techniques was expressed in this context as he deplored the habit whereby 'men study words and not matter,' a focus that led to the study of 'vain matter.' The foulest 'disease' of the day was thus put at the feet of the learned, whose methods, claimed Bacon, risked the destruction of 'the essential form of knowledge.'

Bacon was indulging in no mere exercise of rhetoric in these complaints. The cult of the 'virtuoso' was just beginning to take shape in England, where students at Oxford and Cambridge were being taught, and had begun, to embrace learning for its own sake.[11] Against this trend, Bacon proffered a full-fledged defence of principles of study that were predicated upon the concept of the *vita activa*. But his argument also addressed the wider debate which in the 1580s had encouraged Lipsius to bemoan the growing penchant for what he had called 'vain philosophy.' Lipsius's neostoic treatises affirmed the role of all learning in the present; others in Europe, however, began to focus on just which of the classics were relevant and to what purpose.

Anthony Grafton and Lisa Jardine have recently examined this debate which centred on the academic curriculum and, they argue, resulted in transforming early modern 'humanism' – replete with its moral underpinnings – into the more modern version of 'the humanities.' The shift to a system of study that concentrated on specific disciplines (which was by no means totally effected during the early modern period) was the consequence, they claim, of the age-old dilemma over maintaining the universal values of antiquity while its other culture baggage, specifically its texts and literature, was unabashedly appropriated and rendered domestic. The debate went back at least to the time of Cicero and was revived during the Renaissance. Never satisfactorily resolved, it deeply preoccupied sixteenth-century humanists labouring under the new pressures provoked by religious warfare within states. Grafton and Jardine highlight the acitivities of the French Huguenot scholar Petrus Ramus, who completely repudiated the authority of Aristotle, developed his famous method (or in the words of Grafton and Jardine, 'his infamous *unica methodus*'), and through that technique claimed he could transmit 'the content of any discipline' to students. The classical moral component in *humanitas* – the thread that united and underpinned all Renaissance teaching – was virtually jettisoned by Ramus, Grafton and Jardine claim; consequently, students were taught how to be *good at something* rather than being concerned with acquiring virtue itself. Gabriel Harvey took Ramist theories one step further by inaugurating a system Grafton and Jardine call '*pragmatic* humanism.' Its defining characteristic was the lesson that by pointed and methodical reading one could learn the skills of any particular discipline and use it to achieve social standing. Rhetoric was the key discipline for Harvey; by manipulating Ramist techniques he demonstrated that, in the words of Grafton and Jardine, 'a committed Ramist [found] himself free to pursue the *ars disserendi* [the art of oratory] simply as a route to high government, without worrying about being *vir bonus* (a good man).'[12]

In its elaborate address to the learned, Book 1 of the *Advancement* seems to point directly to this debate over education and the curriculum. What's more, Bacon himself goes on to describe an approach to study closely resembling the pedagogy advocated by Ramus and Harvey. He was at pains to insist, however, that without a civic correspondence learning was an empty venture, affirming, as well, that civics without learning was like fumbling in the dark. He concluded, 'that which will indeed dignify and exalt knowledge, [is] if contemplation and action be more nearly and straitly conjoined and united than they have been; a conjunction like unto that of the two highest planets, Saturn the planet of rest and contemplation, and Jupiter the planet of civil society and action.' He reverted to a common social metaphor to assert his ultimate defence of humanism. Knowledge, he said, was not to act as a courtesan, for pleasure only, or a maid, for the sole use of her master; rather, its function was to act as a spouse to society, 'for generation, fruit, and comfort.'[13]

Bacon's thinking thus stressed the conjunction of learning and action. He never ceased to insist that learning was for use, and, for Bacon, its premier use was its application to political activity – a philosophy which F.J. Levy has dubbed 'political humanism,' and which for Bacon derived from his belief that 'a man's country has some special claims upon him'[14] The *Advancement* was constructed on this very premise. But if Bacon's point of departure there involved a critical debate among humanists, another issue informing the entire work was a crisis of which he had – and would continue to have – personal experience.

### Bacon and the Crisis in Humanism

Bacon first encountered the dilemmas of his brand of humanism some years before the appearance of the *Advancement*, while a member of the Earl of Essex's household. He had become Essex's secretary and advisor in the early 1590s, living at Essex House in London, and accepting Essex's gift of a manor after his hopes for royal service (and remuneration) were stymied as a result of the position he adopted in the Parliament of 1593. The state had requested the levying of an 'extraordinary' tax to support the war effort against Spain; while Bacon accepted the need for the tax, he objected to the means of its proposed implementation.[15] His objections were duly noted by Elizabeth. Henceforth, she obstinately refused Bacon any hope for office. Access to court, she related through Essex, was the most he could now expect. Through Essex she also pointed out that had Bacon's opposition to the royal will occurred 'in the King her father's time, a less offence than that would have made a man be banished his presence for ever.'[16] Her leniency, the message clearly conveyed, was to be wondered at and graciously embraced. It was. Henceforth, Bacon practised 'obsequiesness and observance,' obeying the queen's every command.[17] His endeavours ensured not only the condemnation of Essex for rebellion against the monarch, but included the fulfilment of the order to explain at large why Essex had been executed. As Bacon duly complied, he went on to justify the guilty verdict and vindicate his role in the prosecution.[18] Bacon's crisis as a humanist was thus provoked less by the fiasco of the rebellion (and even less by any deficiency in learning); rather, it was brought about by the unexpected consequences of his success in prosecuting his one-time patron.

That particular service was practically the last required of Bacon during the reign of Elizabeth. Little was left for him to do until he found himself, in 1603, having to once more account for his role in the Essex affair. There were at least two reasons for this new vindication. First, the arrival of James I had not immediately insured an opening for Bacon's services; second, James had been a friend of Essex, who, as we saw earlier, supported the succession of the House of Stuart. Bacon thus had some serious explaining to do. In his *Apology in Certain Imputations Concerning the Late Earl of Essex* (1604), Bacon reviewed his actions, explaining that before the rebellion Essex had spurned all Bacon's moderating advice. He also indicated how he had repeatedly attempted to intercede with the queen on Essex's behalf. He stressed how isolated he had become in attempting to dispel the queen's anger, yet how he was bound 'by the rules of duty' and 'without prevarication' to prosecute his one-time patron to the best of his ability.[19] Elsewhere Bacon also complained that his 'zeal was mistaken for ambition,' a candid admission of the measure of unpopularity he had incurred.[20]

Bacon's apologists tend to note that Bacon acted in a manner similar to others in the Essex retinue, which became radically split over the earl's activities in the years 1599–1601. Like Bacon, Fulke Greville and Robert Sidney distanced themselves from any connection with the rebellion, and Greville and Bacon probably joined forces in the days preceding Essex's execution, each attempting to elicit mercy from the queen.[21] Neither Sidney nor Greville served as witnesses against Essex, however; nor were they called upon to prosecute their former patron. Bacon alone enjoyed that dubious distinction. He took up the challenge in a whole-hearted way, and in the process he broke all the standing rules of client-patron relationships.[22] Thus Bacon has been dubbed a Judas, earning, in Alexander Pope's estimation, the tag 'meanest of mankind.' For some contemporaries, nevertheless, Bacon was 'not the worst friend for being the better subject.'[23] What observers thought of Greville's activities, on the other hand, is difficult to ascertain. He was certainly not viewed as an unwavering friend to Bacon. John Aubrey, writing in the later part of the seventeenth century, recorded that following Bacon's disgrace in 1621, his 'Servants suddenly went away,' which inspired Bacon to compare their abandonment to 'the flying of the Vermin when the Howse was falling.' But it was not only servants who suddenly left him. Greville was described by Aubrey as Bacon's 'great Friend and acquaintance' – that is, while Bacon enjoyed prosperity. When he fell to 'disgrace and want' Greville 'was so unworthy' that he prevented his butler from providing Bacon with any of his 'small Beer,' a drink to which Bacon had become particularly partial. Aubrey remarked that Greville's meanness in this respect 'has donne his memorie more dishonour then Sir Philip Sidney's friendship hath donne him Honour.'[24] Bacon, on the other hand, was clearly a figure whom Aubrey respected; any weaknesses of character on Bacon's part were not noted in his account, and his allusions to the Earl of Essex did not provoke any of the adverse commentary that has marked later scholarship.

Nearer contemporaries like John Chamberlain, as much the inveterate gossip as Aubrey was to become, likewise remarked not so much on Bacon's prior dealings and abandonment of Essex as on the abandonment of Bacon by his colleagues in 1621. 'Many indignities are said and done against him,' reported Chamberlain, 'and diverse libels cast abroad to his disgrace not worth the repeating, as savoring of too much malice and scurrility. God send him patience,' added the observer, 'and that he may make the best use of this affliction.'[25] Chamberlain had not been averse, in earlier commentaries, to making remarks about Bacon's pursuits of office. Throughout his career, Bacon pulled no punches when it came to his career. His rivalry with Sir Edward Coke was particularly long lasting and rancorous. They first clashed in 1594, when both sought the Attorney-Generalship and Bacon lost out. Coke's eventual promotion finally opened the way for Bacon's entry to office. He then worked diligently for Coke's dismissal from the King's Bench, going so far as to make a constitutional issue out of the rivalry when faced by the king's displeasure over his opposition to the proposed marriage between Coke's daughter and the brother of the Duke of Buckingham in 1616. Coke, however, came back with a vengeance. He and Bacon had never seen eye to eye on the English legal system. As Coke took up the cause of the 'ancient constitution,' he became instrumental in reviving the techniques by which Crown officials were to be prosecuted for corruption; in 1621, Bacon, the Lord Chancellor, became the living example of the legal validity of the principle of 'ministerial accountability' – which, in this case, entered the annals of jurisprudence as much the result of an on-going vendetta as the pursuit of justice.[26] A look at Bacon's career helps reveal the attitudes of the English governing elite; an examination of his fall reveals the ambivalence in which he was held by his English contemporaries; many admired his thought but most deplored his political actions.[27]

Bacon's overall experience was something of a duplicate of that undergone by Essex in 1601, with friends and supporters quickly vacating the rotten house before it collapsed. Did Bacon, in making that observation in 1621, see the parallel with his earlier abandonment of Essex?[28] If he did, he never openly admitted it; in his writings, he was more concerned with explaining the principles behind his actions. As early as 1600, he wrote (in a letter to Essex) that he aspired 'to the conscience and commendation first of *bonus civis*, which with us is a good and true servant to the Queen, and next of *bonus vir*, that is an honest man.'[29] The distinction might look a trifle too nice, but it was a stricture that, probably deriving from Cicero, clearly indicated that should a conflict arise between Bacon's obligations, the demands of state took a higher priority than loyalty to friends or gaining respect at large.[30] Bacon's *Apology* had argued precisely that point.

Service to the state was the basic refrain echoing throughout most of Bacon's other major writings, including the *Advancement*, where he presented another vindication of the politics of service. But if Bacon valued only obedience to the Crown, he was clearly concerned about what others thought of him, for the *Apology* was also an exercise in 'forming' public opinion. It would be some time yet before he came to define precisely how opinions and ideas were formed in the mind (to clearly articulate his theory of the false idols of learning), but already in the *Apology* the practice of challenging those idols by contouring the minds of readers to accept a particular view of political behaviour was being rehearsed. Again, judging by contemporary estimations of him, Bacon's efforts were received with ambivalence, at best. It took a certain Thomas Hobbes to do so more successfully, although (again) not in terms that were universally accepted. The amanuensis of the older Bacon and a likely source for Aubrey's favourable comments on Bacon, Hobbes devised his theory of political allegiance without recourse to concepts such as 'good,' 'virtue,' and the like, thereby attempting to establish without question that the 'citizen,' as a result of his natural interest to preserve himself, owed allegiance to his sovereign first and foremost. For Hobbes all other social associations were secondary to that paramount necessity in life.[31]

But for Bacon 'humanist' virtues were the essence of political action, and his own political priorities were imbedded in the earliest edition of his *Essayes*. As F.J. Levy has demonstrated, the *Essayes* reflected Bacon's rejection by the queen after his conduct in the Parliament of 1593, and they offered a consideration on the politics of late Elizabethan England in relation to his humanist assumptions.[32] The ultimate lesson was that political conditions had changed, thus leaving humanism wanting and, as it was commonly understood, with little relevance for current political practices. His second reassessment, partly contained in the *Apology* and worked out more fully in the *Advancement of Learning*, was called forth in the wake of the execution of Essex and in consideration both of his own role in condemning Essex and the accession of James. The program he went on to map out in the *Advancement* endorsed both the message and the method of the *Essayes*. But in this first exposition of the civic value of learning we encounter the measure of the dilemma facing Bacon after his abandonment of Essex.

**The *Advancement of Learning* as Apologia for Tacitism**

Bacon dedicated the *Advancement* to the king, lauding the abilities of the Scottish monarch, and going on to display his own political acumen for the benefit of the king. He also seems to have been concerned to show the king that the brand of humanism he championed was not pernicious to the state. For all his learning (as well as because of it), James I was suspicious of the uses of scholarship, especially its application as political criticism in contemporary Tacitism.[33] The Stuart court included, of course, intellectuals. Isaac Casaubon was one such who was, moreover, quite hostile to Bacon's concept of 'applied humanism.' Casaubon noted that 'the count of Essex's case [was] a tragic example' of the combination of learning and politics, and he insisted that there was danger in '*politicus e libro*,' the 'book-trained politician.'[34] He and Joseph Scaliger, two of the so-called triumvirate of learning in the late sixteenth century, had earlier pounced upon the third member of this trio, their friend, Lipsius, to the same effect. According to Scaliger, writing hot on the heels of the publication of Lipsius's *De Militia Romana* (1595), Lipsius 'is no politician, and he has no power in the State. Pedants have no influence in these matters; neither I nor any scholar would be able to write [sc. anything effective] in political matters.'[35]

But this was precisely the conjunction that Bacon set out to reaffirm. Geoffrey Bullough has noted that Bacon's *Advancement* 'carried on the ideals of the Essex group,' a remark that has some validity but which needs qualification.[36] For one thing, there is no hint in the *Advancement* that Bacon either lamented the passing of that group or considered Essex's fate unwarranted – an attitude which can be contrasted quite sharply with that of other former followers of Essex who neither forgot nor quite got over the debacle of the rebellion. For another, if the conjunction of learning and politics could be constructed as leading to rebellion (which Casaubon subtly suggested), then Bacon had some serious restitution to perform. He would dispel the idea that 'politic knowledge' was subversive by establishing, first of all, that learning was a necessary accompaniment to governance. He would then demonstrate its role in the practice of politics and draw out its promise for inaugurating a new age of wonder and achievement comparable to the earlier examples of Greece and Rome.[37]

Government inevitably prospered under the sponsorship of learning, Bacon declared in the *Advancement*. He noted the deficiencies in contemporary learning by contrasting it to the scholarship of antiquity, first introducing his claim that learning supported governance to counter the criticisms of the 'politiques.' He used virtually the whole of history to sustain this argument, pointing to Aristotle's relationship with Alexander the Great, denoting Julius Caesar the epitome of the conjunction of learning and statesmanship, and reminding his readers that Seneca had been a great statesman as well as a great teacher. He pointed, as well, to the more recent examples of Popes Pius V and Sextus V. These, he noted, were 'esteemed as mere pedantic friars,' but they proved far superior in governing 'than those which have ascended the papacy from an education and breeding [only] in affairs of state and court of princes.'[38] Bacon finally refuted the politiques' claim that experience was the best teacher by simply noting that 'the experience of one man's life [cannot] furnish examples and precedents for the events of one man's life.'[39]

The same line of argument was taken up as Bacon mounted his case against 'the learned.' Where the politiques had denigrated learning, this group claimed a monopoly of the scholarly enterprise which, Bacon declared, resulted in its divorce from any mooring in the civic realm. He pointed to another set of past and current examples, among which Seneca provided a noteworthy instance of the positive results that came from the conjuction of learning and statesmanship – this time with the stress falling on his role as a teacher whose influence permeated the state during the minority of Nero. The true value and dignity of learning could only emerge when it was set to the service of the state, avowed

Bacon, noting that faith and religion were secure when learning flourished in a state. The period between the reigns of Nerva and Marcus Aurelius demonstrated an epoch in which learning was promoted and faith was defended. Bacon had to gloss over the less savoury aspects of this period to hold his point, but he concluded that the Christian church 'for the most part was in peace; so as in this sequence of ... princes do we see the blessed effects of learning in sovereignty, painted forth in the greatest tablet of the world.'[40]

Bacon's main point in addressing the 'learned' was to establish that 'under learned princes and governors there have been ever the best times.' The benefits of learning, he declared, encouraged peace, but peace 'hath no less power and efficacy in enablement towards martial and military virtue and prowess.'[41] The bounty of peace, Bacon insisted, was compatible with military virtue; Lipsius-like, and even reminiscent of Botero, he was referring to the priorities on the home front of a state *vis à vis* its international position. After expounding thus, Bacon concluded with evocative words magnifying the value of learning in the state, affirming, 'there is no power on earth which setteth up a throne or chair of estate in the spirits and souls of men, and in their cogitations, imaginations, opinions, and beliefs, but knowledge and learning.'[42] In short, learning had an inestimable role in society, but it was dependent upon the good graces of the king; bounty and peace could only be had from a prince who resolved to govern with the assistance of knowledge and learning.

Having reached this point, Bacon was ready to embark on his second strategy of delineating the state of learning as it then existed, but already he had accomplished several things. In the first place, he had subtly shifted the tenor of his address, begun with reference to scholars jealous of learning and unwilling to allow its fruits to escape from their halls of study. By contrast, he ends with an appeal for – and to – a philosopher-king. This, perhaps, was only fitting, since Bacon dedicated the *Advancement* to King James, and opened the entire argument by addressing him directly.[43] Hence, it was ultimately to the king that the great figures in whom learning and sovereignty were conjoined were set out as worthy examples.

Second, his agenda for learning was already taking firm shape, as his call for the advancement of learning was centred on those great figures whom Bacon maintained had more to teach than had yet been realized. One of these stood out above all others – Julius Caesar, whose name consistently crops up in the *Advancement*, and whose gift to posterity was the legacy 'both of his power and learning.'[44] Other exemplars owed more to their tutors, particularly Alexander, who 'was bred and taught under Aristotle.'[45] As instructors to kings, Aristotle and Seneca were repeatedly upheld as models. King James, whose motto was *Beati Pacifici* (Blessed are the Peacemakers), hardly aspired to be a latter-day Caesar (although he had himself commended Caesar), or even an Alexander (much less a Nero); these first two were images more in keeping with the vogue that would soon arise at the court of Prince Henry.[46] The point of such examples, nevertheless, was to show readers – and particularly the king – how they displayed 'the glory of learning in sovereignty,' a point with which James would readily agree.[47] Nor would that negate Bacon's candidacy as the new Aristotle, the new Seneca, or the new Caesar of his age. True, the Caesar parallel is somewhat problematic as a model for Bacon; he was hardly a military man and limited the scope of his conquests to that of the minds of men (suggesting that thereafter a conquest of nature would ensue). But he still qualified for two of three aspects of the Caesar image. By virtue of the civic nature of his task and by reference to Caesar's writings, offered as eminently worthy of emulation by Bacon, he could with some plausibility proffer himself as the Caesar of his age. The parallel role he was best fitted to fill, however, was a Seneca-type, or better still an Aristotle, now badly needed to refurbish the paths of learning.

Third, then, as far as the scheme of the *Advancement* was taking shape, Bacon had set out a choice of models for his own potential role in the state. In future writings, he sought to mesh aspects of his portrait of Seneca to some of those depicted in Aristotle, but for the remainder of the *Advancement* it was the Aristotelian role that kept him busy. And as the focus of his argument shifted yet again – this time onto Bacon himself – Bacon can be seen to have been involved in a task preoccupying some contemporaries on the Continent. Twenty years before, Lipsius set out to place scholarship back into the centre of civic activity by demonstrating the contemporary relevance of its legacy. Grafton and Jardine have argued that in the realm of political instruction Lipsius performed a function analogous to Harvey's in the field of rhetoric; thereby Lipsius, too, became an abettor in the movement that transformed 'humanism' into 'the humanities.'[48] Bacon's role in this movement has been suggested recently by Richard Tuck, who posits that Bacon is 'the most spectacular example of an Englishman thinking in terms of the new humanism' which flowered in the first part of the seventeenth century.[49]

A natural question to ask, however, is whether Bacon was attempting to merge two newly created traditions – the one instigated by Ramus and adopted by Harvey, which dissected what had formerly been an all-encompassing humanist educational system, and the other, which raided all learning for use in politics and which had its most systematic expression by Lipsius. We know that Bacon admired Lipsius, considering the *Politica* the best epitome of the subject; he strongly commended the style by which Lipsius 'out of his own reading gather[ed wisdom] for the use of another.'[50] Harvey also used such a technique, which was a manner that Bacon himself adopted, having already put it into practice in his first collection of *Essayes*. But Bacon could not rest content with anything that resembled a mere crash course in politics; the *Advancement* sought to create a firm foundation for redeeming the role of learning in politics. Nor could he ever conceive that learning served the mere personal function of self-advancement. Bacon's thought was too much conditioned by the ideal of political service.

Bacon's ultimate justification for his program of restitution was summed up in the most 'neostoic' statement in the *Advancement*: 'But men must know that in this theatre of man's life, it is left only to God and Angels to be lookers-on.'[51] Time and again Seneca acted the oracle for Bacon; the deficiencies noted in contemporary philosophy, and particularly in the areas of pedagogy, rhetoric, and moral philosophy, were singled out with reference to similar criticisms made by Seneca in Neronian Rome.[52] Seneca, of course, had been a figure of authority to successive generations of pseudo-disciples in the Renaissance and early modern period.[53] But Seneca the proponent of a civic humanism was mainly the result of the efforts of Lipsius, and this was the image adopted by Bacon.[54] Lipsius had raised two other authorities in his neostoic synthesis, Tacitus and 'the divine Epictetus.' What Bacon did with these two ancients differed somewhat from their application at the hands of their foremost champion.

Bacon's Tacitism is one of the better studied aspects in Baconian scholarship. As Kenneth C. Schellhase has remarked, 'Whether for political maxims or for historical information, and whether for moralisms or stylistic examples, Bacon seems to have used Tacitus as a kind of commonplace book of neat lines.'[55] There was also the aspect of Tacitus as an exemplar in the art of history writing, so important in Bacon's program as a means by which to teach civic action.[56] For Bacon, poetry and history fulfilled the same related function of guiding the reader into civic decisions and actions. In his plan for the reinvigoration of learning he called for a new output of these, declaring that 'poets and writers of histories are the best doctors of this knowledge.'[57] Tacitus thus performed two very large functions for Bacon. However, modern interest in Tacitism has tended to overshadow the comparative role of others in Bacon's thought. Indeed, Tacitus may well have vied with Caesar for the uppermost place in Bacon's affections – and with reason.

Bacon hailed Caesar's *Commentaries* as 'the best history of the world,' commending the work for both its 'solid weight of matter' and its style, which was an example of the 'greatest propriety of words and perspecuity of narration that ever was.'[58] Bacon claimed that Caesar's style was 'not the effect of a natural gift, but of learning and precept,' asserting that Caesar 'reduce[d] custom of speech to congruity of speech; and took as it were the picture of words from the life of reason.' Here, in a nutshell, is Bacon's philosophy of language – Ramist in tone, it rejected ornament and artificiality in discourse, offering in their place the aphoristic style, represented in learning by Tacitus and, above all, as his commendation would imply, by Caesar. The extant works of the great Roman dictator suggested to Bacon that 'he did aspire as well to victory of wit as victory of war.' The first of these victories was the sum of Bacon's aim in the program outlined in the *Advancement*.

Classical texts were thus waiting to be harnassed and set to the service of the state, Bacon claimed, and as he sought to extend the range of past authorities he also noted the strengths of particular styles. Genre was a key point for Bacon. Lamenting that Caesar's *Apophthegms* were no longer extant, he was consoled by the idea that that particular genre could be reconstructed by recourse to Caesar's surviving speeches. In 1625, he published his own collection of *Apophthegms*. Both there and in his reworking of the *Advancement* into *De Augmentis Scientiarum*, he noted the ultimate value of the apophthegm:

They serve not for pleasure only and ornament, but also for action and business; being, as one called them, *mucrones verborum*, – speeches with a point or edge, whereby knots in business are pierced and severed. And as former occasions are continually recurring, that which served once will often serve again, either produced as a man's own or cited as of ancient authority. Nor can there be any doubt of the utility in business of a thing which Caesar the Dictator thought worthy of his own labour; whose collection I wish had been preserved; for as for any others that we have in this kind, but little judgement has in my opinion been used in the selection.[59]

The striking feature here is that in the 1620s, and in a tome that was composed in Latin for the purposes of reaching a broad European audience, Bacon reaffirmed his earlier endeavours. And though experimenting in a new literary form, he noted its respectable ancestry to underscore its use for political society. Bacon also championed the study of classical fables. These contained a 'kind of parabolic wisdom,' Bacon argued, which 'was much more in use in the ancient times ... because men in those times wanted both variety of examples and subtilty [sic] of conceit: and as hieroglyphics were before letters, so parables were before arguments: and nevertheless now and at all times they do retain much life and vigour, because reason cannot be so sensible, nor examples so fit.'[60]

These were remarks which Bacon saw fit to repeat in his contribution to the genre by which classical and ancient fables were examined for the secrets they enclosed which might in turn enlighten and be of service to society, his *De Sapientia Veterum*. He also composed a fable of his own, the *New Atlantis* – which continues to intrigue scholars seeking a firm and definitive reading of Bacon's ultimate vision of society.[61] As a fable, however, its wisdom is probably there for the extrapolation – but not in any finalized, definitive form. Bacon was of firm opinions in certain respects only. One was that study must contribute towards civic society, and he went to great length to extend the boundaries of classical learning for his program of learning, seeking always to grant it a greater significance in the civic sphere than (he argued) existed. He maintained that in its current guise, he found 'the wisdom of the ancients to be like grapes ill-trodden: something is squeezed out, but the best parts are left behind and passed over.'[62] In *De Sapientia Veterum*, he demonstrated how wisdom was to be squeezed out of a genre that had so far been largely ignored by scholars. Examining the fable of Narcissus, for example, he concluded that the gifts of nature end in disappointment if not sustained by a disposition for industry. The self-absorption of Narcissus led to 'sloth and listlessness' until he lost 'all vigour and alacrity.' His metamorphosis into the emblem of spring, Bacon noted, was doubly significant, representing in the first place the disappointment of promise unfulfilled. Second, this flower was deemed 'sacred to the infernal deities,' for by his fate Narcissus incurred the judgment of the gods. Bacon thus concluded that the ancients were eminently wise in creating a parable by which to demonstrate that 'anything that yields no fruit ... was ... held sacred to the shades and infernal gods.'[63] Needless to say, in Bacon's hands the moral taught the lesson of the need for political involvement and action.

Such a political interpretation of fables was added criticism of those detractors whom Bacon attacked in Book 1 of the *Advancement*. It was a response, as well, to the complaints of an essayist like Sir William Cornwallis, an ex-colleague of Bacon's in Essex's circle, whose dark reflections in his own collected *Essayes* expressed the on-going disenchantment experienced by many survivors of that group. Cornwallis inveighed against political amorality and the vogue for Tacitus among contemporaries, and he isolated the factor of fables in scholarship as overworked and trivialized by superficial contemporary writers, concluding that the age in which he lived was like the scullery in the structure which housed the history of civilization – now composed only of 'cookes and taylours.' His retort to the ills of the day was the advocacy of obscurity and the solitary life.[64] J.H.M. Salmon has set the pessimism of Cornwallis against the bright conclusions adumbrated by Bacon to suggest the contrast between the English face of 'neostoicism' and that of Tacitism in the first decade of the seventeenth century.[65]

But were these two 'isms' distinct and entirely separate movements? Rather than isolating Cornwallis as a typical neostoic, I would suggest that Bacon better fits the bill. He remained committed to public service in the face of changing conditions, and in the *Advancement* he affirmed the claims of the *vita activa*, setting them firmly within an extended range of scholarship. In the end, Bacon may have failed to satisfy the likes of Cornwallis, who in any case hardly showed any 'constancy' in venting his complaints. Moreover, Bacon reaffirmed the relevance of Seneca and Tacitus in contemporary politics, providing, at the same time, a defence of the philosophy of action deriving from the study of the ancients. Thus he built a firmer foundation for neostoicism by including Greek fabulists and figures such as Julius Caesar as authorities. By raising Caesar to the status of exemplar on a par with Tacitus, Bacon is adding his own distinctive mark to a Lipsian paradigm; Lipsius had considered the works of Caesar to be of minor value, quoting him sparingly in his *Politica*.[66] As well as contributing to a continental movement, then, Bacon was proclaiming a longer pedigree – authenticating the legitimacy, as it were – of the style and mode of learning he endorsed – in a way and in such a manner, moreover, that would not give offence to a king highly suspicious of the political uses of Tacitus in scholarship. Thus, the 'Tacitean' style of his *Essayes*, for example, could be shown to be not a distinctive, innovative practice but the result of Bacon's own ventures into learning and precept, traceable back to the golden age of Rome and exemplified in the writings of Caesar. Politic learning was thus defended against assaults launched by academics at large, by a court scholar like Casaubon, and by a disenchanted neostoic like Cornwallis.

**Bacon and the Stoics**

If the initial measure of Bacon's rethinking the idea of political virtue is found amid the context of his defence of learning, the second falls within the boundaries of his program for its advancement. His great claim here was the need to rid learning of the encumbrances which limited the value of its application. He thus envisaged a complete overhaul of 'rational knowledge.'[67] Despite his claims for providing a general reassessment of human philosophy, however, the striking feature of Bacon's thought is its traditionalism, manifested in his definitions of the major categories of learning and the faculties to which they pertain. His traditionalism is also evident in his essentially organic approach to the nature and end of philosophy.[68] Doctors of knowledge, in Bacon's view, were precisely that, devoted to diagnosing and curing the ills arising in the minds of men. An Aristotelian cast of mind was a common thread linking Bacon to Lipsius, Charron, and other turn-of-the-century thinkers. It was a context familiar enough to readers, too, and Bacon sustained that cast of mind while simultaneously rebelling against what he saw as its shortcomings.

Two villains lurked behind the overall deficiency of knowledge, according to Bacon. The first was Aristotle, deemed guilty for perpetrating various errors which crucially undermined the civic nature of learning. Aristotle's system of logic hardly promoted civics, claimed Bacon, since its propositions and syllogisms resulted in divorcing reason from knowledge. Bacon took something of a Ramist stance against Aristotle; and, again like Ramus, he also complained that Aristotle's system of logic had degenerated further, courtesy of the schoolmen, whose 'art' was 'vicious and incompetent.' Bacon's language even resembled Ramus's earlier diatribes against Aristotelians, especially when he maintained that reason was and should be founded upon nature, and that the role of logic was to bring the relationship between reason and nature closer. And in a very Ramist vein, he pronounced that 'the duty of art is to perfect nature.'[69] Then, Aristotle was charged with having committed a list of other misdemeanours: of promoting study as a contemplative venture; of ignoring the role of rhetoric as a means for instilling virtue; and of passing over the more serious aspects of rhetoric without properly considering their pedagogical and moral value.[70] Learning, in Bacon's view, was to be purged of all these errors.

Bacon's anti-Aristotelianism is well known, but Aristotle was not the sole culprit in his view. A second villain was Epictetus, whose relevance in seventeenth-century England has yet to be ascertained.[71] He was clearly admired, enjoying renewed popularity perhaps due to Lipsius, who made ample use of him in his neostoic synthesis, which incorporated the Epictetan lesson that individuals should ignore those forces which are beyond their control and concentrate on what was in their power to achieve.[72] Such a lesson was particularly repulsive to Bacon, though he displayed a distinct ambivalence towards Epictetus – an ambivalence that also marked his approach to the general legacy of the stoics. Without quite admitting it, Bacon found Epictetan and other stoical teachings ultimately salvageable. He contested some, favoured others, all the while finding that most were eminently adaptable. In fact, Bacon was to make the teachings of the stoics fundamental to a program which, while enhancing the proficiency of learning, became the foundation for his political ethics.

Bacon liked the stoics' attachment to nature. He held that the Aristotelian practice of philosophy resulted in something akin to the disembodiment of reason, concurring with the stoics in positing that the mind, properly and naturally at work, operated according to nature. As he remarked: 'he that shall attentively observe how the mind doth gather [its] excellent dew of knowledge ..., distilling and contriving it out of particulars natural and artificial, shall find that the mind of herself by nature doth manage and act an induction much better than [philosophers] describe it.'[73] Bacon's program was to hang on the observation that learning should teach individuals 'to imitate nature which doth nothing in vain.'[74] Reason had to be grounded in nature; but it also had to be trained to withstand the appetites of the body and the passions of the senses. Thus knowledge had to be restructured to teach both the limits imposed by nature and the approaches by which to live in accordance with it.

Bacon proceeded to indicate how to attain such knowledge by highlighting two categories of learning in dire need of refurbishing. Civil knowledge – the study of political relationships – was virtually non-existent as a field of inquiry, he asserted. But before he treated its requirements he noted that moral philosophy, which he argued was distinct from civics, also needed redress.[75] Bacon's ambivalent attitude towards the legacy of the stoics first emerged in his discussion of moral philosophy, where rhetoric was singled out as its most crucial aspect. The 'duty and office' of rhetoric, he declared, was 'to *apply Reason to*

*Imagination* for the better moving of the will.'[76] The stoics were favourably contrasted with Aristotle (and Plato, in this instance) for their recognition of the importance of rhetoric. But Bacon's praise was brief; he went on to castigate them for their propensity for 'subtilty of argument,' as they sought 'to *thrust* virtue upon men by sharp disputations and conclusions, which have no sympathy with the will of man.' In his view 'the end of Morality is to procure the affections to obey reason, and not invade it; the end of Rhetoric is to fill the imagination to second reason, and not to oppress it.'[77] The rhetoric of the stoics had its specific deficiencies, then, which obstructed its capacity to instil virtue.

Still, the legacy of the stoics was not to be lightly dismissed. Bacon deferred to them in his definition of virtue, holding that it consisted of the twin aspects of duty and activity – activity, because human nature was founded on motion not rest; duty, because individuals formed a social community.[78] Their claim that virtue was the fundamental aim of moral philosophy enabled him to invoke Zeno, Seneca, and Cicero to support his assertion that 'the actions and exercises [of virtue] do chiefly embrace and concern society.'[79] Stoic philosophy thus stood Bacon in good stead in his complaints against particular stoics. Epictetus, who had advocated self-limitation 'lest we be liable to fortune and disturbance,' earned the sneering retort: 'as if it were not a thing much more happy to fail in good and virtuous ends for the public, than to obtain all that we can wish to ourselves in our proper fortune.' Epictetus's way, Bacon suggested, lacked human dignity and (above all) ignored our political nature. While Bacon admitted there was an aspect of 'good,' or virtue, which was private and particular, he held that the 'good which is communicative' was much worthier of emulation. 'The conservation of duty to the public,' he asserted, 'ought to be much more precious than the conservation of life and being.'[80]

Here, referring to the individual encountering the claims of self-preservation in face of the call of public duty, Bacon evokes the conflict of loyalties at issue in the Essex affair. In this context there can be no doubt about where priorities should lie. Moreover, in this instance the 'precious' nature of public duty is set upon a firm moral foundation. In view of his well thought-out theory of moral philosophy it would be a mistake, I think, to hold that Bacon was a proponent of blind self-preservation, or even, as F.J. Levy has suggested, that Bacon sought to divorce public activities from an ethical mooring.[81] His Ramist technique must be remembered, and the political precepts he was about to form hung on the ethical foundation created here. Rhetoric's intrinsic relation to virtue (or public duty) was fundamental to his overall discussion of moral philosophy.[82]

Bacon thus attempted to provide a firm theoretical basis for his subsequent articulation of political virtue; with particular reference to stoic ethics, approached by way of (Ramist) division and dichotomy, he also laid a philosophical foundation for an affirmation of learning in a way that Lipsius had not.[83] Moreover, unlike those of Lipsius, Bacon's political precepts would not follow after a primary rehearsal of God's sovereignty over creation. In the *Advancement*, Bacon had no reason to question what he apparently took for granted.[84] There would be a place for referring to Providence in his argument, but for the moment he rested content with declaring that *'Da fidei quae fidei sunt'* –'Give unto faith that which is owing unto faith.' Indeed, Bacon's main task was to justify the rest of the Christian injunction, render unto Caesar that which is Caesar's – which, of course in Bacon's vocabulary, meant political participation.[85]

Nevertheless, Bacon's task required more than a reaffirmation of humanist principles. Learning had to be overhauled, and the legacy of the stoics showed the way. Bacon was not about to become another mere spokesman for a reinvigorated stoical approach to political knowledge. His program encompassed a system in which 'internal knowledge' led to 'civil knowledge,' and which itself reflected the dualism in Bacon's (stoical) concept of human nature. In the process of establishing its validity, his stoical leanings were transformed into neostoical aspirations.

**Bacon on Fortune, Virtue, and Prudence**

In setting the scope of the internal knowledge required for his program, Bacon asserted: 'First therefore, in this, as in all things which are practical, we ought to cast up [for] our account, what is in our power and what not.'[86] He was referring, of course, to the role of fortune and adversity in life, a topic much in need of attention both because of the uncertainty of politics – as he himself bore witness – and because of the growing fashion for resignation – as represented, for instance, in Cornwallis's pessimistic call for obscurity and the solitary life.

Not that Bacon invoked any such particular points of reference, which were only implicit as he remarked upon the 'deficiencies' in need of rectification. A category of works on 'men's dispositions' would amount to a record of the impressions made upon individuals by nature (that is, the predilections of individual personalities) and fortune (particular individual responses to different situations). Such 'points of nature and fortune' were generally believed to lie outside the command of men, he wrote; yet 'endurance and suffering' were accepted responses to them – a travesty in his view. He then distinguished between 'dull and neglected suffering,' and what he called 'wise and industrious suffering.'[87] Examples drawn from the corpus of history were to furnish the data from which to procure the results he sought.

James Spedding has remarked that Bacon's plea here would result in providing a host of 'moral and mental anatomies,' and it is tempting to thus give Bacon a place in the (future) field of psychology.[88] Bacon, however, was clearly addressing his own tradition of politics and discourse. Twenty years before, Lipsius had addressed issues similar to those facing Bacon, responding with his formula of constancy – the virtue achieved by the mind rummaging through history and discovering that ills have always abounded. In Lipsius's scheme, 'right reason' was the essential agent in the quest for constancy. For Bacon, however, the data upon which right reason depended were still missing, as were the categories of necessary information. His plan of learning, he emphasized, concerned 'the Culture and Regiment of the Mind.' And his goal in accumulating the reservoir of knowledge was 'to make the mind *sound*, and without perturbation; *beautiful*, and graced with decency; and *strong* and *agile* for all the duties of life.'[89] In effect, Bacon was redefining 'constancy.'

He was confident that the observation of examplary attitudes in the past could be transformed into precepts 'for use in life.'[90] And by recognizing the impingements of nature and fortune on individuals, Bacon's readers would be in a position to assert a measure of control after all, if only over their responses to the dealings of life. But it is important to remember Bacon's twofold approach to knowledge, informed by the twin priorities imposed by duty and activity. Inner knowledge was the essential for demonstrating that the first duty of the individual was to society. By itself, however, inner knowledge was insufficient to provide guidelines for the 'outward' aspect of the individual. What was necessary here, Bacon claimed, was a new and thorough corpus of knowledge.

It lay in the realm of 'civil knowledge' – the study of what men do. He divided this branch of learning into three parts: what he called 'conversation,' the study of social behaviour and appearances; 'negotiation,' which comprised political behaviour; and 'government,' which related to the state. The greatest deficiency lay in the second category, argued

Bacon. His great challenge here lay in describing a program to increase civic knowledge while, at the same time, promoting his own concept of 'politic knowledge,' which consisted of a revised rendition of the role of fortune in politics and the necessity for the guiding precept of prudence.[91] His own particular contribution to learning lay here, where he also gave his strongest affirmation of the value of learning to society. Because such politic knowledge had not yet been collected together was no reason, he asserted, for concluding that there was no correlation between learning and wisdom. He had the plan by which to prove it. His technique was a replica of what Lipsius, Harvey, and others had done in scanning the literature of antiquity and extracting lessons and examples for use in the present.[92] Bacon had recommended this method years before he sat down to compose the *Advancement*, but as he went on to prescribe the essentials of the political knowledge so sorely in want, the association between scholarship and action emerged as the fundamental aspect of his text.[93] The 'advancement of learning' thus validated his humanist claims as it simultaneously turned into a handbook for advancement in life.

Before he went on to describe the tenor of the politic knowledge which had so far been neglected, Bacon had to address two necessary preconditions, the fundamental imperatives, of this knowledge. The first was distinction between the qualities required for internal knowledge – for the fashioning of the self, as it were – and the needs for external dealings between individuals. He asserted that in the realm of civic knowledge 'only an external goodness' was required, 'for that as to society sufficeth.'[94] F.J. Levy has noted that Bacon made this distinction in his first collection of *Essayes*, concluding that it represented a shift in Bacon's thought from an emphasis on 'how to "be" with how to "seem."' Levy went on to suggest that this emphasis on 'seeming' was the measure of Bacon's Machiavellianism and hence his rejection of ethics in politics.[95]

'Seeming,' or semblance, or even dissimulation, followed, however, from Bacon's division of human nature into the private and the public – itself in the tradition from which neostoic discourse emerged, underlying both Lipsius's definition of constancy and his discussions on *prudentia mixta*. Charron founded his portrait of the sage on the same feature, although for Charron the division augured the irreconcilable dichotomy whereby his sage made a strict separation between inward and outward virtue. Charron's precepts were highly ambiguous, and in the last chapter we saw how Ralegh reacted to them, particularly as invoked by Robert Dallington. They also lurked in the background of Cornwallis's advice on choosing the 'solitary obscure life' before joining what he called 'fortune mongers' and 'strivers for the world.' Charron had not only adjusted 'the Lipsian paradigm' in highlighting the distinct requirements of the external world; his accomplishment laid the grounds for the repudiation of neostoic teachings as base and unethical.

Bacon would have been keenly aware of the various directions that could result from the strict separation of the private and public aspects of human nature which together, he asserted, comprised the civic individual. And so he posited that the conditions under which civic knowledge was to be applied were distinct from those of moral philosophy – not because of any autonomy enjoyed by the public sphere, he insisted, but because of the outwardness of the conditions and, consequently, the exterior nature of their effects.[96] He also insisted that public virtue was a thing difficult to estimate since it was informed by the greater number of members among whom it operated. Consequently, it was conferred and not a virtue in itself. Furthermore, like learning, and even the concept of honour, public virtue was mostly concerned with the fulfilment of duty in Bacon's argument; indeed, Baconian ethics extolled the practice of public activity.[97] Virtue proper, he insisted, was an internal affair, and it was concerned mainly with intentions and goals.

Bacon was thus concerned to close the discussion on virtue, and attempted to render its more debatable points redundant. Treating it under the heading of moral philosophy, he argued that that was where it ought to stay. Even there, nevertheless, the clear association between private virtue and public duty was imparted in two key lessons. The first was that an 'honest man can do no good upon those that are wicked ... without the help of the knowledge of evil.' This lesson followed quickly on the heels of Bacon's recognition of the value of Machiavelli, to whom, he asserted, 'we are much beholden ... [for writing] what men do and not what they ought.'[98] Neither of these observations resulted in an exoneration of evil or in the claim that in certain areas immoral political action was tolerable. They operated to underline Bacon's 'Lipsian' plea for an increase of study to understand evil, thereby to combat it. The second lesson enjoined the pursuit of 'things which are just in [the] present'; and he added, 'leave the future to the divine Providence' – another instance of his view that earthly events necessitated the exercise of earthly measures.[99] These two lessons – comprised in three observations – functioned as the ethical underpinnings for Bacon's concept of politic knowledge. They also recast Lipsian formulations of the basis for neostoic service to the state, which was founded on action according to reigning circumstances and action devolving from knowledge of good and evil. Thence Lipsius had gone on to define *prudentia mixta*. How far Bacon also affirmed this Lipsian formula will preoccupy us in a moment.

For, not only did Bacon have to consider the concept of virtue as a precondition for politic knowledge, he also had to lay the grounds for the greatest factor that he believed intruded into political behaviour. This was fortune – the decisive power to which everyone was prey, and the overwhelming power to which many succumbed. But according to Bacon, fortune had no inherent qualities, nor was it in any way related to Providence (as, closely allied to fate, it had been for Lipsius). It more properly concerned circumstances and the way in which an individual responded to them. Thus fortune might 'seem adverse and contrary,' but even so might still present a host of new opportunities.[100] Bacon's concept of fortune was erected on what was ultimately a stoic foundation. He consistently avowed the fallibility of the senses as far as fortune was concerned, and he particularly sought to question the responses made by many an unwary victim. Bacon suggested that it was up to reason to make a measured judgment, and, as it did so, to restructure fortune's apparent penalties into incipient bounties.

Where talk of virtue, then, tended to fall out of the picture, the concept of fortune was introduced as of fundamental importance. As he turned to map out the lines of the type of politic wisdom necessary for contemporary purposes, it was the variety of responses to fortune that shaped his venture. He set out eight precepts by which 'to make a better and freer choice of those actions which may concern us' and by which '[we may] conduct them with the less error and the more dexterity.'[101] Each of them began with an axiom taken (in the main) from the stoics, particularly Epictetus. For instance, precept number two held that one should 'look oft in the glass' and know oneself; number three urged 'the endeavour to frame the mind to be pliant and obedient to occasion'; and number four, rendered in Latin, '*Fatis accede Deisque*' – 'take the way which the fates and the Gods offer.'[102] None of the precepts stopped with the message of the axiomatic opening, however; he held (again following the stoics) that human nature was predicated on motion, and his prescriptions for how to circumvent fortune all followed from a natural flow.[103] Thus Epictetus, one of the original purveyors of these teachings, was invoked to show that his views on such observations were highly pertinent – if limited, since his ultimate priority lay in establishing the sovereignty of reason but not as it applied to civic activity.[104] By contrast, Bacon's utmost concern was civic activity – an obsession that delimited the applicability of Epictetus and signalled the shift from a stoic to a neostoic perspective.

Prudence was the key 'virtue' on which each of Bacon's precepts turned; and the possibilities arising from fortune were the crucial factors that guided the direction of those precepts. In exercising the one in light of the other, Bacon settled on dissimulation as the critical aspect in political behaviour: the *modus vivendi* set up for emulation became the maintenance of flexibility in political dealings. Thus he could enjoin, 'the sinews of wisdom are slowness of belief and distrust' – a precept that derived from Cicero but had since become fundamental to the Lipsian formulation of *prudentia mixta*.[105] Readers were urged to observe the basic lesson which his precepts were organized to inform – politic man should be 'politic for his own fortune.'[106] Bacon's key teaching was thus that political advancement should always be pursued, and pursued in accordance with dominant practices. Dissimulation was a factor that Bacon could not ignore. But as he noted, 'the continual habit of dissimulation is but a weak and sluggish cunning, and not greatly politic.'[107] To be greatly politic, on the other hand, a measure of art and flair was required; but the first requirement involved 'the amendment of [the] mind,' for 'the remove of the impediments of the mind will sooner clear the passages of fortune, than the obtaining of fortune will remove the impediments of the mind.'[108]

As he thus articulated what he called 'the honest arts' of political behaviour, Bacon simultaneously advocated his version of *prudentia mixta* – in a tone distinctly his own. He exuded a positive optimism which, in comparative terms, approximates a certain type of literature of our own age, in which people like Dale Carnegie address the rat race of twentieth-century business society in their 'How to' books. Bacon, keenly aware of the ratrace quality of his own courtier-oriented society, set out to examine its features and provide the guidelines for succeeding within it. Positive thinking, a term more clearly related to our age than to seventeenth-century England, was a key lesson Bacon urged in dispensing the politic knowledge he believed to be so necessary for his own day.[109] His strictures on political knowledge emerged from his conjunction of prudence and fortune and acted to justify his own political behaviour. In terms of scholarship, the grand result was a synthesis of Ramist and Lipsian techniques; a Ramist perspective on the 'proficiency' of learning and a Lipsian quest for the 'amendment of the mind' led to Baconian civic action. Lipsius would have understood the terms and goals of each of Bacon's categories; as for Bacon's category of 'amendment of the mind,' Lipsius would have simply called it 'constancy.'

## Bacon and the *Vita Contemplativa*

The *Advancement* thus delineated an ethic of civic activity. Redefining the idea of political virtue, Bacon chastised those whom he considered responsible for divorcing ethics from politics, prominently among them, Epictetus, whom Bacon charged with giving ethics a validity of its own. The *Advancement* responded to the challenge and presented the 'new' learning by which to distinguish what men do from what they ought. But here precisely lay the catch. Asserting the need for a greater awareness of what men do, his goal remained the pursuit of one particular 'ought': the entirety of his work hinged on his desire to procure the pursuit of civic activity and hence prepare the grounds for instituting an epoch equal to and surpassing that of classical times – both in learning and in statehood.[110]

Learning was the key to a view of civic activity which promised the third resurgence of empire. In the *Advancement* and the later *De Augmentis*, Bacon was emphatic on the mutual association he set out and he condemned the instigators of the separation of learning from activity. The *vita contemplativa*, he avowed, was a worthy enterprise only as it applied to the *vita activa*.[111] From personal experience, nevertheless, Bacon could note a certain tension between the claims of the *vita activa* and the contemplative nature of learning. In 1594, in the wake of his disgrace after objecting to the royal proposal for a new tax, he wrote to his patron Essex, proposing to 'retire myself with a couple of men to Cambridge, and there spend my life in my studies and contemplations, without looking back.'[112] Almost thirty years later, after a new disgrace, he again posited the tension between learning and politics. In the *De Augmentis* he wrote that he was 'a man naturally fitted rather for literature than for anything else, and borne by some destiny against the inclination of his genius into the business of active life ...'[113] In both these instances, Bacon was writing as humanist scorned, as one whose main problem lay in reconciling obedience to authority yet seeing no other way beyond the conflict that arose between his concept of civic duty and the claims of humanist learning than by accepting the idea that the *vita contemplativa* had a claim all of its own. In a way, he thus became resigned to the conflicting claims that arose from his 'genius,' as he called it. Such a resignation, however, hardly amounted to a repudiation of his earlier ideals.

After his disgrace in 1621 office was certainly denied him, but scholarship remained not far from that state of deficiency he had decried in 1605 (the year of the publication of the *Advancement*). Studies in natural history (or science) began to occupy a larger proportion of his time after 1621, and John Aubrey tells us that one such experiment cost Bacon his life. In an effort to examine 'why flesh might not be preserved in snow, as in Salt,' Bacon so chilled himself that 'he immediately fell extremely ill.'[114] An incursion into the means of preservation led to Bacon procuring his own demise.

Irony notwithstanding, the striking feature of Bacon's subsequent endeavours is that his view of knowledge for the betterment of society was only a natural extension of his concept of learning as the foundation of politics.[115] Politics, moreover, remained a first priority for him, even during his final years. Immediate upon his fall from grace he composed the *History of the Reign of Henry the Seventh*, an exercise that indicated his continued concern with the exercise of power, not to mention its role in demonstrating his own expertise in such matters. It was also, of course, required as a presentation to the reading public – and especially incipient counsellors – of an example of the genre he had earlier called for in the *Advancement*. The *Advancement* itself was rewritten and rendered into Latin, but Bacon's declining years were also devoted to preparing for publication his collection of *Apophthegms* – inspired, as we have seen, by the example of Caesar and inestimable, claimed Bacon, for their political use.[116] He also devoted time to preparing another edition of the *Essayes*, which duly appeared in 1625 – only months before his death. A much enlarged version of his earlier collections, this edition has been taken to reflect Bacon's growing disillusionment with the idea of acquiring a sure science of politics.[117] It included such essays as 'Of Adversity,' 'Of Gardens' and 'Of Vicissitude of Things,' their very titles suggesting, on the face of it, a greater propensity on Bacon's part for resignation.

Bacon was far from disconsolate, however. For instance, in 'Of Adversity,' he insisted that 'Adversity is not without comforts and hopes;' and in 'Of Vicissitude of Things' he pointed to the natural cycle of growth and decline in nature, people, and states.[118] Moreover, he dedicated the work to the Duke of Buckingham, saying that it formed part of 'the best fruits that by the good encrease ... God gives to my pen and labours.' In the same dedication he mentioned his hope that the Latin version of the work might 'last as long as books them-selves.'[119] Bacon obviously believed he had still much to contribute to the humanist venture.

A dominant theme in these essays was consolation. Not resignation but consolation. An essay influential with the subsequent generation was 'Of Gardens,' in which Bacon described in detail and at great length the most advantageous way a garden should be laid, with proper attention given to the types of flowers, shrubs, and walks that best enhanced a stately residence.[120] His thoughts on gardens were obviously put into practice as, in the many hours political inactivity afforded him, he undertook to refurbish the gardens of his estate at Gorhamberry. John Aubrey, for one, was quite impressed with the outcome. A large part of his 'brief life' of Bacon was given over to describing the layout of Bacon's gardens, and he had nothing but praise for the entire topography of Verulam House.[121] Aubrey seems to have considered Bacon instrumental in creating the fashion for gardening, which he noted became increasingly popular as the century wore on.[122]

Whatever the reasons for such an increase in popularity, Bacon's were clearly set forth in the essay which in length rivalled only three others – those on 'Of Seditions and Troubles,' 'Of the True Greatness of Kingdoms and Estates,' and 'Of Friendship.'[123] Thus he had the most to say on the very public areas of the sustenance and enhancement of the state on the one hand, and, on the other, on the more purely personal areas by which one sustained the self. The crucial lesson afforded by both friendship and gardening, in Bacon's view, was that each provided a means of comfort and place of rest after the hurly-burly of political affairs. Bacon also considered the difficulty princes had in finding true friends. Friendship, he noted, should be distinguished from and kept out of professional life; it should never be an informative principle in the business of state. He wrote:

> It is a strange thing to observe how high a rate great kings and monarchs do set upon this fruit of friendship whereof we speak: so great, as they purchase it many times at the hazard of their own safety and greatness. For princes, in regard of the distance of their fortune from that of their subjects and servants, cannot gather this fruit, except (to make themselves capable thereof) they raise some persons to be as it were companions and almost equal to themselves, which many times sorteth to inconvenience. The modern languages give unto such persons the name of favourites, or privadoes; as if it were a matter of grace, or conversation.[124]

Considering that Bacon dedicated the *Essayes* to Buckingham, he was not loathe in the same volume to include remarks that could be construed as criticism of the power of a Buckingham, since, clearly, they evoked the exalted position he had come to enjoy through the very personal way in which he had been elevated by James. Bacon wrote that Romans had referred to such 'favourites' as *participes curarum*, which he noted was more proper and appropriate to their status, but hardly more commendable insofar as many such *participes curarum* used their ascendancy for treacherous ends. He invoked the examples of Sulla and Pompey, Caesar and Brutus, Augustus and Maecenas, and Tiberius and Sejanus to demonstrate that favourites could prove an unholy influence if not an outright challenge to the power of their patrons. Although the tenor of this part of his discussion on friendship operated to attack the position of favourites in the state, the entirety of the essay pointed less to a critique of Buckingham's position than to two other features in his approach to political society.

In the first place, Bacon seems to have been intent upon classicizing the nature of political relations. In 1616 he wrote to Buckingham and claimed, 'me thinketh I see the image of some ancient virtue, and not any of these times.'[125] Though smacking of sycophancy, this was a sentiment that pervaded Bacon's works, conveying the propriety he saw embodied in classical writings and personified by the ancient Romans.[126] Second, however, Bacon was still, in his later *Essayes*, concerned to firmly establish the distinction he called for between the public and personal spheres of activity, where friendship should hardly be informative in the first, yet could be indispensible in the second. Friendship, he averred, was intended for comfort; among its 'noble fruits' were 'peace in the affections, and support in the judgements.'[127] Above all, he insisted, it pertained to personal and social relations and was rarely fit as grounds for political dealings.

Where friendship had to be cautiously approached by princes, no such hesitancy applied to gardening. 'God Almighty,' Bacon said in introducing the essay 'Of Gardens,' 'first planted a garden.'[128] He went on: '[I]ndeed it is the purest of human pleasures.' The value of gardens, he asserted, was simple: 'It is the greatest refreshment to the spirits of man.' He set forth a description for the 'royal ordering of gardens,' suggesting that such a one as he spoke of would enhance majesty and authority by providing a very visible manifestation of those aspects of power. The ultimate beauty of and pleasure in this garden, however, would be its objective in sustaining the spirit of its royal owner. Here, then, was something that was applicable to every human being, prince and subject alike, and that for princes at least had an assuaging quality by finally comprising a subject that acknowledged their own humanity (while at the same time affirming their relationship to the divine, since God Himself 'first planted a garden'). Friendships princes must always stand aloof from, Bacon advised; but gardens could be their *métier* as well as anyone else's.

Bacon's source for his essay 'Of Gardens' went unacknowledged. Its similarity to the opening of Book II of *De constantia*, however, is too close to be overlooked.[129] The task of classicizing political relationships was something he shared with the now long-dead Lipsius. And in seeking to establish the parameters separating private relationships from public ones and distinguishing the goods of the one from the perils of the other, he was again pursuing a task which had preoccupied Lipsius. Accepting the private part of man's nature – be he a prince, a disgraced courtier, or an established counsellor – did not amount to a repudiation of the public part, however. He promoted gardens for their 'refreshment' value, just as Lipsius had in adopting the concept from the ancients. This retirement ethos went back to the civic ethic championed much earlier by Cicero, and then by Seneca, who in the *Epistles to Lucilius* affirmed that retirement was the due reward of a life of civic activity. 'We have lived in the Stormie Ocean,' Seneca had written to Lucilius; 'let us die in a quiet harbour.'[130] Bacon came to share this sentiment, as Seneca came to wield a greater influence in successive Baconian compositions. He consistently commended the civic spirit of Seneca in the *Advancement* and *De Augmentis*. In the 1612 edition of his *Essayes* he even hailed Seneca as an an early proponent of the 'essay,' in whose tradition Bacon claimed he followed. Finally, in 1625, Seneca was one of the main sources for the accommodation Bacon reached as he recognized that private life could come to the aid of the public.

Gardens symbolized that accommodation for Bacon. Providing shelter and nourishment for the soul, they were praised for their role in preparing servants and princes alike for a more concerted and devoted effort in the public sphere. Bacon always hoped to return to public activity himself, believing his banishment only temporary – like that of Seneca. He appealed to the Senecan precedent when he wrote to King James asking for restitution shortly after his disgrace: 'Seneca [was] banished for divers corruptions; yet was afterwards restored.'[131] One year later, he again invoked the Senecan parallel as reflective of his own plight in a letter to Lancelot Andrewes, bishop of Winchester and counsellor to the king.[132] While unheeded in his dearest wish to be restored to office, he did not desist from proffering political advice whether solicited or not.

Late in 1625, when the newly ascended King Charles was contemplating war against Spain, he wrote to Buckingham, 'I marvel that your Grace should think to pull down the monarchy of Spain without my good help.'[133] With this repeated Senecan hope, Bacon remained the constant political creature to the very end.

# 3

# The Constant Friend:
# Fulke Greville's Life after Sidney

> Mixe not in functions God, and earth together;
> The wisdome of the world, and his, are two;
> One latitude can well agree to neither;
> In each, men have their beinges, as they doe:
> The world doth build without, our God within;
> He traffiques goodnesse, and she traffiques sinne.
>
> <div align="right">(<i>A Treatise of Religion</i>, st. 98)</div>

> Oh wearisome condition of humanity!
> Born under one law, to another bound:
> Vainly begot, and yet forbidden vanity,
> Created sick, commanded to be sound:
> What meaneth nature by these divers laws?
> Passion and reason self-division cause:
> Is it the mark or majesty of power
> To make offenses that it may forgive?
> Nature herself doth her own self deflower
> To hate those errors she herself doth give.
> For how should man think that he may not do
> If nature did not fail, and punish too?
> Tyrant to others, to herself unjust,
> Only commands things difficult and hard.
> Forbids us all things, which it knows we lust,
> Makes easy pains, unpossible reward.
> If nature did not take delight in blood,
> She would have made more easy ways to good.
>
> <div align="right">(<i>Mustapha</i>, Chorus Sacerdotum, ll. 1–18)</div>

Whosoever will be pleased but indifferently to weigh his life, actions, intentions and death shall find he had so sweetly yoked fame and conscience together in a large heart as inequality of worth or place in him could not have been other than humble obedience, even to a petty tyrant of Sicily. Besides, this ingenuity of his nature did spread itself so freely abroad as who lives that can truly say he ever did him harm, whereas there be many living that may thankfully acknowledge he did them good? Neither was this in him a private, but a public, affection: his chief ends being not friends, wife, children, or himself, but, above all things, the honour of his maker and service of his prince or country.   (*Life of Sidney*)

Fulke Greville wrote gloomily of society. Two Senecan dramas, five verse treatises, two prose epistles, a 'dedication,' and over one hundred poems make up his not insubstantial literary output, where rarely does any glimmer of joy or hope ever emerge. Instead, as the epigraphs above suggest, Greville emphasized the irony of the human predicament, and the unhappy paradox of human existence was his continual refrain.[1] Never once, though, did Greville pronounce upon the futility of human endeavour, much less advocate withdrawal from politics or worldly affairs. Imperfection was a basic human trait; upon that fundamental precept Greville developed an approach to political virtue that underscored the vulnerability of human endeavours yet highlighted the necessity of political engagement.

Greville's thinking was distinct, then, by way of its basic structure. In contrast to his contemporaries, Ralegh and Bacon, and in contrast as well to Lipsius, Greville never lost sight of the spiritual dimension of the human plight, which appears to have haunted him, leading him always to distinguish the 'shadows' of mortal experience from the unknown truths augured by eternity and creation. This initial distinction is supplemented by two others. He sanctioned none of his writings for publication during his lifetime (1554–1628); and although a pirated edition of his Senecan tragedy, *Mustapha*, went to press in 1609, Greville's other compositions appeared posthumously, beginning in 1633 with the publication of *Certaine Learned and Elegant Workes*, a collection that included the prose epistles and verse writings, with the exception of the important treatises *On Monarchy* and *On Religion*. In 1652, the 'Dedication to Sir Philip Sidney' was published as *The Life of the Renowned Sr Philip Sidney*, but *The Remains, Being Poems of Monarchy and Religion* did not come on to the market until 1670. According to Greville, the *Life* was intended to preface the published edition of his entire *oeuvre*, but he changed his mind; when his work finally did appear it was submitted to an editorial interference that resulted in its fragmentation and the tendency to isolate and examine only part of his works persists to this day.[2]

Another mark of distinction between Greville and those other authors already considered here is the medium in which he mostly chose to write. Verse was his preferred form, ensuring that when Greville was 'rediscovered' by Morris Croll in the early years of this century he was viewed first and foremost as a poet – that is, a literary figure.[3] The profound, reflective quality of his verse substantiated the value of restoring Greville into the pantheon of seventeenth-century literature from which time and subsequent sensibilities had banished him; and the paradoxical strain in his writings and the tortured quality of his verse led to the widely-accepted view that Greville was a man radically divided between the petty claims of this world and his concerns with the hereafter.[4] Greville had been an engaged politician; yet Greville the thinker came to be distinguished from Greville the courtier – a reading given new emphasis by his most recent biographer, Ronald Rebholz.[5] Greville holds his own among historians mainly by virtue of his participation in the courts of Elizabethan and Jacobean England and by his wide activities as a patron of scholars and intellectuals.[6] The result of this division of labour is that most interpretations of Greville stress one aspect of Greville's endeavours at the cost of the other.

An accurate picture of the priorities in Greville's life is, however, difficult to ascertain if his writings are ignored, and those priorities are often unclear if made solely in reference to literature. The views he expressed are contradictory enough to suggest that he could approach an intellectual problem from various perspectives. *Of Humane Learning*, for instance, at the beginning argues the impossibililty of achieving universal knowledge and points to the vanity of such an ambition; its first part is, in the words of Geoffrey Bullough, 'an undistinguished piece of anti-humanism.'[7] It goes on, however, to qualify the initial position argued and to conclude that learning does, after all, have certain merit and value for mankind. *An Inquisition Upon Fame and Honour* and *A Treatie of Warres* present similar dualistic arguments according to theme of their respective titles. In light of these three treatises, but especially the *Treatise of Religion*, in which Greville's 'dualism' is almost collapsed into a negation of the world, critics have been virtually unanimous in concluding that Greville was always in quest of the absolute, finding the particularities of mortal experience a far cry from what speculation and inspiration led him to believe the ultimate truth of his subjects might be.[8] It is also generally accepted that he nevertheless resigned himself to the very poor second that was the value of human experience. Thus we have been presented with a man who was radically divided between the claims of the world and a propensity for otherworldliness – a soul that was tormented by the rival claims of nature and spirit.

Although there have been calls for a more holistic approach to Greville, to date few historians have rallied to respond.[9] The 'new historicists' in modern literature departments have taken the lead in interpreting Greville's writings as the political commentaries they undoubtedly were, though David Norbrook and Jonathan Dollimore have given the most challenging interpretations to date.[10] Both examine Greville's deep concern with the question of political power, although only Norbrook tackles the question of Greville's style, setting it within the framework of Tacitist discourse. However, Joan Rees's earlier claim that Greville set out to 'evolve a new form of poetic language which would bring poetry out of the pupilage of fiction into the "real" world of "truth"' has so far gone without either challenge or discussion.[11]

Why Greville chose to write (and in his *Life of Sidney* justify his use of) verse as a platform for historical and political commentary provokes some questions that have not yet been fully answered. The success or failure of the technique is less relevant than the choice, especially in view of the growing contemporary debate about the validity of Aristotelian categories distinguishing the real from the fictive, and, in the realm of discourse, the task of the poet in contrast to that of the historian and political commentator. The debate was over the authoritative voice in society. Sir Philip Sidney, whose memory was warmly cherished by Greville, had hailed the poet as preeminent in society; some two decades later, however, Greville's lifelong friend, Francis Bacon, reiterated the claims for the Aristotelian separation of functions to different purpose.[12] As indicated in the last chapter, Bacon promoted the authority of a prosaic but working philosopher in society – one who could harness all learning and apply it to politics and the state.

Greville remained tenaciously attached to his chosen form in the face of this growing debate – and in face, as well, of the defection of poets such as his friend and client, Samuel Daniel. Even Ralegh found prose forms more fitting to the political nature of his task in the changing circumstances of the 1600s.[13] As we saw, that 'last Elizabethan' gave up courtly verse as a mode of political expression once the more prosaic James ascended the throne of England. Greville's predilection for verse, on the other hand, became more and not less pronounced after the arrival of the Stuarts, though hardly in terms comparable to that proto-professional poet, Ben Jonson, who earned his living by the pen. Greville's verse technique is inextricably tied to his political views, and it forms part and parcel of the ambiguity of his legacy. That legacy is best elucidated by recourse to the Lipsian paradigm; Greville himself used a 'Lipsian' vocabulary even while maintaining a distinctive Grevillean voice. His was a voice that incorporated a number of distinctive neostoic perspectives into his description of political virtue, bringing into sharp relief the flexibility of a philosophy which justified subservience to the reigning power while upholding the concept of citizen participation. But just as for Ralegh and Bacon, Greville's particular experiences yield the first clues to understanding how and why he came to adopt a neostoic pose and describe political virtue in his own quite unique way.

## Greville and the *Vita Activa*

According to his own testimony, Greville's vast literary output was a product of his maturity, taking shape in the many hours afforded him by political inactivity.[14] His writings hark to ideals he developed during his early life and education, however, and the conflicts he voiced seem to have followed from his initial and formative experience as the friend of Sir Philip Sidney.[15] Sidney had been Greville's exact contemporary, but had died at the age of thirty-one in 1586 while Greville lived on to the ripe old age of seventy-four. David Norbrook has written that Greville spent his life mourning for Sidney; indeed, the starting point of Greville's political experience was wholly wrapped up in his connection with Sidney.[16]

Although Greville never enjoyed an absolute monopoly of Sidney's friendship, 'togetherness' and communion of ideals were the key features in the singular experience described by Greville.[17] They had met as schoolboys and went on to enter court together; together they enjoyed the patronage of the Earl of Leicester and together they hoped to advance the Protestant cause in Europe; they wrote poetry together, but together they also experienced the frustration of the Protestant 'party' in England. All this was abruptly cut short when Sidney was finally allowed to serve in a military capacity in Europe, there to meet death as a result of a wound he took in a skirmish outside Zutphen in 1586. Greville had been forbidden by the queen to accompany Sidney, and when news of his friend's fate reached him he was devastated by the loss. He confided in a letter: 'The only question I now study is whether weeping sorrow or speaking sorrow may most honour his memory that I think death itself is sorry for.'[18] This last remark was no empty apostrophe; even those whom Sidney had called enemies sent regrets over his death. Twenty-five years might elapse before Greville felt compelled to record the model life of Sidney he set down on paper, but their friendship remained the central experience of his life – as the testimony of contemporaries affirms and as his own several dedications, including that on his tomb, attest.[19]

Thenceforth, like a jilted lover, Greville was left to cope with living as best as he could. The initial shock gave way to a deep depression, which was relieved only when he set himself to preparing Sidney's writings for publication.[20] Perpetuating his friend's memory became a critical factor in restoring his attachment to living. He even became bold enough to slip off to France without royal permission, to lend what support he could to the forces of Henry of Navarre. After seeing the heat of battle and participating in the victory at Coutras in 1587, he returned to England only to encounter the requisite punishment meted out by a queen who frowned upon his setting off without her express permission. For this boldness he was denied royal access for six months. In this period and the months immediately following, Greville came to accept the fact that his forte lay not in trying to replicate Sidney's example as a soldier but in carrying out administrative duties and, as he noted in the *Life*, 'in [performing] such home services as were acceptable to my Sovereign.'[21]

Greville, then, seeking a vindication for continued allegiance to the *vita activa* through an attempt to emulate Sidney – in his own words, the desire 'to sail by his compass' – came to the discovery that Sidney's particular compass – military action – was not for him.[22] But this first crisis in his life had been overcome with the help of Sidney's memory, and thereafter he never again departed from his chosen path – even if, occasionally, it barred itself to him.

At first, little in the way of political compromise was required in his quest for political engagement. The political legacy of Sidney was taken up by the Earl of Essex, under whose auspices Greville achieved office as Treasurer of the Navy. The real end of an era came with the debacle of Essex's rebellion, in which Greville played a curious role. When Essex was committed to 'disgraced isolation' after his unauthorized return from Ireland in 1600, Greville and others were ordered by the court to vacate Essex House; although devoted to Essex, Greville compliantly obeyed.[23] After the aborted rebellion, Greville was among those sent to arrest Essex and his cohorts; again, he fulfilled his royal orders. Subsequently, he continued to enjoy the protection of the queen, but after 1601 he found himself first without a patron, and, on the passing of Elizabeth, without even the prospect of a sympathetic reception at court. The resumption of his career had to await the death of those who probably most impeded his attempt to serve James, namely Robert Cecil – whom Greville did approach only to find Cecil's promises to be hollow – and Henry Howard – a one-time colleague in Essex's retinue who, however, became an implacable enemy to many of his earlier allies.[24] Although not incarcerated, Greville, like Ralegh, would remain something of a political outcast for almost a decade.

His return to court and office was facilitated by the friendship he cultivated with Catherine Howard, wife of the Earl of Suffolk. Rumour had it that a healthy bribe played no small part in ensuring the favourable place he came to enjoy thanks to the Suffolks, who seem to have promoted him to office on the grounds of his malleability, especially in regard to the pro-Spanish policy which they defended.[25] When in 1614 the Suffolks faced disgrace, Greville moved on to court the protection of George Villiers, Duke of Buckingham. If, according to Ronald Rebholz this was 'the obvious source of alternative patronage,' it was a source that Greville pursued assiduously and one to which he remained quite faithful in the remaining years of his political career.[26] There would be a certain poetic justice in the fact that Greville, who wrote so much about the shadowy nature of mortal life and had himself moved in the shadow of patrons, should have his own death overshadowed by that of his last patron. Both Buckingham and Greville in quick succession fell at the hands of assassins, but in terms of political importance it was Buckingham's death that gained attention.[27] Little in the way of public mourning came to Greville, who was quietly buried away from London, in Warwick.

His later career thus seems to manifest a betrayal of the Sidney political legacy, which was characterized by an anti-Spanish policy and a Protestant, European involvement. It cannot be denied that Greville's involvement in politics depended on the prevailing system of patronage, which demanded that he subsume any cherished political ideals for the opportunity to be an actor at court. Outwardly, he made this compromise with ease. But contemporaries, noticing what they took for a lack of political integrity, remarked upon it. In 1612, Sir John Holles remarked to a correspondent that 'though Northampton [Henry Howard] and he [Greville] speak ill one of the other, this Nicodemus yet visiteth him ... at midnight.'[28] Perez Zagorin has recently demonstrated that the tag of 'Nicodemism' applies to early modern *religious* dissimulation, used for purposes of avoiding persecution; Holles's comment, however, invites a secular understanding of the term, even indicating the transferability of religious, political, and moral terms.[29] Moreover, the remark was hardly meant as a clever insight into the way Greville ticked; rather, it conveys the notion that Greville was a hypocrite. But if so, when exactly did Greville first take on the attributes of dissimulation? When did he quite decide to appear a 'Nicodemus'? And if a 'Nicodemus,' why not 'constant' in the Lipsian sense? He had undergone a series of crises about civic participation, and after the collapse of Essex's circle he was outwardly able to resist any personal preferences he might have cherished for the higher claim, as it were, of simply participating as a royal servant. Henceforth, I suggest, 'constancy' characterized his stance, becoming, it would seem, the guiding precept of his political career. But what did such 'constancy' mean to Greville, and how faithfully did he regard it an embodiment of proper and moral virtue? To answer the latter question we will have to widen the grounds of our discussion, but we can begin to answer the first by exploring Greville's intellectual and social milieu during the early part of his career.

It was as a friend of Sidney that Greville first came to public life and it was doubtless as a member of the Sidney circle that Greville first engaged with contemporary European intellectual trends. Sidney had made contacts far and wide, having been in close correspondence with thinkers as diverse as the Fleming Lipsius, the Frenchman du Plessis-Mornay, and the Scotsman Buchanan, these last two being counted among the 'monarchomach' theorists of Protestant Europe.[30] They all shared a keen interest in and an intellectual debt to the Stoics; but whereas Lipsius constructed neostoicism with little reference to Christian theology, Christianity pervaded the work of the others, in particular that of du Plessis-Mornay.[31] His *De la Verité de la Religion Chrétienne* was greatly admired by Sidney, who began its translation into English, a task completed by Arthur Golding.[32] Although it assimilated stoicism into a Christian framework, its militant theological argument was hardly comparable to the irenicism of Lipsius. *De constantia* offered a defence of the pagan doctrines du Plessis-Mornay attacked as it simultaneously rejected the zeal with which the French Huguenot promoted the Reformed Christian faith. Three factors, I think, led Greville away from Sidney's interests in du Plessis-Mornay, attracting him instead towards a Lipsian perspective.

The first was Greville's own cautious personality. He was never naturally an adventurous spirit; whatever adventures he had undertaken had been either in Sidney's company or inspired by Sidney's example. Thus, following Sidney, he had attempted to steal away on a sea voyage with Drake in 1585 to attack the Spanish in the West Indies; thus similarly he went off to France without permission after the death of Sidney, seeking thereby to resurrect in some way the spirit of his lost friend. Thus also, much later, he devised the plan to erect a huge tomb as a memorial to Sidney – one which would house his own remains along with those of Sidney. In the end he heeded the advice of John Coke, the friend who came closest to occupying the place left vacant by Sidney in Greville's life, and abandoned the plan; he was so stricken by Coke's criticisms of both the pagan-like tomb and the verses he prepared to inscribe there that the occasion seems to have prompted his own inquiry into the human desire for fame.[33]

Greville was perpetually confronted with what others – monarchs and friends alike – considered the inappropriateness of some of his most cherished opinions. He came to terms with his own limitations shortly after his unauthorized excursion to France, finally accepting that he was a follower and not a leader. In one poem in *Caelica*, Greville also confessed: 'I in thy wanton Visions ioy'd to languish. / ... Thy playes of hope and feare were my confession.'[34] These lines suggest that the militant Protestant cause he had espoused in his early, Sidney years might well have been something less than a matter of fundamental principle. It had been championed by many powerful, illustrious, and flamboyant men, and the intoxicating passion of Sidney's adherence to it could not have but spilled over onto Greville, who admired his friend above all others. Then Sidney died, and his death was followed by that of the other leaders of the Protestant cause in England – Leicester and Walsingham. Although Essex took up the banner of the militant Sidney legacy, the Spanish menace came to be overshadowed by the question of the succession, in which Essex was also deeply immersed.[35] Notably, two Grevillean pieces generally accepted to have been composed during Elizabeth's twilight years – the Senecan dramas – are devoted to just such a question.

Those tragedies, along with the *Letter to an Honourable Lady*, also suggest the ideological justification of Greville's practices in his new-found political life. Before turning to examine this question, however, we need to note that besides a natural reticence of character and the shift that occurred in English political priorities in the 1590s, a third factor operated to steer Greville towards a Lipsian perspective. This was the matter of seeing Sidney's writings through to print, the experience which not only helped Greville find a reason for living on after Sidney's death but led to the eruption of some hostility between Greville and Sidney's sister, Mary Herbert, the Countess of Pembroke. The disagreement began with Greville's attempt to forestall the appearance of what he called a 'mercenary' edition of Sidney's *Arcadia*. The threatened publication concerned the 'Old' *Arcadia*, an early version of the work, which was submitted for licensing not a month after news of Sidney's death reached England.[36]

According to Greville, Sidney had 'bequeathed no other legacy but the fire to this unpolished embryo.'[37] But he had also left a revised version of the work in Greville's hands, and Greville insisted that this one, although unfinished, was closer to Sidney's ultimate intention. In his *Life of Sidney*, he recorded that Sidney's purpose in *Arcadia* was to 'limn out such pictures in the mind that any man, being forced in the strains of this life to pass through any straits or latitudes of good or ill fortune, might (as in a glass) see how to set a good countenance upon all the discountenances of adversity, and a stay upon the exorbitant smilings of chance.'[38] Here, Greville portrayed Sidney in the manner of a stoic sage; shortly after Sidney's death, he set out to make sure the public would perceive him thus. Overseeing the publication of *Arcadia*, he reorganized its chapters and ecologues, inserting chapter summaries to guide readers in properly interpreting the work. This edition ended abruptly at the point at which Sidney had left the revisions, never to return to complete them. Greville insisted that the work should appear in just this way.[39]

Mary Herbert, however, for whom Sidney originally composed the work, thought Greville's editorial work full of 'fault' and 'defect.' She insisted that Greville's emendations 'disfigured' the entire composition 'wherewith the beauties therof' had been 'unworthely blemished.'[40] With the help of Hugh Sansford, her husband's secretary, she set about producing another version which, building on Greville's revised version but dispensing with his additions, incorporated some of Sidney's earlier and more lighthearted passages and restored the original ending. Remarking on the rival versions of *Arcadia* that appeared within three years of each other, Joan Rees has summed up the nature of the disagreement thus: 'Viewing *Arcadia* as he did, Greville would hardly be likely to accept as a satisfactory memorial of his friend the mixed version which the Countess offered. She, on the other hand, was anxious that nothing of her brother's should be lost and was perhaps angered by what may have seemed like Greville's contempt for the version that was so especially hers.'[41]

This episode affords us an insight into the debate over the nature of the Sidney legacy as, quick on the heels of his demise, a public debate arose over his image among posterity. The role of literature in Sidney's life was the key issue addressed by Greville and the countess, whose influence might well have been thought pernicious for the idea of Sidney that Greville wished to perpetuate. On the death of her brother, she adopted a stance of Christian resignation. Her translation of the Senecan tragedy, *Antonius*, composed in French by Robert Garnier, and of du Plessis-Mornay's *A Discourse of Life and Death*, which as Michael Brennan has noted 'concerned itself ... with the futility of courtly ambition,' manifested this resignation.[42] She also endorsed an image of Sidney that stressed his piety and was suggested from his devotional poetry, comprising translations of the verse of the Protestant du Bartas and his own versification of many Psalms. Greville agreed that Sidney should 'have all those religious honours which are worthily due to his life and death.'[43] But the countess's obsession with promoting her brother's sanctity at the expense of his equally strong devotion to politics jarred with Greville's own devotion to Sidney's memory. It was probably as a result of this disagreement that Greville began, privately, to record what he considered the image of the Sidney he knew, in what eventually became his *Life of Sidney*. There, Sidney's devotion to religion was subtly offset, and neatly balanced, by his devotion to his prince. Moreover, Sidney's literary achievements were the first item on Greville's agenda for setting to rights the picture of Sidney he endorsed. As he insisted, 'the truth is, [Sidney's] end was not in writing even while he wrote, nor his knowledge moulded for the tables or the schools, but both his wit and understanding bent upon his heart to make himself and others, not in words or opinions, but in life and action, good and great.'[44] In effect, Greville's Sidney resembles the figure who represented *virtus* and *doctrina* for Lipsius in 1585, provoking the Fleming's warm admiration. It was this very image of his friend that Greville set out to reassert.

The disagreement with Mary Herbert which followed quickly on other personal disappointments thus seems to have encouraged Greville to consider more closely the grounds of both his own passionate devotion to Sidney and the active life manifested by Sidney. His *Letter to an Honourable Lady* certainly addressed both these issues. It also signals Greville's engagement with the Lipsian paradigm while rehearsing the ambiguity that marked his engagement with neostoicism and his definition of political virtue.

## Right Reason and Grevillean Constancy

The *Letter to an Honourable Lady* purports to advise its addressee on how to comport herself in view of her husband's infidelity. Greville opened his address with a sympathetic overview of the happy beginnings of a marriage that had deteriorated into a 'Laberinth' of deception. The relevant point of comparison is between the state of marriage and that of society, and Greville posited that each undergoes a departure from an initial golden age 'onelie govern'd by the unwritten lawes of nature.'[45] That was a period of happiness, but Greville set its passing as inevitable 'since in the vicissitude of thinges, and times, there must of necessitie followe a *Brasen* age.' This is characterized by the emergence of 'unconstant proportions of power, and will.' According to Greville, the result is that 'reciprocall love' yields to inequality in 'liberty ... and power,' where the emerging principle is the manipulation of 'Hope and Fear' – hope by which to lull the unsuspecting to act upon desires, and fear by which to maintain power.[46] Greville used biblical allusions to account for the fateful decline in which 'selfeseekinge arts' come to predominate over that once reigning reciprocity, and in which the 'fall of mindes' becomes equated to the fall of man.[47]

Sympathy then turns to counsel as the Lady is urged, first, to come to terms with the loss of something that was precious to her but that she can never retrieve. Her golden time having passed, she is now prey to the 'false rudders of hope and fear,' which are only 'cloudy pillars,' the tools of the 'leakinge shippe of humane power,' which is itself described as 'an encroachinge power.'[48] She must learn to recognize and avoid these 'tributes of Tyranie,' which dominate in what Greville calls this 'unhopinge time.'[49] Her only recourse is to attempt to avoid a deterioration which is, nevertheless, wholly natural because change is the governing characteristic of life and living relationships. He tells the Lady, 'remember that the metall you are made of is earth, your habitacion a world; both mortal; and so no perfection at all is to be expected in them'[50] Thus, the Lady must lessen her expectations of others.

Greville's first piece of advice, then, is the acknowledgment of natural change and inevitable decline, and by means of a political analogy he depersonalizes a specific (and personal) loss by setting it among a larger pattern of social relationships. At the same time he establishes the public aspect of all private relationships. Comfort is to be gained from the one point of view, while responsibility and the lessons of duty emerge from the other. This explanatory scheme forms the basis from which Greville goes on to urge the Lady to remain a dutiful wife – even while he ascribes the decline of her marriage to the husband, who has yielded to passion and vanity. He is described as weak, but Greville, less in a misogynist tone (I think) than a view to the universality of human weakness, maintains that the Lady must not attempt to judge and punish him. On the contrary, she must be guided by her 'Arcke of dutie' and 'Let God, the searcher of harts; and time[,] the discoverer of faults[,] move those lincks of shame, and punishment.'[51]

Neither vengeance nor punishment are rightly within her compass, Greville insists. The Lady's role is likened to that of a subject under a prince as she, 'under the yoke of a husband,' is urged to make obedience the guiding principle of her behaviour. Greville accepts the fact that hierarchy and governance are warranted according to both the customs of nations and the laws of nature, and goes on to ask: 'those excesses which arise out of authoritie, are they not either rodds of trialls, which we inferiors must kisse, and that God onelie may burne which made them; or els mistes of mutinouse self-love which deceive, and make man as well misunderstand his diseases, as their remedies? And so by misplacinge equalitie, and inequality, at once ruin both publique, and private securitie.'[52] The Lady is acknowledged to be superior in 'love, chastity, piety, and sincereness,' but these virtues are no grounds for any mutiny against her husband's authority, which is based upon his acknowledged liberty and power. If her options are thus limited, she must yet remain dutiful and obedient and steel her mind to a world which is sadly lacking in the virtue she represents. She must learn to 'distinguishe vertue from vertue, right from right,' and Greville urges that her only recourse is to avoid error by seeking 'inwardlie for the fruite of true peace.' She must attempt to cultivate 'a steddie mind.' Thus 'against, and amongst all storms' she might have refuge in 'a calmed, and calminge *mens adepta*.' The promise of the *Letter* is that the Lady will find the way towards attaining a state of 'discreete constancie' whereby she might yet fulfil her duties while coming to terms with adversity and even conquering it.[53]

Greville's advice to the Lady comes close to an advocacy of patient resignation in the face of a hostile environment produced by factors outside the Lady's control. While critics are undecided whether there actually was an 'honourable lady' whom Greville might have had in mind, there is general agreement that in form and tone he adopted a Senecan approach in this work, and that the letter belongs to the humanist tradition of the epistle.[54] To classify the *Letter* as neo-Senecan is to indicate its relationship to a movement in which Lipsius was the renowned master.

The particular terminology of the *Letter*, moreover, alerts us to the view that this is no orthodox Christian resignation – much less Calvinist pessimism – that Greville has advocated.[55] The language echoes that of Lipsius's dialogue, *De constantia*, replete with its stress on the pursuit of constancy or the resolute mind (*mens adepta*). And as in *De constantia*, the *Letter* urges that the cultivation of inward detachment from the world has to be offset by continued outward engagement, where, again echoing Lipsius, Greville notes that one type of virtue applies to one sphere of action while another pertains to the other. Activity remains all-important in either realm as the bridge between the two worlds, and the two types of virtue are achieved by the quest for a *mens adepta*, where virtue itself dissolves into the key tenet of obedience and is maintained by what Greville calls the practice of 'discreet constancie.' This is to realise that hope and fear are but tools for manipulation. Greville sums up his case for the pursuit of constancy by noting, 'so subject is our life to the oppressions of power, chance, and negligence, as the practise of times will shewe, that he who cannot endure to loose, can much more hardlie endure to live.' Thus Greville domesticates the political dictum: *qui nescit dissimulare, nescit regnare*.[56]

This stress on loss (and the attempt to come to terms with all that it entails) suggests a personal aspect to the *Letter* – and its function as a rite of passage in Greville's experience. The golden age when Greville shared Sir Philip Sidney's companionship and ideals has been succeeded by a 'brazen' age in which 'reciprocall love' can no longer be the bond that will seal his commitment to any patron or policy. Henceforth, obedience and subservience would actually characterize his quest for political patrons, as he came to recognize that the appearance of virtue and right, based on sanctions of public convention, hardly accorded with their private and personal manifestations. His own obedience and subservience, then, might well have developed from *his* own quest for 'right reason,' which in Lipsian terms resulted from the dictates of the *mens adepta* and taught the practice of 'constancy.' Contemporaries thus might have gossiped about his political malleability, but the three lessons imparted by the *Letter* – the acceptance of change, the necessity of obedience, and, most importantly, the call for constancy – suggest that Greville had constructed a philosophy of action that enabled *him* to persevere in the fallen world he now inhabited.

The *Letter*, however, is one of the few places where Greville uses the idea of 'constancy' – and the term itself – in a Lipsian sense and without equivocation. In many poems of the *Caelica* collection, it was rather 'inconstancy' that preoccupied him. Complaints against the fickleness of a mistress in these poems convey the orthodox meaning of its opposite term, which stood for fidelity and immutability – that constancy which, in fact, the 'Honourable Lady' possesses but which Greville advises should be supplemented by another variety in order that she might persevere through the changed days of her present 'unhopinge time.'[57] David Norbrook has demonstrated that the poems of *Caelica* do share with the *Letter* an intense concern with the theme of political subjection and the nature of obedience. He sees a debt in Greville to Étienne de la Boëtie, the great friend of Montaigne, whose devotion to de la Boëtie resembled Greville's own devotion to Sidney. Greville, Norbrook has suggested, 'may well have been attracted [to de la Boëtie] by the elegaic aspect of Montaigne's writings.'[58] How far those same writings might also have affected Greville's concept of 'constancy' demands some attention. For indeed, Lipsian impulses in his language and thought, while frequent, are often offset by a sceptical streak that points to Montaigne.

This appears in the Senecan dramas, *Alaham* and *Mustapha*, where Greville portrays characters driven by passion and inhabiting a world in which chaos threatens to erupt at any moment. Reason barely triumphs in the sordid worlds of these plays, and when it does it is compromised and lacks any vestiges of a natural reason that might be universally available. The finally triumphant reason in *Mustapha*, for example, is 'right' only in that it urges the faithful counsellor, Achmat, to compromise his belief in the existence of universal justice. Greville sets 'stoic' precepts against 'neostoic' ones in this play, where stoical 'consistency' gives way to the acceptance of a neostoic idea of 'constancy.' Both, however, come up short.

The title character in *Mustapha* is the worthy heir of Soliman, whose legacy is sought by Soliman's wife, Mustapha's stepmother, Rossa, for her own son. She plants seeds of doubt and fear in Soliman about the loyalty of Mustapha; and as Soliman, out of his desire for Rossa, succumbs to them, Mustapha is put to death. At this point the people rise in rebellion. Achmat is torn between his sympathy for the uprising and his duty to the state he serves – even while that state has come to languish under the perverted rule of a now 'dotard king.' Achmat's dilemma is only reluctantly resolved as he considers both sides of the question:

And shall I help to stay the people's rage
From this estate, thus ruined with age?

> No, people, no. Question these thrones of tyrants.
> Revive your old equalities of nature.
> Authority is more than that she maketh.
> Lend not your strengths to keep your own strengths under.
> Proceed in fury. Fury hath law and reason
> Where it doth plague that wickedness of treason.
> For when whole kingdoms surfeit, and must fall,
> Justice divides not there, but ruins all.
> Besides of duties 'twixt the earth and sky
> He can observe no one that cannot die.
> But stay! shall man, the dam and grave of crowns
> With mutiny pull sacred sceptres down?
> People of wisdom void, with passion filled,
> While they keep names, still press to ruin things.
> Freedom dissolves them; order they refuse.
> Worth, freedom, power and right while they destroy,
> Worth, freedom, power and right they would enjoy.
> What soul then, loving nature, duty, order,
> Would hold a life of such a stateless state,
> As made of humours, must give honour fate?[59]

Achmat finally decides to support the state in quelling the rebellion. For him the worst of the two evils unleashed by Mustapha's death is the threat of social disorder, a problem which takes precedence over the problem of tyranny. Outward chaos in society is avoided by internalizing the chaos of nature, symbolized as the chaos of language and represented first by Achmat's words on fury (properly a passion but for Achmat devolving from a righteous and rational quarter), and then by the distinction he voices between words and things. Achmat recognizes that terms such as 'worth, freedom, power and right' pertain only to the system of order they uphold; separated from it they threaten anarchic dissolution. Without the established state, they have little reference to anything fixed and tangible.[60]

The character of Soliman is an even more forceful representation of the internal chaos which drives the world of *Mustapha*. Soliman alternates between a state of rational lucidity and one of impassioned jealousy; his tyranny is the result of his inward chaos, where passion finally overwhelms his reason. Achmat concludes that tyranny is less of a menace than the unleashing of full-scale chaos. He finally adopts a Lipsian position of constancy, although the play as a whole is infused by a strong streak of Montaigne's sceptical teachings on the fallibility of reason, the absence of any universal reason, and the need for the imposition of outward order as a means of controlling nature's otherwise anarchic tendencies. As such, Greville appears to have been using *Mustapha* as a platform for hammering out the implications of Montaigne's political prescriptions.[61]

If Greville thus evokes Montaigne, we should remember that Montaigne set out to discover difference – that is, the individuality of human beings, a point that held little interest for Greville, who looked for characteristics common to all in the plight for political survival under an all-encompassing monarchy.[62] Moreover, if Greville showed a propensity for universalizing human experiences and thus a tendency for abstractions, he never comes across, as does Montaigne, as a detached observer of human emotions and weaknesses. Instead, he seems keenly aware of and involved in every passion he describes.[63]

He also shows reservations in propounding Lipsian constancy. For example, in *Mustapha*, 'right reason' proves painful in the gaining for Achmat; nor is the Lady's quest in the *Letter* shown to be an easy task. In short, 'constancy' proved worthy of cultivation because it justified continued public participation, but a sacrifice of sorts is one of the incontrovertible aspects in Greville's construction of political virtue. Obedience is its most pronounced characteristic. In the name of obedience and by virtue of 'constancy,' the Lady must submerge her ideal of love and expect less of her husband; to the same end and according to the same means, Achmat is led to compromise his principles of good governance and order to ensure the continuation of governance itself.

But there is a higher principle involved. In *Mustapha*, by the end of the play, the murdered prince, who personified private virtue and integrity and who died true to himself, becomes a crucial figure who brings to a head the threat to society. Greville seems to be saying that those whose virtue results in death (that is, are dead heroes) are in fact hardly worthy exemplars and that self-sacrifice, far from being admirable, has effects that are positively dangerous. 'Constancy,' if not right reason, emerges to provide the rationale for the sacrifice of principle needed for the sake of the obedience that Greville demands. Notably, though, the *Letter to an Honourable Lady* is left unfinished; and *Mustapha* concludes with Achmat adopting a stance of 'constancy' but with passion and unreason still threatening at every quarter. Such conclusions – or lack of them – strongly suggest that Greville continued to grope for a satisfactory resolution to the problem of political virtue.[64]

In several of his treatises, moreover, he further engaged with Lipsian vocabulary, but only to question the precept of right reason and challenge the validity of the concept of *mens adepta* as an adequate means of discovering any certainty that might exist. The *Treatise of Humane Learning* begins by considering the impossibility of complete and universal knowledge, at least for the human intellect. The stoics' system of knowledge is treated with ambivalence as Greville avows our natural subjection to the senses, only to affirm *their* unreliability since they present (often) false and (always) inconclusive knowledge to the mind. He then argues that the evidence of the senses is never wholly overcome; it continues to operate on the various faculties of human apprehension: imagination, memory, and understanding. As such, the senses are the bastion of misinformation instead of something to be conquered as reason establishes itself as the source of infallible knowledge and as 'true' reason emerges triumphant over them. In fact, Greville summarily rejects any great function for reason as he contemptuously remarks:

> ... none agree
> What this true Reason is; not yet have powers,
> To leuell others Reason unto ours.[65]

In the *Treatise of Religion*, Greville's sceptical estimation of the power of human reason is virtually complete. Here, he repudiates all claims that human power can achieve true virtue and knowledge and, again with something resembling contempt, questions the value of a stoic's epistemological stance. Insisting that 'Without God there was no man ever good,' he declares that true virtue can only come as God's gift. He rejects all claims for

> ... heathen vertue, which they doe define
> To be a state of minde, by custome wrought,
> Where sublime reason seemeth to refine
> Affection, perturbation, everie thought
>   Unto a *Mens adepta*, which worck spent
>   Halfe of the dayes to humane *Hermes* lent.[66]

In light of such strong repudiations of what in the *Letter to an Honourable Lady* Greville seemed only ready to take on, we might want to ask what (if any) final position did Greville hold on the issue of human reason.

Two approaches, I think, can help us. One requires us to see the entirety of each of the treatises and weigh remarks such as the above within their formal (or rhetorical) context; the other demands setting these pieces in a larger humanist context. As to the first, the *Treatise of Humane Knowledge* and the *Treatise of Religion* have as a starting point that repudiation of human efforts noted above. But each then goes on to mark the measure of what is within human power and to insist that human abilities should always be put to use. Greville's conclusion is best stated in that stanza of the *Treatise of Religion*:

> Mixe not in functions God, and earth together;
> The wisdome of the world, and his, are two;
> One latitude can well agree to neither;
> In each, men have their beinges, as they doe;
> > The world doth build without, our God within;
> > He traffiques goodnesse, and she traffiques sinne.

Many literary scholars have seen in these lines evidence of that dualism for which Greville has become renowned. Still, if we remember the contours of the Lipsian paradigm, it looks as if Greville is again giving a rendition of constancy, the starting point for which is the espousal of a fideistic position and a refusal to engage in theological debate. At the same time, Greville's lines evoke the Lipsian dictum, *prudentia mixta*, which was validated by the view that political action had to be based on the recognition that we inhabit not the commonwealth of Plato, but the dregs of the state of Romulus. Greville's terms are clearly different from those of Lipsius, but then so too is the context of discussion. The Lipsian paradigm was shaped in response to the crisis provoked by the European Wars of Religion. Greville, in these treatises at least, explicitly addressed the question of learning, in one, and religion, in the other. If the context which formed the backdrop to the *Letter* and the Senecan plays was Greville's readjustment to a changing world which no longer included Sidney, the crisis he addressed in his treatises was of a different character; the dissolution Lipsius had striven to avoid in his repair of humanism had clearly come to pass. Thus we should turn to the larger humanist context addressed in Greville's treaties.

**Greville, Knowledge, and Prudence**

One of the consequences of Essex's rebellion was the strong suspicion that fell upon certain types of learning. Works that could be read as having relevance to the activities of Essex – from Sir John Hayward's *Henry*

*IIII* to Daniel's *Philotas* and Jonson's *Sejanus* – were considered suspect by a council that was becoming increasingly alert to critiques of the court, whether presented under the guise of learning or of entertainment.

There was a certain irony in the fact that with the coming of James suspicion of 'politic' learning intensified rather than eased. After all, the king was a scholar himself and a known patron of letters. The prevalence of a critical approach to Tacitism, however, was virtually guaranteed by continuity among the council membership.[67] But the threat to learning in general, and Tacitism in particular, was now heightened by several other factors, not least of which was the attitude of the king. As noted in earlier chapters, James spearheaded a campaign to discredit the validity of Tacitus as the only historical authority of value, advancing scholars less partial to the attractions of techniques that characterized Tacitists.[68] Others, like William Camden, made the necessary adjustments and submerged overtly Tacitist methods thus maintaining their privilege to write.[69] The Stuart court's special vigilance over the tenor of historical publications played no small part in helping divorce scholarship from politics – at least in a critical and public guise. Ralegh's *History of the World* was temporarily withheld as much for its sauciness towards princes as, no doubt, its didactic intent. And Ben Jonson's experience in 1605 of being hauled off to answer for having written *Sejanus* was repeated in 1611 after the appearance of *Catiline*. Thenceforth, Jonson wrote no more historical tragedies. If one mark of Tacitism was its avowal of the centrality of learning and scholarship in the arena of political action and, conversely, of the centrality of contemporary politics to literature, King James tried his best to limit such literary expressions.

Amidst this aspect of the crisis in English humanism, Greville was among those who sought to redefine the relationship between literature and politics – much as he did in his discussion of Sidney's writings in the *Life*, when faced with the interpretation of Mary Herbert. But politic learning was more closely associated with Tacitism, and Greville's lifelong commitment to Tacitism was only made manifest in the closing months of his life. Nevertheless, since at least 1615 he had planned to institute a chair of History at Cambridge, which finally materialized, however briefly, in late 1627.[70] At that point, Greville not only picked the man – a thoroughgoing Lipsian Tacitean who had been educated at Leiden and would later go on to serve in the English Commonwealth – but the topic of the inaugurating lecture itself – Tacitus and the origins of political power – and this in the unsettled political climate which was soon to lead to the presentation of the Petition of Right. Matthew Wren, a protégé of William Laud, was among the listeners; he found the topic subversive and believed 'it was stored with ... dangerous passages ..., so applicable to the exasperation of these villainous times.'[71] Wren was instrumental in having Dorislaus's appointment rescinded. The whole matter of the history lectureship at Cambridge thus ended rather ignobly, leaving Greville, at the end of his life, a failed patron of Tacitism.

But before patronage, there had been engagement. The *Treatie of Humane Learning* experiments with literary Tacitism, as Greville considers the general question of the relationship of learning to politics while also reflecting upon several aspects of the debate as it was then being articulated.[72] Bacon, as we saw in the last chapter, keenly participated in the same debate, vindicating Tacitism in his *Advancement of Learning* by establishing the outline for an enlarged program of learning. He reaffirmed the value of scholarship to political society and made a strong case for the practical application of a classical program of education, which he promoted against rivalling claims for the autonomy of learning, on the one hand, and the total repudiation of it in terms of its value for statesmen, on the other. Bacon's was a program that established his position as a proponent of what Isaac Casaubon later disparaged as the 'book-trained politician.'[73] At the same time, Bacon made two optimistic predictions: his program would lead to the uncovering of the secrets of nature; and universal knowledge was entirely possible.

If Bacon's was the voice that gave the most thorough affirmation of Tacitism, his was only one side of that argument. Samuel Daniel, another close friend of Greville, represented a quite different point of view. In *Musophilus*, a poetical treatise first published in 1599, Daniel announced that he offered 'a generall defence of all learning.' The title character is a lover of the muses who affirms knowledge to be the 'soule of the world,' hails the virtues of literature, and proclaims the immortality that is invested in works of learning. This optimistic assessment is challenged throughout the poem by Musophilus's cynical counterpart, the worldly-wiseman Philocosmus.[74] D.R. Woolf has recently indicated that *Musophilus* 'is a colloquy, not a debate. It raises questions rather than resolving them ...'[75] Notably, though, the poem was dedicated to Greville; and it was probably Greville's views of learning that were portrayed, although *in extremis*, through the character of Philocosmus. Knowledge to Philocosmus was limited by the nature of human capacity and understanding; the prime justification for the pursuit of learning was its functional and very temporary use.

In his own discussion of 'Humane Learning' Greville stood somewhere between the views propounded by Daniel's Philocosmus and those championed by Bacon. According to his verse treatise, Greville saw much that could be challenged in both Bacon's hymn of praise to learning and Daniel's apostrophe to the muses. The problem with Daniel's argument was the autonomy implicit in human knowledge and the power accredited to human eloquence, with the further implication of learning being pursued for its own sake.[76] Bacon's defence of learning challenged this latter phenomenon, but Bacon too raised learning to levels to which Greville objected.[77]

The arguments of Bacon and Daniel point to a debate that was occurring within the confines of English humanism, that also referred to a wider political context. The fate of Essex, of course, was the common denominator linking the two, and Daniel's poem also stands as representative of the voices that had been competing among Essex's advisors. Philocosmus echoes the dominant refrain of those days, while Musophilus speaks in terms of a more personal view that reflected, among others, the voice of Daniel's one time patroness, the Countess of Pembroke. We have already noted that following the death of her brother, Sir Philip, Mary Herbert sought retreat and consolation in literature. She would return to be an active courtly lady, particularly after the succession of the Stuarts. The 'internalization' of learning that she advocated was Charronian in tenor; it may have played no small measure in winning the favour of James towards her family.

Daniel was thus also instrumental in forging a rationale for the internalization of knowledge, by which learning was seen as a private, personal affair. During his years at the Pembroke's estate at Wilton, he participated in the vogue for Senecan drama – properly called 'closet drama,' as much for its repudiation of a transference to the stage as for its private quality.[78] Daniel subsequently migrated into the sphere of Greville, who, perhaps prodded by Daniel, soon experimented with this form of stoic discourse. In Greville's hands, it manifested sceptical impluses but was predominantly neostoic in tenor; Daniel, much more than Greville, fell under the spell of Montaigne – to the effect that he came to question the validity of applying works he considered to be of timeless value to the particularities of temporal events.[79] His own literary outlook did not save him from suspicion when contemporaries noted, in 1605, that his tragedy *Philotas* looked very much like a critical representation of the fate suffered by Essex in 1601. In Daniel's mind, however, literature was personal rather than political, and for him history taught broad lessons, and did not have strict applicability to a present event. Above all, as Musophilus declared, literature enjoyed the status of being the immortal, 'blessed letters.'[80]

If Daniel's *Musophilus* provided his own view while also entertaining Greville's, it was the former that appealed to many survivors of the Essex debacle after 1601. But learning as consolation competed with yet another view. Championed by Sir William Cornwallis this alternative totally repudiated the value of the classics – particularly Tacitus – for contemporary life.[81] In contrast to Bacon, Cornwallis had adopted Montaigne's essay form and made it a vehicle not for contemplating the function of learning in society but to undermine that relationship. Moreover, neither learning nor society escaped criticism at the hands of Cornwallis. Essex's failure and his own bitterness led him to cast an ominously bleak verdict on any accomplishments of his fellow men. The temporary retreat promised in the attitude of a Pembroke became, in the hands of Cornwallis, the call for resigned and complete withdrawal from the active life of politics. Cornwallis's work probably provoked Bacon to reissue his own collection of *Essayes*. Much enlarged by 1612, Bacon's *Essayes* were very much designed to counter the challenge to the *vita activa* issued by Cornwallis.

The moral framework that Greville constructed before finally launching into his own defence of learning in the 'Treatie' addresses not only the defence made by Daniel for all learning and the grand plan laid out by Bacon, but also that disheartened pessimism expressed by Cornwallis. As such, it also reflected his own perusals of the humanist assumptions he shared with other contemporaries. It had become painfully obvious that the optimistic notion of the close relationship between learning and action had backfired – that political wisdom did not necessarily follow from a 'politic' reading of literature. Thus Greville reiterated throughout his verse treatise the view that man is 'finite both in wit, time, [and] might,' while 'Knowledge doth itselfe farre more extend, / Than all the minds of Men can comprehend.'[82] After repeatedly insisting on the false arrogance of inflated claims for learning and scholarship he could then go on to discuss the positive role the limited resources of human learning could nevertheless hold for both political society and individual moral regeneration.[83] Baconian precepts of learning were then embraced – but always with the reminder that the several branches of learning should 'serve, and not possesse our hearts.'[84]

Greville's repudiation of the ideas of unbounded knowledge and the intrinsic value of literature was given in the language of Calvinism. Whatever the precise nature of his own religious beliefs (and in many of his poems in *Caelica* they emerge deep and strong), both his Calvinism and his scepticism were also powerful literary devices mobilized to address the critical juncture at which English humanism found itself at the turn of the seventeenth century. The Calvinist strain merged with a neostoic one to underscore the mutability of earthly existence, underline the transience of all human experience, and stress the fallibility of that experience. It also grafted on to Greville's Lipsian leanings the religious impulse – the fideism – that was submerged in Continental neostoicism and that, especially after Charron, was little emphasized. At the same time, it drew attention to the affinity that even Calvin had felt for the writings of the Stoic Seneca.[85] Although Greville's pessimistic overtones have caused some critics to note that in places Greville 'out-Calvins Calvin,' they also operated as a foundation from which Greville could go on to justify the pursuit of learning – that in his life as a patron certainly occupied his time.[86]

His favourite religious metaphors also operated to vindicate scholarship. Greville repeatedly made use of the Pauline description of human reason, and his verse, including the treatises, resounds with the idea that we 'see through the glass but darkly.' After his brief foray into the powers of human reason in the *Letter to an Honourable Lady*, Greville refrained from proclaiming the sovereignty of reason, based on the sanction of theological authorities. But the same biblical sources did not by any means negate the quest for knowledge, even if such knowledge could never quite approximate the substance of truth. Greville accorded that only to the Divine. This ontological perspective gave him a firm basis upon which to promote his limited claims for learning. More important for contemporary purposes, however, it enabled him to articulate his own specific version of *prudentia mixta*: if human knowledge can only discern shadows of the real and divine truth, shadows are yet better than nothing; however wrong or false human knowledge must be, it yet serves a purpose and is all we have to work on.

His adaptation of the Lipsian precept occurs, in one instance, when he discusses the role of the Church in *Humane Learning*. He insists that human doctrinal positions – the result of reason applied to study – could never reflect the true substance of faith. Thus any earthly church was essentially false. But even a false church has a semblance of what it is supposed to represent:

For though the World, and Man can never frame
These outward moulds, to cast Gods chosen in;

> Nor giue his Spirit where they give his Name;
> That power being neuer granted to the sinne;
> > Yet in the world those Orders prosper best,
> > Which from the word, in seeming, varie least.
>
> Since therefore she [the Church] brookes not Diuinity,
> But Superstition, Heresie, Schisme, Rites,
> Traditions, Legends, and Hypocrisie;
> Let her yet forme those visions in the light,
> > To represent the Truth she doth despise;
> > And, by that likenesse, prosper in her lies.[87]

These lines help us see how Greville could become, late in life, patron to the puritan John Preston, while having earlier protected and advanced Lancelot Andrewes – hardly a devout Calvinist, but rather one whose views came closer to Arminianism.[88] And while Greville discoursed much on the depravity of human nature, he clearly saw room for the place of ceremony and outward ritual in effecting piety. Not that such features could promote faith, he would say; much like music and poetry, 'outward Church-rites if applied, / Help moue thoughts, while God may touch the hearts / With goodnesse, wherein he is magnified.'[89]

More than a demonstration of Greville's flexible activities as a patron and a Christian, however, these same lines indicate Greville's place in the dialogue over political virtue. If Bacon had established, through his *Essayes*, the idea of 'seeming' as a measure of political virtue, Greville, much more in keeping with the mixed prudence advocated in the Lipsian paradigm, restores the value of seeming to the public sphere, where, in the case of the Church and also in the realm of law, governance, and the arts, it has the function of catering to a greater good.[90] His idea of 'mixed prudence,' however, was far from Robert Dallington's aphoristic version. According to Dallington,

> So goodly a thing is vertue in it selfe, as even her shadow, if it be in Princes, doth much good: to particular men, by imitation; and to the publicke, by participation. Wherefore, though *simulation* of what is good, and *dissimulation* of what is evil, be vices in a private man, yet in a publicke person they are necessary evils. In whom to be ouvert in expressing his nature, or free in venting his purpose, is a thing of dangerous consequence.[91]

Whereas Dallington considered the state's security the justification for simulation/dissimulation, Greville countered with the view that simulation was the most that was within man's capacity to achieve and that *dis*simulation was the best to be expected on earth, no matter what a man's station. His view stemmed from a philosophic/theological perspective; being of the world, man must needs be a 'traffiquer in sin.' Human wisdom, for Greville, was the ability to recognize and practise such dissimulation.

Unlike Bacon, moreover, who argued that the public benefits of the practice of mixed prudence were of paramount importance, Greville considered above all its applicability in the private sphere. Nor was dissimulation a matter of alternatives for Greville. Rather, it accorded with the nature of mortal things and was fundamental to the human context. In constructing his justification for dissimulation, Greville differed from most of his contemporaries, not least Ben Jonson. As we shall see, Jonson's Lipsian prescriptions were expressed with the *gravitas* of classical diction. Greville, by contrast, 'spoke' with a dark religiosity that was as much a literary convention (or a rhetorical tool) as a pointer to his beliefs and a symptom of his character.[92] But it was this specific voice that enabled him to establish the great discrepancy between real (human reason and knowledge) and ideal (divine knowledge and truth), thereby to distinguish mortal aspirations from divine omniscience. In Greville's terms, it is only the 'ideal' that is real; what we might consider the real remains, for Greville, but a collection of shadows. Yet these were the grounds on which he could proceed to rescue the role of learning from extinction in political society. The same discursive feature also allowed him to affirm the validity of social institutions as they existed – even as he pointed to their fallible nature. Just as political virtue was in some ways compromised, so the order of society, based on imperfection as it was established, must be maintained. This amounted to what a later generation would term 'defactoism.'[93]

Greville's theory of knowledge led to a repudiation of the dogmatic adherence to any particular set of religious dicta and denied the idea of a slavish attachment to any prescribed forms of policy – in either the domestic or the foreign arena. In these very respects, however, the *Treatie of Humane Learning* stands in stark contrast to the *Treatise of Monarchy* and the *Life of Sidney*, which are more pointedly concerned with establishing a particular political program and thus with Greville promoting himself as the councillor he ultimately became. Still, the *Treatie of Humane Learning* reiterated the advice Greville gave to the Honourable Lady and echoed the position adopted by Achmat at the end of the Senecan drama, *Mustapha*. The application of public virtue in those works – in effect, Greville's reformulation of *prudentia mixta* – was given its fundamental vindication in the theory of knowledge expressed in *Humane Learning*.

## Greville, Virtue, and Counsel

Greville's initial distinction between private and public virtue could well have been provoked by his own need for a ready justification for the compromises he had decided upon – compromises which indicated an early departure from Sidney's political example. Interestingly, though, Greville's portrait of Sidney in his 'Dedication' also represents a resolution to the difficulties implied in the portrayal of Achmat and the advice to the Lady – although it could equally represent, as indicated earlier, a portrait that was begun in order to justify his own vision of Sidney, begun as a corrective to the pious and privately devoted image of her brother adopted by the Countess of Pembroke. Whichever the case, in the *Life* Greville came up with a portrait of a hero, one less troubled and troubling than an Achmat, and one drawn much more in recall of less complicated days, loss of which is lamented in his consolation to the Honourable Lady.

Sidney emerges as an exemplary figure, one wholly at ease with his convictions, who, constant in the older sense of the term, is equally constant in his obedience to the queen. He is the paragon of virtue, unmatched in 'the real and large complexions of those active times.'[94] What made the times exemplary and heroic was the threat (and promise) of England's involvement in a war of survival against the peril of the Catholic forces of Europe – meaning mostly Spain and the Jesuits, but including the French as well. In the *Life*, Greville provides an apologia for the war party of the 1570s, which proved a thorn in Elizabeth's flesh, but whose spokesman in those days was increasingly Sir Philip Sidney. Greville cannot deny that Sidney was thus a critic of the royal policy; at one point he refers to him as 'our unbelieved Cassandra.' The point, however – in the portrait of Sidney, at least – is to show that 'he so sweetly yoked fame and conscience together in a large heart,' and that 'he did so constantly balance ambition with the safe precepts of divine and moral duty as no pretence whatsoever could have enticed that gentleman to break through the circle of a good patriot.'[95]

Fame and conscience, ambition and duty – these qualities are uniquely balanced in the character Greville sets up for remembrance and emulation. They are also, he strongly suggests, disparate and more likely to be found separately. And indeed, contemporaries were accustomed to remarking upon an individual's predilection for one above the other. Ben Jonson, for example, remarked to William Drummond of Hawthornden 'that Sir Walter Ralegh esteemed more of fame than of conscience.'[96] In a previous chapter we saw that (Jonson's comment notwithstanding) Ralegh was himself deeply involved in discussing the type of political virtue required in post-Elizabethan England, and that he managed to reintegrate virtue from its two distinct manifestations.

Greville adopts a similar scheme in his 'Dedication.' In Sidney, private virtue is indistinguishable from public virtue, and it is undivided because 'after mature deliberation, being once resolved, [Sidney] never brought any question of change to afflict himself with, or perplex the business, but left the success to His will that governs the blind prosperities and unprosperities of chance, and so works out His own ends by the erring frailties of human reason and affection.'[97] Despite the disclaimer on the reliability of human reason, Greville suggests that it was actually the practice of right reason – 'mature deliberation' – that brought Sidney to the constancy implied in this description. The same statement provides the reader with the fundamental source of Sidney's virtue – his trust in God's ultimate sovereignty of the world.

Greville's Sidney, then, is drawn from a providentialist perspective. Thereby Greville resolved the issue of virtue as something dichotomous, insisting that Sidney's commitment to public service and his demands of conscience both devolved from the operations of right reason, which itself began with an acknowledgment of the power and direction of Providence. Notwithstanding the question of when Greville might have actually begun to sketch out this portrait of Sidney, it would be intriguing to discover if, as he developed and completed his portrait, he engaged in some sort of exchange with Ralegh. It is generally taken that Greville was, in fact, working on what became the *Life* during the years in which Ralegh was composing his *History of the World*; and there are some remarkable similarities between the two works, most notably the stress on virtue and the emphasis on the necessity for an aggressive policy against the Catholic powers of Europe. Ralegh had himself admired Sidney and had composed a eulogy wherein he lamented the death of 'the Scipio ... of our time.'[98] Greville chooses the same analogy; his portrait of Sidney climaxes with the epithet 'this Briton Scipio,' a parallel which signals the reconciliation he achieved in the virtue represented by Sidney.[99] This parallel is also an appeal to *similitudo temporum* as Sidney's exploits on behalf of England are implicitly set against those of Scipio the Younger on behalf of Rome. But if so, and in light of the Raleghean connection (tenuous as it appears), could this 'Dedication' be something other than a personal testament to the friendship Greville shared with Sidney? Such a reading of the work depends upon a number of some external factors worth considering.

The internal evidence of the *Life* has encouraged most commentators to estimate that it belongs to the period 1610–11. Greville refers to Henry IV of France as already dead, and that king was assassinated in 1610.[100] Then, there are the digressions which are concerned with vindicating Essex and exploring the greatness of Elizabeth as monarch, together with an excursion into her regal way of conducting policy and selecting advisors.[101] Greville might well have launched into these issues once Robert Cecil, then the Earl of Salisbury, subverted his plan to write a history of the period. Cecil had been a long-time rival, who, apparently suspecting Greville's memory of Leicester and Essex (both of whom had been patrons of Greville and the political rivals of Cecil), put obstacles in the way of Greville's access to the state papers.[102] Cecil's dominance in the England of James I thus not only kept Greville on the fringes of political action, it prevented him from paying homage – through literature – to the queen he had served and the age he had lived through.

As it turned out, the *Life*, with those sections that lauded Elizabeth's style of governance, became everything the authorities (or rather Salisbury) sought to prevent. Thus, perhaps, was justified another instance of the Jacobean phobia against, and repression of, a likely Tacitean text. However, while Greville composed a not-so-veiled critique of contemporary governance he did not attempt to publish it. Perhaps just as well! But to what purpose was the feature of *similitudo temporum* that Greville so clearly invoked? As a mere (and well recognized) tool of criticism it could only operate to land him at the mercy of the authorities. Greville, alert to the peril involved in this type of criticism, refrained, on the whole, from using it elsewhere in his writings; his historical invocations were less a full-scale transference onto the contemporary scene than a means by which to illustrate a particular point.[103] Might Greville, then, have had another less threatening end in mind? One that, as things turned out, proved to be elusive and thus required Greville to keep his work out of publication?

A key point to bear in mind is that this period was one of hiatus in Greville's political career. Dismissed from office in 1604, Greville was kept out of it until his return to favour in 1614. Ronald Rebholz has argued that Greville occupied his time by concentrating on domestic business, rebuilding Warwick Castle, recording his tribute to Sidney, and undergoing a religious conversion – all roughly in that order.[104] But we are still left with a strange gap in our knowledge of Greville's activities, and it is difficult to believe he may have ignored contemporary politics. For a committed political actor it seems odd that he would quietly while away his time in Warwickshire. Though there is as yet little evidence of it, might not he have been drawn towards the household of Prince Henry, as so many other survivors of Essex's circle were? In 1611 Greville was the dedicatee of an epistle by Joseph Hall, at this time a chaplain to the heir presumptive.[105] There are other indications to suggest that Greville's 'Dedication' might actually have been intended as a means to promote, if not herald, his come-back into political life via this route.

His *Treatise of Monarchy*, for instance, which contains the most fulsome treatment of Greville's view of kingship and governance, was meant to be included in the publication for which the 'Dedication' was to act as a preface. It would be interesting to know whether Greville also intended a more initial dedication, which would precede the preface which the account of Sidney was intended to have been. Unlike Bacon, whose record of his intention to dedicate the second edition of his *Essayes* to Henry has survived, Greville's legacy is mute on this subject; as with so many of Greville's intentions, we are left to fumble in the dark. What emerges from *Of Monarchy*, nevertheless, is its resemblance to the hand-book literature of the time, even though it was composed in verse. There, Greville, in a long poem of almost seven hundred stanzas, considered the art of kingship, giving particular attention to the arts by which strong governors keep or lose their power and their subjects' loyalty.

Greville devotes specific sections to considering the role of the Church, the laws, the place of commerce, policies of peace and of war, and the comparison of monarchy to aristocracy and to democracy. The 'excellencie' of monarchy is reiterated in the last two sections of a poem that was much reworked – causing Sir William Davenant, Gerville's protégé, to lament his patron's tendency to revise and thus spoil what might have remained 'a dainty thing.'[106] Nevertheless, the final, all-inclusive version is of interest because, besides much else, it echoes – in sections which were probably among the original 'Declination' part of the poem – much of what Lipsius, in his *Politica*, isolated as the prime requirements for governors.[107] The moral foundation of governance, the need for *prudentia mixta* in governors, and the strict distinctions between the forms of dissimulation – between what is permissible and what not – are among the prime lessons Greville would impart.[108] In the sections devoted to peace and war, Greville proclaims peace to be 'the most perfect state of governmente,' but holds that war is often necessary; preparedness, a disciplined army, and 'a well fram'de Navie,' are thus urged upon the politic and martial prince he probably had in mind.[109]

In its individual parts and as a whole, the *Treatise* takes the shape of a manual of instruction fit for a martial and virtuous monarch in the making. The political grooming of Henry was largely in the hands of the frustrated English 'war party,' to which not only Ralegh but also Greville, at that time, seem largely to have subscribed. But from the very form of his discourses and from the tenor of his 'Dedication,' Greville, like Ralegh, seems to have had some reservations about how that grooming was taking place. In an earlier chapter, we noted that Robert Dallington whole-heartedly adopted the view that public virtue was distinct from private morality and advocated a type of *raison d'état* by stressing that 'the generall good and safetie of a State is the Center in which all ... actions and counsailes must meete: To which men cannot alwaies arrive by plaine pathes, and beaten waies.'[110] Charronian in tenor, Dallington's work endorsed a strict departure from the realm of normal morality while promoting that stance of acquiescence and withdrawal on the part of subjects that was urged by Cornwallis. Like Ralegh, Greville would not have approved of the radical dichotomy ascribed to virtue by those writers – especially as their advice went to one so young as the prince, whom Greville would have considered to be in the midst of his own 'golden age.' Thus Sidney provided a perfect model to demonstrate the reunion of virtue – if only on the part of a subject. That reintegrated virtue also acted as a precondition for Greville's strictures on 'mixed prudence' in the *Treatise of Monarchy*, which adhered above all to the considerations of an overriding moral scheme in force in political society.[111]

Greville and Ralegh might thus have been mutually engaged in rescuing the concept of political virtue from Charronian and 'statist' constructions. From Greville's point of view, such a contribution to the 'mirror for princes' literature served two vital functions. By propounding an aggressive anti-Hapsburg policy it established his credentials as one fit to sit (beside Ralegh) at a future council table headed by a new monarch. And this new monarch would also, courtesy of Greville's (and Ralegh's) lessons, be well versed in the redefined and redirected forms of virtue and warfare. If these speculations have any warrant at all, two conclusions follow inevitably. The first is that the *Life of Sidney* and the *Treatise of Monarchy* only became 'literary attacks on the [Jacobean] government' by virtue of losing their *raison d'être* as manuals of instruction, on the death of Prince Henry in 1612.[112] The second is that these texts allowed Greville to retrieve the principles of the Protestant party of the 1570s and 1580s. When any flicker of hope associated with the pending accession of Henry was extinguished, Greville came to be known for his pacific and cautionary stance. As he became firmly entrenched in the council membership of James it was his 'consideration' of vital issues that was always noticed.[113]

Thus having again resigned himself to abandoning the Sidney legacy it was little wonder that Greville, in turning to prepare his 'Dedication to Sidney' for publication, made it clear how far he – and England – had travelled from Sidney's political legacy:

The difference which I have found between times, and consequently the changes of life into which their natural vicissitudes do violently carry men, as they have made deep furrows of impressions into my heart, so the same heavy wheels cause me to retire my thoughts from free traffic with the world and seek rather comfortable ease or employment in the safe memory of dead men than disquiet in a doubtful conversation among the living ...[114]

On one level, these lines can be taken at face value as a reflection of the intermittent melancholy to which Greville seems to have been prone. On another, however, that melancholic tone is itself a device and convention, for Greville was as keenly attached to the idea of state service as ever. The year 1612 might have brought the death of one hope – the prospective coming of a militant Protestant king; the same year, however, also saw a real revival of hope as Greville's indomitable foe, Salisbury, died. The door to state office, so firmly closed for a decade, finally presented an opening through which Greville, in the space of two years, would enter.[115]

### Greville, Authority, and Obedience

In the absence of more substantial evidence, the idea that a number of Greville's writings were intended for Prince Henry must depend on his indisputable faith in literature as praxis. Provoked by the crisis in English political humanism, he came up with his specific version of political virtue which suggested his changing political goals while affirming his ongoing commitment to service. The biblical imagery that punctuated his discussions of virtue gave them a spiritual aspect, and his often melancholic voice operated to enhance the objectivity he sought to infuse into his own very personal, subjective attachment to political action. In this sense, irony is never far below the surface of Greville's works. Throughout his treatises Greville was promoting his own services and expertise. But to dwell only on the self-interest implicit in Greville's writings is to ignore the larger framework against which they were set.

I have isolated two main debates to which Greville's writings have application. Both revolve around the position of the political 'outs' of the early Jacobean period, and both concern the working out of the legacy of Essex (and of Sidney), especially in view of the altered political conditions brought about by the accession of the Stuarts. Thus the essential problem confronting Greville was one shared by his contemporaries – and not only those who had been specifically attached to the Earl of Essex. He shared with Ralegh, for instance, the concern to define an idea of political virtue suitable to both the times (in view of contemporary debates) and the promise (while it lasted) of a future with a courageous young monarch. Unlike Ralegh, however, and more in line with the legacy of Essex which he shared with Bacon, Greville remained a firm if cautious Tacitean.

A crucial problem confronting him, and which was in turn confronted by him, was less the division between spirit and flesh (proclaimed in *Mustapha* and many of his short lyrics) than the distance between subject and prince, and the resulting misinterpretations that could arise from that distance. Greville saw around him a political system bedevilled by conflicting interests at court and an England suffering from a crisis of counsel, both provoked by the gap between human communication and mutual understanding. Greville's literary career was devoted to addressing that perceived gap – which only deepened as the Stuart dynasty rested its claims for obedience on the authority of God. Greville's Calvinist discourse gains force in light of the resurgence of divine-right theories of governance; as a literary device it simultaneously upholds a particular rendering of political virtue and offsets the inflated claims for monarchy made by James I.

Not that Greville was thus a critic of the Stuarts in principle. He definitely was not. Rather, much like Tacitus, Machiavelli, Lipsius, and many of his own contemporaries, Greville regarded the order guaranteed by a strong prince – a unifying *pater patriae* – essential for keeping at bay the anarchy threatened by a vacuum in the political and social sphere.[116] But as he consistently avowed, society was an artificial construct designed to enhance the safety and ease of its members.[117] Language, too, was invented, prone to the reason that created it and susceptible to the unfixed rules of human predilections.[118] Thus language could not for Greville, as it did for Ralegh, denote either virtue or its opposite, nor did it act as a reliable guide to conduct, much less truth. The very inconsistency of the orthography of the day might show the vulnerability of the state of language – of the vernacular – in the early modern period. All was in flux, as far as Greville could gauge, and amid that flux one greatly disconcerting feature figured prominently. Political society, in his view, was 'metamorphizing' into a 'precipitate absoluteness,' which in turn could provoke a revolution.[119] In the *Treatise of Monarchy*, he warned:

> Princes againe ore'rack not your creation,
> Least power returne to that whence it began;
> But keepe upp scepters by that reputation
> Which raised one, to rule this world of man:
>   Order makes us the body, you the head,
>   And by disorder anarchie is bred.[120]

Anarchy and disorder were the component parts of the nightmare haunting Greville, who was Achmat-like in his Aristotelian assumptions about order. And 'orderly' thinker that he was, he had no great problem reconciling his views of the origins of government with the reality of monarchy. Ever alert to the dictates of necessity, he could also submerge principles and ideals for the demands of the moment. The uppermost problem confronting him, however, remained the means by which he might convey his advice to an authority that did not necessarily seek it nor particularly want it.

How then to give advice where it was least desired? Greville responded to this question by turning to the most artificial form of discourse and communication available – verse. To be sure, Sidney, Spenser, and others had in Elizabethan times made claims for the superiority of the poet and his medium, but even Greville's Elizabethan verses avow the artificiality of the form, as they bemoan the artificiality of Elizabethan political culture.[121] In the more prosaic Jacobean period, Greville's attachment to verse could only underline how much more artificial he considered the Stuart monarchy to be. He thereby registered a protest against his ostracism from a court in great need of the counsel he could give.

Greville's poetic adherences thus signal an aspect of his Tacitist leanings. His Tacitism embraced vestiges of the 'black' Machiavellian type, as it sought to alert his prince to the desirability of manipulating 'hope and fear' in order to procure greater power, thus to maintain stability and augur domestic peace.[122] The arcana of power and majesty were well upheld, for instance, in the treatises of *Monarchy* and *Religion*, where the very form that expressed Greville's political theories was the arcane medium of poetry. But Greville's Tacitism also evokes its 'red' application. Composing verse in a prosaic environment is a mode of protest and dissent. Greville, in fact, dissented more from the politics of the time than he cared to acknowledge.

He could not escape, for instance, the view that reason (not to mention many classical authors) taught the lesson: 'If the feet knew their strength as we know their oppression, they would not bear as they do.'[123] So spoke Greville in Parliament in 1593, and so he reiterated, in various ways, in many of his verse treatises, where he consistently drew attention to the threat posed to society should the bonds of trust, or the illusions of power that upheld authority be seriously undermined.[124] Speaking in the *Treatise of Monarchy* of the danger of factionalism and favouritism when practised by a monarch, he warned:

> For to make bodies stronge, proves heads are weake,
> And soe twoe sects prepared in one Realme,
> Which doth the beauty of obedience breake ...[125]

Remembering that this verse treatise might have been intended as a source of instruction for Prince Henry does not negate the possibility that it was also designed to point a finger at the practices by which the Jacobean monarchy provoked much criticism. Greville clearly, however privately, participated in this critique. Still, he never thereby issued or concealed a call for rebellion. That, much as he expressed it through Achmat's dilemma in *Mustapha*, he could never condone. But the dangers of bad government ought to be remedied. While he enjoyed place and office, he doubtless believed his presence and participation in 'the debatements of all serious designs' contributed to stability in the state. When barred from the political process, both Tacitism and the teachings of Tacitus himself seem to have presented themselves as the best means of conveying the requisite lessons to an erring monarch.

In late 1627, now old and firmly banished from political involvement in the highest sphere, Greville made explicit his until then covert and private Tacitism by inaugurating a History Chair at Cambridge and installing Isaac Dorislaus as its first incumbent.[126] We noted earlier the failure suffered by Greville in this bold attempt. If he thus ended as a failed patron as well as a failed politician, he finally showed his fidelity to what he considered the true Sidney legacy of being a 'general Maecenas of learning.'[127] Greville, who was so quick to scuttle the militant ideology personified in Sidney, lived up to this aspect of Sidney's example, and he adhered at the same time to what he considered Sidney's true intent in his sponsorship of literature and study – to have them always at the service of politics and the state.[128] In 1586, Sidney had hoped to bring Lipsius, the prime authority of Tacitus, to England.[129] In 1627, Greville sponsored one of Lipsius's intellectual heirs, and attempted to install him at Cambridge. Whatever the tenor of his failure, Greville did succeed in clarifying his position as a Tacitist in the Sidney mould. Greville's own legacy would bear fruit among the subsequent generation that had to confront more urgently the question of obedience – to a government that had no precedent in English history. At that point Dorislaus was engaged to draft the charges of tyranny against the king, and infringing upon English precedents was not among those changes for which Charles went to the block. Still, as Greville had said in that Parliament of 1593, 'Why should you stand so much upon precedents? The times hereafter will be good or bad: if good precedents will do no harm; if bad, Power will make a way where it finds none.'[130]

# 4

# A Neostoic Scout: Ben Jonson and the Poetics of Constancy

Ill Fortune never crush't that man, whom good Fortune deceived not. I therefore have councelled my friends, never to trust her fairer side, though she seem'd to make peace with them: But to place all things she gave them so, as she might aske them againe without their trouble; she might take them from them, not pull them: to keepe always a distance betweene her, and themselves. He knows not his own strength, that hath not met Adversity. Heaven prepares good men with crosses; but no ill can happen to a good man. Contraries are not mixed. Yet, that which happens to any man, may to every man. But it is in his reason what hee accounts it, and will make it.

(Jonson, in his commonplace book, *Timber, or Discoveries*)

Ben Jonson earned the distinction of being called 'the Roman poet' for his lifelong attempt to revive the classicism of those whom he claimed as predecessors. He aspired to be a latter-day Horace to James I's Augustus, a parallel which greatly appealed to the first Stuart monarch in whose court Jonson became a sometime and unofficial laureate. The peace, union, and empire achieved by the first Roman emperor were aspects of the 'self-fashioning' image of the Stuart court which Jonson helped create.[1] Jonson was also a self-conscious moralist who borrowed from the pages of Juvenal and Martial – satirists and social observers of the Rome of Domitian – seeking thereby to expose the vanities and vices of the society of which he was a part. He admired Lipsius's attempts to adapt the literature, historiography, and stoic morality of the early Roman Empire to the needs of contemporary European society, seeking himself to apply the Lipsian paradigm to England. If the form and the manner of his teachings on political virtue harked to a broad classical inheritance, the essential Jonsonian message derived from his rootedness in a philological culture of which Lipsius was the most prominent exemplar; it was one to which Jonson gained entry as a young man in London, a prominent experience in the varied and eclectic lifestyle he enjoyed.

## Life and Circle

The opening epigraph is a Senecan sentiment, one of many that filled Jonson's commonplace book.[2] It neatly captures what a large amount of his writing sought to convey, and is a sentiment to which he was probably attracted in view of his own brushes with adversity. His misfortunes were many and derived largely from his unconventional personality– which itself stands in stark contrast to the poise and decorum of much of his writing. He was from a humble family, and was first a bricklayer and then a soldier before taking up the pen for a living in the late 1590s.[3] Almost immediately he fell foul of the law. In 1597, he was imprisoned for his role in writing and acting in *The Isle of Dogs*, a play that has been lost but which was probably a satire on the court of Elizabeth's declining years.[4] Then, in 1598, he was involved in a duel in which he killed a fellow actor, Gabriel Spencer. He was charged with murder and only escaped a penalty harsher than a branding on the thumb by pleading benefit of clergy. In 1603, he was brought before the Privy Council to answer to charges of 'popery and treason' arising from the production of his Tacitean tragedy, *Sejanus*. In 1605, he was again imprisoned, this time for writing *Eastward Ho*, a play which mocked Scottish courtiers. Jonson apparently feared for his life on this occasion, although later in the same year he was summoned, after the discovery of the plot to blow up king and Parliament, to help uncover the identity of Guy Fawkes's fellow conspirators. He might well have been suspected of complicity in the plot himself; early in 1606 he was cited for recusancy, and it was not until 1610 that he returned to the fold of the established English church, from which he had departed twelve years before.[5]

Jonson's religious outlook is a key factor in indicating the Lipsian perspective he came to adopt in his own life, although defiance was prominent in him as well . The favour he came to enjoy from the first two Stuart monarchs was repeatedly threatened by the enmities he incurred among both courtiers and the fellow artists who vied with him for royal favour. The Earl of Northampton and the Duke of Buckingham, successive favourites of James I, were, Jonson considered, his enemies.[6] His rivalry with the poet Samuel Daniel resulted in his temporary expulsion from the court in 1604; that with Inigo Jones, master architect and surveyor of the court of King Charles, ultimately led to his eclipse in courtly circles. He finally died in 1633 in abject poverty, his life characterized by the predominance of a deeply rebellious and independent nature.

But personality and lifestyle by themselves do not wholly define Jonson. For, side by side with his rebelliousness lay his scholarly and 'civil' interests, making him aspire to impress on a chosen readership a classical approach to society. His intellectual interests brought him into a philological culture whose most famous recent member and exemplar was Lipsius, although Jonson's route to it lay closer to home. William Camden was the teacher who, for a brief two years in the 1580s, introduced him to learning, instilling in him the training of mind and memory of which he would later boast.[7] Camden became renowned for *Britannia*, his study of England, Scotland, and Ireland, in which he surveyed the British Isles and argued, through archaeological and philological analysis, the essential continuity between Roman and contemporary Britain. Completed during the years in which James VI of Scotland was attempting to negotiate his inheritance of the English crown after Elizabeth, its promotion of the concept of a single entity – Britain – over distinctions of polity between England and Scotland was one which greatly appealed to James, who, in the event, became 'King of Great Britain.'[8] In its stress on Britain's Roman ancestry, it also prefigured the royal iconography promoted by James and adopted by Jonson – replete as it was with images of peace and empire.[9] Kevin Sharpe has noted that it was Camden 'who first brought to English historical studies the humanist interest in the classical world.'[10] Camden's humanist and intellectual aspirations linked him with a number of European contemporaries. And like Lipsius, Camden had his own circle of students – his own 'contubernium' – and his concern with reviving the classics bore great fruit among his pupils; Jonson was only one of these, but he paid tribute to Camden by calling him the 'most reuerend head, to whom I owe / All that I am in arts, all that I know.'[11]

Camden's circle included John Selden, whose scholarship was also renowned throughout Europe. In the preface of his *Titles of Honor* (1614), Selden acknowledged a debt to his 'beloued friend that singular Poet M. Ben Ionson, whose speciall Worth in Literature, accurat Iudgement, and Performance, known only to that Few which are truly able to know him, hath had from me, euer since I began to learn, an increasing admiration.'[12] Jonson reciprocated by composing a verse tribute commending both the book and its author. In this 'Epistle to Master John Selden,' Jonson praised Selden above all for his scholarly integrity, applying to him the image of the perfect working compass which 'keeping one foot still / Upon your Center, doe your Circle fill.'[13] The compass was the symbol of constancy, the concept appropriated by Lipsius but an emblem associated especially with the Flemish city of Antwerp, a centre of scholarship and learning.[14] Jonson's own *impresa* was a compass whose outer leg was broken, signifying, as he told William Drummond of Hawthornden, *'Deest quod duceret orbem'* [that which should guide the circle is missing.][15] David Riggs has noted that the absence of a vital part of the outer leg implied 'Jonson's lack of full control over the nature and scope of his own work.'[16] Indeed, as the 'Epistle' to Selden admitted, Jonson 'too oft preferr'd / Men past their termes, and prais'd some names too much.' Ever prey to the exigencies of his situation, Jonson frequently sent complimentary verses to those about whom he had moral reservations. The Earl of Salisbury was the recipient of several epigrams, frugal as far as commendatory verses go and containing hints of Jonson's reservations about his subject. 'What need hast thou of me, or of my Muse / Whose actions so themselves doe celebrate?' So wrote Jonson in his first verse tribute to Salisbury. He went on to give judgment on the fallen state of poets in his day, obliquely referring to Salisbury's own role in overlooking the arts – 'Tofore, great men were glad of Poets: Now, / I, not the worst, am couetous of thee.'[17] Jonson was indebted to Salisbury for his release from the prison term he earned as a result of the production of *Eastward Ho*; his method of payment was the epigram – which in the event spoke more of Jonson than it did of Salisbury.

Throughout his career, Jonson resorted to composing many 'epistles mendicant,' whether to repay a favour or to request one. One way around the predicament was to appeal to the humanist principle of *laudando praecipere* – to teach by praising. According to Francis Bacon, who examined this precept among the many subjects of his *Essayes*, poets were required to 'represent to [kings and great persons] what they should be' – not necessarily what they were.[18] Yet Jonson still wrote that he committed through his verse 'most fierce idolatrie' to many a 'worthlesse lord'; he would have preferred 'to write,' as he confessed in 'To my Muse,' 'Things manly, and not smelling parasite.'[19] In the 'Epistle' to Selden he reiterated that in his own practices he fell far short of his ideals. Selden, by contrast, embodied those ideals for him.

Robert Cotton, once Camden's student and then his colleague in the Society of Antiquaries, was another close friend. Cotton was one of the premier 'political aides' of the Jacobean and Caroline years, a client first of the Earl of Northampton and, later, of the Earl of Arundel. His home

5 *Impresa* of the Plantin Press from C. Cornelius Tacitus, *Opera quae extant*. Courtesy of The Library, University of King's College, Halifax, Nova Scotia. Photography by Findlay Muir, Instructional Media Services, Dalhousie University.

in London was a centre for political humanism, its vast library serving the needs of many contemporaries (including, in the Tower, Sir Walter Ralegh). In his own quest for authenticity, Jonson borrowed many a Cottonian manuscript when composing his royal masques.[20] Jonson and Cotton became even more closely associated in the 1620s, as the pre-eminence of the Duke of Buckingham incurred widespread disillusionment.[21] Political tensions climaxed in the assassination of Buckingham in October 1628, and after the parliamentary polarization in late 1628 and early 1629, many of Jonson's friends, including Cotton and Selden, were remanded to the Tower. Selden was imprisoned for having attacked the Speaker at the closing of the session of 1629. He was later charged along with Cotton and others in the Star Chamber with circulating a seditious tract.[22] Although they ultimately went free, in the period immediately following their citation at Star Chamber no one could be sure of the extent of the court's leniency. As Kevin Sharpe has written, they had 'co-operated [in Parliament] against Buckingham ... and against them the friends of Buckingham sought to exact their revenge.'[23] An order of closure was issued on Cotton's library; and Jonson, who was a regular visitor at Cotton's house in this period, was himself suspected of inciting the assassination of Buckingham by composing subversive verses.[24] In all likelihood he did not lament the deed; but he managed to convince Attorney General Heath that he was innocent of any complicity in the murder and no further action was taken against him.

Jonson's attitude towards Buckingham was not without its ironic side. He and Buckingham first tasted fortune's favours as something of a team, since both he and the future duke came to court under the auspices of the Earl of Pembroke. In the struggle for influence in 1615–16, Pembroke had promoted the advancement of the unknown George Villiers in an attempt to break Somerset's hold over the king. Jonson, a long-term client of Pembroke's, wrote *The Golden Age Restor'd*, the masque in which Villiers made his important first impression upon the king. The masque celebrated the beginning of a new age of peace and plenty; translated into political terms, it signified that James's domestic and foreign policies would now begin to reap the fruits of their seed. James had withdrawn England from active involvement in the European theatre of war and, in late 1614, had proclaimed that 'all Our Lieutenants and Noblemen' should 'repaire unto their severall Countreys to attend their service there, and to keepe House and Hospitalitie.'[25] Jonson's masque envisaged the outcome of such policies: henceforth harmony, the arts, and, of course, the harvests would flourish. The role played by Villiers in

*The Golden Age Restor'd*, and his carriage of it, won the approval of the king. Time would show that the promotion of Villiers succeeded all too well. He went on to win the confidence of James and later Charles to the exclusion of virtually all others. In 1616, however, Pembroke also basked in the king's favour. He was made Lord Chamberlain and took his place as a member of the Privy Council. And Jonson, after contributing a second acclaimed Twelfth Night masque in succession to *The Golden Age Restor'd*, was rewarded with a royal pension.[26] His own star now enjoyed its ascendancy; but this was one of the gifts of a 'fortune' upon whose bounty he could never entirely rely. Court life dealt him various blows and as the years went by, the pension, as often as not, went unpaid.

Jonson never wholly dominated the poetics of James I's court. Nor was his aim that of merely serving princes and blindly endorsing court policies.[27] Aristotle described the poet as an instructor to society; Jonson certainly sought to 'delight and teach,' and through his royal masques to 'faine a Common-wealth' to inspire emulation in the real world.[28] But in 1617–18, Jonson succeeded neither in teaching nor in delighting. The central lesson of that year's masque, *Pleasure Reconciled to Virtue*, was that the wise king and courtier lived by moderation – and this in a court whose consumption habits were remarked upon. The masque was received as a moral admonition to which James was reportedly the first to object. As one contemporary remarked, 'The maske on 12th night is not commended of any. [T]he poet is growen so dull that his devise is not worthy the relating, much less the copying out. [D]ivers thinke fit he should retourne to his ould trade of bricke laying againe.'[29] Jonson was not about to give up writing, much less return to a long past way of life; he responded by taking a walking trip to Scotland.

On this occasion, as on many others, Jonson was able to assert his independence. If he displeased the court by his productions, he might make a brief foray into the world beyond England. In 1612, after the failure of his Roman play, *Catiline*, he left Britain altogether and travelled to France and the Netherlands as tutor to young Wat Ralegh, son of Sir Walter. Usually, though, Jonson had two other outlets for his talents and teachings which also provided alternative means for making a living. One was the London public theatre, in which he had served his literary apprenticeship and to which he often returned; the other was the retreat offered by friends and patrons. Cotton and Selden were sources not only of support but of inspiration for Jonson. Many of Jonson's patrons fulfilled a similar function. For most of his career he enjoyed the patronage of members of the Sidney family. The series of verses addressing the Sidneys comprise, as we shall see, an important aspect of Jonson's strictures on political virtue. Along with the more immediate members of the Sidney family – Sir Robert, Sir William, Lady Mary Wroth, and Sir Philip's daughter, Elizabeth, Countess of Rutland – Jonson's connections reached out into the broader circle of nobles which included the Pembrokes and the Bedfords. William Herbert, Earl of Pembroke, gave him lifelong support, providing him with a yearly income with which to buy books.[30] When Pembroke died in 1630, Jonson became, with Thomas Hobbes and others, a client of William, Lord Cavendish. In the 1620s and 1630s Jonson also gravitated towards the circle of Lucius Cary, 2nd Viscount Falkland, and was an eager participant in Falkland's intellectual circle at his Oxfordshire home, Great Tew. Graham Parry has noted that 'Jonson never lacked for noble patrons, nor did he lose the gift for modulating patronage into friendship.'[31] As we explore in subsequent sections Jonson's attitudes to religion and his views on politics and the function of literature we shall see that perhaps one good reason for this affability among patrons and friends alike, and the common denominator linking the various branches of his personal associations, was the classical perspective that he proffered as England entered a crisis period quite different in character from those experienced by previous generations.

**Learning, Humanism, and Religion: Jonson's Road to Constancy**

Part and parcel of Jonson's unconventional personality was a particular attitude towards religion – an aspect of Jonson's thought largely unexamined, although his comedic representations of Puritans and religious extremists are well known. In comedies, Jonson rejected out of hand groups or individuals that challenged the hegemony of the established Church. His models were the Roman satirists Juvenal and Martial, and in his aversion to fanaticism and dogma he resembled Lipsius, himself an admirer of the Roman satirists, writing his *Antiquae lectiones* (1576) as commentaries on the comedies of Plautus and including in many of his *epistolae* satirical barbs culled from Juvenal and others.[32] Thus sharing with Lipsius an acute interest in the satiric and critical strains in Roman imperial culture and borrowing from him many an idea and theme, Jonson wrote satires that barely concealed his views on the social and political ills at large in England in his own day. In his entire *oeuvre*, the satires complemented, even as they counterbalanced, his poetry of praise, as Jonson harnessed the Roman satirists much as Lipsius had Tacitus, in creating his neostoic synthesis. Jonson's goal also resembled that of Lipsius; in whichever medium he chose to write he sought to procure civility and revive the classicism of the Roman world he so admired.

In *The Alchemist* (1610), the character of Tribulation Wholesome was portrayed as a canting hypocrite; in *Bartholomew Fair* (1614), Zeal-Of-The-Land Busy was the target. In his *Discoveries*, Jonson condemned outright what in his comedies he merely, if savagely, exposed:

> A Puritan is a heretical hypocrite, whose balance of mind has been disturbed by his confidence in his own perspicuity, because of which he flatters himself that – with a few others – he has found out certain flaws in Church dogma, as a result of which he – urged on by a sacred rage – fights insanely against the civil authority, believing that he is, in this way, showing his obedience to God.[33]

Jonson often took issue with religious zealots, condemning the extent to which religious inspiration led to unrest in both civil and ecclesiastical society. He was addressing a very real contemporary issue in which disputes were arising over the extent of ecclesiastical jurisdiction, and where theological debate succeeded in reawakening disputes over doctrine, discipline, and the question of uniformity within the English ecclesiastical institution.[34] But Jonson's aversion to doctrinal factionalism was not confined to condemning puritan zealots and separatists. In Paris in 1612, he witnessed a debate between theologians on the question of transubstantiation – the doctrine of the presence of the blood and body of Christ in the Eucharist – an episode that helped inspire his presentation of Zeal-of-the-Land Busy in *Bartholomew Fair*. Although Busy was portrayed as a separatist, Jonson showed his dislike of all forms of religious dispute by satirizing extremists but collapsing others into their positions. The implicit parallel with other churchmen did not escape John Selden. Referring to a scene in which an argument develops over the most instructive uses to which time might be put, Selden remarked that the scene 'satyrically express'd the vain Disputes of Divines.'[35] In his *Discoveries*, Jonson alluded to such 'vain disputes' as he recorded his view in a more direct fashion:

> Some Controverters in Divinity are like Swaggerers in a Taverne ... Their Arguments are as fluxive as liquour spilt upon a Table; which with your finger you may draine as you will. Such Controversies, or Disputations, (carried with more labour, then profit) are odious; where most times the Truth is lost in the midst, or left untouch'd. And the fruit of their fight is that they ... are both defil'd. These Fencers in Religion I like not.

Such a characterization of religious debate showed the intensity of Jonson's abhorrence for what he regarded as matters without certain resolution:

Man is read in his face: God in his creatures: but not as the Philosopher, the creature of glory, reads him: But, as the Divine, the servant of humility: *yet even hee must take care, not to be too curious.* For to utter Truth of God (but as hee thinkes onely) may be dangerous; who is best knowne, by our not knowing.[36]

Jonson clearly had no blind animosity towards 'divines'; what he questioned was the extent of their inquiries and their doubtful – if not spurious – claims of infallible truth. On the other hand, he wholly lauded the humanist quest for knowledge. The last part of the quotation above was a borrowing from Lipsius. Jonson owned a number of Lipsian works, including the *Politica*, which provided him with various quotations for his commonplace book.[37] It is the source for this next extract, which shows that Jonson was keenly attracted to the Lipsian re-articulation of humanism:

Truth is mans proper good; and the onely immortall thing, was given to our mortality to use. No good Christian, or Ethnick, if he be honest, can misse it: no States-man, or Patriot should. For without truth all the Actions of mankind, are craft, malice, or what you will, rather then Wisdome.[38]

These excerpts and many more that could be extracted from other Jonsonian compositions reveal that Jonson, like Lipsius, believed that learning should be concerned with the realm of the knowable – that is, with an exclusively human sphere. Excursions into the mind of God were impossible, Jonson insisted, and the objects of learning were thus limited. Still, in the range yet left to scholars, learning promised much bounty. The 'Epistle to Master John Selden' stated Jonson's positive view of the aim of scholarship:

> What fables have you vext! What truth redeem'd!
> Antiquities search'd! Opinions dis-esteem'd!
> Impostures branded! and Authorities urg'd!
> What blots and errours have you watch'd and purg'd
> Records, and Authors of! how rectified
> Times, manners, customes! Innovations spide!
> Sought out the Fountaines, Sources, Creekes, paths, wayes,
> And noted the beginnings and decayes!

Here Jonson addressed Selden's accomplishment in *Titles of Honor* (1614). The same might have been said about the later and more famous *History of Tithes* (1618), in which Selden set forth a scholarly response to the clergy's claim for autonomy in its fiscal policies. Through antiquarian research and his knowledge of languages Selden demonstrated that, contrary to clerical claims, no authority for tithes was asserted in the Scriptures; he went on to prove that their origins could be fixed in distinct historical circumstances. As Selden engaged in these issues, Jonson contrasted the integrity of his scholarship to that of 'pernitious' enemies of truth and learning whom he charged with 'favouring' in books 'what is there not found.' Jonson isolated the issue of learning as one under threat as a result of a renewed conjuction of religion and 'reformation.'[39]

The issue of scholarship was thus a vital factor drawing Jonson towards a Lipsian approach to society; his hostility towards religious debate should be seen primarily in this light. In his 'Execration upon Vulcan,' Jonson lamented the passing of his library in a fire that in 1623 claimed 'twice-twelve-yeares stor'd up humanitie.' Among his collection had been 'humble Gleanings in Divinitie, / After the Fathers, and those wiser Guides / Whom faction had not drawne to studie sides.'[40] Considering that the patristic authors had had axes of their own to grind in their respective interpretations of the faith, a hint of irony might be detected in Jonson's invocation. As Dewey Wallace has explained, however, the Church fathers had come to be held as moderating authorities in face of the current theological debates over the predestinarian doctrine of grace and its definitive place in the English Reformed and Established Church.[41] The issue which tended to divide theologians, and which resulted in the drafting of the Lambeth Articles in 1595 and the subsequent silencing of other, dissenting voices, was this idea of grace as an act wholly attributable to the will of God. It gave a certain assurance of salvation for God's elect, who, without any necessary intercession of good works, could not in any respect fall away from their salvation.[42] The corollary of the benefits for the elect was that reprobates were doomed; no amount of good works could intercede to prevent their condemnation for their sins.

Proponents of a more moderate strain of the doctrine of grace arose to challenge this harsh formulation, finding that the ancient fathers offered a more humane alternative. In his study which traces the various threads which made up the 'more moderate theology of grace than that enshrined in Reformed scholasticism,' Wallace remarks that it emerged 'partly under revived humanist impulses emanating from the Continent and partly from a renewed patristic interest.'[43] Margo Todd has recently argued that the Erasmian humanist tradition was sustained in the broadly-based 'Puritan' effort to effect moral and 'godly' rule in England.[44] But as we have noted in the Introduction, above, Erasmianism itself underwent a metamorphosis at the hands of Lipsius. Jonson adhered to the Lipsian reformulation, condemning, in his 'Execration Upon Vulcan,' the metaphorical fires that burned within the hearts of proponents of an entrenched Reformed tradition in the church as much as the physical fire that burned his books. He saved a stronger indictment of claims based on religious authority for the radical separatists – whom Jonson claimed rejected scholarship altogether.[45] In *Bartholomew Fair*, Busy is indicted as one who 'derides all Antiquity; defies any other Learning, then Inspiration.'[46] In the face of the two-pronged attack on learning, Jonson vigourously maintained the principles of classical scholarship and endorsed the efforts of Selden and others in their pursuit of knowledge and what he might call disinterested truth – truth that was discerned by reason, enshrined in the teachings of antiquity, and derived from the morality of the ancients. And the same attacks brought him even closer to Lipsius, as he shared with the Fleming a fundamental belief in the value of learning in society and a basic abhorrence for its misuse at the hands of factional interests. A defence of the basic principles of humanist study attracted Jonson towards the Lipsian paradigm, with its focus on the defence of humanism and, in this instance, its affirmation of an Erasmian ideal.

Lipsius also appealed to Jonson on the level of personal religious professions, where, oddly enough, Jonson's own leaps of conscience have passed with the minimal amount of comment. Although he was born into the English parish system, he converted, when in his 20s, to Catholicism, remaining there for a decade and more until, in 1610 he finally returned to the state church. Religion, posterity readily accepts, was peripheral to his view of society. Also accepted, almost without reservation, is the testament provided by William Drummond of Hawthornden, who recorded that Jonson was 'for any religion, as being versed in both.'[47] And if posterity has been very understanding and sympathetic towards Jonson, both contemporaries and modern critics have made much of the 'inconstancy' of Lipsius's religious affiliations. Something of a double standard is evident in the selective principle implicitly applied. Jonson's religious career deserves some note. It is particularly interesting because he evidently came to support the hegemony of the established English Church. This was not always the case.

Jonson converted to Catholicism while awaiting sentence for the murder of Gabriel Spencer in 1598. According to William Drummond, to whom Jonson related the story of his religious affiliations, 'Then he took his Religion by trust, of a priest who Visited him in prison. Thereafter he was twelve years a papist.'[48] Catholicism might have appealed to him because its simple promise of forgiveness contrasted sharply with the sentence of death he could expect from the state.[49] This act of conversion, however, was made by a man who had courted danger and had even sought it out as a soldier. David Norbrook has suggested that Jonson's conversion was in the manner of that made by Lipsius, 'whose writings he greatly admired.' Norbrook goes on: 'Lipsius had become a Catholic because of his profound antipathy to the social and political disorder which seemed an inevitable consequence of Calvinist fanaticism.'[50] Whether Lipsius isolated Calvinism as fanatical is perhaps a point to ponder; after all, Catholics under the command of the Duke of Alba had been equally fanatic in their destruction of the Netherlands, and yet Lipsius ultimately went over to them. In terms of analogies, moreover, Norbrook's assessment overlooks the factor of chronology. Jonson did not become a public 'anti-Calvinist' – if we can use that term – until twelve years after his conversion to Catholicism. Furthermore, in regard to Lipsius, the elements of war and peace must be taken into consideration. The disorders resulting from the Earl of Leicester's heavy hand in Leiden provoked Lipsius to remove himself to the more peaceful climes of Louvain, where the established religion, once the area had been tamed by the Duke of Parma, was Catholicism.[51] In reconverting to the Church of Rome, Lipsius only practised the prime directive he had himself articulated for obedient and peace-loving subjects – that it was incumbent upon subjects to adhere to the laws of the land. And the law of the Spanish Netherlands demanded that its subjects be Catholic.

Jonson, by contrast, became and remained Catholic by contravening the laws of England. His was hardly an act of a dutiful and obedient subject of the Protestant realm in which he resided. Indeed, because he repudiated the official, government-enforced religion, it is the political nature of his conversion that stands out; what looked to be probably his last deliberate act was one of ultimate rebellion. And here, the exact nature of his rebellion calls for explication. For if Jonson finally came to support the state church, the rationale for his views about religion and the state clearly underwent a change.

The initial period of Jonson's voluntary departure from the church of England coincided with the years in which Catholics suffered the most severe persecution since the early days of the English Reformation. In

1595 the English Jesuit and poet, Robert Southwell, was hanged, drawn, and quartered. Despite his claim that Catholics were loyal subjects – an argument forcefully made in a tract he circulated in 1591, and which was published in 1601 – he was tortured and dealt the standard punishment for traitors.[52] Other priests suffered equally, and after the discovery of the Gunpowder Plot the conspirators against the new king and his government were liable to the same treatment. But as James announced, no retribution would be exacted on those Catholics 'who yet remaine good and faithfull Subjects.'[53] On this occasion, Jonson was called to perform a civic duty. His Catholicism being known, he was charged by the Privy Council to help uncover the whereabouts of a certain suspected priest. Jonson complied with the order but had little success. He was plainly against treason and the regicidal aims of the conspirators, writing to Salisbury; 'For my selfe, if I had bene a Preist, I would haue put on wings to such an Occasion, and have thought it no aduenture, where I might have done (besides his Maiesty, and my Country) all Christianity so good service.'[54] Still, even in these dark days for Catholicism, Jonson was not averse to remaining associated with his adopted church; six months after he wrote to Salisbury promising to perform his services to the king with all integrity, he had to answer to a charge of recusancy. If Jonson was against the revolutionary formulation of Catholicism in its call to arms against Protestant monarchs, what then, we might ask, was the nature of his conviction in adhering to the faith of Rome for twelve years?

The first clue to Jonson's religious position comes from his attitude towards Robert Southwell. Jonson told Drummond 'that Southwell was hanged; yett so he had written that piece of his ye burning babe, [that Jonson] would have been content to destroy many of his.'[55] 'The Burning Babe' was one of Southwell's most Catholic and spiritual poems, the beauty and intensity of which appear to have made Jonson believe many of his own verses far inferior. It perhaps inspired his own 'Hymn on the Nativity of My Saviour' – a poem certainly less adoring in tone than Southwell's, but equally stressing the element of supreme sacrifice.[56] If Jonson did not actively seek to emulate Southwell, there can be no doubt that he admired him. As well, Jonson's reference to Southwell's fate contained an implicit criticism of the state by suggesting that for his intellect and art (at least), the priest ought not to have been executed. In view of the fact that Southwell had also fiercely avowed his loyalty to the English crown, Jonson must have viewed him as the victim of Protestant and corporate paranoia. Southwell had addressed his 'Supplication' to the queen in terms of freedom of conscience; in the wake of threats on

Elizabeth's life he had argued that politics was a separate issue from the claims of conscience, and that charges of treason against Catholics muddled both religion and politics by confounding spiritual faith and secular fidelity.[57] Although Southwell could not quite pass for an early proponent of religious toleration, he wrote against the perpetration of torture. While grounded in his assumptions of the infallible truth of his Catholic beliefs, his tract could well have been read by one such as Jonson as a defence of the autonomy of the individual in the face of state repression.

Jonson's own approach to religion seems to have followed this rationale. He first departed from the established religion while languishing in jail, awaiting penalty. True, he had killed a man, but as John Whitgift, the Archbishop of Canterbury, had recently drawn up the Lambeth Articles as a test for proper doctrine, Jonson probably expected the state itself to view him as a reprobate, without chance for parole or any means to have his crime pardoned. By contrast, the Church of Rome offered at least the opportunity for remorse and, after penitence, the promise of forgiveness. A second incident, seven years on and with a new monarch at the helm of the ship of state, found him in a similar situation. We noted earlier the trouble Jonson incurred in 1605 for his part in writing and performing *Eastward Ho*, the comedy that lampooned the Scots, so many of whom had recently arrived in the train of the new king. He and George Chapman were 'hurried to bondage and fetters' without 'examininge, without hearinge, or without any proofe, but malicious *Rumour*.' 'Delivery' finally came, but not before 'the report [went about] that they should ... have their ears cut and noses.'[58]

As Jonson faced the prospect of torture he cannot have become any more enamoured of a system that so infringed upon what he seems to have considered the prerogatives of the artist in exposing the vices at large in society. His means of protesting the censorious activities of a coercive state was to maintain his religious independence. After the suspicion that fell upon Catholics as a result of the Gunpowder Plot, he returned, it is true, to habitual attendance at his parish church. It was not, however, until 1610, the year, notably enough, of *The Alchemist* (featuring Tribulation Wholesome), that he returned to the fold of the English church.

Drummond recorded that 'at his first communion, in token of true Reconciliation, he drank out all the full cup of wyne.'[59] This was a gesture replete with Jonsonian theatricality and independence – hardly one indicative of humility and submission. But the important point about the reconversion, or as Jonson would have it, his reconciliation, was that it conveyed Jonson's view that no longer was the monopoly of coercion against consciences held by the state authorities (and Protestant state authorities at that). By 1610 the greater threat emerged from individuals demanding doctrinal purity. That same year, a 'puritan' monk had brought down Henry IV of France, who in the 1590s had embraced Catholicism as a means of restoring order and stability in France, and whose political acumen Jonson had long admired.[60] His own adherence to Catholicism coincided with the period when Henry presided over the French religious settlement guaranteed by the Edict of Nantes. Henry IV's assassin, François Ravaillac, however, was affronted at the bland prostitution of his faith and the king's grant of toleration to Huguenots. Ravaillac proved uncompromising in his faith and fanatic to the point of realizing his beliefs according to a doctrine of resistance, which had been given theoretical formulation by the Catholic cardinals Bellarmine and Mariana.[61]

King James himself was frequently provoked to repudiate the resistance theory promoted not only by such Catholics but by Calvinist spokesmen such as his old mentor, George Buchanan, who had written a justification for the deposition of his mother, Mary, Queen of Scots, after she had been expelled from her Scottish throne in 1567. 'Jesuits,' complained the king, 'are nothing but Puritan-papists.'[62] The problem with these papists, he pointed out, was that they laid 'an excellent ground in Divinitie for all rebels and rebellious people.'[63] As Jonson's comments on puritans (quoted earlier) indicate, he came to see things much as the king; by the year 1610, he had come to accept that only the established church constituted a barrier to the repression he believed to be inherent, on the one hand, in the programs of religious reformers (who purported to dictate how society should be governed according to their own methods of justification) and, on the other, in the claims of religious purists (who stopped at nothing to live up to their beliefs). In the face of these threats, Jonson turned to embrace the confession of the established English church, and did so with a great deal of panache.

Public religious affiliation remained preeminently a matter of politics for Jonson. As for his personal beliefs, it is not so much any Christianity that stands out as his rational approach to religion. In his later years he joined Lord Falkland's circle at Great Tew.[64] John Aubrey was later to record that Falkland 'setled and rested in the Polish [Church],' adding in parenthesis that by this he meant Socinianism. Aubrey also noted, however accurately, that Falkland 'was the first Socinian in England.' One of the distinguishing features of Socinianism was its propensity to put matters of faith to the test of reason; for this, Falkland and his friends were attacked by one of the foremost heresiographers of the 1640s, Francis Cheynell. Cheynell devoted three tracts to exposing the threat he perceived to the Protestant religion by the 'rise, growthe, and danger of Socinianisme.'[65] Falkland was killed in battle in 1643; it then became the turn of his colleagues, William Chillingworth and Henry Hammond, to be targeted by Cheynell for their beliefs in the power of reason, obedience, and good works – rather than the grace of Christ – to effect justification. Much to the distress of Cheynell, Chillingworth maintained that justification was always conditional.[66] The main threat to orthodoxy discerned by Cheynell and others, however, was the Socinian teaching on the moral effort required of its adherents. This autonomy seemed, in the words of Dewey Wallace, 'to destroy the very notion of redemption by grace' – the fundamental premise upon which Protestantism and the English Church had been built.[67]

Socinianism also had other features; yet if Jonson was at all associated with this faith of his friends, it would have been in keeping with the rational basis of the morality he espoused elsewhere. He composed only a few religious poems; otherwise Christian theology hardly intruded into his verses. Instead, he gave voice to precepts of integrity deriving from Horace and Seneca and based upon the tradition of natural law and reason. The 'Epigramme to Sir Thomas Roe' is a case in point:

> Thou hast begun well, Roe, which stand well too,
> And I know nothing more thou hast to doo.
> He that is round within himselfe, and streight,
> Need seeke no other strength, no other height;
> Fortune vpon him breakes her selfe, if ill,
> And what would hurt his vertue makes it still.
> That thou at once, then, nobly maist defend
> With thine owne course the iudgement of thy friend,
> Be alwayes to thy gather'd selfe the same:
> And studie conscience, more then thou would'st fame.
> Though both be good, the latter yet is worst,
> And euer is ill got without the first.[68]

Although an occasional poem, written perhaps in commendation of Roe's appointment as ambassador to the Grand Mogul in 1614, there is no ephemeral quality to this adaptation of a moral admonition first composed by Horace before the dawn of the Christian era.[69] Dignity and classicism are its most outstanding features, and in many ways it typifies the task Jonson set out to accomplish – to transfer the values of antiquity to the England of James I. In the most belligerent of his satires, the most poignant of his epitaphs, and the most angry of his vituperative verses, Jonson's concern was to acclimatize Latin borrowings to the English context. The ancients taught him both the method and the goal, and he sought to faithfully follow them to expose greed, hypocrisy, and envy on the one hand, and to encourage virtue and nobility of spirit on the other. Without exception, Jonson's verses can be deemed hymns to, and commentaries upon, life. In a broad sense, of course, religion of a sort is thus pervasive; his moral didacticism gives his work its religious flavour. But his was a morality which concerned the mortal sphere of men. This is consonant with Jonson's own confessional practices and goes a long way in explaining his ability to befriend and win the trust of both committed Protestants, like the Sidneys, and suspected Catholics, like the Earl of Arundel.

**Politics and the Poetry of Constancy**

Jonson thus came late to adopt a Lipsian attitude of obedience to the prince in matters of religion. After a period of unequivocal rebelliousness, he was won to the established church as a result of the flaring of religious disputes. The radical implications of the religious individualism inherent in the actions of separatists, on the one hand, and of disgruntled Catholics on the other was enough to encourage Jonson to curb his own individualism. He remained by temperament a non-conformist, though, and in every book he acquired he inscribed the Senecan motto 'tanquam explorator,' suggesting that in his approach to the recorded wisdom of others he ventured 'as a scout.' In commenting upon Jonson's motto as a guide in establishing his approach to classical authorities, Katharine Maus remarks that 'the exploring mind refuses to commit itself too firmly even to a system it finds congenial, for fear of restricting its own openness and flexibility.'[70] Although Jonson, again following Seneca, declared he was 'neither Author, or Fautor of any sect,' we can safely propose that as he dismissed contemporary religious positions he simultaneously adopted alternatives suggestive of the Lipsian paradigm.[71] Even before the question of the church manifested itself to Jonson he was drawn towards neostoicism, and, in two respects at least, he showed himself an emulator of Lipsius: in the attempt to revive Roman

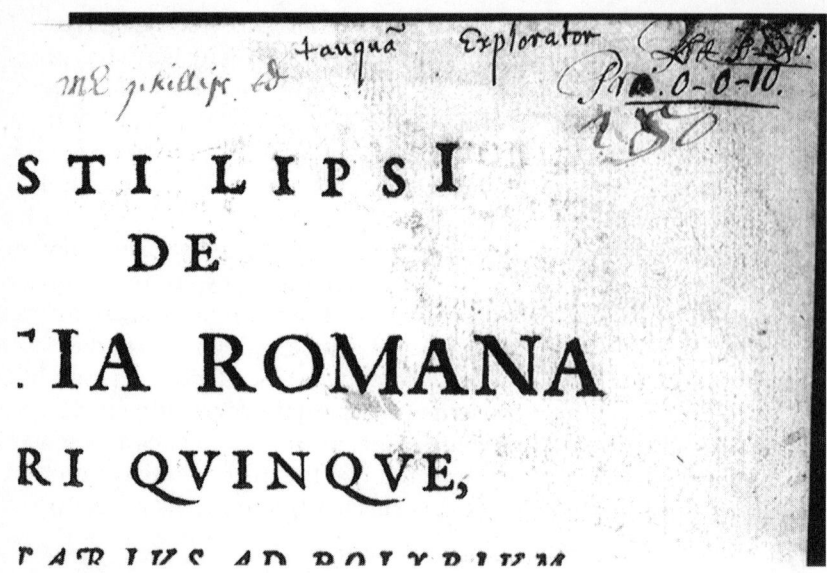

6 Jonson's autographed motto on his copy of Lipsius, *De Militia Romana*. Reproduced by permission of the Houghton Library, Harvard University.

codes of conduct in his readers and in the adoption of both a Senecan view of society and a Tacitean approach to politics. Although he composed no political treatises, Jonson consistently promoted his own variation of a Lipsian paradigm. If in his reading he proceeded as a scout devoted to exploring any and all intellectual currents, through his verses Jonson acted as another kind of scout might – one who, trained in recognizing the vital signs imbedded in uncharted grounds, proceeds in the vanguard to map out the route for subsequent travellers.

Jonson thus addressed Sidney family members in *The Forest*, a compilation of commendatory verses written much earlier than their 1616 publication date. Up until that year, the Sidneys, along with Pembroke, the Russells and others, were conspicuous for their frustrated alienation from the court. The monopoly of the king's confidence enjoyed first by Salisbury and then by the Howards prevented Sir Robert Sidney and Sir William Herbert from establishing themselves at court. A more fundamental obstacle was a familial tradition of anti-Spanish leanings carried on in the face of James' deliberate policy of friendship with Spain. Their royal associations were maintained, but mainly through the households of the queen and – until his death in 1612 – Prince Henry; up until 1616, the year of Pembroke's rise to favour, it was their disaffection with royal policies which stood out.[72] These were the years, too, in which their bonds with Jonson were forged. Their proud aloofness from the pro-Spanish policy promulgated by the king matched the position Jonson himself displayed in the matter of religion prior to 1610. On one important level, therefore, Jonson's most important patrons shared with their client the status of self-imposed outcast.

It was not the anti-Spanish principles of the Sidneys which Jonson chose to highlight, however. In 'To Penshurst,' Jonson praised the simple pattern of life conducted by Sir Robert Sidney's family, gradually shifting his scrutiny from the exterior of the Sidney dwelling – 'Thou art not, Penshurst, built to envious show' – to the interior – the Sidney spirit – that made Penshurst a model of country living. At Penshurst, according to Jonson, nature was harmonious because of the proper balance of priorities displayed by its owners. In 'To Sir Robert Wroth,' an address to the husband of Sir Robert Sidney's daughter, Mary, Jonson drew a portrait of a man facing the temptation to follow the trend for display and ostentation, but who resists it in order to 'live long innocent' away from the vices of the city and the court. A lesson on the classical virtues of modesty and study was addressed to Sir William Sidney in a poem commemorating his coming of age; and in the 'Epistle to Elizabeth, Countess of Rutland,' Jonson addressed Sir Philip Sidney's daughter to lament the reign of 'almighty gold,' regretting that in its ascendancy 'all virtue now is sold.' In all of these poems Jonson shows a marked concern with the market value being placed upon civic service. By this means one particular aspect of the Sidney detachment from the Anglo-Hispanic accord did get aired: as supporters of the royal policy were rewarded with so-called 'Spanish' pensions, the Sidney family fortune waned; and as Sidney family homes threatened to fall into disrepair, royal officials like Salisbury and Sir Edward Sackville could flaunt the fruits of the royal favour shown them by converting wealth into stone and glass. Theobalds, the sumptuous dwelling that Salisbury bestowed on the king, was close to the Wroth family property at Enfield; Sackville's prodigy-house at Knole was close enough to Penshurst to emphasize its visible signs of aging.[73] As Jonson invoked a virtue/wealth dichotomy, he set his focus upon the integrity of the Sidney family and the honour of their name, contouring the poems to provide several and repeated lessons on the vanity of outward display. He used their enforced frugality as the standard against which to measure both the shallowness of others and their inward and true nobility.

But Jonson did not force the issue of the politics of wealth; his criticisms were directed against the misuse rather than the fact of wealth. And rather than endorsing the political stance of the family, the Sidney poems turn on the well-known theme of 'the centred self.'[74] The stoic impulse informing these and so many other Jonsonian compositions needs no repetition here; I want to suggest that Jonson's concern with the centredness of individuals can betaken as none other than an appeal for the political virtue of 'constancy.'

Lipsius had reworked that Renaissance commonplace, making it resonate with political overtones. In the neostoic framework, constancy augured a commitment to civic participation but required as a prime duty obedience to the sovereign. This political edge need not disturb the ethical aspect of integrity. Fulke Greville, we saw in the last chapter, noted the critical tensions involved in attempting to reconcile integrity and obedience, alleviating that tension through recourse to Calvinist language, replete with the view of a strict dichotomy between worldly and unworldly, outward and inward, things. Jonson, by contrast, ignored Christian discourse and metaphors; he was not troubled by problems such as those confronting Greville.

Indeed, he lauded and encouraged the independence of character that enabled the subjects of his verse to withstand the pressures to succumb to current practices; but simultaneously – and unobtrusively – he introduced the question of political obedience by portraying the Sidneys as dutiful subjects of both nature and England in 'To Penshurst.' The Sidneys were entreated not to rest upon the laurels of a family name. Sir William was advised that virtue was not hereditary; to show his true nobility he must first cultivate it by fulfilling his social and educational responsibilities. Wroth, in his turn, was urged 'To do thy country service [by doing] thyself right.' The concept of civic virtue invoked by Jonson entailed the view that service to the state began with service to the self, not in terms of material self-interest, which was last on Jonson's list of priorities here, but in terms of familial responsibility and duty – a concept with a tradition that went back to Roman stoic thought.[75] While his stress fell on the Sidneys' need to persevere in the cultivation of honour and integrity, however, Jonson was far from conveying a message of mere stoic consolation. Obedience, for Jonson, did not imply a placid resignation in the face of hostile cirumstances. Even when he wrote to offer political consolation, as in his epigram to John Williams, Bishop of Lincoln, after his dismissal from the office of Lord Keepership in 1625, his consolation took the form of a militant critique of the immorality of court practices.[76] He insisted that what might be taken for minor service (the peaceful running of one's country estate) or even no service at all (the pursuit of an education instead of living it up among royal servants) was in fact where true service to the state began.

Jonson's views of civic virtue had some radical implications. In the first place, the service or obedience so advocated implied a concept of the state that transcended peculiarities of political organization. This was a feature in humanist thinking that facilitated the transfer of classical precepts to the monarchical systems of sixteenth-century Europe by Erasmus, More, and others, but which derived from the assumptions of the Roman republican tradition, in which the state was the sum of its citizens.[77] In view of this ancestry, the classical concept of civic virtue awaited only a number of requisite circumstances (and they emerged in the 1640s and 1650s) to provide the basis for a revival of 'classical republicanism' (which was espoused by some members of Rump Parliament in the wake of the execution of the king).[78] Second, although the rejection of heredity as qualification enough for title was a restatement of Erasmian teachings and would later grow to be a fundamental precept among the radicals of the late 1640s, Jonson's particular version of it lauded heredity as it simultaneously promoted the greater responsibilities that heredity must entail. A more purely classical and more faithful rendering of the politico-stoical teachings of Cicero and Seneca, this view represented a shift away from the Erasmian teaching on virtue as devolving from merit rather than birth and contained an implicit criticism of practices of governance in which natural-born rulers were overlooked when the monarch made his choice of intimate councillors.[79]

Traces of this view were later expressed by Algernon Sidney, great-nephew of Sir Philip and sometime radical later in the century, who upheld the merits of birth.[80] For Jonson, however, the implications of his advice to the Sidneys went unexplored. And according to his views they need not be explored since the unspoken assumption in his Sidney poems was that the current state of politics – its vicissitudes, Bacon would say – did not give one leave to opt out of the performance of one's civic duty. Jonson's advice closely resembled the teachings of Lipsius on the subject, affirming the value of participation, however regional. Thus he, too, countered the challenge of Charron, whose *De la sagesse* was translated by the Sidney client, Samson Lennard, and whose teachings could lead to political withdrawal.

Tensions of the sort that plagued Fulke Greville thus did not arise in

Jonson's thought, where the pursuit of individual liberty of thought loomed large, but where questions of political freedom did not necessarily follow.[81] But Jonson was also altering the tenor of the humanist legacy he shared with patrons and contemporaries; maintaining a Lipsian emphasis on the role of the teacher in mediating the association between learning and politics, he encountered the legacy of Sir Philip Sidney and met the challenge head on.

Sidney had been committed to political action first and foremost. Literature was the expression and analysis of politics, and served as praxis.[82] Thus Sidney elevated the role of the poet in his *Defense of Poetry*, but after his death in 1586 his reputation centred largely on his poetics. Jonson was ambivalent towards Sidney, commending to Drummond of Hawthornden the poetry of the Countess of Rutland as 'nothing inferior to [that of] her father, S[ir] P[ilip] Sidney.'[83] Since Jonson also came to enjoy the patronage and confidence of so many of the Sidney family, any claim to be literary heir to Sidney had some substance. But Jonson had strong reservations about Sidney, both as a poet and as a courtier – functions which for Sidney became inseparable after he first turned to poetry as a vehicle for exploring particular policies, most notably those which supported Protestant militancy in Europe. Jonson's motivation for writing was 'apolitical' by comparison. Certainly, he sought out patrons by appealing to their political views, and without doubt he alluded to policy matters, most pointedly perhaps in the masques, but also in his non-dramatic verse. In the epigram 'On the Union,' for instance, he lauded the idea of the political unification of England and Scotland, a measure which caused much debate in the wake of the accession of James VI of Scotland and I of England.[84] And in the 'Epistle Answering to One that Asked to be Sealed of the Tribe of Ben,' a poem of the late 1620s, he mirrored the growing anti-Spanish feeling that Buckingham and Charles were currently cultivating.[85] However, hearts and minds were his main preoccupation. If Jonson was spokesman for any particular cause, it was his own; by and large, his main concern lay with promoting a manner of living, not with advocating the pursuit of a particular policy – nor even, as we shall see, with championing the policies which his benefactors supported.[86]

On the other hand, Jonson clearly agreed with Sidney's idea of the poet. He insisted that his particular art was the superior branch of the humanities, 'the Queene of Arts,' as he called it, 'which had her Originall from heaven, received thence from the 'Ebrewes, and had in prime estimation with the Greeks, transmitted to the Latines, and all nations, that profess'd Civility.'[87] Jonson's art sought to heighten the 'civility' of England. To that purpose he maintained that a poet should have 'the exact knowledge of all vertues, and their Contraries; with the ability to render the one love'd, the other hated, by his proper embattling them' – a statement at once a revelation of his own personality as well as the theoretical basis for his poetics.[88] His aim was to elevate the role of the poet and ensconce him as acknowledged teacher and guide of society. If Lipsius rendered philology philosphy, Jonson's writings were devoted to rendering poetry the vehicle of moral instruction in all social relationships.

In his early play *Cynthia's Revels*, Jonson juxtaposed the poet / scholar and the courtier, promoting the first over the second in terms of their contribution to the court, that microcosm of society. The protagonist of the piece, Criticus, arrives to find the court populated by 'mimiques, jesters, pandars, parasites / And other such prodigies of men,' and discovers that 'pride and ignorance' seem to be the 'two essential parts of the courtier.' His position is finally vindicated when Cynthia recognizes the value of the poet as censor and promotes Criticus to 'impose what paines you please: / Th'incurable cut off, the rest reforme.'[89] In *Poetaster*, it is the personna of Horace who wins out at the end and goes forth to inaugurate a new golden age, both in letters and in morals. To Jonson, Horace was 'the best master, both of vertue and wisdom,' with a fitting reputation for judgment based on the knowledge he gleaned 'out of use and experience.'[90] Jonson strove to emulate Horace. As early as 1603, the playwright Henry Chettle referred to him as 'the English Horace'; on his death, Sidney Godolphin eulogized him as 'the best Judge of what was fit; / The deepest, plainest, highest, clearest Pen; / The voice most eccho'd by consenting Men.'[91] Jonson's poetic career may not have been all smooth sailing. From the beginning, however, he saw his task clearly; through his writings he would guide society, exposing and attempting to correct its errors and evils.

Still, he continually confronted the legacy of Sidney, the sole place free from its shadow being the Jacobean court. As Jonson told Drummond, 'The king said Sir P. Sidney was no poet.'[92] Jonson seems to have taken a perverse pleasure in attempting himself to undermine the reputation of his 'predecessor.' Sidney had been portrayed as handsome and gallant, the epitome of the perfect courtier; Jonson informed Drummond, however, that he 'was no pleasant man in countenance, his face being spoiled with pimples.'[93] Nor were his much-praised verses beyond reproach; Sidney was first on Jonson's list of poets who needed censuring for their main failing 'in making everyone speak as well as himself.' Thus Sidney neglected decorum, the single most important element in Jonson's poetics.[94] By giving each his due voice, and by making his addresses in the terms most fitting to any intended audience, Jonson hoped to not only classicize his endeavour, but to have the required effect upon his readers. Mobilizing decorum in satires, comedies and dramatic tragedies, Jonson ultimately hoped to 'shame the ill from vice'; by a different application of the same feature in masques and commendatory verses he also sought to 'teach while delight.'

A philosophy of poetry was thus one of the issues upon which Jonson and Sidney ultimately differed. Nor did policy matters on the whole perturb Jonson as they did Sidney. Two political issues, however, continually preoccupied him, and Jonson's response to them distinguished his view of the poet from that championed by Sidney. One was the matter of counsel, the other the subject of kingship. They both concerned him intimately since, in the first place, his philosophy of politics was based upon the humanist dictum (used by Lipsius in dedicating his *Politica* to all governors): 'a Prince without Letters, is a Pilot without eyes'; then, in the role of royal poet, Jonson presented himself as the eyes of the pilot, 'the interpreter, and arbiter of nature, a teacher of things diuine, no lesse than humane, a master in manners.'[95] In the second place, political society for Jonson fell into two main categories – the rulers and the ruled. Harbouring a fundamental distrust of the judgment of most subjects Jonson held that the arcana of government were mysteries best kept from the prying eyes of the ignorant. In his political outlook, Jonson thus favoured reason of state. But he was also something of a Tacitist, though hardly in the same mould as Sidney had appeared in the 1570s and 1580s, or as Essex had been in the 1590s. On the one hand he could be outraged that 'ripe statesmen ... grow in euery street,' who, since 'They carry in their pockets Tacitus', the 'councils, proiects, practises they know, / And what each prince doth for intelligence owe.'[96] On the other hand, he could commend Sir Henry Savile, the English translator of Tacitus, in the very same terms:

> We need a man, can speake of the intents,
> The councells, actions, orders, and euents
> Of state, and censure them: we need his pen
> Can write the things, the causes, and the men.
> But most we need his faith (and all haue you)
> That dares not write things false, nor hide things true.[97]

Jonson's applause of the implied statesmanship of Savile stands in stark contrast to his satirical attack upon the popularity of Tacitus. According to Annabel Patterson, Jonson's marked ambivalence towards Tacitus was an exercise in the ongoing 'hermeneutics of censorship,' the result of Jonson's early connection with Essex, and his subsequent experience and involvement with the prosecution of the Gunpowder conspirators. Jonson then referred to Tacitus as 'a model of subversion'; in the circumstances of 1600–1, by contrast, he had been the model for the approach to 'things true' (and probably the best approach for exposing the travesty of Ralegh's trial for treason).[98] Jonson's estimation of the Roman historian might well have changed over time and according to differing circumstances. Yet the dissemination and widespread appropriation of Tacitus was his greatest complaint. Mysteries of state such as those revealed by Tacitus were not, in Jonson's view, for general consumption, and his single disavowal of Tacitus stands against his several acclamations of him.[99] As late as 1618–19, Jonson commended Tacitus for exposing 'the secrets of the Councill and Senate.'[100] He saved his highest praise, however, for Tacitus's language, signalling his own goal of recontouring virtue, making it fit the Jacobean audience he had in mind.

This audience included the prominent Tacitist, and one of his own patrons, Sir Robert Sidney. A friend and correspondent of Lipsius, Sir Robert was drawn to 'red' Tacitism which has been called a covert form of republicanism.[101] Jonson's 'To Penshurst' might be taken as a response to Sir Robert's potentially revolutionary Tacitism (not that Jonson therefore subscribed to the 'black' version – Tacitus as a disguised Machiavellian). Indeed, Jonson's views resembled those of Bacon, with whom, incidentally, Jonson shared the same mixed favour extended by the court (both experienced the role of royal golden boy, which alternated with that of black sheep). Close to Jonson's heart were his Roman plays, *Sejanus* and *Catiline*, both of which were virtually booed off the public stage and liked little better by court audiences, provoking the authorities to call for explanations of their intent.[102] Jonson's attempt to Romanize the English failed miserably. He responded by turning to print. Paradoxically, it was this medium – which he charged with creating a mass of Sir Politic Would-bes – to which he entrusted his work for discerning readers in his own and later times. But Jonson was somewhat disingenuous in his disavowal of the effects of the printing press. He had more faith in the reading public than an audience, and for an author famed for his 'plain style,' he was ever at pains to seek out a discriminating readership, saying: 'Pray, take care, that tak'st my book in hand, / To read it well: that is to understand.'[103]

If Jonson's historical tragedies were 'box-office' failures, it was not because of the choice of topic – plots of treason and subterfuge were a pretty safe bet among Jacobean audiences. The reason lay in the style and assumptions manifested in the plays. Jonson prided himself on his classical scholarship, but his fidelity towards his sources did not make for easy entertainment. *Sejanus* contained speeches lifted directly from Lipsius's edition of Tacitus's *Annals* and followed the interpretation of the reign of Tiberius given not only by Tacitus but by his editor.[104] *Catiline* presented a Cicero lifted from the pages of Machiavelli and Lipsius, although Machiavelli cared less for that Roman's famed humanist ideals and oratory than the practical statesmanship he displayed in uncovering the conspiracy of Catiline, while Lipsius admired above all Cicero's mastery of language.[105] Neither of the plays was easy entertainment; though decorously embroidered on a fabric lifted from antiquity, Jonson's Roman plays are stringent commentaries upon the 'wretchednesse of greatest states ...! / That cannot keepe what they doe gain; / And what they raise so ill sustaine!'[106] They appealed, in short, mainly to the learned, to those versed in the subtleties of the classical sources and their more recent interpreters. Which is to say, they appealed to those who could discern their political application in contemporary contexts.[107]

Both *Sejanus* and *Catiline* examined reason of state and the conjunction of principles of rule with those of morality. The title characters of each play are the villains of the piece who succeed (while they do) by perverting language and power for their own ambitious ends. Virtuous men find no room for action in *Sejanus* (1603), the play that the Earl of Northampton suspected alluded to Sir Walter Ralegh's recent trial for treason, and which, as J.H.M. Salmon has noted, was a story without heroes.[108] But *Catiline* – reflecting, perhaps, Henry IV's recent rule in France – tells a different story. Here, the noblest Roman of them all is Cato, whose earnestness and nobility of spirit, however, is too severe in view of the threat facing Rome in the shape of the Catilinian conspiracy to overthrow the Senate. Cato's desire to search out and destroy all who are merely suspected of complicity holds no promise for a restoration of the safety of the republic. By contrast, Cicero manages both to win the support of Caesar (whom Cato would destroy, but whose political clout is invaluable in the Republic) and to infiltrate and expose the conspiracy. His means for accomplishing the latter is the use of double agents. Fulvia, the prostitute, and Curius, a conspirator, are won over by Cicero, who triumphs over Catiline through an exercise of *prudentia mixta*. While nowhere explicitly mentioned in the play, mixed prudence is applied by Cicero, who turns the vices of his informants to a noble end. Cicero's integrity, moreover, is not impugned by his manipulative techniques; at the play's close, he has his creator's full approval. After giving thanks for the outcome of events, Cicero ends by saying:

> Romans, I now am paid for all my labours,
> My watchings, and my dangers. Here conclude
> Your praises, triumphs, honours, and rewards,
> Decreed to me: only the memorie
> Of this glad day, if I may know it liue
> Within your thoughts, shall much affect my consience,
> Which I must alwayes studie before fame.
> Though both be good, the latter yet is worst,
> And euer is ill got, without the first.[109]

In *Catiline*, Jonson puts into Cicero's mouth what in other places he himself avowed as the fundamental guide in social and political relations. This inward / outward parallel characterizes the basis of his teachings on virtue to the Sidneys; it was also the central message of the 'Epigramme to Sir Thomas Roe,' which, as we saw earlier, Jonson probably wrote as Roe was about to take up his appointment as ambassador to the Great Mogul in 1614. Jonson's advocacy of the precept of 'the gathered self,' which adhered above all to 'conscience' rather than 'fame,' was the main teaching he imparted to the leaders of his society. And within a framework of uprightness and integrity, he also avowed, as *Catiline* loudly declared, that political priorities necessitate the use of mixed prudence.

*Catiline* rendered in a dramatic form Jonson's poetics of constancy, which repudiated a strictly stoical stance in relation to politics. By highlighting the use of language as a means of procuring public safety, *Catiline* was also a response to adherences to Tacitism as a critique of governance. The use of language was thus brought into sharp relief; for Jonson, words were very much the matter of 'matter.' They were the poet's tools. And it was above all to the issue of the poet as the guide and conscience of society that Jonson's literary talents were devoted.

He recorded in his commonplace book that poetry 'offers to mankinde a certain rule, and Patterne of living well, and happily; disposing us to all Civil offices.'[110] He spent his literary career living up to this Aristotelian dictum – whether through the medium of satire, the panegyric style of his royal masques, or through the vast number of occasional verses he composed. As such, Jonson is a prime example of one who frequently enjoined the principles of political humanism but was himself mainly concerned to be a teacher. Holding that the teacher was an intrinsic member of society and the poet the teacher writ large, Jonson personified the humanist belief in the power of the written word, even exemplifying the use of language as a form of action. In his undeviating belief in the power of literature to serve society, however, Jonson also succeeded in sundering the concept of action into two component parts. Literature had an autonomous aspect in his view, and the poet had to be above (rather than involved) in hammering out issues of state.

For the greater part of his life, Jonson adhered to the role he mapped out for himself. He attracted a following of young poets to whom he acted as mentor.[111] Here lay the fundamental difference between Jonson and his own 'mentor,' Lipsius, who sought to train future statesmen, not second-hand through his own interpretation of the classics (as Jonson was doing in his poetry of praise), but by instilling firsthand familiarity with the Roman texts and authors, set out in a meticulous regime of intellectual training.[112] It has not been Jonson, founder of the Tribe of Ben, who has concerned us here, however, as much as the Jonson whose training and associations encouraged his firm belief in the autonomous power of literature and its service to society. Ultimately, his concept of the poet undermined the humanist endeavour as championed by Sidney; it also challenged the validation of that same form of humanism on the part of Ralegh, Bacon, and Greville. Yet it remained troublesome enough to the authorities of the day. When *Catiline* was published in 1611, it was dedicated to the Earl of Pembroke. 'In so thick, and darke an ignorance, as now almost couers the age,' wrote Jonson, 'I craue leaue to stand neare your light: and, by that, to bee read.'[113] The reference to ignorance was probably meant to evoke the hostile reception which greeted *Catiline*. Did it also, however, invoke the reaction to the play's lessons on politics? These certainly appear to have angered both Salisbury and King James. The former seems to have seen – and not liked – himself as the model for the presentation of Cicero as the exposer of plots; while the king, it has been suggested, was miffed for not having a parallel role assigned to him in the great unmasking.[114] The dedication itself would not have helped Jonson's standing with the rulers of England in late 1611; Pembroke was addressed as a man above the rest, discerning and honourable in the extreme. But Pembroke was a nobleman conspicuous for being overlooked for office of state. Whatever the exact tenor of royal and official disapproval, Jonson, in the event, found it prudent to embark on a European tour after *Catiline* was published – even though, in contrast to the reception of *Sejanus*, no charges ensued. No treason, in fact, was to be discerned in Jonson's politics as stated either in his Roman tragedies or in his private notebook.

According to his dramas, public rabble-rousers of the ilk of a Catiline held no promise for good government. Nor did Jonson believe that institutions were themselves the cause of the failures of government. *Catiline* was set in republican Rome, and here any prince, of course, was entirely absent. That did not prevent the rise of conspirators and plotters intent on subverting the state. In *Sejanus*, set during the Empire, Tiberius could be perceived as largely ineffectual; when he acted, his were the deeds of a tyrant. But the problems of empire and rule in *Sejanus* did not derive so much from the system of government as from the nature of character. The essential problem which confronted Jonson (and which he could not resolve) was that political systems were defined by the personalities of the officers of state. As we have seen, Jonson subscribed to the principles of civic virtue which were the legacy of Roman republican – and stoical – thought. Nevertheless, as a member of the post-Reformation European community and an England undergoing the pangs of economic expansion and threatening a revival of religious dissension, he wholeheartedly concurred with a Bodinian concept of indivisible sovereignty, taken to inhere in monarchy.[115] His 'defence' of monarchy (if defence it can be called) derives from the typical Jonsonian stress on intellectual freedom. 'Learning needs rest,' he recorded in his commonplace book; 'Soveraignty gives it.'[116] His adherence to moderate and humane absolutism – based on precepts lifted from classical sources and more recent writers ranging from Machiavelli and Vives to Lipsius and Bacon – filled pages of his private notebook and provided the basis of the teachings he imparted to his readers. Prominent among these was the injunction: 'After God, nothing is to be lov'd of man like the Prince: He violates nature, that doth it not with his whole heart. For when hee hath put on the care of the publike good, and common safety; I am a wretch, and put of man, if I do not reverence, and honour him: in whose charge all things divine and humane are plac'd.'[117]

The state of monarchy was thus all-important to Jonson. But so too were its responsibilities. Seneca and Lipsius were quoted for the qualities the prince should display. One was the perception to select worthy advisors. Men good and honest, learned and respected, should be sought out for the important role of councillor; the prince, moreover, was to be 'the Pastor of the people. He ought to sheere, not to flea his sheepe; to take their fleeces, not their fels ... No, let him keepe his owne, not affect his Subjects: strive rather to be call'd just, than powerfull.'[118] In light of the Stuarts' never-ending financial woes and the political dilemmas they provoked, Jonson's words on kingship and counsel are suggestive. In 1610 the failure of the Great Contract left the king maintaining his right to collect duties that many considered unconstitutional; from 1626 to 1628 the Forced Loan levies were seen as trespassing upon the property rights of subjects. Jonson's commonplace notations were made (or remade) after the fire which gutted his library in 1623. They indicate that, by the 1620s at least, he stood with the government's critics on these issues, suggesting as well that his presence at Cotton's house in the late 1620s owed less to reasons of mere affable companionship than to the political issues which dominated those gatherings. Yet the point of Jonson's remarks on kingship are that they give attention to what he considered the proper duties of officers of state – including those of the king.

Not that Jonson therefore offered either James or Charles explicit political advice. His approach to his prince was more discreet. On the one hand, he spoke to the monarch through both masques and poetry of praise, which, although panegyrics, were informed by the humanist dictum on teaching through praising. (We noted earlier that Jonson's didacticism was not always pleasing to the king.) On the other hand, as he urged obedience in discontented and alienated members of the court, he reserved the right to endorse those whose advice the king chose to ignore, including, as we have seen, Tacitean historians. Jonson admired Bacon above all his contemporaries, writing in his commonplace book that he reverenced 'him for the greatnesse, that was onely proper to himselfe, in that hee seem'd to mee ever, by his worke, one of the greatest men, and most worthy of admiration, that had beene in many Ages.'[119] As well, Sir Walter Ralegh's *History of the World* was praised by Jonson even as it was banned by James in 1614, and his laudatory commendation became, as Annabel Patterson has pointed out, an eloquent epitaph on Ralegh after his execution in 1618.[120] Ralegh was 'not to be contemn'd,' wrote Jonson in his *Discoveries*, 'either for judgement, or style.'[121] Notably, Jonson placed this vindication of Ralegh between that of two other major Tacitists whom he singled out for admiration, 'The Earl of Essex, noble and high,' and 'Sir Henry Savile, grave and truly letter'd.'[122] One of Jonson's closest intellectual friends and allies, Sir Robert Cotton, heretofore unremarked for any Tacitist leanings, has claims to be considered one. His *Short View of the Long Reign of King Henry the Third, King of England* (written perhaps in 1614 but unpublished until 1627), was a history full of political precepts affirmed by Lipsius and since adopted in English by John Speed, Ralegh, and Bacon.[123] A contemporary noticed a basic Tacitean motif governing Cotton's history and remarked, 'There is a little booke published comprising severall passages of state historically related, as they were carried in the long raigne of King Henry 3rd with some *observations of application to our state at this present* which by reason of *favourites & discontented peeres resembles* in many things that ancient government.'[124] Thus, Cotton also was concerned to contribute to the dialogue which was coming to dominate, in growing proportions, the tenor of English political discourse.[125] His penchant for the Lipsian paradigm emerged in his consideration of Sir John Eliot, who languished in the Tower for his part in the Parliamentary disturbances of 1629. Cotton sent him a copy of Lipsius's *De constantia*.[126] Eliot was to spend his last years composing *The Monarchy of Man*, in which he pleaded with the regal power to stem the growth of political and ecclesiastical innovations which threatened, Eliot rightly if precipitously claimed, the peace and stability of England.[127] Neither James nor Charles heeded the advice proffered by English Tacitists. It is arguable that had they done so, the circumstances which led to civil war might have been averted.

Jonson did not live to see that calamity. Nor is it by any means certain that had he lived he would have become a die-hard Cavalier. Although many of the young poets whom he met and influenced – the 'sons of Ben' – became intransigent supporters of the king, Jonson's own patrons' families straddled both sides of the royalist / Parliamentary divide, as he might have done. He had been as much a 'civic' as a 'courtly' poet; often as much a critic as a panegyrist of the Stuart kings.[128] In 'A New Year's Gift Sung to King Charles.1635,' a pastoral celebration of the monarch, he depicted the king in the role of 'great shepherd.' In light of his commonplace entries and the king's financial expediencies during the 1630s, it appears that this 'shepherd' was being called upon (rather than accepted) to be 'great.' The effects of the Forest Laws, the enclosing of land, and the series of bad harvests in the previous years undermined Jonson's singing voice, which proclaimed:

> Where e'er he goes upon the ground,
> The better grasse, and flowers are found,
> The sweeter Pastures lead hee can,

> Than ever PALES could, or PAN;
> Hee drives diseases from our Folds,
> The theefe from spoyle, his presence holds.

The last line of the chorus of this pastoral lyric praises Charles as 'the author of our peace.'[129] The phrase evokes Charles's English withdrawal from the European theatre of combat, where the Thirty Years War was raging. But England's neutral position was criticized by many and was a source of discontent rather than tending to harmonize the conflicting attitudes towards Europe among the English nobility. Moreover, peace did not exactly reign within British boundaries; Laud's ecclesiastical reforms compounded discontents which festered in the wake of innovative official fiscal endeavours.[130] Jonson appeared to suggest, then, that the king fell far short of the mandatory role of being 'author of our peace.' How he would have reacted as King Charles raised the banner of civil war at Nottingham in 1642 remains an intriguing, if moot, question.

What is indisputable is that Jonson's aim had been to transfer the values of Roman civic virtue to 'modern' England by thoroughly naturalizing – and Anglicizing – the principles and values of classical verse. David Norbrook has argued that Jonson's classicism led him to partake in the movement towards the 'aestheticization' of political culture, in which the court, with little reference to the world outside itself, became deaf to the grievances of the country.[131] Norbrook is right insofar as he argues that Jonson's aim was predicated upon the desire to dignify politics through poetry and, in the process, classicize the nature of political relations between prince and subjects. Jonson's poetics manifested the motto which Lipsius had appropriated in the 1580s – 'Moribus Antiquis': for the morality of antiquity; and Jonson's political attitudes can be described as closely resembling, if not entirely derived from, those expressed by Lipsius. Conditioned by his overwhelming love of learning, his authorial voice called for peace and harmony in the state: from the Stuart kings he sought to procure wise rule; from subjects he sought to elicit obedience and service. In his approach to kings and to subjects, he sought above all to inspire in them the lessons he imparted from the elevated place he claimed as a poet. If he thus challenged the shape of the political virtue being expresssed by some of his contemporaries in England, he still sought to instill a type of civic virtue, proceeding himself as a 'neostoic' scout.

# 5

# Joseph Hall and 'That Proud Inconstant Lipsius': The English Face of Neostoicism?

> If Seneca could have had grace to his wit, what wonders would he have done in this kinde? what Diuine might not have yeelded him the chaire for precepts of Tranquillity without any disparagement? As he was, this he hath gained: Neuer any Heathen wrote more diuinely: never any Philosopher more probably. Neither would I ever desire better Master, if to this purpose I needed no other Mistris than Nature. (*Heaven Upon Earth*, 1606)

> What Stoick could his steely brest containe
> (If Zeno self, or who were made beside
> Of tougher mold) from being torne in twaine
> With the crosse Passions of this wondrous tide?
> Griefe at ELIZAES toomb, orecomme anone
> With greater ioy at her succeeded throne?
> (*The Kings Prophecie, or Weeping Ioy*, 1603)

> We are here in a perpetual warfare, and fight we must: surely, either fight or die. (*Holy Self-Conferences*, 1650)

> Thou art afraid of death: thou mistakest him: Thou thinkest him an enemy; he is a friend; if his visage be sowre and hard, he is no other than the grim Porter of Paradise, which shall let thee in to glory. (*Christian Moderation*, 1640)

> As Kings are to the World, so are good Kings to the Church: None can be so blind, or enuious, as not to graunt, that the whole Church of God vpon earth, rests her-selfe principally (next to her stay aboue) upon your Maiesties royall supportation. (*A Recollection of ... Treatises*, 1615)

Joseph Hall was renowned as a moralist. His use of the meditation as a vehicle for moral instruction brought him fame, and he later adopted the epistle and the character sketch to the same purpose and effect. Above all, his literary reputation rested on his adaptation of Seneca. In *Heaven Upon Earth* (1606) he announced that he followed Seneca as a philosopher but went beyond him as a Christian. 'True peace and tranquilitie of minde,' as the work was subtitled, could not be achieved courtesy of Athens (or Rome); Hall insisted that only Jerusalem could teach this lesson. By 1610 he was being hailed in France as 'le Senèque Chrestien,' while in England Thomas Fuller proclaimed him 'our English Seneca.'[1] The 'Senecan turn' of *Heaven Upon Earth* permeated Hall's *Meditations* and was the distinctive feature of his subsequent and voluminous moral writings, including those of the 1640s and 1650s. His lessons on quiet internal fortitude became the key stance of many on the defeated Cavalier side during the 1650s. An examination of individual English commonplace books, moreover, reveals an ongoing popularity for the lessons on pious self-sufficiency that his writings were designed to convey.[2]

Hall is best known to posterity for his so-called 'Christian stoicism.' Forty-five years ago he was judged 'the most thorough-going of seventeenth-century Neo-Stoics,' though nowadays critics question just how 'stoic' his writings actually were or argue about just how original his thought might have been. Recently, there has also been a defence of the 'intrinsic excellence' of his writings, especially when examined in relation to 'the religious, social, and political problems of their time.'[3] What does not attract much attention is the politics of ambition which shaped his career, thought, and by extension, his literary output. The literary and political contexts of Hall's formative years demonstrate how crucial they were to his subsequent success as a Christian moralist; there is a greater unity than has generally been recognized between the professional and the literary goals he espoused, a unity that encapsulates Hall's brand of 'neostoicism.' For his teachings on political virtue may be better understood – and their impact is best gauged – against the writings of the Flemish philologist Justus Lipsius and some of his counterparts in England.

### The Making of 'our English Seneca'

Hall was a recently graduated young clergyman when James VI of Scotland came to the English throne in 1603. He would eventually rise to the position of bishop, preferment beginning in 1611 and culminating in

1628. In 1640, he was translated from Essex to the bishopric of Norwich, only to be ejected during the Civil War, finally to die, in 1656, 'bishop of no place.'[4] His clerical career had been long and arduous, and both its zenith and its nadir came during the reign of Charles I (1625–49). But clerical advancement was perhaps secondary to his main aspiration in life. Hall always believed his special destiny lay in the role of legislator of social mores, an ambition that ran like a thread throughout the corpus of his writings, from his first publication in 1597, down to his autobiography, written in the 1650s.[5]

The theological and rhetorical training he received at Cambridge certainly qualified Hall for such a role.[6] Yet in 1603 he lacked the stature needed for such leadership and strove under a certain handicap, since his first experiment in teaching society was made while he was still a student (in 1597). The particular work, the *Virgidemiae*, was banned by the Bishop of London, Richard Bancroft.[7] Moreover, his earliest patron had been Henry Hastings, the third Earl of Huntingdon, who was renowned for his protection of reformist clergymen and his support of programs for an educated clergy.[8] Hall's affiliation to the reformist cause may have made him doubly suspect in the eyes of Bancroft, who was promoted to the primacy of the church in 1604 but has remained notorious for his hammering of the Puritans during an incumbency which lasted until 1611.[9] Hall had to await the death of Bancroft before enjoying clerical preferment – the prerequisite for the authority to which he ultimately aspired.

Still, throughout a literary career which took firm shape in the first decade of the Jacobean reign, Hall seems to have been less concerned with the question of an educated clergy than with the cause of a learned, pious, and obedient laity, and in 1601 he became village rector at Hawstead, Suffolk. He won this position through the good offices of Lady Anne Drury, niece of Sir Francis Bacon and wife of Sir Robert Drury.[10] Hall's association with Sir Robert was rather unhappy (and perhaps, as we shall see, regretted), but his sojourn at Hawstead provided him with several inestimable opportunites which ensured that his aspiration of becoming moral legislator to the English became inevitably tied in with his appropriation of the teachings of Seneca.

First, he began writing and publishing his work – in order, he later wrote, to supplement the meager income he derived from his pastoral position.[11] His first Jacobean piece was the congratulatory hymn of praise to James I, newly enthroned in England. It was entitled *The Kings Prophecie, or Weeping Ioy,* and three verses of that poem draw attention to what in the marginalia Hall describes as his imitation of 'Virgil's fourth

Ecologue translated and applyed to the birth of Hen. the Prince.'[12] If his words are to be trusted, Hall declared himself the first to foresee that 'these golden dayes' of James/Augustus would 'succeed' and 'freshlie reuiue' Elizabeth's England.[13] Howard Erskine-Hill has remarked that if Hall indeed drew that early 'on the Augustan myth as a way of thinking about the new reign,' he was the first to do so – but 'was far from being the last.'[14] However, Erskine-Hill has also noted that James, while still king of Scotland, applied the parallel of the Augustan age to the English context and was thus the first to render an English application of Augustus to Elizabeth. He applied the analogy in *Basilikon Doron* (1599), inspired, Erskine-Hill suggests, from his reading of Elyot's *Book Named the Governour*, which graced the shelves of the Scottish royal library.[15]

Whatever King James's reasons for – and originality in – applying the analogies he chose, it has often been remarked that Joseph Hall himself was anything but an original or innovative thinker. His sermons fade before those of a Donne or a Lancelot Andrewes; his poetry fares little better beside that of his contemporaries; even his satires were as nothing beside those of Donne or the personal venom coming from a pen like Milton's.[16] Alternatively, if not an original, he has been esteemed to belong 'in the intellectual mainstream of his time,' representative, that is, of his age and perhaps also exemplary of some of its best features.[17] How attuned, though, was he to the prejudices of James I? In subsequent writings, Hall showed himself keen to adopt both Solomon and Constantine as analogies for the king, analogies appropriated by James in *Basilikon Doron* and assumed in his many other princely compositions.[18] In sermons preached before the Jacobean court, Hall, like other court preachers, would address 'our Constantine' or allude to the contemporary British Solomon.[19] In 1609, he published *Solomon's Divine Arts*, a handbook of social mores. The work was dedicated to the young Earl of Essex, and Hall noted that it was based on the writings of 'the royalist philosopher and wisest king,' a description ambiguous enough to encourage F.L. Huntley to comment that it was one 'James no doubt applied to himself.'[20] Much earlier, Hall probably also picked up on the Augustan parallel, applying it not – as James had done – to Elizabeth, but to James himself.

*Basilikon Doron*, moreover, was a mine for aspiring authors, and in 1603, due to his dire financial straights if nothing else, Hall was certainly one of these. In this regal testament the king instructed the young heir presumptive in his duties to God and to his charge (when it would come). James listed the virtues Henry should cultivate and the vices he should shun. 'Filthie proud hypocrisie' and 'deceitfull dissimulation' were the greatest vices to which Henry was alerted; on the other hand, he was urged to 'embrace trew magnanimitie,' 'foster trew Humilitie,' 'keepe trew Constancie,' 'use trew Liberalitie,' and 'exercise trew Wisdome.'[21] True constancy was the virtue that James repeatedly insisted upon. It was also an idea that had provoked renewed discussion among contemporaries ever since 1584, when Lipsius published his little dialogue on the subject.

One imagines that at first James had few qualms about either Lipsius or the *Constantia*. With its message of fortitude, perseverence, and adaptability, and in its innovative use of classical sources, it was a runaway best seller. Considering the tenor of his advice to his son, James's hostility to Lipsius emerged after 1589, when Lipsius published the volume that sought to instruct 'princes, monarchs, and emperors' in their duties and argued that deceit and dissimulation were necessary techniques in the art of governing well. Then, to cap it all, Lipsius, born a Catholic and educated by Jesuits, had adapted to the Reformed religion while at Leiden (where he composed both *De constantia* and the *Politica*), only to publicly avow his adherence to Catholicism in 1592 and move back to Louvain, the seat of Jesuit training. Because of their meddling in politics, particularly their criticisms of kings, James held the Jesuits in the highest contempt. He also told his son that 'bookes are [live] Ideas of the authours minde' and, insisting that 'constancy' was nothing less than consistency, he repudiated the Lipsian argument that outward profession need not match inward belief. Lipsius was in the same league as other authors of 'infamous libels,' as far as James was concerned, and hardly to be relied upon, as he told his son. In urging Henry to keep 'trew constancie,' he had noted that he certainly did not mean the version advocated by 'that proud inconstant LIPSIVS.'[22]

The second opportunity offered by Hall's Hawstead employment, therefore, was to become acquainted with some of the stylistic patterns and literary predilections of the new king. Henceforth, Hall made the regal judgment on Lipsius the basis of his future teachings. First he declared war on contemporary 'stoics' – as the second epigraph at our introduction, an excerpt from *The King's Prophecie*, suggests. Then he entered into literary combat with Lipsius himself, launching his first offensive through one of the very few Latin compositions he ever wrote.

This was *Mundus Alter et Idem*, which on one level is a satire on travel and the folly of the curious, and on another a critique of contemporary scholarship.[23] The 'hero' of the *Mundus* is the narrator, Mercurius, who

7 Parody of Lipsius in *Mundus Alter et Idem* (1643 edition; first published 1605). Courtesy of Special Collections, Dalhousie University Libraries.

sets off on a ship, *Fantasia*, to visit four kingdoms in the Antipodes: Crapulia, Viraginia, Moronia, and Lavernia – respectively the lands of gluttons, shrews, fools, and thieves. Each stop he makes on his travels produces several encounters which demonstrate how topsy-turvy is the world of the Antipodes, and a crescendo gathers to climax in the third port of call. This is Moronia, land of fools. Mercurius discovers that two of its several provinces, the 'Paradise of Moronia Felix' and the western region, Moronia Pia, are the havens of Moronia's spirituality and religious beliefs. Mercurius describes what readers would have recognized as a parody of Continental Catholicism, replete with superstitious pilgrim sites and miracle centres. But in the same land we encounter the province of Variana, or Moronia Mobilis, the land of inconstant fools. Here variability and mutability reign. Here, also, Mercurius, very matter of factly, describes a recent excavation of 'antique' coins, including one which bears the likeness of 'someone in a toga, nearly middle aged.' As Mercurius describes the 'someone,' 'His right hand rested on the head of a very attractive little dog; his left hand held a half-open book. The other side [of the coin] displayed a chameleon in all its various colours, and above was the inscription CONST. LIP., "Constant Lipsius."'[24] This was not the only sardonic reference to Lipsius in the *Mundus*, although it was the most direct and the most caustic.[25] Lipsius' love for his dog was well known, and his flexible religious adherences had also been well documented.[26] That Hall was making a satirical jibe at his

8 Portrait of Lipsius, frontispiece to his edition of Seneca's *Opera Omnia* (Antwerp, 1605). Courtesy of the Department of Rare Book and Special Collections. Princeton University Library.

famed love for learning and antiquity is also evident in the brief and suggestive description. All Lipsius's supposedly good points were represented on one side of the coin; but those very good points are negated by the obverse – with its picture of a chameleon, the reptile that changes colours to blend into any environment in which it finds itself. It is not just the flip-side of the coin, though, that reveals how Hall would have Lipsius characterized. If Lipsius's dress invokes antiquity and book wisdom, the sinister nature of Lipsian learning is suggested by the details specified in Mercurius's commentary. The traveller asserts that the left hand holds the book, and the left – the *sinistre* – is the 'unnatural' side of human physiognomy according to Galenic theory. The book, moreover, is only half-open, suggesting – in this satirical framework – a critique of Lipsius's scholarly methodology. During his lifetime, Lipsius produced not only authoritative editions of the works of Tacitus and Seneca, tracts on 'Constancy' and 'Politics,' and commentaries on Roman traditions; after his reconversion to Rome, in 1591, he went on to write scholarly expositions on and proofs of miracles.[27] From Variana Mercurius proceeds to explore the Moronian 'Paradise' and Moronia Pia, where the (Catholic) devotion to miracles is caricatured. As such, the whole of Mercurius's Moronian experience in *Mundus Alter et Idem* looks very much like an extended satirical commentary on a variety of Lipsian compositions. The exercise as a whole shows Hall addressing Lipsius with an indirect but bellicose challenge.

Modern scholars have not interpreted the *Mundus* in quite this light. Richard McCabe, for example, argues that the *Mundus* belongs to the tradition of More's *Utopia*, remarking that for Hall, the Lipsian coin symbolized 'the seduction of spiritual constancy by the vagaries of the physical world.'[28] Coming to the text from an entirely different perspective, Leonard Tourney has suggested that the *Mundus* was produced during Hall's Cambridge days and 'must not be taken too seriously; undoubtedly it provided Hall with a much needed vacation from academic routine.'[29] Neither of these commentators has noticed that little was spared when it came to Hall's attestation of the veracity of King James's verdict on the inconstancy of Lipsius. The *Mundus* was also composed entirely in the Senecan prose style – for which Hall later became renowned. But whether that stylistic mode was first adopted to parody Lipsius 'his hopping style' is a question that has not preoccupied modern commentators. That the style became characteristic of Hall's later writings serves as a testament to the success of the early Lipsian parody.[30]

That the work was addressed to a learned community that included Lipsius appears incontrovertible, appearing as it did in Latin.[31] The *Mundus* was a composition never acknowledged by Hall as his own, but he never entirely disowned it either.[32] Published in 1605, it is only assumed to have been written during Hall's Cambridge days. The precise date of composition becomes irrelevant since we know that Hall attended Cambridge from 1589 to 1601, and that Lipsius had become very *à la mode* ever since the publication of his edition of Tacitus; we also know that a number of contemporaries were promoting a Lipsian type of exegesis throughout the 1590s, while James of Scotland was at the same time berating the Fleming for his switches of religion.[33] What is significant is that in 1605, the very year the *Mundus* was published, Lipsius's authoritative edition of Seneca's *Works* appeared, and Hall undertook a journey to the land of the Flemings.

Hall's trip coincided with an official English state visit to the court of the Archduke Albert. He seems to have gone on impulse, after an invitation from his friend, Sir Edmund Bacon, whose inclusion in the visit was unauthorized and whose position was thus quite unofficial. Bacon wanted to take advantage of the newly afforded opportunity to visit the Low Countries, and Hall's reason for enthusiastically responding to Sir Edmund's offer was, he later claimed, the opportunity it afforded him to know better the Catholic enemies of his Protestant faith.[34] Such a visit, though, also offered the promise of acquainting himself better with the author who was about to become his lifelong literary nemesis. The archduke whose court provided the destination of this visit was himself a fervent admirer of Lipsius.[35] An intriguing question is whether Hall was impelled to embark on this journey in the hope of meeting and chatting with Lipsius himself – disputing perhaps with the man in person. From Hall's own description of the trip, written in a letter shortly after the fact, we know that his interest in going was neither wholly academic nor totally in the interests of dispassionate understanding. He was driven by an intense and belligerent curiosity, and he later revealed that Sir Edmund's familial credentials were, on one occasion at least, needed to bail him out of trouble.[36] Although he says nothing of any encounter with Lipsius, Hall managed the next best thing. He met and disputed with Jesuits (whom Lipsius, in these years, was keen to convince of his own religious orthodoxy); and in disputations he managed to invoke and repudiate (successfully, he considered) Lipsius's *Diva Virgo Hallensis*, his latest scholarly enterprise that attested to recent miracles performed locally by the Virgin Mary.[37]

The publication of *Mundus Alter et Idem* followed upon his return from the excursion, and whether the work included something of a self-portrait – reflecting the fact that personal experience now told him of the folly of travel – provides another interesting point to ponder. Yet despite his hostility to what he was coming to perceive as the hypocrisy of the teachings of Lipsius, Hall could not help but agree with Lipsius that travelling was of no instrinsic value to individuals. After all, the lessons of *De constantia* all follow after the 'Lipsius' of the story has searched far and wide for the answers to his troubles. It is finally Langius who enlightens him about the idea that peace and tranquility proceed from within, and that no amount of travel will assuage internal turmoil.[38] Hall's advice on travelling was similarly constructed. He was an inveterate critic of the fashionable and growing trend in England for the European tour.[39] In 1617 he condemned the fashion outright in his pamphlet, *Quo Vadis*. He, as much as Lipsius, sought to convey the message that strength, enlightenment, and above all, a 'constant mind,' were to be acquired from the internal processes of thought and contemplation. Travel, argued Hall, only offered examples of dissolute behaviour and always threatened the unwary with impious, foreign ideas.[40]

Hall's journey to the Low Countries, I would suggest, was a major milestone in his life and intellectual development. He experienced at first hand examples of 'dissolute' behaviour, and he encountered and disputed 'impious' ideas – of Jesuits and of their archapologist, Justus Lipsius. His prejudice against Lipsius was confirmed in that voyage of discovery, which also provided him with the opportunity to affirm the Protestant faith into which he had been born. On his return, he was convinced that his task in life was to do more than merely attack foreign influences like that of Lipsius. 'Methinks God pulls me by the sleeve,' he wrote to a friend when he was first invited to become rector at the Drury patrimony of Hawstead.[41] After the 1605 voyage, he was more certain of his destiny.

It was then that he began to carve out his own moral program, replete with his own construction of political virtue. *Heaven Upon Earth* was its first and most fundamental building block, followed by *The Arte of Divine Meditation*, several and subsequent 'decades' of *Epistles*, and his *Characters of Vertues and Vices*. Throughout his life Hall would write many more treatises defending the English Church, promoting a reduction of 'Christianitie to practise,' and magnifying the authority of his monarch.[42] These four works, however, together with his three books of *Meditations and Vowes*, comprise the central corpus of his alternative to

9 Frontispiece, Joseph Hall, *The Shaking of the Olive-Tree* (London, 1660). Photo courtesy of the Newberry Library.

the Lipsian paradigm and to alternative English variations that were becoming available to his contemporaries. That it was directed first and foremost as an alternative to Lipsius is to be discerned through his qualified endorsement of the place of Seneca's teachings in his writing. Hall set himself to show his contemporaries that despite the many good lessons to be gleaned from the philosophy of Seneca – newly available in an up-to-date edition produced by Lipsius – Seneca had been, and remained, a pagan. The opening paragraph of *Heaven Upon Earth* stated:

When I had studiously read over the moral writings of some wise heathen, especially those of the Stoical profession, I must confess I found a little enuy and pity striuing together within me: I enuied Nature in them, to see her so witty in deuising such plausible refuges for doubting and troubled minds: I pitied them, to see that their careful disquisition of true rest led them, in the end, but to mere unquietness. Wherein, methought, they were as hounds swift of foote, but not exquisite in the scent; which in a hasty pursuit take a wrong way, spending their mouths and courses in vaine. Their praise of guessing wittily they shall not lose; their hopes, both they lost and whosoever follows them.[43]

True tranquillity, or the quest for 'heaven upon earth,' Hall's entire treatise went on to show, could never derive solely from a dependence on the writers of classical antiquity. 'Not Athens must teach this lesson,' he affirmed, 'but Jerusalem.' He went on to demonstrate the central role of the Christian message for any Christian seeking eternal peace and mortal happiness.

The real challenge thus issued to Lipsius was Hall's assertion about Christianity and his emphasis on its crucial place in any contemporary moral philosophy. The Lipsian paradigm was constructed on a body of writings that neatly side-stepped Christian revelation; to this Hall replied that alone, and in a Christian society, pagan authorities would never suffice.[44] He turned to Patristic authors and the Scriptures to augment and correct the pagans. But he wholeheartedly adopted the Senecan-Lipsian writing style. Henceforth, he was to be renowned as one of its prime English practitioners, and it was the vehicle by which he taught readers how to channel their thoughts towards consideration of personal experiences and their devolution from God's omnipotence.[45] In the *Meditations and Vowes* and the *Arte of Divine Meditation*, Hall's Senecan style augured the pursuit of pious hearts. As a result, the afterlife, peripheral in a Lipsian scheme (where society was constructed to protect its individual members), was implicitly brought to the fore in the alternative that Hall was constructing. Yet Hall's primary concern remained the moral code appropriate for *this* life; through the infusion of Christian teachings, his curt 'neo-Senecanism' taught a lesson that countered and, in a Christian context, superseded Senecan 'tranquility.'

It must be emphasized, however, that it was not Seneca, with his message of tranquillity and stoical poise, whom Hall perceived to be the real threat to contemporary morality. Seneca's teachings might have only limited applicability to a Christian society, but Seneca could be corrected and brought up to date – and he was – by Hall and several others.[46] The real enemy that Hall identified was Lipsius. He never ceased to mention Lipsius in later writings, speaking disparagingly of him even in his memoirs.[47] In one of his *Epistles* (in volume I, which was first published in 1608), it was Lipsius's 'inconstant' example in religion that served Hall as the prime model his readers should reject. Profession and devotion were inseparable in Hall's teachings, and unswerving allegiance to one church was the measure of virtue in his eyes.[48] In the *Characters of Vertues and Vices* (also first published in 1608) the worst vices – expressed in 'The Hypocrite' and 'The Unconstant Man' – seem to have been associated with Lipsius. Of the first Hall said, he 'hath a cleane face and garment, with a foule soule.' The hypocrite's religion is but skin deep and only feigned for the purposes of appearances.[49] Of the second, 'The Unconstant Man,' Hall wrote:

... it is a woonder if his loue or hatred last so many dayes as a wonder. His heart is the Inne of all good motions, wherein if they lodge for a night it is well; by morning they are gone and take no leaue, and if they come that way againe they are entertained as guests, not as friends. At first like another Ecebolius he loued simple truth, thence diuerting his eyes hee fell in loue with idolatrie; those heathenish shrines had neuer any more doting and besotted client ...[50]

In this sketch Hall went on to expose the unconstant man's malleability in religion. Knowing his disdain for Lipsius's apologia for miracles, it is not unlikely that Lipsius, the articulator of what Hall saw as false constancy, was his model here.

It is therefore of no small significance that quick on the heels of the appearance of Lipsius's authoritative edition of the works of Lucius Annaeus Seneca, Hall embarked on his challenge to Lipsian constancy.[51] Notably, in his epistolary, Senecan, style Hall deliberately dropped that other figure whom Lipsius had harnessed beside Seneca for his neostoic synthesis – Tacitus. Hall certainly had recourse to the occasional use of dark, obscure passages, which signalled the Tacitist technique of style. But Hall's purpose in his usage of it was as far from the original thrust of Tacitism as could be possible. If his style, then, augured a challenge to Lipsius by promoting what he considered the most fitting approach to a contemporary *Christian* society, so too did another aspect of Hall's first neostoic writings: where Lipsius wrote treatises and also, with the publication of his *Epistles*, what he considered manifestations of his own practice of neostoicism, Hall followed suit by turning to a variety of genres – including the epistle and the character-sketch. But the same feature of elevating the place of Christian revelation was also explicit in his rival adaptations. Hall's formula of stressing that the moral basis of all encounters lay in a devotion to the promise of biblical revelation was a counter to the 'classicism' of Lipsian *epistolaie* (which served as the basis of much imitation from the 1590s onward).[52] It also, of course, followed logically from one of his specific vocation. Whether Hall's Christian-neostoicism resulted from a deeply rooted pious conviction, or whether in fact it followed naturally from professional leanings (not to mention a desire to please and impress the king) cannot, of course, be absolutely ascertained. But what can hardly be disputed is that Hall sought to reclaim Seneca from his perfidious application at the hands of Lipsius; he also promoted a system to rival that of the 'inconstant Lipsius.' It was one that was not only informed by faith but was also wholly, and would be consistently, Protestant – or Reformed – in its expression. Thus, by extension, it was nationalistically English.[53] By 1608 Hall's neostoicism had taken firm shape. His first volume of *Epistles* appeared in that year, followed in a few months by another volume, and yet another in 1611. Meanwhile, his *Characters of Vertues and Vices* had also been published. The flowering of the alternative he was thus establishing, however, can be set against yet other constructions of virtue based on 'constancy,' those being expressed and discussed in England itself.

**Competing Moral Paradigms: Hall versus Bacon**

Lipsius was only one of Hall's two main targets. Francis Bacon was among the earliest advocates of an approach to political society that resembled that of Lipsius, and a number of authors dedicating their tracts to Prince Henry aspired to the same league. Hall's writings comprised a challenge to them all.

The very 'spirituality' of Hall's writings provides the most telling evidence of his disagreement with Bacon. In his *Essayes* of 1597 and *The*

*Advancement of Learning* of 1605, Bacon promoted the idea of the centrality of *outwardness* in individuals as they related to society and, based on the type of learning he recommended, he advocated a secularization of political relationships.[54] Hall strongly dissented from such an approach. In fact, he hardly subscribed to any Baconian view, although he certainly agreed with one – the idea of total allegiance to the monarch. The adulatory tone of such expressions was frankly admitted by Bacon, who as a minor courtier dedicated his *Advancement of Learning* to King James with fulsome praise. An even more minor person in the social scale, Hall rehearsed the same tone as he sat down to compose his congratulatory poem on the occasion of James's accession. Postponing for a moment a closer glance at Hall's attitude towards authority, we should note that whereas Bacon certainly swore (and very audibly) fidelity to the monarch, in the years 1603–5 he was in the midst of one of the periods of limbo that punctuated his political career. Until 1607 he was unwanted by a court that favoured his arch-rival, Sir Edward Coke. And although we do not know precisely if or when Bacon might have presented a copy of his revised and enlarged *Essayes* to young Prince Henry, he made several overtures for employment to him and intended to dedicate the published second edition to the prince.[55] Those *Essayes* discussed the unique nature of political dealings. Bacon also reiterated his view that, in effect, external acts and behaviour were the all-important elements of an individual's political comportment – be he prince or subject.

The aspirations entertained by Bacon to be both teacher and counsellor to governors (and future governors) must have galled Hall's sensibilities. That he believed the influence of Bacon pernicious and considered that all efforts should be used to prevent it, is suggested in many of his early *Epistles*, including that 'to Mr. Newton, Tutor to the Prince.' Hall stressed that a prime lesson Newton should instil in his royal pupil was the never-ending quest for upright self-knowledge. 'How happy a service shall you doe to this whole world of ours, if you shall still settle in that princely mind a true apprehension of himself; and shall teach him to take his own height aright; and euen from his childhood to hate a parasite, as the worst traitor,' wrote Hall. He went on to urge the tutor to encourage the prince 'To break those false glasses, that would present him a face not his owne: To applaud plaine truth, and bend his browes vpon excessive praises. Thus affected, he may bid vice doe her worst.'[56]

This epistle, which was published in 1608 but probably written sometime earlier, appears quite general in its admonitions, and its warning against flattery is common enough. Moreover, to see it as aimed against one specific individual – Bacon – is to risk the charge of reductionism. Indeed, Bacon may not have been the only target in this instance, but that a Bacon-Hall debate was taking place is suggested from the specifics of Hall's advice. He isolated two evils that Henry's tutor should be alert to, flattery and treason. Each was part and parcel of the other, claimed Hall, since flattery taught internal treason – treason against the self. Where Bacon considered such pious sentiments redundant in the world of political affairs, Hall's lesson, by contrast, resembled the advice given by the poet Jonson, who was to urge one of his patrons to do 'thyself right' and another to 'be always to thy gathered self the same.'[57] Unlike Jonson, however, who was perhaps too inclined towards the authority of classical heathens for Hall's literary liking, Hall's teachings on integrity depended on his fusion of Seneca and Christianity.[58] Integrity was all-important since ultimately the Christian had to answer to God.[59]

The more one examines the mere forms of composition that Hall adopted, the more Hall's teachings appear intended as a counter to Bacon's views on 'politic wisdom,' conceived even as he also took up the challenge of repudiating the lessons of Lipsius. Not long after being installed in the Drury patrimony of Hawstead, Hall began what can best be described as a 'tinkering' with neostoic forms of composition. His first experiments were devoted to the highly successful, and essay-like, meditation. Bacon himself had experimented with that form by publishing several (misnamed) *Religious Meditations* along with his first edition of essays in 1597.[60] In these early years at Hawstead, Hall began to write his *Meditations and Vowes*, which were in effect little meditative and moralistic snippets. The full title of the work, which appeared in two books in 1605 (and a year later was extended to include a third) was *Meditations and Vowes Divine and Morall. Serving for Direction in Christian and Civil Practice.* The very title alerts us to the christianizing process upon which Hall came to settle in advocating his alternative to the Lipsian paradigm. But with its twinning of 'Christian and Civil' it also announces its challenge to Bacon, whose collection of *Essayes* and *Meditations* pertained to 'moral and civil' life.[61] Notably, Hall ignored the term 'essay' altogether, but many of the early meditations exemplify how far he went along with Bacon's 'Lipsian' bent – both in style and thought – and where and how Hall's path became distinct. One example is the quite long Meditation Number 83:

Euerie man hath a kingdome within himselfe: Reason as the Princesse dwels in the highest & inwardest roome: The sences are the Gard and attendants on the

Court; without whose ayde nothing is admitted into the Presence: The supreame faculties as will, memorie & c. are the Peeres: The outward parts and inward affections are the Commons: Violent Passions are as Rebels to disturb the comon Peace. I would not bee a Stoick to haue no Passions; for that were to ouerthrow this inward gouernmet, God hath erected in me; but a Christian to order those I haue: and for that I see that as in commotions, one mutinous person drawes on more, so in passions, that one makes way for the extremitie of another ... : I will doo as wise Princes vse, to those they misdoubt for faction, so holde them downe, and keepe them bare, that their very impotencie & remisnesse shall affoorde me security.[62]

In this and many other meditations, Hall experimented with short and pithy sentence structures and tried out the 'hopping' feature characteristic of Lipsian prose and of the early Baconian essay as well.[63] Here, Hall also exuded what was to become his typical but qualified admiration of stoical precepts – especially the elevation of the human faculty of reason. His denigration of the stoics' *utter* dependence on reason, however, is prominent; and his resort to the Christian message as a means to combat the heathen (and sinful) nature of that dependence was also being rehearsed.[64] Nevertheless, F.L. Huntley has noted that Hall's early meditations were 'indeed more ethical than devotional, more Senecan than biblical, more little Baconian essays on proper conduct than fervent pleas to God in secret for aid in arousing one's self from earthly lethargy to contemplation of heavenly things.'[65] Huntley's remark addresses an issue in modern scholarship, where some students of Hall argue his engagement with fashioning a 'form of meditation for Protestants,' resulting, by the end of his life, in the creation of a form 'that would match in effectiveness the Jesuistical contributions of the Counter-Reformation.'[66]

In the end, and seeing his work as whole, Bishop Hall did indeed produce a Protestant form of meditation. In the years 1603–5, however, when Hall was still far from becoming a bishop and was first drawn to experiment with the genre, his objectives may well have lain elsewhere. Contrary to Bacon in his meditations and essays, Hall declared that he would *follow* the example of 'wise princes,' not attempt to show that he knew better and thus impart wisdom to them. In contrast to Bacon, as well, Hall's meditations took examples of external actions and applied them as aids in the quest for internal composure. The spiritual, contemplative, and the physical, active sides of life were completely interrelated, Hall insisted. As he would write in a later epistle (to a fellow 'neostoic,' Fulke Greville), 'All our safetie or danger ... is from within.'[67]

Hall, therefore, took 'Senecan' models already adapted by Bacon, re-adapted them, and sought to undermine certain principles they conveyed. He refused to participate in any discussion on political wisdom; spiritual and ethical self-understanding were as far as his lessons went. Still, his work came into demand; capitalizing on its popularity he composed the methodical *Arte of Divine Meditation*. In the preface to its second edition he remarked on the dearth of such works, concluding that the main reason for the success of this piece was its provision of lessons 'which concerneth devotion and the practice of true piety.' His meditations filled an existing void, he claimed, a void only deepened by the prevalence of polemical books, the angry tenor of which did little to assuage the need for moral direction. He also mentioned that 'respecting the Reader, I sawe the braines of men neuer more stuffed, their tongues neuer more stirring, their hearts neuer more emptie, nor their hands more idle.'[68] With works like those of Bacon around, he neglected to say, a call to spiritual devotion and pious self-knowledge was sadly overdue among his contemporaries.

Why Hall should have challenged Bacon looks obvious enough. In view of his pastoral station and attachment to the teachings of the Scriptures, what else was a man of the cloth to do than attempt to disavow teachings that could easily be construed as atheistic?[69] Hall's disagreement with Bacon, however, may have developed from an animosity based on personal and ideological differences. In order to explore the roots of the challenge, therefore, we must turn to Hall's experiences in the crucial period immediately before and after Essex's rebellion.

Bacon, we will remember, forsook Essex and went on to play an important part in his prosecution. He thereby alienated forever the good faith he enjoyed with many of his contemporaries. Those henceforth wary of Bacon included Hall's first patrons, the Hastings family. Sir Francis Hastings, surviving brother of the third Earl of Huntingdon (Hall's earliest benefactor), lamented Essex's folly in attempting to raise a rebellion against Elizabeth. While disassociating himself from that act he nevertheless refused to relinquish his adherence to the Essex legacy.[70] Neither, for that matter, did Sir Robert Drury, Hall's first employer. Drury owed his knighthood to Essex, and under the Stuarts he maintained the pose of a frustrated military man.[71] It had been at Sir Robert's London residence – Drury House – that the plot to take the City had been hatched among Essex's followers. In the aftermath of the rebellion

Sir Robert had some serious explaining to do.[72] Extricating himself from all suspicion on that occasion, he would hardly have been enamoured by the disloyalty shown to Essex by his own kinsman by marriage, Sir Francis Bacon, who first prosecuted Essex, and then later wrote an apologia for his actions; even Drury's wife, the niece of Bacon, might have had reservations about her uncle, despite the many favours she owed him.[73] She and her brother, Sir Edmund Bacon, descended from the same paternity as Francis, but their branch sprang from Sir Nicholas Bacon's first wife, whereas Francis and his brother, Anthony, were from the Lord Keeper's second marriage. Sir Nicholas had known that the Bacon patrimony was not large enough to provide for all the children; Anthony and Francis were quickly ear-marked for public service, for which they demonstrated talent enough.[74] Was there, however, a certain rivalry between the offspring of Sir Nicholas Bacon, the elder, between those who had been accounted for financially and those who had not? Did a certain coolness descend on the two branches of the Bacon family after the death of Essex, so that there existed a familial animosity and antagonism in which Joseph Hall found himself a not unwilling participant?[75] If any of these questions are at all viable, Hall's literary challenge to Bacon, which began shortly after he arrived at the Drury rectory, took on the aspect of a critical renunciation of one whose reliability, credibility, and good auspices were being discussed at large. Even without such an interpretation, however, it is clear that many of Hall's writings as a divine were designed to offset and repudiate the teachings of Bacon, a *politique* before anything else.

Whereas Bacon proposed (praising Machiavelli) that study should uncover for readers 'what men do and not what they ought,' Hall was to spend a lifetime drawing attention to the 'ought' of the matter.[76] Moreover, where Bacon would use Machiavelli as a model for 'studied action,' Hall could turn to the same source to find teachings of a quite different sort. In 'An Holy Panegyrick,' a sermon delivered to the court in 1613, Hall avowed that great things were in store for England in view of the 'continued succession of vertuous princes.' These, he affirmed by calling upon Machiavelli in his *Discoursi*, '(*fanno grandi effeti*) cannot but doe great things.'[77] Hall thereby showed that even 'politic' sources could be invoked for eminently 'pious' purposes.

Hall may have thought little of Sir Francis Bacon; he devoted a considerable amount of energy to combating his teachings. But he had not remained entirely happy with his first employer for long either. As well as being reluctant to pay Hall his due stipend, Drury was much too disposed towards maintaining his former military career than Hall perhaps thought fitting for a loyal subject of a newly enthroned pacific king. Widely known for his persistent anti-Spanish attitude, Drury was also suspected of being something less than a devoted husband and father, spending much time off in search of adventure and continually seeking employment in foreign lands.[78] Such predilections could not have endeared him to Hall, who came to berate travel, and, in any case, owed his position at Hawstead to the invitation extended by Sir Robert's long-suffering wife, the Lady Anne.[79] Hall's association with Drury was reaching a breaking point that was only averted by the timely offer of employment from Sir Edward Denny, future Earl of Norwich.

Hall's association with Denny was one of the most important factors in his career. His employment as rector of Waltham lasted until 1611, when ecclesiastical preferment came his way. Indeed, Hall chose to remain a rector rather than to take up the offers extended by Prince Henry, who not only invited Hall to become his principal and permanent chaplain, but promised 'to obtain for him such preferments, as should yield him full contentment.'[80] Drury's connections with members of the prince's court seem to have been vital in preparing for the warm acclamation of Hall's works there – although in his memoirs Hall implied that he had been one who, wholly unsolicited by himself, enjoyed many 'divine providences.'[81] He wrote that humility prevented him from taking up the princely offer in its entirety. His testament indicated, nevertheless, that he had been quite worthy of such 'providences' since he committed his life first to God, and secondly to his monarch – directives that, in one of the most important of his collected *Epistles*, he urged were incumbent upon 'a good and faithful courtier.' The following is part of the advice he imparted to 'The Gentlemen of his Highnesses Court':

The Court is as nigh to Heauen as is the [religious] Cell, and doth no lesse require, and admit strict holineses. I banish therefore hence all impietie, and dare presage his ruine whose foundation is not layed in goodnesse. Our Courtier is no other than vertuous, and serues the God of Heauen as his first Master, and from him deriues his dutie to these earthen gods; as one that knowes the thrones of heauen and earth are not contrary, but subordinate, & that best obedience springs from deuotion: his abilitie and will haue both conspired to make him perfectly seruiceable, and his diligence waits but for an opportunity. In the factions of some great riualls of honor, he holds himselfe in a free neutrality, accounting it safer in vniust frayes to looke on, than to strike; and if necessitie of occasion will needs winde him into the quarrell, he chuses not the stronger part, but the better.[82]

Again, as in (or as part and parcel of) his challenge to Baconian teachings, this particular *epistle* looks the natural advice of a pious man of the cloth. Hall the ambitious scholar had clearly melted into such a persona in the years 1605–8, never henceforth to abandon it. The striking features of this epistle, nevertheless, are twofold. In the first place, it reveals something of Hall's predisposition to remain aloof from total involvement in the court of Prince Henry, whose precocious personality made his household a centre of attraction for those who remained aggrieved with the ascendancy of Salisbury and Northampton with the king.[83] In view of Hall's reluctance to whole-heartedly commit himself to Henry, and in view also of his later 'arrival' to the king's attention, the last sentence in the above quotation looks rather autobiographical in nature. From the perspective of the English concern with (and debate over) political virtue, however, it is crucial to note that in this advice to courtiers we see Hall pose a challenge to contemporary Tacitism, which had many adherents among Henry's courtiers, and, of course, derived in large part from the popularity of the Lipsian construction of Tacitus.

## Hall and Theophrastus versus Tacitus

Hall's hostility to Lipsius, as we have seen, was a lifelong obsession that probably originated with James's denunciation of 'that inconstant Lipsius' in 1599. With the help of the Christian message Hall had little trouble in seconding the verdict of the king, both in showing how shallow was Lipsian constancy for the needs of a Christian society, and in demonstrating what he considered as the hypocrisy of the Lipsian tenet. In the quest for constructing a private, personal philosophy, therefore, and one relevant to contemporary needs, Hall's task of rendering Lipsius redundant and unsuitable for Protestant England appeared easy enough.

The Lipsian paradigm in all its manifestations, however, functioned as a philosophy of action, geared to participants in the public sphere. It was here that 'constancy' became so important, for in a shifting world individuals had only to adjust their outward carriage to meet prevailing circumstances while inwardly acknowledging that nothing was permanent in this world of flux. Lipsius had engaged the authority of Tacitus to drive home this point. It was here, too, in the lessons for political action, that Bacon found the means by which to press the importance of seeking to find out what men did over what they ought. This was the realm in which Tacitus had an application unrivalled among teachers and examplars from both antiquity and recent history. And it was precisely here that Hall found the greatest challenge he was to face in advocating his neostoic alternative as the only viable vindication of public action and the only fitting moral philosophy for public conduct. Henceforth, if Hall was to have his way, Tacitus was to be dropped from English neostoicism and his place taken by the classical Greek moralist, Theophrastus – an ancient teacher much more amenable to Christianization than Tacitus.

In 1608, Hall adopted the Theophrastan character sketch and composed his short collection, *Characters of Vertues and Vices*. He drew portraits of eight particular virtues his contemporaries should aspire to emulate, sketching as well fifteen vices to be avoided. We saw above that Lipsius could have provided the model for at least two of the latter – the hypocrite, whom Hall averred embodied the very worst type of vice that could exist, and the unconstant man. It was only natural, I suspect, that an avowed Christian author would account vices more numerous than virtues. But his characters of virtue consisted of typically Christian virtues – wisdom, honesty, faith, humility, valour, patience, true friendship and true nobility.[84] Then, Hall added another portrait, which was also drawn in typically Christian fashion. This was 'Of the Good Magistrate,' whose qualities, unsurprisingly enough, were headed by a faithful devotion to his 'Maker.' He was the most dutiful servant of God, according to Hall. The portrait concluded with the affirmation that the good magistrate 'is the guard of good lawes, the refuge of innocencie, the Comet of the guiltie, the pay-maister of good deserts, the champian of iustice; the patron of peace, the tutor of the Church, the father of his Countrey, and as it were another God vpon earth.'[85]

'What one notices as one studies the descriptions of Hall's virtuous types,' writes Benjamin Boyce in examining the role of the Theophrastian character in English literature, 'is that they are all developments of one basic type, the Stoic-Christian wise man, calm and steadfast in a devout trust and with an absolute morality deduced from it.'[86] Yet Hall's virtuous types culminate in the description of the Good Magistrate, a sketch that (rather than depicting the epitome of the 'Stoic-Christian') operates in two distinct ways. In the first place, it further suggests Hall's indebtedness to the original edition of the *Basilikon Doron* by King James, whose concept of kingship was rendered as if into a nutshell by the skillful literary artist, Hall.[87] The key to Hall's resort to Theophrastus lies in this very familiarity, which he seems to have cultivated with all James's prejudices and pet peeves.

In 1592 Isaac Casaubon had drawn the attention of the academic world to Theophrastus, 'that ancient Master of Morality.'[88] Hall's own penchant for satire probably drew him early towards a reading of Casaubon's rendition of the Greek's characters, each of which was a comic representation of a particular vice. However, it wasn't until 1608 that he tried his hand at the genre. Casaubon also appealed to King James, who had attempted to lure Casaubon to his Scottish court, succeeding instead in bringing him, in 1610, to England. The first invitation was addressed 'to his dearest Casaubon, telling him that, besides the care of the church, it was his fixed resolve to encourage letters and learned men, as he considered them the strength, as well as the ornament, of kingdoms.'[89] By 1608, after James was well installed on the English throne, Casaubon's fame derived not only from his popularization of the classics but his defence of the Protestant Church. His views on church hierarchy and the episcopal form of church government matched those espoused by James. In that same year, it was also reported that on being presented with a copy of Casaubon's latest ecclesiastical offering, *De Liberate Ecclesiastica*, James 'had been so delighted with it, that for many days he could talk of nothing but Casaubon.'[90]

Here, then, I would suggest, we come to the why of Hall's late but timely resort to Theophrastus as a model for moral instruction. James not only favoured certain scholars, such as Casaubon and his type of exegesis, but frowned upon others. He disapproved of certain features in contemporary Tacitism, dismissing the belief that Tacitus 'was a master of political wisdom.' He favoured scholars with tastes like his own. Prime among these was Casaubon, who himself had nothing but contempt for the concept of the 'book-trained politician' that Francis Bacon, for one, spent a lifetime attempting to legitimate.[91] Scholarship certainly had a place in society, Casaubon strongly believed; but scholars should not themselves have political ambition. Himself a scholar content to dedicate his life solely to scholarship, he considered the mixing of careers anathema. From this perspective, of course, the duty inherent in one's station and calling in life was the factor that should guide one's participation in society. Thus a scholar should restrict himself to scholarly enterprises, kings to kingly ones, and moral and religious leaders to the specific tasks of propagating moral and religious teachings.

Joseph Hall clearly shared Casaubon's assumptions about station, vocation, and their limits. Moreover, having been introduced into Prince Henry's court, he could not have failed to notice the vogue among some of its members for Lipsian and Tacitean scholarship, replete with its tendency to make the *arcana* of government available for discussion, not to mention making it accessible to the public.[92] 'Minor' literary figures such as Robert Dallington, Samson Lennard, and John Healey, did just that, and, of these, Hall was at enmity with Dallington and Healey. The latter enjoyed the protection of the Earl of Pembroke, who, while no mean figure in the political culture of the day, was in the midst of his political impasse. From 1607 until 1612, while Salisbury and Northampton acted as helmsmen for the ship of state, Pembroke was excluded from the court, and built instead an association with Queen Anne and the young Prince Henry. In this period, as well, he was busy maintaining the position of prominent patron of English Tacitism at the court of the prince.[93]

The quarrel between Hall and Dallington and Healey took the shape of a series of public and literary ripostes which, individually and on the face of it, look innocuous enough. Dallington had been a Norfolk schoolmaster who aspired to be a *politique*. As early as 1604, after winning employment with the Earl of Rutland, he began to publish travel literature commending the education to be acquired by visits to the Continent.[94] Hall believed that fashion to be pernicious, and he wasted no time in arguing that travel was detrimental to all well-intentioned Englishmen. Not only was his *Mundus Alter et Idem* designed to satirize Lipsius, but in this context of the claims advocated by Dallington for the sophistication to be earned by voyages abroad, it had application even closer to home. Dallington did not limit himself solely to the promotion of travel, however. He had entered the household of Prince Henry, there to embrace the vogue of Tacitism. In 1609, he presented the prince with his manuscript, modelled after Guicciardini and borrowing heavily from Lipsius, *Aphorismes Civill and Militarie*.[95]

Hall's challenge to Dallington was both subtle and of a piece with his repudiation of Bacon. It can be seen in several of his *Epistles*, especially those urging modesty, caution, and uprightness if travelling abroad, and in the *Meditations*, less concerned with travel, but generally comprehending individual ethical conduct. Above all, it appeared in his 'Epistle to the Gentlemen of his Highnesses Court' and his *Characters of Vertues and Vices*, both of which implicitly repudiated the Tacitist concern with revealing (not to mention understanding) the operations of politics and governance. Individual moral uprightness, Hall's *Characters of Vertues and Vices* affirmed, was the goal for which learning should be harnessed. Society had its God-given magistrates to worry about the problems of politics, he seemed to say, especially in the portrait he drew of the 'Good Magistrate' – which was a composite sketch evoking a type of mini-God, embodying all the other virtues Hall had spent half his book describing. In this way, 'The Character of the Good Magistrate' operates not only as an indication of the source of Hall's political ideas (which derived from the king); it also attests to his challenge to Tacitist writers and his attempt to redirect opinion about the character of politics.

Hall's challenge to the Tacitists was not lost on contemporaries. In 1609, John Healey, a client of Pembroke, published an English translation of Hall's *Mundus*, which appeared in that year under the title, *The Discovery of a New World*. Healey took a great many liberties in his translation, and, in particular, he relished elaborating on the political systems Hall had only subtly and minimally described in the original.[96] Healey's English version thereby took on the aspect of a Tacitist discourse, a feature quite absent in the original. He also clearly intended to embarrass Hall by rendering the satire public and available at large. In the introductory epistle he announced, 'I.H. the translator, unto I.H. the Author,' which knowing readers would have no difficulty in translating into 'Iohn Healey' and 'Ioseph Hall' respectively.[97] Healey went on: 'Sir, if the turning of your witty worke into our mother tongue doe distast you, blame not any but your selfe that wrote it: Language doth not alter the state of any thing.'[98] Much as Hall had originally engaged in a parody of Lipsius, Healey now turned the tables on Hall. The satirical mode Healey faithfully adopted in this case was a belligerent act made, perhaps, in response to the growing Tacitean reaction (in England and elsewhere). Healey's response was not unique; in 1612 Traiano Boccalini, reacting to the wave of anti-Tacitism in Europe, released his *Ragguagli di Parnaso*, in which Tacitism and Lipsian neostoicism were reaffirmed with the aid of satire.[99]

The decision to translate and publish Hall's *Mundus Alter et Idem* thus probably arose from a debate over the nature not only of English Tacitism but of English neostoicism (and Hall's position towards both). Healey made clear his adherences by dedicating his translation to the Earl of Pembroke and going on to produce his own version of Theophrastan character-writing and an English translation of the *Manual* of Epictetus – whom Lipsius had called 'the Divine,' and who Bacon, as we have seen, harnessed for advancing his own conception of 'constancy.'[100] Healey had strong reasons for embracing 'constancy' himself; he might well have been the son of a Catholic recusant and was earlier implicated in the Gunpowder Plot of 1605.[101] Whatever the religion of his heart, he became attached and remained faithful to Pembroke until his death in Virginia some few years later. Together with Prince Henry, not to mention in close association with him, Pembroke had come to be viewed as the natural heir to the Sidney/Essex legacy.[102] Hall, as a dutiful subject of the only 'earthen god' he could admit, James, could not and would not become a permanent member of the prince's entourage. Healey and Dallington recognized both his insipid association with Henry's court and his subtle but obstinate criticism of the Tacitism and neostoicism which they embraced.

**Hall, Obedience, and Authority**

By 1611, the year in which his complete edition of *Epistles* appeared, Hall's alternative to Lipsius and others was fully formed. He had appropriated parts of the Lipsian paradigm, adjusted what he perceived to be the objectionable aspects of Lipsian teachings, and completely shed others. He also adopted the idea of 'retiredness and secrecy' from Tacitism – the object of his application being, however, not prudential politics but the conditions that best favoured contemplation.[103] In effect, nevertheless, and quite ironically, the constancy he taught came closer than that of any of his English contemporaries to Lipsius, for the obedience to authority he urged upon all faithfull subjects closely resembled that established in the Lipsian paradigm. In 1605, for example, he recognized that the royal overtures for peace with Spain met with a mixed reaction from the king's subjects. He wrote to Sir Edmund Bacon, who was averse to gestures of friendship towards the Spaniards, and virtually congratulated him on the temporary disgrace that he was then experiencing (probably for the unauthorized trip to Belgium, earlier that year). Thus he was spared the headaches and potential hazards of politics, Hall noted. 'It is an happinesse,' he wrote, 'not to be a witnesse of the mischiefe of the times; which is hard to see, and be guiltlesse.'[104] This was a distinct version of political dissimulation, based on the idea of withdrawal, which was preferable, in Hall's view, to the risk of political division consequent on debate.

Yet he never ceased to call for peace, unity, and harmony in the political nation. In sermons and tracts addressed to separatists and Scottish Presbyterians, Hall defended James's dictum, rendered famous at the Hampton Court Conference, 'No Bishop, No King.' Much as he inspired

Hall's political strictures, James, it seems, also played no small part in shaping Hall's views on church government. Much of Hall's posthumous reputation rests on his strong defences of episcopacy, first made at the behest of James in 1617 in answer to the Scots' apprehension about the imposition of episcopal government on their national church. Hall was not so much commissioned as commanded to reply to the Scots – an order with which he dutifully complied. A similar scenario later formed the immediate backdrop to Hall's encounter with Milton in the aftermath of Hall's obedient response to Archbishop Laud's command that he justify the Laudian Church.[105] Laud saw what King James had earlier discovered; Hall was not so much a born controversialist as a devoted and dutiful servant. Sir Henry Wotton, too, recognized Hall's propensity for 'obedience at any price' when he wrote about Hall's *volte face* concerning the 'reconciliation' between the Churches of Scotland and England. In 1637, after Hall's defence of Laud's view of the church, Wotton remarked to a contemporary,.'I could not but somewhat wonder to find our spiritual Seneca (you know whom I mean) among these reconcilers, having read a former treatise of his (if my memory fails me not) of a contrary complexion.' The irony in Wotton's allusion to Hall as 'our spiritual Seneca' should not be missed – even if the epithet is usually quoted out of context.[106]

That is not to say that acquiescence to each and every policy advocated by his royal or spiritual governors had always characterized Hall's practice. He shunned and despised Tacitist discourse, but there were times when he considered he should alert King James to certain particular responsibilities. While most frequently occupied in praising and magnifying the king, he found occasions to remind the king about the integrity of England and its Protestant church.

Hall made his opposition to Catholicism apparent in both his moral writings and those pamphlets which were direct contributions to religious polemical debate.[107] The issue of Catholicism, however, became critical for Hall after King James entered into negotiations with the Count of Gondomar for a Spanish bride for Prince Charles. Diplomatic overtures began in 1615, and it was not until almost a full decade later that the spectre of such a Spanish match was finally laid to rest for concerned contemporaries. Throughout that period, Hall used every opportunity, and numerous religious parallels from the Old Testament, to alert the devout – including, presumably, the king – of the danger in pursuing this policy, as he began to use the genre of 'contemplation' as a platform for political commentary. Samson and Solomon, both of whom had married out of their faith and, according to the Scriptures, thus brought corruption to the religion of their fathers, were two figures readily harnessed to Hall's purpose. In one of his *Contemplations* of 1615, he expounded upon the case of Samson and stressed the lament of Samson's parents: 'Shall our deliuerance from the Philistims begin in an alliance? Have we bin so scrupulously carefull, that he should eate no vncleane thing, and shall we now consent to an heathenish match?'[108]

The most powerful parallel available for any purpose of regal instruction, however, was that of Solomon, the wise king of old whom James considered a model for his own brand of kingship. In 1609, Hall published *Solomons Divine Arts*, a treatise devoted to explaining the wisdom of Solomon; and on the death of James, he and others would praise him as the British Solomon.[109] In the 1620s, though, Hall was keen to note that even Solomon had been, in the words of Richard McCabe, 'led astray by foreign wives and the result not surprisingly [was] the perversion of true religion.'[110] Hall went to great length to show that, while Solomon himself remained to true to his faith, 'so farre was the vxorious King blinded with affection, that he gaue not passage onely to the Idolatry of his heathenish wiues, but furtherance.' Their 'sins,' as Hall saw it, were Solomon's, because he 'winkt' at their idolatry, and 'his hand aduanced it: Hee that built a Temple to the liuing God, for himselfe and Israel in Sion, built a Temple to Chemosh ... in the very face of Gods House.'[111]

The parallel operating throughout this contemplation is clear enough. Israel could be England, the Temple the Reformed religion of Protestants, Solomon the king, etc., etc. Less obvious in its application is one of *Contemplations* of 1623:

Israel soiourned in Egypt, and brought home a golden calfe: Ieroboam soiournes there, and brought home two; It is hard to dwell in Egypt vntainted; not to sauour of the sinnes of the place we liue in, is no lesse strange, then for wholesome liquor tund up in a musty vessell, not to smell of the cask: The best body may be infected in a contageous aire: Let him beware of Egypt that would be free from Idolatry.[112]

These words can easily be construed to form part of a personal meditation, an admonition to private vigilance lest one's faith wander. Such, after all, was the usual tenor of Hall's *Meditations* and those *Epistles* discussing the perils of travel and teaching the route by which to achieve his brand of fortitude.[113] A number of his *Contemplations*, however, a series of eight volumes appearing between 1612 and 1625, proclaimed their application to the public sphere by the topicality of their analogies. In 1623 Prince Charles and the Duke of Buckingham left on their clandestine trip to Spain in the hope of winning the infanta and returning with her as Charles's bride. In that same year, Hall published his seventh volume of *Contemplations*, which included the words of warning excerpted above. He also performed another act indicating his place in the public dialogue over royal policy. In 1623 he published a sermon delivered to the court, 'The Best Bargaine,' with a dedication to the Earl of Pembroke.

Hall humbly requested that Pembroke 'receiue from the Presse what you vouchsafed to require from my pen.'[114] Conditions and circumstances had obviously altered Hall's attitude towards one who at one time could be esteemed an unworthy patron. In the period of his chaplaincy at the court of Prince Henry, Hall had been at odds with several members of Pembroke's entourage. In those days, and as a patron of Tacitist writers, Pembroke had probably incurred only suspicion from Hall. In the 1620s, Hall's relationship with Pembroke had become more amicable. Not that Pembroke's political stance had altered greatly. Nor for that matter had Hall's. He wholly applauded all the measures advanced by King James in his quest for international peace among nations of diverse religious persuasions. In 1605, as the epistle to Edmund Bacon suggests, Hall might have had reservations about peace with Spain, as he spoke about 'the mischiefe of the times.' Still, he considered that the king's business and in 1613 praised James by noting that he was 'like another Augustus, before the second coming of CHRIST that becalmed the world and shut the iron gates of warre.'[115] What Hall thought about the outbreak of the Thirty Years War is to be discerned from his relative silence on the subject. The sole arbiter for war or peace, he would have said, was the king; in 1624, while so much public discussion was taking place over events in Europe, Hall presented a sermon to the court entitled, 'The True Peace-Maker.'[116]

Hall was only being true to his convictions by refusing to participate in the public dialogue in these instances. He avowed that 'Nothing is more odious, than to make Religion the stalking horse to Policy.'[117] A Catholic match for England's Protestant heir to the throne, however, was a different matter. Crown and Church had mutual duties to each other, he affirmed, and both owed their first allegiance to God and to His worship (through the Reformed Church, which hardly needed stating). Accordingly, in one of his *Contemplations* of 1618, he cautioned that:

Where the Temporal and Spirituall State combine not together, there can follow nothing but distraction in the people: The Prophets receiue and deliuer the will of God, Kings execute it: The Prophets are directed by God, the people are directed by their Kings. Where men doe not see God before them in his Ordinances, their hearts cannot but faile them, both in their respects to their superiors, and their courage in themselues.[118]

The threat posed to the English Church by a royal marriage with Spain thus acted as a catalyst drawing Hall towards Pembroke. The royal authority badly needed some guidance over this issue, which provided one of the rare instances where Hall drew his attention away from his usual task of counselling subjects on how to become model and obedient servants of the king.

Whereas Fulke Greville might have lamented that obedience to authority owed less to love of the sovereign than fear, Hall insisted that fear and love were complementary in a God-fearing society.[119] This he sought to instill in his readers, who eagerly purchased editions of the *Meditations*, *Epistles*, and *Characters* that repeatedly appeared in print.[120] And where Ralegh had been so concerned to promote the validity of royal criticism by insisting that the policy of peace with Spain went against both God and the interests of a Protestant England threatened by Catholic Spain, Hall thought long and hard on how to respond, finally rejecting such an argument by asserting the doctrine of separate spheres. 'Dominion and propriety,' wrote Hall in his *Cases of Conscience* (not published until 1649), 'is not founded in Religion, but in a naturall and civill right.' He went on:

It is true that the Saints have in Christ, the Lord of all things, a spirituall right in all creatures ... but the spirituall right gives a man no title at all to any naturall or civill possession here on earth; yea Christ himself, though both as God, and as Mediator, the whole world were his, yet he tells Pilate, My Kingdom is not of this World; neither did he (though the Lord paramount of this whole earth) by vertue of that transcendent soveraignty put any man out of the possession of one foot of ground which fell to him either by birth or purchase.[121]

By enjoining that the concerns of governance and politics rested solely on the shoulders of magistracy, Hall consistently issued a challenge to the government's critics.

Hall's writings thus appear to amply support Margaret Sampson's claim that by the middle of the seventeenth century, and via 'their preference for preaching up an unrealistic and rigoristic morality,' the English clergy had yielded to secular political thinkers the role of guide of the laity.[122] But perspective, in this case, is all. Hall's teachings were well received by his contemporaries, his influence both far-reaching and long lasting. The extent of the dissemination of his anti-Lipsian teachings – rigoristic morality that they might exude – and their appeal to poets and *literati* have been long known to literary scholars; and his position within the pantheon of English writers can be gauged from a contemporary's observation that 'All men honoured the Doctor, though some loved not the Bishop.'[123] These words give credence to Hall's own view that religion and politics do not mix. Ironically, however, his dual reputation resulted from Hall's lifetime subservience to authority; when he acted upon his own tenets in the 1630s and 1640s, obeying Laud in the defence of the episcopal church, he incurred the wrath of the five Presbyterians who signed themselves 'Smectymnuus' – not to mention John Milton, who proceeded to launch a vehement attack against Hall, suggesting that Hall had not always been the pious divine he purported to be.[124] This episode in the Root and Branch campaign to extirpate episcopacy is famous in the annals of Whig historiography and Miltonian scholarship. But to conclude a study of Hall here is to miss much of Hall's participation in the ongoing events of the day.

By insisting that Hall developed an adaptation of the Lipsian paradigm, the rationale for his actions during the crisis of the 1640s and 1650s becomes clear and those actions look, indeed, very fitting. He obeyed Laud for as long as Laud was there to be obeyed; thereafter, he obeyed the king – again, for as long as the king himself was there to be obeyed. His fidelity to the established power was such that he needed no compulsion to defend Laud's claims of episcopacy by divine right, although for his part in the Parliamentary debates over the place of bishops in the Lords he earned a four-month jail term. While in prison, he composed a testimony called *The Free Prisoner*. The poet Richard Lovelace used an idea in this piece to create lines that would soon become the defeated Cavalier swansong:

> Stone walls do not a prison make,
>     Nor iron bars a cage;
> Minds innocent and quiet take
>     That for an hermitage:
> If I have freedom in my love,
>     And in my soul am free,

> Angels alone that soar above,
>     Enjoy such liberty.[125]

How far these words, even his own *Free Prisoner*, accurately captured Hall's ongoing attitude to events, however, is open to question.

For on his release Hall took up his duties at Norwich, to which he had only just been transferred (before his imprisonment) by King Charles. Hall thought that critics of the king were factional; until royalism was thoroughly defeated in the field and the king executed and episcopacy abolished, he remained faithful to what he considered the 'better part' in the dispute wrenching the nation, not the 'stronger,' as his *Epistle* 'To the Gentlemen of his Highnesses Court,' written so long before, had adumbrated. Not that it was absolutely clear, until 1648 when the king faced his upcoming trial, which in fact would prove the stronger part.

It was, of course, Parliament that emerged victorious. The king was executed, episcopacy was abolished and Hall was deprived of his livings. For what remained of his life (and he did not die until 1656) Hall remained a bishop in all but name, income, and official recognition.[126] Many modern critics would have it that Hall was a man overtaken by time and events, and they suggest that for the days left to him he would remain a relic to a bygone age.[127] But whether history and democracy were indeed on a progressive march, as those same critics have assumed, is quite open to question. What is more certain is that events and circumstances conspired to create the illusion that Hall became a living martyr to the royalist and episcopal cause in the 1650s. True, he was deprived and expelled from his episcopal see. Also, by the late 1640s he was an old man in his seventies – too old, perhaps, to shed old loyalties in order to comply with the dictates of a new authority in the realm, and too public a figure to even contemplate it. The real problem, however, was that nothing was substituted once episcopacy was abolished. Many Englishmen of the time abhorred the vacuum; in the absence of a viable alternative they remained committed, either actively or covertly, to the forbidden practice of 'Anglicanism.'[128]

And what of Hall? These years saw a new outpouring of writings, which were more devotional than ever. It appears that he turned more and more to his own constructed 'hermitage,' his place of 'retirednesse and secrecy,' there to consider and prepare himself for eternity.[129] The question that lingers is whether this was through choice or the circumstances of the day.

In the 1640s, besides his provocative participation in the episcopal debate, Hall had also concerned himself with advocating peace and reconciliation, and with offering spiritual consolation to those who were troubled by the divisions splitting the country. *The Peace-Maker; Laying forth the Right Way of Peace in Matters of Religion* appeared in 1645, and as the title suggests, it concerned the first of his priorities; *The Balme of Gilead: or comforts for the distressed both moral and divine*, concerned the second, and was first printed in 1647, to be reissued in 1655 and 1660. The fateful year of 1649 saw the publication of his *Cases of Conscience*. In it, he examined forty of 'the most common and practical cases,' ten of which were devoted to questions of profit and traffic, ten to life and liberty, another ten to piety and religion, and the last ten to matrimony. We noted above that in one of his cases of piety and religion, Hall appeared to endorse the official peaceful foreign policy and argued against the claims of 'imperialists' following in the footsteps of a Ralegh. Here, as elsewhere, Hall displayed his willingness to divorce religion from politics – if only in consideration of foreign affairs. As long as the Reformed faith was unquestioned at home, Hall saw little reason for allowing matters of disagreement to overflow into separatism, much less civil war.[130] Of greater significance, from the perspective both of Hall's political malleability and the circumstances of the day, is one of his commentaries from his cases of life and liberty.

He considered the very topical issue of 'Whether and in what cases it may be lawful for a man to take away the life of another?' Considering that this piece was published after England had endured seven years of civil war and that the king had recently been executed, it is perhaps surprising that Hall's inquiry was discussed in abstract terms and mainly given over to a host of questions like duelling for honour, abortion, suicide, and bearing witness against others.[131] Even more surprising was Hall's conclusion. He combined the Christian argument of charity with the natural law argument of self-preservation to aver that in a case where a thief or assailant threatened violence to human safety or property, 'the blood that followes is but the unwilling attendant of my defence.'[132] Hall appears to have been acquiescing in the outcome of the Civil Wars. He was not among those numberless royalists who spent the Interregnum in retreat and in lament for the collapse of their cause; the designation 'martyr' was applied to – rather than claimed by – Hall. During those last years of his life he held himself aloof from political discussion and continued to preach and guide his flock through both the written and the spoken word. That he might have been prepared, after all, to come to terms with the outcome of the war is a possibility that has seldom been considered. A tract he composed to address the reaction inspired by Laudian measures in the 1630s, however, is suggestive.

In 1639, in *Certain Irrefragable Propositions* 'concerning Oaths and Covenants,' Hall considered the validity of the Scottish Covenanters' bond to resist the king in his attempt to introduce an English style prayer book into the Church of Scotland and impose Laudian forms onto its pattern of worship. Hall contested the Scots' recourse to a solemn covenant mainly in terms of prior and 'sworn allegeance' to the sovereign. In the summary, he stated:

If therefore any *sworne subject* shall by pretences and perswasions, be drawne to binde himselfe by Oath or Covenant, to determine, establish, or alter any act concerning *matter* of *Religion*, without, or against the allowance of *Soveraign Authority*, the *act* is unlawfull and unjust, and the *party* so ingaged is bound in conscience to reverse and renounce his said act.[133]

Hall was arguing that religion followed from the dictates of the sovereign. The question of Protestantism was not at issue, but the authority of the king was. Many years earlier, and repeatedly, Hall had avowed that religion owed its safety to the king, whose prime responsibility was to safeguard and support it.[134] For subjects to band together to dispute the king's authority and endanger religion was anathema to him. The point that needs stressing, however, is Hall's insistence on 'the allowance of Soveraign Authority' – in this instance, unquestioningly assumed to belong to the king. With the Civil War, and particularly after the king's execution, the problem of defining the locus of sovereign authority took on immense proportions and became a matter of general discussion.[135] Hall's only part in those subsequent debates was indirect, when he examined the validity of killing in general terms and affirmed the right of self-preservation.

During the Interregnum, Hall implicitly accepted the sovereign authority of the Commonwealth. He meekly walked away from his bishop's palace; he ceased to argue for the primacy of episcopacy. He did not fall into any state of apathy and despondency, however; nor did he succumb to frustrated resignation. He remained committed to participation in society and continued to fulfil his pastoral functions; he also began to prepare for a death which held no dread for him.[136] If in 1603 Hall had denied the 'stoical' stress on overcoming the passions, by 1649 his passions, if they were felt, were in 'his steely brest' contained.

Hall outlived those contemporaries with whom he had discussed

English society and politics and argued the merits of a paradigm exemplified by Lipsius. In the end, he alone came close to abiding by the original Lipsian teachings. The irony runs deep. Hall was Lipsius's most indefatigable enemy; relentlessly, he conceived of Lipsius as his most pernicious rival. In his last days, did he finally come to understand and recognize the validity of Lipsian 'constancy'? The European Wars of Religion had provoked Lipsius to assemble his neostoic concept of constancy; the English Revolution, which could not avoid a religious dimension, finally provided the context in which Joseph Hall adopted 'constancy' – the form of civic virtue that enabled him to persist in the changed world that was Interregnum England.

# Epilogue

# Constancy in the English Revolution

With the writings and teachings of Joseph Hall we have come virtually full circle in examining the relevance of the Lipsian paradigm in English political thinking in the late sixteenth and early seventeenth centuries. The thinkers treated here were by no means the only commentators on the virtue of 'constancy,' and on the question of political activity there were specific points of disagreement among those who discussed it – the most critical perhaps arising over the practice of public virtue. But one consistent feature in the writings of the five Englishmen considered here, a feature linking each to the other in the general movement which was English humanism, and serving as well to link their thought back to Lipsius himself, was their unrelenting adherence to political survival and participation – to the precept of the *vita activa*, infused as it was with assumptions about the role of learning in society. The threat to it had provoked the Lipsian synthesis in the first place, when Lipsius was confronted with the traumatic effects of the European Wars of Religion in the 1580s. The tumultuous equivalent in England came in the 1640s with the Civil Wars. As war gave way to a peace that culminated in the establishment of the Commonwealth, the revolutionary outcome was the execution of the king and the abolition of monarchy and the House of Lords. These events precipitated a crisis without precedent in English political culture, provoking the emergence of 'Lipsian' neostoicism in public (and published) polemics. While space precludes a full treatment of this subject here, I would like to point out its application to a republican England in at least two distinct ways.[1]

The first is in the resurgence of 'Tacitism' and its manifestation as the language of open and proud republicanism.[2] Isaac Dorislaus, the Dutch scholar whom Fulke Greville had hoped to install in the first Chair of

History at Cambridge in 1627, helped draw up the charge of treason against Charles I for tyranny over his people. Dorislaus's career in England almost epitomizes the fortunes of English Tacitism. After his dismissal in 1627 for lecturing on 'many dangerous passages' in Tacitus, political debate entered a period of decline which was hastened by the king's dissolution of Parliament in early 1629.[3] In the aftermath of that event came the imprisonment of Sir John Eliot, who had earlier compared the Duke of Buckingham to the devious and sycophantic Sejanus portrayed by Tacitus in his *Annals*. Eliot's invocation of the Sejanus parallel in 1626 was not only the first nail in Eliot's coffin but a critical threat to many 'book-trained' politicians in Caroline England. Eliot suffered imprisonment at the time for the implicit parallel that was extended to the king; if Buckingham was Sejanus, then, Charles believed, he must be taken for Tiberius.[4] Incarcerated again for his misdemeanours in the Parliament of 1629, Eliot was sent a copy of Lipsius's *De constantia* by Sir Robert Cotton. The treatise may well have served as consolation, but Eliot was to die not four years later, still a prisoner in the Tower. Between the two episodes resulting in Eliot's imprisonment, Dorislaus, too, had been to all intents and purposes silenced.[5] Until the eve of the Civil War, Joseph Hall's brand of neostoicism prevailed – and as we have seen there was little of the Tacitist in Hall, who became a bishop in the very year of the royal crackdown on Tacitism. Neostoicism had begun to dissolve into its component parts; Senecan constancy and Tacitean political observations no longer formed part and parcel of the same discursive paradigm.

With the defeat of the king all that changed. His trial was set and charges of tyranny were drawn up by Dorislaus, a Tacitist of the first order. Charles was eventually executed. Nor had Dorislaus been entirely out of the picture in the intervening years. In the words of C.V. Wedgwood, 'since the beginning of the war he had given the benefit of his excellent brain and profound classical and legal knowledge to the King's enemies.' Subsequently he was appointed ambassador of the English Commonwealth to The Hague, where, however, he was 'savagely murdered' by Royalist exiles.[6] Although Dorislaus thus perished soon after he applied (and brought to vivid representation) a Tacitist critique of the reign of Charles I, Tacitism would long outlast this scholar, one of its most devoted proponents.[7]

Two of the most renowned Tacitists of the English Commonwealth period were John Milton and Algernon Sidney. As we saw earlier, it was Milton who recovered Ralegh's Lipsian compilation, *The Cabinet-Council*, and made it public in 1658. Milton hailed Tacitus as 'the greatest possible enemy to tyrants,' and his considered opinion became strengthened in the belief that kingship, or monarchy, in effect produced tyranny.[8] Algernon Sidney became, like Milton, an unrepentant republican during the Commonwealth period. As Jonathan Scott has demonstrated, however, Sidney was by no means the ideologically committed republican that Milton proved to be. In time, he would be as eager to offer his services to the restored Charles II. Although his biographer thus calls his political sensibilities 'relativist,' one of the striking features of Algernon Sidney's activities was his fidelity not to any one form of government, but to the legacy of a family tradition dating back to the 1580s and to Sir Philip, a legacy informed by a critical approach to politics yet an overwhelming commitment to participation.[9]

If the Tacitism that was resuscitated in 1648 was characterized by a sense of republican liberation, that was nevertheless only one of the two faces of political 'constancy' as it was invoked in the wake of the military defeat of the king. By far the most important challenge of the day was the government's need to convince the nation of the validity of the outcome of the Civil War and provide itself with a broadly recognized legitimacy. England's history was closely wrapped up in monarchy; never, not even in folk-memory, had England been without a king.[10] The novelty of the situation and its precariousness was such that the government of the Rump Parliament promulgated a law requiring all members of the political nation to subscribe to an engagement to be 'true and faithful to the Commonwealth of England as it is now established without a king or House of Lords.'[11] Thus was instituted the notorious 'Engagement,' which provoked the most divisive campaign of the century, and which probably superseded the earlier controversies over going to war against the king, disturbing enough to many as they had been.[12]

Into this fray entered Anthony Ascham, Marchamont Nedham, Andrew Marvell, and a certain R. Fletcher – each of whom produced, in one way or another, a neostoic response to the dilemma of the Engagment. Ascham, whose tone was melancholic and detached in his important pamphlet, *Of the Confusions and Revolutions of Governments* (1649), combined a dark Christian religiosity with a blatant call for self-preservation in the face of hostile circumstances. This was Ascham's adaptation of the precept of 'constancy,' in which his polemical voice resembled that of Fulke Greville in his discourse on loyalty, *Letter to an Honourable Lady*. The question Ascham addressed was, of course, the issue of obedience to the *de facto* government then exercising power; de factoism was, as we have seen, implicit in Greville's political thinking.[13]

Despite his rhetoric of disillusionment, Ascham was a firm proponent and a clear example of the commitment to political participation. Like Dorislaus, he met his doom at the hands of Royalist assassins, this time in Spain, where he was about to take up his post as the Commonwealth's ambassador.[14] Ascham's career, however, stands in strict contrast to that of Marchamont Nedham, a survivor of the first order. A journalist and a pithy writer, Nedham used his talents to serve first the party of Parliament, then that of the king, then the Commonwealth, and, later still, the restored monarchy. His flair for what we would call propaganda was based on his use of history, most particularly Roman history, which he diluted with a good dose of biblical *exempla*. Although it has been said that Nedham 'did not so much explore Roman history as raid it,' his technique was clearly the unabashed use of *similitudo temporum*; he applied this in both the government newspaper for which he was editor, *Mercurius Politicus*, and his pamphlet of 1650, *The Case of the Commonwealth of England, Stated*, to convey the need for allegiance to the government of the Rump.[15]

Nedham was a colleague of Milton in these heady days of the Commonwealth's inception, and as Blair Worden has shown, his optimistic republicanism was derivative of Machiavelli, perhaps as much as his historical technique was reminiscent of Lipsius – although one contemporary thought him more a 'politick Shuttle-cock' than a chameleon.[16] Was there also something of the Baconian – not to mention traces of Ralegh – in his style and political outlook? What is certain is that his ebullient prognostication for republican England's role as heir to classical Rome was one of the vital means by which to procure obedience to the government. Another was the discreet use of the idea of *prudentia mixta* –applied less to governors than to subjects, and addressed in particular to those who perceived England's new polity as an oppressive regime that owed its institution to a defiance of all standards of law and right. In the last chapter, we saw that Joseph Hall not only despised Lipsius, he also repudiated similar teachings advanced by others. And he had decried the lamentable perversion of the (horrendous enough) Tacitean precept, *qui nescit dissimulare, nescit regnare*, which in other hands became *qui nescit dissimulare, nescit vivere*. This particular dictum was also mobilized as an argument for obedience. Andrew Marvell, in his 'Horatian Ode,' preferred to evoke the original: the Cromwell he portrayed in the poem is full of the skills that demonstrate 'how fit he is to sway.'[17] Another poet, the enigmatic R. Fletcher, preferred the adaptation, and in a poem of twenty-six stanzas (which he called 'A Short

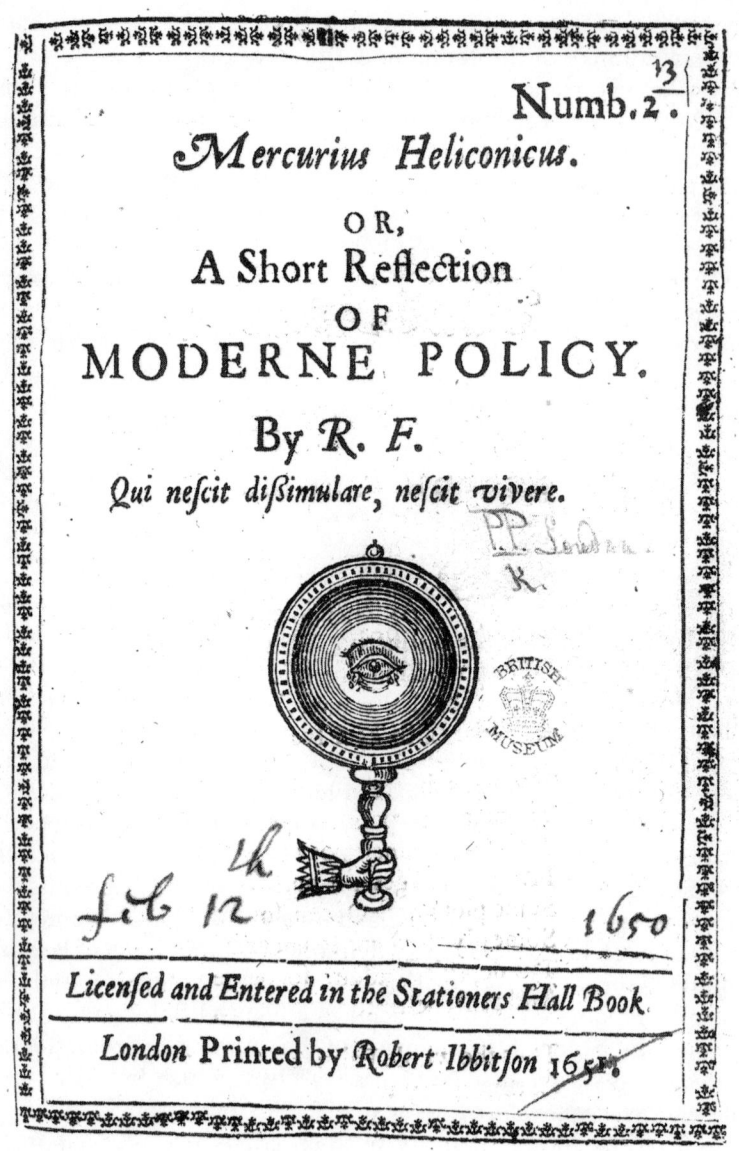

10 Title-page, R. Fletcher, *Mercurius Heliconicus, Or a Short Reflection of Moderne Policy* (Numb. 2) (London, 1650). Thomason Collection, E623 (13). By permission of the British Library.

Reflection of Moderne Policy') argued that obedience was by far the safer response to the new government than outright recalcitrance.[18]

Fletcher's long delineation of the prudential adoption of dissimulation came nowhere close to the sophistication of Marvell's subtle suggestion for obedience, but he shared with all these other polemicists, and if not with Ascham in his writings, at least in his actions, one common feature. Again, as in the common denominator linking the earlier English thinkers, that element was the avowal of the *vita activa* by means of a wealth of historical illustration and the application of scholarship to confirm it. During the Interregnum, and particularly in the wake of the Engagement, this was the principle to be defended, as Royalists, in defeat and despair, sought political oblivion and argued political retreat.

Applications of the Lipsian paradigm in England, therefore, helped maintain not the power of the state, but the idea of the state as being constituted through a body of healthy and fully participating members. From the initial reception of Lipsius by the English in the 1580s and 1590s, to the various 'constant minds' articulated in the first half of the seventeenth century, to the variety of neostoic resolutions to the crisis that descended on the English in the aftermath of the Civil War, the approach to politics first crystallized by Lipsius proved less an instrument to the creation of absolutism, as it did in France; it became, above all, a method by which to evoke the classical form of republicanism, which itself was predicated on and informed by the application of learning to civic participation.

# Notes

**Prologue**

1 The term 'Lipsian paradigm' is borrowed from R.J.W. Evans, who applies it in a very different sense in *Rudolph II and his World: A Study in Intellectual History 1576–1612* (Oxford, 1973), p. 96.
2 See Thomas Kuhn, *The Structure of Scientific Revolutions* (Chicago and London, 1962), pp. 10–11, where he speaks of 'coherent traditions of scientific research,' and goes on: 'The study of paradigms ... is what mainly prepares the student for membership in the particular scientific community within which he will later practise.' From this perspective (and strictly speaking), Lipsius himself participates in a 'humanist paradigm,' as do all others treated in this study.
3 The debate over humanism is discussed below; for the inclusion of 'amateur gentlemen' among its ranks, see David Starkey, 'England,' in *The Renaissance in National Context*, ed. Roy Porter and Mikulas Teich (Cambridge, 1992), p. 153; for leisurely patricians, see David Quint, 'Humanism and Modernity: A Reconsideration of Bruni's *Dialogues*,' *Renaissance Quarterly*, 38 (1985), pp. 423–45.
4 Lipsius's life can be followed in Jason L. Saunders, *Justus Lipsius: The Philosophy of Renaissance Stoicism* (New York, 1955), chap. 1; Mark Morford, *Stoics and Neostoics: Rubens and the Circle of Lipsius* (Princeton, 1991), provides by far the most sensitive and up-to-date account of Lipsius's professional goals and the controversies that surrounded them. For Lipsius's belief in the staying-power of his work, see below p. 26 and n. 111.
5 Saunders, *Justus Lipsius*, p. 22; Gerhard Oestreich, *Neostoicism and the Early Modern State*, trans. David McLintock (Cambridge, 1982), pp. 13, 58. Of course, Latin remained the language of scholarship and diplomacy well into

the seventeenth century, but for an example of the growing preference for the vernacular and widespread interest in the cultivation of languages other than the native and Latin, see *Letters of John Holles 1587–1637*, 3 vols., ed. Peter Seddon (Nottingham, 1975–86). Praise of the vernacular became a cardinal point in much nineteenth-century nationalist scholarship, but more recently, Richard Helgerson has scrutinized the imperial/nationalistic assumptions of a number of important English vernacular writings in *Forms of Nationhood: The Elizabethan Writing of England* (Chicago and London, 1992). Hereafter, to stress the classical nature of Lipsius's endeavour, I use the abbreviated Latin titles of his neostoic texts (*De constantia* and the *Politica*) while quoting from their contemporary English translations.

6 Cf. the epigraph at the opening, which comes from Lipsius's autobiographical letter to Johannes Woverius (October, 1600), in *Justi Lipsi Opera Omnia* (Wesel, 1675), II, pp. 309–15. I have used Saunders's translation (*Justus Lipsius*, p. 57) of the passage at p. 314: 'Corpus & facies non indecora ... os probum, animus verecundus: ingenium docile & capax omnium, excipio Musicam: judicatio collineans & recta: memoria non sine praeceptorum miraculo, etiam in peuro: quae nunc, etsi elanguit, non defecit. Eloquentia nobis prompta, nec sine venere, in publico: privatum, restrecti magis, & minus amoeni. Stili & inventionum faciles: ... In culto, gestu, sermone modici: & exterorum qui Lipsium videbant, saepe requirebant ... ' Cf. also figure 1, showing Lipsius flanked by *Doctrina* (learning) and *Virtus* (virtue), and being crowned by *Fama* (Renown) and *Gloria* (Glory). Lipsius's personal motto, *Moribus Antiquis* (for the morality of antiquity) appears above Lipsius's portrait, and the caption at the bottom speaks of Lipsius's diligence in learning and the pursuit of virtue, and of becoming himself the very image of *Modestia* (Equanimity). This posthumous verse ends by noting that now Lipsius securely wears the plaited crowns of Fame and Glory, while Envy and Odium are suppressed under the feet of the Modest Virgin – an allusion to the controversies in which Lipsius became embroiled over his own religious adherences. For my own approach to the Lipsian texts, see 'A Note on Texts, Sources, Translations and Conventions,' above, pp. xv–xvii.

7 Such an interpretation of Montaigne is challenged by David Lewis Schaefer, *The Political Philosophy of Montaigne* (Ithaca and London, 1990).

8 On the revival of stoicism see below. Tuck, it should be said, fruitfully explored the relationship between Renaissance stoicism and scepticism, indicating its political importance in 'Scepticism and Toleration in the Seventeenth Century,' *Justifying Toleration*, ed. Susan Mendus (Cambridge, 1988), pp. 21–36, and 'Humanism and Political Thought,' *The Impact of Humanism on Western Europe*, ed. Anthony Goodman and Angus MacKay (London and New York, 1990), pp. 43–65.

9   The quotation is from J.H. Elliott, 'Yet Another Crisis?' in *The European Crisis of the 1590's*, ed. Peter Clark (London, 1985), p. 310. See also, I.A.A. Adams, 'The Impact of War,' ibid., p. 276, and for the study on which such assessments are based, Oestreich, *Neostoicism and the Early Modern State*. Such a 'Lipsian moment' is perhaps more historically valid than J.G.A. Pocock's Machiavellian original, argued in *The Machiavellian Moment: Florentine Political Thought and the Atlantic Republican Tradition* (Princeton, 1975). See Cesare Vasoli's review of Pocock, '*The Machiavelian Moment*: A Grand Ideological Synthesis,' *Journal of Modern History*, 49 (1977), pp. 661–70.
10  '... unius tamen Machiavelli ingenium non contemno, acre, subtile, igneum: et qui utinam Principem suum recta duxisset ad templum illud virtutis et honoris.' *Politicorum sive civilis doctrinae libri sex* (London, 1590; STC 15700.7), pp. 8–9. ('Yet I do not belittle Machiavelli's singular genius, which is sharpe, subtle and fiery; and he who rightly uses his *Prince* will be guided to that temple of virtue and honour.') Machiavelli's impact on early modern readers has recently been revisited by Victoria Kahn in *Machiavellian Rhetoric. From the Counter-Reformation to Milton* (Princeton, 1994).
11  'Stoicism and Roman Example: Seneca and Tacitus in Jacobean England,' *Journal of the History of Ideas*, 50 (1989), pp. 199–225; cf. Blair Worden, 'Constancy,' *London Review of Books*, 20 January–2 February 1983, pp. 13–14. In his otherwise excellent study *Politics and Ideology in England 1603–1640* (London, 1986), J.P. Sommerville has nothing at all to say about the relevance of Lipsian doctrines, a major omission in a book that highlights the main traditions of English political discussion prior to the outbreak of the Civil War; more recently Lisa Ferraro Parmelee has offered something of a rejoinder to Professor Salmon through her 'Neostoicism and Absolution in Late Elizabethan England,' in *Politics, Ideology and the Law in Early Modern Europe*, ed. A.E. Bakos (Rochester, 1994), pp. 3–19.
12  See, for instance, Jill Kraye, 'Moral Philosophy,' *The Cambridge History of Renaissance Philosophy*, ed. Charles B. Schmitt et al. (Cambridge, 1988), pp. 370–4; cf. Giles D. Monsarrat, *Light From the Porch: Stoicism and English Renaissance Literature* (Paris, 1984). The literature on the subject goes back at least to L. Zanta, *La Renaissance du Stoïcisme au XVIe Siècle* (Paris, 1914).
13  Robert P. Adams, *The Better Part of Valor: More, Colet, and Vives, on Humanism, War, and Peace, 1496–1535* (Seattle, 1962), p. 9, goes so far as to characterize humanism as a 'neo-Stoic' phenomenon. For how far stoic principles pervaded life-writing in the early modern period, see *The Rhetorics of Life-Writing in Early Modern Europe*, ed. T.F. Mayer and D.R. Woolf (Ann Arbor, 1995). Cf. also Peter Burke, 'Tacitism, Scepticism, and Reason of State,' *Cambridge History of Political Thought 1450–1700*, ed. J.H. Burns with Mark Goldie (Cambridge, 1991), pp. 479–98.

14 *The Life and Letters of Sir Henry Wotton*, ed. L.P. Smith (Oxford, 1907), II, p. 370.
15 My justification for this approach will emerge in the following discussion. The principle of 'unintended consequences' has, of course, been applied by (among others) Christopher Hill in his revision of the impact of early-modern radicalism on England's post-1660s history. See his 'A Bourgeois Revolution?' In *Three British Revolutions: 1641, 1688, 1776*, ed. J.G.A. Pocock (Princeton, 1980), pp. 109–39.
16 Mark Morford, *Stoics and Neostoics*, pp. 78–84, analyses the basis of these attacks, especially that launched by Pieter Burman in the early eighteenth century, which characterizes Lipsius's posthumous reputation.
17 P.O. Kristeller summarizes his interpretation in 'Humanism,' *Cambridge History of Renaissance Philosophy*, ed. Schmitt, et al., pp. 113–37. The classic statement on civic humanism is Hans Baron, *The Crisis of the Early Italian Renaissance*, 2nd ed. (Princeton, 1966); for a useful summary of both the criticisms provoked by Baron and a modification of his thesis, see Anthony Grafton, 'Humanism and Political Theory,' *Cambridge History of Political Thought*, ed. Burns, pp. 9–29. For Bouwsma, see *The Culture of Renaissance Humanism* (Washington, 1973), and 'The Spirituality of Renaissance Humanism,' *Christian Spirituality*, vol. 2, ed. Jill Raitt (New York, 1988), pp. 236–52. Javitch's variation is expressed in *Poetry and Courtliness in Renaissance England* (Princeton, 1978); and for Levy's adaptation, see Francis Bacon, *The History of the Reign of King Henry the Seventh*, ed. F.J. Levy (Indianapolis, 1972), p. 2, n. 1. Delio Cantimore, 'Rhetoric and Politics in Italian Humanism,' trans. Frances A. Yates, *Journal of the Warburg and Courtauld Institutes*, I (1937–8), pp. 83–102, remains of enduring value.
18 Alistair Fox, 'Facts and Fallacies: Interpreting English Humanism,' *Reassessing the Henrician Age: Humanism, Politics and Reform 1500–1550*, ed. Alistair Fox and John Guy (Oxford, 1986), pp. 9–33.
19 Cf. Charles Trinkaus, 'Introduction,' *The Scope of Renaissance Humanism* (Ann Arbor, 1983), pp. xviii–xix, and his 'Renaissance Ideas and the Idea of the Renaissance,' *Journal of the History of Ideas*, 51 (1990), pp. 667–84.
20 David Starkey, 'England,' *The Renaissance in National Context*, ed. Porter and Teich, pp. 146–63.
21 James D. Tracy, 'Humanism and the Reformation,' *Reformation Europe: A Guide to Research*, ed. Steven Ozment (St. Louis, 1982), p. 40.
22 Cameron, 'Humanism in the Low Countries,' *The Impact of Humanism on Western Europe*, ed. Goodman & MacKay, p. 155.
23 See Alistair Fox, 'Facts and Fallacies,' pp. 27–8.
24 Andrew Lockyer, '"Traditions" as Context in the History of Political Theory,' *Political Studies*, 27 (1979), p. 216. Cf. Trinkaus: 'What should be remembered,

though frequently forgotten, is that humanism must inevitably be studied individual by individual, generation by generation, region by region, aspect by aspect.' In 'Renaissance Humanism, Its Formation and Development,' *The Scope of Renaissance Humanism*, p. 21.

25 See Trinkaus, ibid., pp. 27–8, and Brian Vickers, 'Leisure and Idleness in the Renaissance: The Ambivalence of *Otium*,' *Renaissance Studies*, 4.1 (1990), pp. 1–37, and 4.2 (1990), pp. 107–54. Cf. the difference between Lipsius and Machiavelli in regard to this point and as suggested in the Introduction to *Machiavelli and the Discourse of Literature*, ed. Albert Russell Ascoli and Victoria Kahn (Ithaca and London, 1993), pp. 5–8.

26 J.H. Elliott, *Richelieu and Olivares* (Cambridge, 1984), p. 25; J.G.A. Pocock, 'The Concept of a Language and the *Métier d'Historien*: Some Considerations on Practice,' *The Languages of Political Theory in Early-Modern Europe*, ed. Anthony Pagden (Cambridge, 1987), p. 21.

27 The study of 'influence,' while itself an issue of current controversy, is something of a futile endeavour since the concept of imitation was pervasive in the early modern period and few writers acknowledged their intellectual debts. For the current controversy, see Conal Condren, *The Status and Appraisal of Classic Texts: An Essay on Political Theory, Its Inheritance, and the History of Ideas* (Princeton, 1985). For the problem of relating 'outside' ideas to English thinkers in light of current historiographical trends, see Johann P. Sommerville, 'English and European Political Ideas in the Early Seventeenth Century: Revisionism and the Case of Absolution,' *Journal of British Studies*, 35 (April, 1996), pp. 168–94.

28 The charge of rigidity can be made against Pocock's method and has often been levied against Quentin Skinner's, which is in a constant state of refinement. His most important methodological essays have been collected in *Meaning and Context: Quentin Skinner and his Critics*, ed. James Tully (Princeton, 1988). Under the editorial eye of Skinner and others, Cambridge University Press has devoted a whole series to such 'Ideas in Context.' Launched in 1984, two recent titles bear upon themes I pursue in this study but reflect the 'transformation / transmutation over time' approach characterized by Skinner and his students. See Maurizio Viroli, *From Politics to Reason of State: The Acquisition and Transformation of the Language of Politics 1250–1600* (Cambridge, 1992), and Markku Peltonen, *Classical Humanism and Republicanism in English Political Thought 1570–1640* (Cambridge, 1995). To bolster the linguistic approach to the history of ideas but prevent in particular a resemblance to Nietszche's 'prison-house of language,' Andrew Lockyer has proposed the idea of continuing discourse in '"Traditions" as Context.' Condren offers the alternative of 'usage,' which allows more scope for adapta-

tions of language by receivers (see *The Status and Appraisal of Classic Texts*, pp. 133–8).

29 Kevin Sharpe discusses this theme in his Introduction to *Faction and Parliament: Essays in Early Stuart History*, ed. Sharpe (Oxford, 1978); see also Mark Curtis, 'The Alienated Intellectuals of Early Stuart England,' *Past and Present*, 23 (1962), pp. 25–43, and the important collection of essays in *The Reign of Elizabeth I: Court and Culture in the Last Decade*, ed. John Guy (Cambridge, 1995).

30 Kenneth Burke, *The Philosophy of Literary Form: Studies in Symbolic Action*, 3rd ed. (1941; Berkeley, 1973), p. 1. Emphasis in the original.

31 As T.F. Mayer has noted in *Thomas Starkey and the Commonweal: Humanist Politics and Religion in the Reign of Henry VIII* (Cambridge, 1989), p. 10, 'the vital point is that emphasis throughout must fall on redressing the balance between individual and tradition, as Condren insists, on how [an author] used the materials available to him, not the materials.' Mayer's subject, of course, is Starkey; his reference is to Condren's *Status and Appraisal of Classic Texts*, p. 136.

32 Lockyer, '"Traditions" as Context,' p. 219. For the importance of a *Sitz-im-Leben* approach, see Tracy, 'Humanism and the Reformation,' p. 42; Richard Tuck, *Natural Rights Theories*, (Cambridge, 1979), p. 4; and Mayer, *Thomas Starkey and the Commonweal*, p. 9. And for a recent restatement of the relevance of non-discursive contexts for recovering unspoken assumptions, see David Wootton (ed.), *Divine Right and Democracy: An Anthology of Political Writing in Stuart England* (Harmondsworth, 1986), p. 13.

33 This has recently been reiterated by Cleanth Brooks, *Historical Evidence and the Reading of Seventeenth-Century Poetry* (Columbia and London, 1991). Offsetting this approach, and offering some pertinent comments about it, are Terry Eagleton, *Literary Theory: An Introduction* (Oxford, 1983), and Anthony Easthope, *Literary into Cultural Studies* (London, 1991). Beyond theory, though taking account of it, see the recent essay by Christopher Wortham, 'Shakespeare, James I and the Matter of Britain,' *English* 45. 182 (summer, 1996), pp. 97–122.

34 The relation between an author's life and the text is particularly condemned by followers of Derrida's brand of deconstruction (see Dominick LaCapra, 'Rethinking Intellectual History and Reading Texts,' *Modern European Intellectual History*, ed. LaCapra and Steven L. Kaplan (Ithaca and London, 1982), pp. 60–1). For a response and a reminder of the aesthetic question, see Donald R. Kelley, 'What is Happening to the History of Ideas?' *Journal of the History of Ideas*, 51 (1990), pp. 20–2.

35 Harold Bloom, 'The Breaking of Form,' *Deconstruction and Criticism*, ed.

Bloom et al. (London, 1979), p. 7; Dante's guide is cited by B. Reynolds, Introduction, *The Divine Comedy, vol. 3, Paradise* (Harmondsworth, 1962), p. 45.
36 Sharpe and Lake (eds.), *Culture and Politics in Early Stuart England* (London, 1994), p. 13.
37 Jonathan Scott, *Algernon Sidney and the English Republic, 1623–1677* (Cambridge, 1988), p. 15. Emphasis added.
38 See *Oxford Today*, vol. 8, no. 2 (1996), p. 3.
39 If my overall argument is at all persuasive, historians and literary critics concentrating on the later part of the seventeenth century will have to rethink their own assumptions. For instance, Derek Hirst has recently written that: 'The conviction that hypocrisy was the very stuff of politics drives Samuel Butler's *Hudibras* of 1663, a work that caught the national mood ... Butler's conviction would have been untenable a generation earlier.' See Hirst, 'Locating the 1650s in England's Seventeenth Century,' *History* vol. 81 no. 263 (July, 1996), p. 368. Also of relevance to such a view is Katharine Eisaman Maus, *Inwardness and Theater in the English Renaissance* (Chicago and London, 1995).

## Introduction

1 For Lipsius's works and their various editions, see F. van der Haeghen, *Bibliographie Lipsienne*, 3 vols. (Ghent, 1886–88). Lipsius as a philosopher is examined by Jason Lewis Saunders, *Justus Lipsius: The Philosophy of Renaissance Stoicism* (New York, 1955); and his life and teachings receive a sensitive yet critical treatment in Mark Morford, *Stoics and Neostoics: Rubens and the Circle of Lipsius* (Princeton, 1991). For Lipsius as a political philosopher and the founder of a movement that changed the face of early modern politics, see Gerhard Oestreich, *Neostoicism and the Early Modern State*, ed. Brigitta Oestreich and H.G. Koenigsberger, trans. David McLintock (Cambridge, 1982).
2 The pervasive nature of these ideas is brought out in many of the essays in *The Rhetorics of Life-Writing in Early Modern Europe: Forms of Biography from Cassandra Fedele to Louis XIV*, ed. Thomas F. Mayer and D.R. Woolf (Ann Arbor, 1995).
3 See the introductory remarks by Kirk in *Tvvo Bookes of Constancie Written in Latine by Iustus Lipsius*, Englished by Sir John Stradling, ed. Rudolph Kirk (New Brunswick, N.J., 1939), pp. 13–30. Stradling's, in 1595, was the first English translation of *De constantia*, and he noted in his 'Epistle to the Reader' the 'unaccustomed yet most familiar manner' of the work (*STC* 15695). In 1654, the title-page of a new translation by 'R.G.' entitled, *A Discourse of Constancy: In Two Books. Written in Latin by Justus Lipsius* (*STC* [ed. Wing] L 2359), carried a quotation from Boethius.

4 For the revival of stoicism in the sixteenth century, see L. Zanta, *La Renaissance du Stoïcisme au XVIe Siècle* (Paris, 1914). Hiram Haydn, in *The Counter-Renaissance* (New York, 1950), discerns two major kinds of stoicism in Renaissance Europe; for his definitions, see p. 55. The pervasive influence of stoicism in early modern political thought is charted in Quentin Skinner, *The Foundations of Modern Political Thought*, 2 vols. (Cambridge, 1978), and Richard Tuck, *Philosophy and Government 1572–1651* (Cambridge, 1993); Margo Todd, *Christian Humanism and the Puritan Social Order* (Cambridge, 1987), chaps. 2–3, charts the incorporation of stoicism into humanist (and later, Puritan) social and educational programs.

5 *Of Clemencie*, in *The Workes of Lvcivs Annaevs Seneca*, trans. Thomas Lodge (London, 1614; STC 22213), Book I, chaps. 3–4, pp. 585–6. For more on this theme, see Margo Todd, 'Seneca and the Protestant Mind: The Influence of Stoicism on Puritan Ethics,' *Archiv für Reformationsgeschichte*, 74 (1983), pp. 182–99.

6 See Marjorie O'Rourke Boyle, *Rhetoric and Reform: Erasmus' Civil Dispute with Luther* (Cambridge, MA, and London, 1983); cf. Victoria Kahn, *Rhetoric, Prudence, and Skepticism in the Renaissance* (Ithaca and London, 1985), pp. 89–114 and passim. For the view that Erasmian humanism scarcely exhibited the features of a movement, see the essays by Alistair Fox in *Reassessing the Henrician Age: Humanism, Politics and Reform*, ed. Alistair Fox and John Guy (Oxford, 1986).

7 See Jozef Ijsewijn, 'The Coming of Humanism to the Low Countries,' *Itinerarium Italicum: The Profile of the Italian Renaissance in the Mirror of Its European Transformations*, ed. Heiko A. Oberman with Thomas A. Brady, Jr. (Leiden, 1975), pp. 193–301.

8 See G.W. Pigman III, 'Imitation and the Renaissance Sense of the Past: The Reception of Erasmus' "*Ciceronianus*",' *Journal of Medieval and Renaissance Studies*, 9 (1979), pp. 155–77; cf. Charles Trinkaus, '*Antiquitas* versus *Modernitas*: An Italian Humanist Polemic and Its Resonance,' *Journal of the History of Ideas*, 48 (1987), pp. 11–21. The factor of 'modernity' in humanists, *quatroccento* and Northern European alike, provokes literary critics like David Quint and Victoria Kahn to chart the demise of humanism. See Quint, 'Humanism and Modernity: A Reconsideration of Bruni's *Dialogues*,' *Renaissance Quarterly*, 38 (1985), pp. 423–45 and Kahn, *Rhetoric, Prudence, and Skepticism in the Renaissance*.

9 Lipsius, *A Discourse of Constancy in Two Books*, trans. Nathaniel Wanley (London, 1670; STC [ed. Wing] L 2360), 'Justus Lipsius To the Reader.' Lipsius's prefaces to *De constantia* were not included in any English translation until this edition appeared; the 'Ad Lectorum' in the 1584 edition of *De Constantia*

began by drawing attention to 'this new way of writing' ('in nouo hoc scribe[n]di genera' [sig. *3]). Lipsius also noted that others would have to confess their indebtedness to him for setting out this method and manner of writing: 'Rem, inuentionem, ordinem videant: Mihi ea debere fatebuntur.' Lipsius's method, and the importance of its novelty, will be treated below.

10 *Tvvo Bookes of Constancie*, trans. Sir John Stradling (1595; *STC* 15695), I, v, p. 10. Further references in the text refer to this edition.
11 A useful summary of the stoic concept of reason is given by Giles D. Monsarrat, *Light from the Porch: Stoicism and English Renaissance Literature* (Paris, 1984), pp. 9–19.
12 See Eco Haitsma Mulier, 'The Language of Seventeenth-Century Republicanism in the United Provinces: Dutch or European?' in *The Languages of Political Theory in Early-Modern Europe*, Anthony Pagden (Cambridge, 1987), pp. 175–95; Herbert H. Rowen, 'The Dutch Revolt: What Kind of Revolution?' *Renaissance Quarterly*, 43 (1990), pp. 570–90, and the same author's 'The Dutch Republic and the Idea of Freedom,' in *Republicanism, Liberty, and Commercial Society, 1649–1776*, ed. David Wootton (Stanford, 1994), especially pp. 310–14. See also Geoffrey Parker, *The Dutch Revolt* (Ithaca, 1977), and from a sociological point of view, Sherrin Marshall, *The Dutch Gentry, 1500–1650: Family, Faith, and Fortune* (New York and London, 1987).
13 In *Philosophy and Government*, pp. 52–6, Richard Tuck prefers to stress Lipsius's engagement with Renaissance (or psychological) scepticism, but for Lipsius's ongoing interest in reconciling Christianity and stoicism, see Saunders, *Justus Lipsius*, chap. 4; Henry Ettinghausen in 'Neo-Stoicism in Pictures: Lipsius and the Engraved Title-Page and Portrait in Quevedo's "Epicteto y Philocilides",' *Modern Language Review*, 46 (1971), pp. 94–100, and in *Francisco de Quevedo and the Neostoic Movement* (Oxford, 1972), argues that not Lipsius but his Spanish disciple succeeded in reconciling the two doctrines.
14 I quote from and refer in the notes to the English translation by William Jones, *Six Bookes of Politickes or Civil Doctrine, Written in Latine by Iustus Lipsius* (London, 1594; *STC* 15701). Quotations at I, ii, p. 2.
15 See Étienne Gilson, *Reason and Revelation in the Middle Ages* (New York, 1966); Robert Hoopes, *Right Reason in the English Renaissance* (Cambridge, MA, 1962), pp. 96–114; Haydn, *The Counter-Renaissance*, passim; and Kristin Zapalac, *'In His Image and Likeness': Political Iconography and Religious Change in Regensburg, 1500–1600* (Ithaca & London, 1990), chap. 2. In '"Have You Read Lipsius?": Thomas Middleton and Stoicism,' *English Studies*, 77.5 (1996), pp. 401–21, A.A. Bromham discusses the perpetuation of the same issue among the English, courtesy of the influence of Lipsius's writings.
16 Cf. Robert Bireley, *The Counter-Reformation Prince* (Chapel Hill and London,

1990), p. 77: 'Lipsius's doctrine on providence is most important if he is to be understood as an anti-Machiavellian.'
17 While he did not ignore the older Greek variety, Lipsius favoured Roman stoicism, particularly as it had been enunciated by Cicero, Seneca, and Epictetus. For the shifts and debates that occurred in the stoic concept of 'God,' see J.M. Rist, *Stoic Philosophy* (Cambridge, 1969), pp. 152–79; see also Robert B. Todd, 'Monism and Immanence: The Foundations of Stoic Physics,' *The Stoics*, ed. John M. Rist (Berkeley, Los Angeles and London, 1978), pp. 137–60, and Michael Lapidge, 'Stoic Cosmology,' ibid., pp. 161–85.
18 See for example *Tvvo Bookes of Constancie*, trans. Stradling, I, xviii, p. 45 and II, ii–iiii, pp. 65–9. I take up this argument below.
19 Boyle, *Rhetoric and Reform*, passim; cf. Zapalac, '*In His Image and Likeness*,' and James D. Tracy, 'Two Erasmuses, Two Luthers: Erasmus' Strategy in Defense of *De Libero Arbitrio*,' *Archiv für Reformationsgeschichte*, 78 (1987), pp. 37–59.
20 The garden setting, or an equivalent, had become almost de rigeur in Renaissance humanist dialogue, which originated with Cicero. See Michel Ruch, *Le Préamble dans les Oeuvres Philosophiques de Ciceron: Essai sur la Genèse et l'Art du Dialogue* (Paris, 1958), pp. 80–2, 197–202.
21 *Institutes*, III, viii, 9. For the tensions in Christian stoicism, see W.J. Bouwsma, 'The Two Faces of Humanism: Stoicism and Augustinianism in Renaissance Thought,' *Itinerarium Italicum*, ed. Oberman and Brady, Jr., pp. 3–60; and for Calvin's relationship with humanism, see Bouwsma, *John Calvin: A Sixteenth Century Portrait* (New York, 1988).
22 For instance, the work of du Plessis-Mornay, which is briefly discussed below, chap. 4. See also, for English Calvinists, Geoffrey Aggeler, '"Sparkes of Holy Things": Neostoicism and the English Protestant Conscience,' *Renaissance and Reformation*, 26. 3 (1990), pp. 223–40.
23 See, for example, *Tvvo Bookes of Constancie*, I, vii and I, xii. In his address to the reader, Lipsius inveighed against his contemporaries, who he said, 'use philosophy as a diversion, not as a medicine.' ('Habent eam ut oblectamentum, non ut remedium.' *De Constantia* (Antwerp, 1584), Ad Lectorem, n.p.) Mark Morford, in *Stoics and Neostoics*, pp. 14–95, notes that the father–son conceit, understood as the Roman concept of 'contubernium' (pp. 15–16), was the informing principle in Lipsius's most valued relationships. For the father-son technique in humanist dialogue, cf. the argument by David Quint in 'Humanism and Modernity,' and Ernst Robert Curtius, *European Literature and the Latin Middle Ages*, trans. Willard R. Trask (New York, 1953), pp. 98–101. For more on the medical analogy, see below, pp. 15–16.
24 For humility as a literary technique, see Curtius, *European Literature*, pp. 83–5, and Kahn, *Rhetoric, Prudence, and Skepticism in the Renaissance*, p. 77.

25 Hadrian Saravia certainly concluded so, in a letter to James I, in 1608. See Leon Voet, *The Golden Compasses: A History and Evaluation of the Printing and Publishing Activities of the Officina Plantiniana at Antwerp*, 2 vols. (Amsterdam, London, and New York, 1969), I, p. 23. See also Leonard Forster, 'Lipsius and Renaissance Neostoicism,' *Festschrift for Ralph Farrell*, ed. Anthony Stephens, H.L. Rogers, and Brian Cloghan (Bern, 1977), pp. 201–20, and cf. Anthony Grafton, 'Portrait of Justus Lipsius,' *American Scholar*, 56 (1986–87), pp. 382–90. Jason Saunders, *Justus Lipsius*, pp. 19 and 58, argues that religion meant little to Lipsius.

26 H.N., *An Introduction to the Holy Understanding of the Glasse of Righteousnesse* (Cologne, 1575; rept. London, 1649), pp. 7, 20, as quoted and cited in William C. Johnson, 'The Family of Love in Stuart Literature: A Chronology of Name-Crossed Lovers,' *Journal of Medieval and Renaissance Studies*, 7. 1 (1977), pp. 95–112. See also Rufus M. Jones, *Studies in Mystical Religion* (London, 1909); George H. Williams, *The Radical Reformation* (Philadelphia, 1962); Alistair Hamilton, *The Family of Love* (Cambridge, 1981); Jean D. Moss, *'Godded with God': Hendrik Niclaes and His Family Of Love* (Philadelphia, 1981); Christopher W. Marsh, *The Family of Love in English Society, 1550–1630* (Cambridge, 1994); and for the Netherlands in particular, B. Rekers, *Benito Arias Montano (1527–1598)* (London and Leiden, 1972).

27 J. Lecler, 'Les Origines et le Sens de la Formule *Cujus Regio, Ejus Religio*,' in *Recherches de Science Religieuse*, 38. 1 (1951/52), pp. 119–31. 'Whereever he rules, his is the religion of state.' Cf. Rowen, 'The Dutch Republic and the Idea of Freedom,' *Republicanism, Liberty, and Commercial Society*, ed. Wootton, p. 314, noting the particularities of religion in the Netherlands.

28 Besides those sources given in n 26, above, see also Perez Zagorin, *Ways of Lying: Dissimulation, Persecution, and Conformity in Early Modern Europe* (Cambridge, MA, and London, 1990), pp. 116–30.

29 This point is heavily stressed by Oestreich in *Neostoicism and the Early Modern State*, but by referring to the later *Manductio*, Tuck argues that Lipsius deftly avoided engaging with justice as a cardinal virtue. See *Philosophy and Government*, pp. 50–6, where Tuck argues Lipsius's position in exploring an ideology of self-interest. Tuck's argument here is based less on references found in Lipsius's writings than those from Cicero and others. For Lipsius's discussion of the issue, see *Tvvo Bookes of Constancie*, I, xx–xxii, pp. 51–7, quotations at p. 57.

30 Malvezzi, *Davide Perseguitato* (Bologna, 1634), p. 3. For the context of this quotation, see Carlo Ginzburg, 'High and Low: The Theme of Forbidden Knowledge in the Sixteenth and Seventeenth Centuries,' *Past & Present*, 73 (1976), pp. 28–41. In another work written towards the end of his life, Lipsius

maintained that religion was the cement that held society together. Without religion, he wrote, 'the Prince cannot perform his office ... ; without it society cannot exist, for where there is no faith, there is no justice, no virtue, but only fraud, license, perversity, and, in a word, confusion among mankind and all things.' (*Monita et Exempla Politica Libri Duo* (1605), in *Opera* (1675), IV, p. 129: 'Sine ea, non Princeps officium suum ... ; sine ea, societas non erit, quia non fides, non Justitia, non virtus; sed fraus, licentia, protervitas, &, uno verbo, confusio hominum ac rerum.')

31 Cf. Zagorin, *Ways of Lying*, pp. 7, 122–5; for the emergence of religious ideology, see Donald R. Kelley, *The Beginning of Ideology: Consciousness and Society in the French Reformation* (Cambridge, 1981).

32 See the standard approach to toleration in Henry Kamen, *The Rise of Toleration* (London, 1967), Joseph Lecler, *Toleration and the Reformation*, trans. T.L. Westow, 2 vols. (New York, 1960), and D.P. Walker, *The Decline of Hell* (London, 1964).

33 Mario Turchetti, 'Religious Concord and Political Tolerance in Sixteenth- and Seventeenth-Century France,' *Sixteenth Century Journal*, 22 (1991), pp. 15–25; Benjamin J. Kaplan, 'Dutch Particularism and the Calvinist Quest for "Holy Uniformity",' *Archiv für Reformationsgeschichte*, 82 (1991), pp. 239–55, and the same author's *Calvinists and Libertines: Confession and Community in Utrecht, 1578–1620* (New York, 1995); Delio Cantimore, 'Submission and Conformity: "Nicodemism" and the Expectations of a Conciliar Solution to the Religious Question,' trans. and ed. Eric Cochrane, *The Late Italian Renaissance 1525–1630* (New York and London, 1970), pp. 244–65; and James D. Tracy, 'With and Without the Counter-Reformation: The Catholic Church in the Spanish Netherlands and the Dutch Republic, 1580–1650,' *Catholic Historical Review*, 71 (1985), pp. 547–72. Cf. W. Nijenhuis, 'Variants Within Dutch Calvinism in the Sixteenth Century,' *The Low Countries History Yearbook*, 12 (1979), pp. 48–64.

34 *Sixe Bookes of Politickes*, IV, iii, pp. 64–5; see also Richard Tuck, 'Scepticism and Toleration in the Seventeenth Century,' *Justifying Toleration*, ed. Susan Mendus (Cambridge, 1987), pp. 21–36, and cf. Bireley, *The Counter-Reformation Prince*, pp. 74–5, who, however, does not take into account the strong possibility of Lipsius's attachment to Familism. Lipsius's pronouncements on the issue sparked the controversy examined by (among others) Francine De Nave, 'De polemiek tussen Justus Lipsius en Dirck Volckertsyn Coornheert (1590),' *De Gulden Passer*, 48 (1970), pp. 1–40; see also below, p. 15.

35 In stressing the role of philosophical scepticism in Lipsian thought, Richard Tuck underestimates, I think, Lipsius's general address to a Christian audience; and in neglecting the role of both Tacitus and Tacitean language in *De*

*constantia*, Tuck himself overlooks both the role of rhetoric in Lipsius's writings and how the marriage of Tacitism and stoicism was actually effected by Lipsius. See *Philosophy and Government*, pp. 45–64.

36 Cf. Blair Worden, in his review of *Neostoicism and the Early Modern State*, in *London Review of Books*, 20 January – 3 February 1983, pp. 13–14. The eclectic nature of early modern borrowings (for which see Hanna H. Gray, 'Renaissance Humanism: The Pursuit of Eloquence,' *Journal of the History of Ideas*, 24 [1963], pp. 506–7) renders our search for philosophic consistency in Lipsius, who never claimed to be a stoic, somewhat redundant.

37 This is not to say that it was all or in most part good. In both his biography of his father-in-law, *De Vita Ivlii Agricolae*, and his *Annals*, Tacitus considered the stoics as lacking in the qualities that Rome required, qualities, moreover, that Agricola had personified. See, B. Walker, *The Annals of Tacitus: A Study in the Writing of History* (Manchester, 1952), pp. 176–239, and Ronald Syme *Tacitus*, 2 vols. (Oxford, 1958), II, pp. 520–65.

38 Quentin Skinner, 'Thomas Hobbes: Rhetoric and the Construction of Morality,' *Proceedings of the British Academy*, 76 (1990), pp. 9–10. On this issue, see also Mark Morford, 'Tacitean *Prudentia* and the Doctrines of Justus Lipsius,' in *Tacitus and the Tacitean Tradition*, ed. T.J. Luce and A.J. Woodman (Princeton, 1993), pp. 129–51, who notes how far Lipsius falls from the standards set by Tacitus.

39 Lipsius's efforts to maintain relations with both sides of the religious divide can be seen from his letters; see A. Gerlo and H.D.L. Vervliet, *Inventaire de la correspondence de Juste Lipse, 1564–1606* (Antwerp, 1968). His correspondence to Spaniards has been collected, edited, and translated by Alejandro Ramirez: *Epistolario de Justo Lipsio y Los Espanioles (1577–1606)* (Madrid, 1966). Morford's *Stoics and Neostoics* gives the fullest description of Lipsius's relationships with statesmen, churchmen, and students.

40 Indispensable on this issue is *'Attic' and Baroque Prose Style: The Anti-Ciceronian Movement. Essays by Morris Croll*, ed. J. Max Patrick and Robert O. Evans (Princeton, 1966).

41 Montaigne, 'A Consideration upon Cicero,' Bacon, *Advancement of Learning*, both quoted in Croll, 'Attic Prose: Lipsius, Montaigne and Bacon,' in *'Attic' and Baroque Prose Style*, ed. Patrick and Evans, pp. 178, 189. The attack on Ciceronian style was closely associated with the campaign against the Aristotle of scholastic tradition, which Bacon was concerned to overcome in his *Advancement* (see below, chap. 2).

42 Croll, 'Attic Prose,' p. 185.

43 Ben Jonson, *The Complete Poems*, ed. George Parfitt (London, 1988), pp. 463, 437. See also below, chap. 3.

44 Lipsius's role in constructing a 'Tacitean' Cicero is discussed by J.H.M. Salmon, 'Cicero and Tacitus in Sixteenth-Century France,' *American Historical Review*, 85 (1980), pp. 323–4. The ongoing importance of Cicero to early-modern European and English political thought is reiterated by Peter N. Miller, *Defining the Common Good: Empire, Religion and Philosophy in Eighteenth-Century Britain* (Cambridge, 1994).
45 Croll, 'The Baroque Style in Prose,' *Essays*, ed. Patrick and Evans, p. 219.
46 Oestreich, *Neostoicism and the Early Modern State*, pp. 29–30.
47 See Croll, 'Attic Prose,' passim; George Williamson, 'Senecan Style in the Seventeenth Century,' *Seventeenth-Century Prose: Modern Essays in Criticism*, ed. Stanley Fish (New York, 1971), pp. 112–46; George Williamson, *The Senecan Amble* (Chicago, 1951).
48 See John Christian Laursen, 'Michel de Montaigne and the Politics of Skepticism,' *Historical Reflections*, 16 (1989), pp. 91–133, who argues that Montaigne aimed at 'the demolition of Stoic theories of universal natural law' by juxtaposing the contrary customs and laws evident in the world (pp. 113–14). For a more radical reading of Montaigne's observations, see David Lewis Schaefer, *The Political Philosophy of Montaigne* (Ithaca and London, 1990). The rhetorical aspect of Montaigne's thought is treated by L.D. Kritzman, *Destruction / Découverte: Le Fonctionnement de la Rhétorique dans les Éssais de Montaigne* (Lexington, 1980); Kahn, *Rhetoric, Prudence and Skepticism in the Renaissance*, pp. 115–51; and Skinner, 'Thomas Hobbes: Rhetoric and the Construction of Morality,' pp. 27–8.
49 Lipsius to Montaigne, 3 September 1589: 'In Europa non inueni, qui in his talibus sensu mecum magis consentiente': In *Ivsti Lipsi Epistolarum Centuriae Duae* (London, 1593; *STC* 15699), II, no. 59, p. 51. (Also in *Iusti Lipsi Opera* [1675], II, p. 176 [however, it is *Epist*. II no. 55, in this edition]). Without even considering Lipsius, John Michael Archer's discussion of Montaigne's *Essais* brings out the fundamental similarity between Montaigne's and Lipsius's political ideas. See his *Sovereignty and Intelligence: Spying and Court Culture in the English Renaissance* (Stanford, 1993), chap. 1.
50 Lipsius, 'Ad I. Hautenum, Non Esse Aptum se Belgicae Musae.' '... ego quid nisi iocum / Risumque nautis debeam & cauponis?/ Fallace ut olim cecidit ales Icarus / Penna levatus....' *Delitiae poetarum belgicorum* (1614), III, p. 305: as cited and reprinted (in full) in J.A. van Dorsten, *Poets, Patrons, and Professors: Sir Philip Sidney, Daniel Rogers, and the Leiden Humanists* (London, 1962), pp. 204–5. The translation given in the text is van Dorsten's: ibid., p. 37.
51 See *Tvvo Bookes of Constancie*, I, x–xii. At p. 25, the distinction is set when Langius notes the 'contention about the name.' He goes on, 'let vs come

neerer to the thing it selfe.' Cf. Tuck on the same issue, *Philosophy and Government*, pp. 51–5.
52 See Peter Burke, 'Tacitism,' in *Tacitus*, ed. T.A. Dorey (New York, 1969), p. 152.
53 *Iusti Lipsi, Ad Annales Corn. Taciti liber commentarius sive notae* (Antwerp, 1581), Ep. Ded. [to the States of Holland]: 'Cornelii Taciti Historiam ... Non adfert ille vobis speciosa bella aut triumphos, quorum finis sola voluptas legentis sit; non seditiones aut conciones Tribunicias, agrarias frumentariasve leges; quae nihil ad saecli huius usum: reges ecce vobis ey monarchas, et velut theatrum hodiernae vitae. Video alibi Principem in leges et iura, subditosque in Principem insurgentes. Invenio artes machinasque opprimendae, et infelicem impetum recipiendae liberatis. Lego iterum eversos prostratosque tyrannos, et infidam semper potentiam cum nimia est. Nec absunt etiam reciperatae libertatis mala, confusio, aemulatioque inter pares, avaritia, rapinae, et ex publico non in publicum quaesitae opes. Utilem magnumque scriptorem, deus bone! et quem in manibus eorum esse expediat, in quorum manu gubernaculum et reip. clavus.' I am deeply indebted to Mark Morford for his help in ascertaining the publication details of this hard-to-find dedication, and for sending me a copy of the entire text. The reasons why the piece is so elusive are explained by Professor Morford in *Stoics and Neostoics*, pp. 149–54; see also ibid., pp. 96–138. The translation of the quoted excerpt is from Grafton, 'Portrait of Justus Lipsius,' p. 386.
54 Arnaldo Momigliano, 'The First Political Commentary on Tacitus,' *Journal of Roman Studies*, 37 (1947), pp. 91–101; cf. Kenneth C. Schellhase, *Tacitus in Renaissance Political Thought* (Chicago, 1976), pp. 135–40.
55 See Burke, 'Tacitism,' *Tacitus*, ed. Dorey, pp. 149–71 and 'Tacitus, Scepticism, and Reason of State,' *Cambridge History of Political Thought 1450–1700*, ed. J.H. Burns with Mark Goldie (Cambridge, 1991), pp. 479–98. The changing fashion for historical authorities is charted by Burke in 'A Survey of the Popularity of Ancient Historians, 1450–1700,' *History and Theory*, 5 (1966), pp. 135–52.
56 Francesco Guicciardini, *Ricordi*, cited in Burke, 'Tacitism,' p. 163.
57 Burke, 'Tacitus, Scepticism and Reason of State,' p. 484, referring to G. Toffanin, *Machiavelli e il Tacitismo* (Padua, 1921). Tuck, in *Philosophy and Government*, passim, discusses the longer pedigree of Tacitism; Ronald Mellor, however, notes that Lipsius was the greatest Tacitean of the time, in *Tacitus* (New York and London, 1993), pp. 143–4.
58 Bacon, *Temporis Partus Masculus*, in *The Works of Francis Bacon*, ed. James Spedding et al (London, 1858–61), III, p. 538; Schellhase, *Tacitus in Renaissance Political Thought*, p. 160.

59 Einar Lofstedt, 'On the Style of Tacitus,' *Journal of Roman Studies*, 38 (1948), p. 3; Walker, *The Annals of Tacitus*, p. 53; Syme, *Tacitus*, I, p. 304.
60 Seneca, *Epistles*, 114, in *Workes*, trans. Lodge, p. 458.
61 See Kirk, ed., *Tvvo Books of Constancie*, p. 31; Voet, *The Golden Compasses*, I, p. 192; Williamson, 'Senecan Style,' p. 118.
62 *Sixe Bookes of Politickes*, IV, iii, p. 64, citing both Seneca, *De Beneficiis*, 3. 7, and Cicero's Ninth Philippic, one of the last orations, written against Mark Anthony and given in the heat of Cicero's final defence of the Roman Republic after Caesar's assassination. For the relationship between rhetoric and medicine, see Walter J. Ong, *Ramus, Method, and the Decay of Dialogue: From the Art of Discourse to the Art of Reason* (Cambridge, MA, 1958), pp. 225–8. For the Coornhert–Lipsius quarrel, see G. Güldner, *Das Toleranz-Problem in der Niederlanden im Ausgang des 16 Jahrhunderts* (Lubeck, 1968); Morford, *Stoics and Neostoics*, pp. 112–17. I plan to revisit the debate between Lipsius and Coornhert in another study.
63 See *Tvvo Bookes of Constancie*, pp. 14, 28, 105, 108–9, for Languis as the physician; and for God, pp. 73–84. Other analogies for God are that of the gardener, pp. 61, 86, and that of the playwright, tragedian, and composer, p. 92. Morford, *Stoics and Neostoics*, p. 128, n. 134, notes that Lipsius used the metaphor *ure et secari* as early as 1573 in a Jena oration calling for the end of discord among academics.
64 Lipsius to Sidney, Utrecht, 30 August 1586: 'dissidia interna nos ducent rapidi & torrentes isti ... Asseri habenas vobis plene & firmiter probo, suadeo; tempestive modo id fiat & cum quodam tractu: in corpore tam aegro, omnia paucis mensibus curatis? opus est diaetae.' *Epistolae ecclesiasticae et theologicae*, ed. P. a Limborch (Amsterdam, 1684), no. 2. Cited and reprinted in van Dorsten, *Poets, Patrons, and Professors*, pp. 217–18. Translation in the text is van Dorsten's, ibid., p. 149.
65 *Sixe Bookes of Politickes*, IV, iii, p. 65; see also IV, ix, p. 79, when he recommends that 'seueritie is to be used in respect of the commonwealth, without which no Citty can be well gouerned. Wee knowe that it is better to cut off the finger, then to let the Gangrena gaine the arme.' Lipsius set the requirement for severity beside the need to be constant and restrained. To this end, at IV, xiiii, p. 119, he writes, 'And as in the application of medicines [princes] do with approbation mingle venimous drugs for the good of the patient, so these things do seeme profitable as it were a medicine.'
66 *Sixe Bookes of Politickes*, IV, i, xiii, xiiii, pp. 59, 113, 123.
67 Ibid., IV, xiiii, p. 117. In France, *politiques* were advocating the same rule, claiming, however, the example of Louis XI. See Adrianna E. Bakos, 'The Historical Reputation of Louis XI in Political Theory and Polemic During

the French Religious Wars,' *Sixteenth Century Journal,* 21 (1990), pp. 3–32, and '"*Qui nescit dissimulare, nescit regnare*": Louis XI and *Raison d'État* During the Reign of Louis XIII,' *Journal of the History of Ideas,* 52 (1991), pp. 399–416.

68 Innocent Gentillet's *Discours ... contre Nicholas Machiavel Florentin* (1576) is representative of this view of Machiavellism. See Donald Kelley, 'Martyrs, Myths and the Massacre: The Background of St. Bartholomew,' *American Historical Review,* 77 (1972), pp. 1323–41; see also Friedrich Meinecke, *Machiavellism,* trans. Douglas Scott (New Haven, 1957) and Peter S. Donaldson, *Machiavelli and Reason of State* (New York, 1988). A recent discussion of the effect of the massacre is James R. Smither, 'The St. Bartholomew's Day Massacre and Images of Kingship in France: 1572–1574,' *Sixteenth Century Journal,* 22 (1991), pp. 27–46.

69 *Sixe Bookes of Politickes,* IV, xiii, p. 114; and for what follows, ibid., IV, xiiii, pp. 115–23.

70 Felix Raab, *The English Face of Machiavelli* (London, 1964), p. 120; Bireley, *The Counter-Reformation Prince,* pp. 72–100; and J.H. Elliott, *Richelieu and Olivares* (Cambridge, 1984), p. 27. Victoria Kahn has re-examined this issue in 'Rhetoric and Reason of State: Botero's Reading of Machiavelli,' in her *Machiavellian Rhetoric. From the Counter-Reformation to Milton* (Princeton, 1994), chap. 3.

71 Robert Hariman, 'Composing Modernity in Machiavelli's *Prince,' Journal of the History of Ideas,* 50 (1989), pp. 12, 13, 19. Cf. Kahn, *Rhetoric, Prudence, and Skepticism in the Renaissance,* pp. 186–7; Quentin Skinner, 'Machiavelli's *Discoursi* and the Pre-Humanist Origins of Republican Ideas,' *Machiavelli and Republicanism,* ed. Gisela Bock, Quentin Skinner, and Maurizio Viroli (Cambridge, 1990), pp. 121–41; and Maurizio Viroli, 'Machiavelli and the Republican Idea of Politics,' ibid., pp. 143–71.

72 Useful on this point is Delio Cantimore, 'Rhetoric and Politics in Italian Humanism,' trans. Frances A. Yates, *Journal of the Warburg and Courtauld Institutes,* 1 (1937–38), pp. 83–102. See also Albert Russell Ascoli and Victoria Kahn's Introduction in *Machiavelli and the Discourse of Literature,* ed. Ascoli and Kahn (Ithaca and London, 1993), especially pp. 5–9, and Kahn, *Machiavellian Rhetoric,* chaps. 1–3.

73 *Sixe Bookes of Politickes,* Author's Epistle, n.p.

74 Ibid., 'An Alphabet of the authors contained in this worke,' n.p. The original stated: 'inter eos eminet Corn. Tacitus extra ordinem dicendus: quia unus ille nobis contulit, quam ceteri omnes.'

75 Giovanni Botero, *Reason of State,* trans. P.J. and D.P. Waley (London, 1956); for Ammirato, see Eric Cochrane, *Florence in the Forgotten Centuries 1527–1800* (Chicago, 1973). Among the now numerous studies treating reason of state,

see especially Maurizio Viroli, *From Politics to Reason of State* (Cambridge, 1991).
76 *Sixe Bookes of Politickes*, I, viii and ix, pp. 12–14.
77 Ibid., III, v, pp. 47–8; and cf. Salmon, 'Cicero and Tacitus,' p. 324. Notably, in the 'Ad Lectorem' of *De Constantia* Lipsius appealed to the nautical metaphor in explaining his task in that work. After dismissing those who abuse philosophy by not extracting from it lessons for life, he goes on: 'Ad mihi alia mens, qui nauim semper auertens ab illis argutiarum salebris, velifectione[m] omnem direxi ad unum tranquilla mentis portum.' *De Constantia* (Antwerp, 1584), n.p.
78 *Sixe Bookes of Politickes*, IV, xiii, p. 112.
79 See Jerrold Seigel, *Rhetoric and Philosophy in Renaissance Humanism: The Union Of Eloquence and Wisdom From Petrarch to Valla* (Princeton, 1968), chap. 1; for the question of whether Ciceronian republicanism or Ciceronian rhetoric was at issue during the Italian Renaissance, see the debate between Seigel and Hans Baron in *Past & Present*, 34 (1966), pp. 3–48, and 36 (1967), pp. 21–37; see also Quint, 'Humanism and Modernity.'
80 Skinner, 'Thomas Hobbes: Rhetoric and the Construction of Morality,' p. 3.
81 Tacitus, *Agricola*, chap. 30, section 5, ed. R.M. Ogilvie and Sir Ian Richmond (Oxford, 1967), p. 112: 'auferre trucidare rapere falsis nominibus imperium atque ubi solitudinem faciunt pacem appellant.' For the translation I have used *The Agricola and Germany of Tacitus and The Dialogue on Oratory*, trans. Alfred John Church and William Jackson Brodribb (London, 1877), p. 29.
82 *Agricola*, chap. 42, sections 3–4, in Ogilvie and Richmond, p. 120; Church and Brodribb, *The Agricola and Germany of Tacitus*, p. 42.
83 Skinner, 'Thomas Hobbes: Rhetoric and the Construction of Morality,' pp. 23–5; Eugene Garver, *Machiavelli and the History of Prudence* (Madison, 1987).
84 Cf. the relationship between language and history as described by Nancy S. Struever, *The Language of History in the Renaissance: Rhetoric and Historical Consciousness in Florentine Humanism* (Princeton, 1977), p. 38.
85 Hariman, 'Composing Modernity,' p. 18.
86 Croll, 'Attic Prose,' in *'Attic' and Baroque Prose Style*, ed. Patrick and Evans, p. 66.
87 *Sixe Bookes of Politickes*, I, x, p. 15; cf. *Tvvo Bookes of Constancie*, I, xviii, p. 45.
88 *Sixe Bookes of Politickes*, I, x, p. 15.
89 See *Tvvo Bookes of Constancie*, I, xviii, pp. 46–7, where stoic epistemology as set forth by Zeno and others is argued and advocated by Lipsius. For the stoic concept of wisdom as prudence, see E. Vernon Arnold, *Roman Stoicism* (New York, 1958), pp. 301–29.

90 On the debate between philosophy and rhetoric, see Brian Vickers, *In Defence of Rhetoric* (Oxford, 1988), especially chaps. 2–3, and Struever, *The Language of History in the Renaissance*, chap. 1 and passim.
91 For Melanchthon, see Vickers, *In Defence of Rhetoric*, pp. 189–96, quotation at p. 195; Lipsius stated his admiration of Melanchthon in his Jena oration of 1573, calling him and Luther 'divine heroes.' Morford, *Stoics and Neostoics*, p. 129, suggests this is part of the hyperbole that marks that speech.
92 *Sixe Bookes of Politickes*, I, x, p. 15; 'doctrine' was the quality Lipsius also required in public figures, noting that his friend Busbecq (Ogier Giselin van Busbeke, diplomat and scholar in the service of Emperor Ferdinand II) personified that attribute as well as 'virtus.' See Morford, *Stoics and Neostoics*, pp. 86–7, and below, p. 34.
93 Cf. J.H. Salmon, 'Cicero and Tacitus,' p. 324.
94 *Tvvo Books of Constancie*, II, xxii–xxvi.
95 Cf. Timothy Hampton, *Writing From History: The Rhetoric of Exemplarity in Renaissance Literature* (Ithaca and London, 1990), which charts the ongoing tensions in the appeal to historical *exempla*, finding that these tensions ultimately lead to a repudiation of history.
96 There is a vast literature on this issue, of which I have found the following the most useful: Kahn, *Rhetoric, Prudence, and Skepticism in the Renaissance*; Seigel, *Rhetoric and Philosophy in Renaissance Humanism*; Gray, 'Renaissance Humanism,' pp. 497–514; George M. Logan, 'Substance and Form in Renaissance Humanism' *Journal of Medieval and Renaissance Studies*, 7 (1977), pp. 1–34; C.J.R. Armstrong, 'The Dialectical Road to Truth: the Dialogue,' in *French Renaissance Studies 1540–70*, ed. Peter Sharratt (Edinburgh, 1976), pp. 36–51; and Seth Lerer, *Boethius and Dialogue: Literary Method in the Consolation of Philosophy* (Princeton, 1985).
97 As Morford, *Stoics and Neostoics*, p. 107, notes, this is Lipsius's method in the *Politica*; it is also amplification of Lipsius's challenge to contemporary humanism. In view of his technique, Lipsius would probably be in accord with at least one of Victoria Kahn's conclusions. In *Prudence, Rhetoric, and Skepticism in the Renaissance*, she argues that the goals of humanist rhetoric collapsed 'in the Northern Renaissance' (pp. 46–54). This collapse came about less because of any disengaged philosophical issue, however, than the circumstances of the day. It is to his circumstances that Lipsius responds with his alternative form of humanism, exemplified in Lipsian 'doctrine.'
98 For the metaphor of 'theatrum mundi,' see Curtius, *European Literature and the Latin Middle Ages*, pp. 138–44; for its importance in stoicism, Monsarrat, *Light From the Porch*, pp. 11–18, 29. For historical similitude, G.W. Trompf, *The Idea of Historical Recurrence in Western Thought* (Berkeley, 1979); Donald R.

Kelley, 'The Theory of History,' *Cambridge History of Renaissance Philosophy*, ed. Schmitt et al., pp. 746–61; and Hampton, *Writing From History*.

99 See Grafton, 'Portrait of Justus Lipsius,' p. 388. For Bodin's approach to Tacitus and the classics, see Salmon, 'Cicero and Tacitus,' pp. 317, 320–1; and for his place in a broader context, D.R. Kelley, *Foundations of Modern Historical Scholarship: Language, Law and History in the French Renaissance* (New York, 1970), and George L. Mosse, 'The Influence of Jean Bodin's *Republique* on English Political Thought,' *Medievalia et Humanistica*, 5 (1948), pp. 73–83.

100 Andrew Lockyer, '"Traditions" as Context in the History of Political Theory,' *Political Studies*, 27 (1979), p. 202.

101 Guiseppe Toffanin, *La fine dell 'Umanesimo*, (Milan-Torino-Rome, 1920); for Toffanin's place in the debate over humanism, see William J. Bouwsma, *The Interpretation of Renaissance Humanism* (Washington, 1966), p. 8.

102 See *Tvvo Bookes of Constancie*, II, iiii, p. 68 and passim; and important on this point is Brian Vickers, 'On the Practicalities of Renaissance Rhetoric,' *Rhetoric Revalued*, ed. Vickers (New York, 1982), pp. 133–41, reprinted and expanded in his *In Defence of Rhetoric*, pp. 254–93.

103 In his use of the word 'Zeno' Lipsius partakes in the convention by which stoic argument was understood as dogmatic and overly subtle. For this point, see Boyle, *Rhetoric and Reform*, especially pp. 47–9.

104 See figure 2, which, however, comes from the 1675 edition of his *Opera* and is a poorer representation (as well as a mirror image) of the original, prepared for the first, 1637, edition of Lipsius's *Opera*. Morford, *Stoics and Neostoics*, reproduces the original at plate 17; Morford also provides a fine analysis of the symbolism, ibid., pp. 141–3.

105 Grafton, 'Portrait of Justus Lispsius,' p. 390.

106 Cf. Oestreich, *Neostoicism and the Early Modern State*, pp. 90–4, and Anthony Grafton and Lisa Jardine, *From Humanism to the Humanities: Education and the Liberal Arts in Fifteenth- and Sixteenth-Century Europe* (Cambridge, MA, 1986), pp. 197–9.

107 On who had to make such a declaration and the many of whom it was not required, see Peter J. van Kessel, 'The Denominational Pluriformity of the German Nations at Padua and the Problem of Intolerance in the 16th Century,' *Archiv für Reformationsgeschichte*, 75 (1984), pp. 256–75.

108 See R.J.W. Evans, *The Wechel Presses: Humanism and Calvinism in Central Europe 1572–1627*, *Past & Present. Supplement 2* (1975), p. 48. Lipsius's 'official' publisher remained the Plantin Press in Antwerp and he remained very close to the Plantin family; see Voet, *The Golden Compasses*, I, pp. 21–137, 362–95; II, pp. 255–78.

109 *Basilikon Doron: Devided into Three Bookes* (Edinburgh, 1599; STC 14348), p. 117.

110 Morford, *Stoics and Neostoics*, chaps. 2 and 3, describes the classicization of attitudes and behaviour among Lipsius's circle of friends and students.
111 Lipsius to Johannes Woverius, November 3, 1603: 'ego ad Sapientiam primus vel solus mei aevi Musas converti: ego e Philologia Philosophiam feci.' And about his books: 'vide *Constantiam* meam ... vide *Politica* ... & hoc utrumque opus est, cui vita fortasse cum Latinis litteris manebit.' ['See my *Constantia* ... see my *Politica* ... ; and each of these works will last perhaps as long as Latin literature itself.'] *Epistolarum ... Miscellaneae* IV, no. 84, in *Opera Omnia* (1675), vol. II, p. 413.
112 Seneca, *Epistles*, no. 108, in *Workes*, trans. Lodge, p. 442. On Lipsius's ongoing dialogue with Seneca, see Morford, *Stoics and Neostoics*, pp. 157–80.
113 In 1595, Lipsius published his *De Militia Romana*, which was followed by a study of military techniques, *Poliorceticon*, both of which were to inspire the princes whom he called upon in the *Politica* to emulate the Roman example. For the impact of Lipsius's military ideas, see Oestreich, *Neostoicism and the Early Modern State*; J.R. Hale, *Renaissance War Studies* (Hambledon, 1983); and Geoffrey Parker, *The Military Revolution* (Cambridge, 1988).
114 For a convincing statement of the revival of Roman imperial ambitions among Europeans, see Elliott, *Richelieu and Olivares* and his *The Count-Duke of Olivares: A Statesman in an Age of Decline* (New Haven and London, 1986); and William F. Church, *Richelieu and Reason of State* (Princeton, 1972). Lipsius's role in this process is noted by I.A.A. Thompson, 'The Impact of War,' *The European Crisis of the 1590s*, ed. Peter Clark (London, 1985), pp. 261–84; J.H. Elliott, 'Yet Another Crisis?' ibid., p. 310.
115 See Theodore G. Corbett, 'The Cult of Lipsius: A Leading Source of Early Modern Spanish Statecraft,' *Journal of the History of Ideas*, 36 (1975), 139–52; cf. J.A. Fernandez-Santamaria, *Reason of State and Statecraft in Spanish Political Thought, 1595–1640* (New York and London, 1983), chaps. 3 and 6–7.
116 Tuck, *Philosophy and Government*, pp. 41–3; 82–94.
117 Oestreich, *Neostoicism and the Early Modern State*, p. 105.
118 Cf. Tuck, 'Scepticism and Toleration in the Seventeenth Century' who argues the 'pragmatic' nature of such policies. On Henry's attempt to maintain his warrior-like image in the subsequent French peace, see Edmund H. Dickerman and Anita M. Walker, 'The Choice of Hercules: Henry IV as Hero' *Historical Journal*, 39. 2 (June, 1996), pp. 315–37.
119 As quoted in Nannerl O. Keohane, *Philosophy and the State in France: From the Renaissance to the Enlightment* (Princeton, 1980), p. 134.
120 *The Moral Philosophie of the Stoicks*, trans. Thomas James (1598), ed. Rudolph Kirk (New Brunswick, N.J., 1951), p. 115. On du Vair as a political philosopher see Keohane, *Philosophy and the State in France*, p. 134, and Hans Baron,

'Secularization of Wisdom and Political Humanism in the Renaissance,' *Journal of the History of Ideas*, 21 (1960), p. 148; and on du Vair as a nationalist, see Church, 'France,' in *National Consciousness, History, and Political Culture in Early-Modern Europe*, ed. Orest Ranum (Baltimore, 1975), p. 47. Cf. Skinner's view of du Vair as an opponent of political resistance, in the *Foundations of Modern Political Thought*, II, pp. 277–82.
121 See Baron, 'Secularization of Wisdom and Political Humanism in the Renaissance,' pp. 148–50.
122 See *Of Wisdome. Three Bookes. Written in French by Pierre Charron*, trans. Samson Lennard (London, 1608 [?]; *STC* 5051), I, p. 1. Book 1 was devoted to the subject of self-knowledge. Charron's repudiation of external authorities was captured in the allegorical device he created to serve as frontispiece in his work. See figure 3 and contrast the Charronian concept of naked, natural wisdom with the representation (based on Rubens's design) of Lipsian wisdom (in figure 2, above, p. 25).
123 *Of Wisdome*, II, pp. 222–3.
124 Ibid., p. 229.
125 Ibid., III, p. 351. Cf. *Six Bookes of Politickes*, IV, i, pp. 59–60.
126 See Paul F. Grendler, 'Pierre Charron: Precursor to Hobbes,' in his *Culture and Censorship in Late Renaissance Italy and France* (London, 1981), chap. 8; cf. Quentin Skinner – in neither *The Foundations of Modern Political Thought* nor, more recently, 'The State,' (*Political Innovation and Conceptual Change*, ed. Terrence Ball, James Farr, and Russell L. Hanson [Cambridge, 1989], pp. 90–131), does he notice Charron's role in regarding the state as a distinct entity.
127 Keohane, *Philosophy and the State*, p. 143.
128 Jean Duvergier, *Question Royalle et sa Decision* (Paris, 1609) quoted and cited in Keohane, *Philosophy and the State*, p. 125, and Church, *Richelieu and Reason of State*, pp. 22–3. See also Jean Orcibal, *Saint-Cyran et le Jansenisme* (Bourges, 1961), p. 6.
129 Cf. Bakos, 'Louis XI and *Raison d'État* During the Reign of Louis XIII,' pp. 406–7.
130 Elliott, *Richelieu and Olivares*, pp. 25–6.
131 Cf. Schellhase, *Tacitus in Renaissance Political Thought*, p. 156. For the impact of the *Germania* on Giambattista Vico, see Donald R. Kelley, '*Tacitus Noster*: The *Germania* in the Renaissance and Reformation,' in *Tacitus and the Tacitean Tradition*, ed. Luce and Woodman, pp. 165–7.
132 Church, 'France,' p. 53.
133 See Orest Ranum, *Artisans of Glory: Writers and Historical Thought in Seventeenth-Century France* (Chapel Hill, N.C. 1980). Authors could also maintain their independence by adhering to techniques exemplified by Lipsius.

François de Mézeray, writing in the age of Colbert, produced histories which, as William Church ('France,' p. 55) remarks, 'retained their popularity for more than a century ... Graced by a highly readable style, they also contain many pithy comments concerning men and events, and Mézeray did not hesitate to question the actions of men in high places when their policies seemed contrary to the general good.' Mézeray lost his position as royal historiographer for exposing too many abuses in his *Abrégé chronologique*.

134 See Jonathan Goldberg's analysis of the 'Roman Actor' in *James I and the Politics of Literature: Jonson, Shakespeare, Donne, and Their Contemporaries* (Baltimore and London, 1983), chap. 4; cf. Jenny Wormald, 'James VI and I: Two Kings or One?' *History*, 68 (1983), pp. 187–209.
135 William Loe, *Vox Clamantis: A Stil Voice to the Three Thrice-Honourable Estates of Parliament* (London, 1621; STC 16691), p. 61.
136 Van Dorsten, *Poets, Patrons, and Professors*, p. 120, speculates that Louvain provided the setting for the first meeting between Sidney and Lipsius.
137 Sidney to Robert, October, 1580, in *The Correspondence of Sir Philip Sidney and Hubert Languet*, ed. and trans. Steuart A. Pears (London, 1845), p. 201.
138 His copy of Tacitus is held at the British Library, London; for a brief analysis of Sir Robert's political assumptions, see Blair Worden, 'Classical Republicanism and the Puritan Revolution,' *History and Imagination: Essays in Honour of H.R. Trevor-Roper*, ed. H. Lloyd Jones, V. Pearl, and B. Worden (London, 1981), pp. 185–7.
139 Leiden University Library, MS Lips. 4. Sidney to Lipsius, 14 September 1586: 'Novi te gratissimum fore nostrae Reginae et multis alliis imo omnibus aliis.' Cited and reprinted in van Dorsten, *Poets, Patrons, and Professors*, pp. 151 and 218. I have used van Dorsten's translation, in ibid., p. 151.
140 *The Correspondence of Sir Philip Sidney and Hubert Languet*, ed. Pears, passim.
141 *A Letter written ... to Queen Elizabeth ...*, in *Miscellaneous Prose of Sir Philip Sidney*, ed. Katherine Duncan-Jones and Jan van Dorsten (Oxford, 1973), pp. 46–67.
142 See David Norbrook, *Poetry and Politics in the English Renaissance* (London, 1984), chap. 4; cf. Andrew D. Weiner, *Sir Philip Sidney and the Poetics of Protestantism: A Study of Contexts* (Minnesota, 1978). See also Katharine Eisaman Maus, *Inwardness and Theater in the English Renaissance* (Chicago and London, 1995), p. 74 and pp. 85–6, 187–8, where the author discusses the *Arcadia* in relation to England's gendered politics. Cf. Archer, *Sovereignty and Intelligence*, chap. 2, and Catherine Bates, *The Rhetoric of Courtship in Elizabethan Language and Literature* (Cambridge, 1992), pp. 110–33.
143 Sidney revised his original draft of *Arcadia* to stress the political compo-

nent. For the different emphasis in the two versions, see Norbrook, *Poetry and Politics*, pp. 92–108, and for the contest over the authoritative version, below, chap. 3. Daniel Javitch, *Poetry and Courtliness in Renaissance England* (Princeton, 1978), pp. 48, 92–104, gives a good account of Sidney's writing as an exercise in *serio laudere*, linking Sidney to an Erasmian form of humanism, as well as to the Italian courtly model set out in Castiglione's *Book of the Courtier*.

144 Annabel Patterson argues that such allusions were used because of the inquisitive and censorious eyes of the court. *Censorship and Interpretation: The Conditions of Writing and Reading in Early Modern England* (Madison, 1984), chap. 1.

145 Michael Brennan, *Literary Patronage in the English Renaissance: The Pembroke Family* (London, 1988), pp. 45–54, John Buxton, *Sir Philip Sidney and the English Renaissance*, 3rd ed. (London, 1987), chap. 5, and F.J. Levy, 'Philip Sidney Reconsidered,' *English Literary Renaissance*, 2 (1972) pp. 11–15, discuss these preoccupations, but see also the studies cited at n. 142, above.

146 'A Dedication to Sir Philip Sidney,' *The Prose Works of Fulke Greville, Lord Brooke*, ed. John Gouws (Oxford, 1986), p. 12. Cf. Kahn, *Rhetoric, Prudence, and Skepticism*, p. 189 where examining humanism as instruction through *reading*, she neglects the role of *writing* as praxis.

147 Sidney's priorities in life (as opposed to the myths that have come to surround him), are discussed in *Sir Philip Sidney. 1586 and the Creation of a Legend*, ed. Jan van Dorsten, Dominic Baker-Smith, and Arthur F. Kinney (Leiden, 1986). See, in particular, the essays by W.A. Ringler, van Dorsten, and Marjon Poort.

148 *De constantia*, I, xiv. This idea is considered part of a 'Machiavellian' tradition of republicanism. See J.G.A. Pocock, *The Machiavellian Moment: Florentine Political Thought and the Atlantic Republican Tradition* (Princeton, 1975). See also Martin van Gelderen, 'The Machiavellian Moment and the Dutch Revolt: The Rise of Neostoicism and Dutch Republicanism,' in *Machiavelli and Republicanism*, ed. Bock et al., pp. 205–23. English republicanism is discussed by Blair Worden in a chapter by that title, in *Cambridge History of Political Thought, 1450–1700*, ed. Burns, pp. 443–75.

149 The Leicester episode is discussed by F.G. Oosterhoff, *Leicester and the Netherlands 1586–1587* (Utrecht, 1988); Lipsius's involvement in Leiden politics is briefly suggested by Jean Jehasse, *La Renaissance de la Critique: L'Essor de L'Humanisme Erudit de 1560 à 1614* (Saint Étienne, 1976), p. 251.

150 *Iusti Lipsi De Recta Pronunciatione Linguae Latinae Dialogus* (1586), dedication to Sidney; British Library, Burney MS 370, f. 35 (Lipsius to Jan Dousa, 1 September, 1585): 'felix hac quoque dote Anglia, quod nobilitas in ea vere nobi-

lis, culta studiis virtutis et doctrinae.' I have used the translations of Jan van Dorsten, *Poets, Patrons, and Professors*, p. 118.
151 Cf. Morford, *Stoics and Neostoics*, pp. 86–7.
152 For Essex's conception of the office, see Mervyn James, 'At a Crossroads of the Political Culture: the Essex Revolt, 1601,' in his *Society, Politics and Culture: Studies in Early Modern England* (Cambridge, 1986), p. 450.
153 Walter B. Devereux, *Lives and Letters of the Devereux, Earls of Essex, in the Reigns of Elizabeth, James I and Charles I, 1540–1646* (London, 1853), p. 187. One of Essex's secretaries later wrote that Essex had been 'a bad courtier,' and 'had a spirit too great for a Subject.' See Henry Wotton, *A Parallel Betweene Robert late Earl of Essex and George late Duke of Buckingham*, in *Reliquae Wottonianae: or a Collection of Lives, Letters, Poems, with Characters of Sundry Personages*, 2nd ed. (London, 1654; *STC* [ed. Wing] W3649), pp. 41 and 54. (*The Parallel* has its own separate pagination.)
154 Francis Bacon on behalf of his brother, Anthony, to Essex: in Devereux, *Lives and Letters of the Devereux*, p. 278. Essex's circle has been called 'a circle of malcontents' and a 'bitter circle,' with many of its members pressuring Essex for advancement. See Paul E.J. Hammer, 'Patronage at Court, Faction and the Earl of Essex,' in *The Reign of Elizabeth I: Court and Culture in the Last Decade*, ed. John Guy (Cambridge, 1995), pp. 65–86 (quotations from p. 76 and p. 72, respectively); see also Guy's 'Introduction' to the same volume, ibid., pp. 1–19, and Natalie Mears, ibid., pp. 46–64, in her chapter entitled '*Regnum Cecilianum*? A Cecilian Perspective of the Court.'
155 See Anthony Grafton and Lisa Jardine, '"Studied For Action": How Gabriel Harvey Read His Livy,' *Past & Present*, 129 (Nov. 1990), pp. 30–78.
156 Essex's circle is described in Wotton, *A Parallel*, in his *Reliquiae Wottonianae*, pp. 14, 25, 31–3, and passim. The careers of Cuffe, Savile, and Wotton are sketched in the *DNB*; for Cuffe, see also A.L. Rowse, 'The Tragic Career of Henry Cuffe,' in his *Court and Country: Studies in Tudor Social History* (Brighton, 1987), pp. 211–41. For Perez, see Gustav Ungerer, *A Spaniard in Elizabethan England: the Correspondence of Antonio Perez's Exile*, 2 vols. (London, 1974–6).
157 *John Aubrey, Brief Lives*, ed. Oliver Lawson Dick (London, 1949), p. 11; *The Letters and Life of Francis Bacon*, ed. James Spedding (London, 1862–74), III, p. 143. See also Robert Lacey, *Robert, Earl of Essex: An Elizabethan Icarus* (London, 1971), pp. 95, 244.
158 See F.J. Levy, *Tudor Historical Thought* (San Marino, 1967), chap. 7; and his 'Hayward, Daniel, and the Beginnings of Politic History in England,' *Huntington Library Quarterly*, 50 (1987), pp. 1–34.
159 'A.B.' suggests Anthony Bacon, but for Jonson's ascription see his 'Conver-

sations with William Drummond [1619],' in *Ben Jonson: The Complete Poems*, ed. Parfitt, p. 471.
160 Tacitus, *The Ende of Nero and the Beginning of Galba, Fower Bookes of the Histories of Cornelius Tacitus, The Life of Agricola*, trans. H. Savile (Oxford, 1591), 'A.B. to the Reader.'
161 Malcolm Smuts, 'Court-Centered Politics and the Uses of Roman Historians, c.1590–1630,' in *Culture and Politics in Early Stuart England*, ed. Kevin Sharpe and Peter Lake (London, 1994), pp. 25–30, quotation at pp. 26–7.
162 Savile's 1591 edition of *Tacitus* had appended to it *A View of Certaine Militarie Matters, or Commentaries Concerning Roman Warefare*, a tract in which he took issue with Lipsius over Roman administrative habits. His dialogue with Lipsius was extended in other studies, including a 'Report of the Wages Paid to the Ancient Roman Soldiers, Their Vitayling and Apparel, in a Letter to Lord Burghley' (1595); in *Somers Tracts: Collection of Scarce and Valuable Tracts ... of the Late Lord Somers* (16 vols., 1748–52), ed. Sir Walter Scott (London, 1809–15), vol. 1, pp. 555–7.
163 See Wallace T. MacCaffrey, 'The Court: The Revival of Faction,' Part 4 of his *Elizabeth I: War and Politics 1588–1603* (Princeton, 1992); and for an analysis of Essex's political activities, see Mervyn James, 'At a Crossroads of the Political Culture: The Essex Revolt, 1601.' See also the essays in *The Reign of Elizabeth I*, ed. Guy.
164 *Letters and Life of Francis Bacon*, ed. Spedding, II, p. 127, and III, p. 146.
165 A typescript of the letter from Egerton and of Essex's response is on deposit at the West Sussex Record Office, Chichester, in a volume entitled 'Copies of Certain Letters in the Possession of the Earl of Winterton, volume 1,', pp. 1–7 (R.O. reference, Lib. 5650). I wish to thank Richard Childs, County Archivist, for his courtesy and speedy response to a query about the Essex Letter. In the text, I quote from a mid-seventeenth-century printed source, *Cabala: Sive Scrinia Sacra. Secrets of Empire in Letters of Illustrious persons* (London, 1654; *STC* [ed. Wing] C 184), p. 28 (Egerton on Seneca) and p. 30 (Essex on Seneca).
166 Wotton, *A Parallel* in *Reliquiae Wottonianae*, pp. 23–4.
167 These were Attorney General Coke's objections, as quoted in Levy, 'Beginnings of Politic History,' p. 17.
168 Ibid.
169 As quoted in Levy, 'Beginnings of Politic History,' p. 1; cf. below, chap. 3, pp. 75–9.
170 See Levy, 'Beginnings of Politic History,' pp. 15–21, and Grafton and Jardine, 'How Gabriel Harvey Read His Livy,' pp. 33–5.
171 For a more sympathetic treatment than is generally accorded Cuffe, see

Rowse, 'The Tragic Career of Henry Cuffe,' in his *Court and Country*, pp. 211–41, and for the rebellion in general, Lacey, *Robert, Earl of Essex: An Elizabethan Icarus*, passim, and James, 'At the Crossroads of the Political Culture: the Essex Revolt of 1601.'

## 1 The Constant Courtier: Sir Walter Ralegh in Jacobean England

1 *James I by his Contemporaries: An Account of his Career and Character as Seen by Some of his Contemporaries*, ed. Robert Ashton (London, 1969), p. 214; *Aubrey's Brief Lives*, ed. Oliver Lawson Dick (London, 1949), p. 206. (Emphasis in both quotations is mine.) Ralegh's ongoing popularity can be gauged from Christopher M. Armitage, *Sir Walter Ralegh: An Annotated Bibliography* (Chapel Hill, 1987), pp. 29–47; see also Edward Thompson, *Sir Walter Ralegh: The Last of the Elizabethans* (London, 1935), pp. 354–8, and more recently Stephen Coote, *A Play of Passion: The Life of Sir Walter Ralegh* (London, 1993).
2 For Ralegh's life I rely on the works already mentioned and the following: Edward Edwards, *The Life of Sir Walter Ralegh*, 2 vols. (London, 1868), hereafter, Edwards *Life*, I, or Edwards, *Letters*, II; Philip Edwards, *Sir Walter Ralegh* (London, 1953), hereafter, Edwards, *Ralegh*; and Robert Lacey, *Sir Walter Ralegh* (London, 1973).
3 See J.W. Daly, 'The Idea of Absolute Monarchy in Seventeenth-Century England,' *Historical Journal*, 21 (1978), pp. 227–50; J.P. Sommerville, *Politics and Ideology in England 1603–1640* (London, 1986); *Divine Right and Democracy: An Anthology of Political Writings in Stuart England*, ed. David Wootton (Harmondsworth, 1986), pp. 22–38; and Christopher Haigh, *Elizabeth I* (London, 1988).
4 G.M. Trevelyan, *History of England*, 3rd ed. (London, 1945), p. 388. Cf. D.R. Woolf, 'Two Elizabeths? James I and the Late Queen's Famous Memory,' *Canadian Journal of History*, 20 (1985), pp. 184–8.
5 The politics of courtiership was not lost on contemporaries like Sir Robert Naunton, who recorded many instances of its operation in *Fragmenta Regalia* (1641), in *Somers Tracts: Collection of Scarce and Valuable Tracts ... of the Late Lord Somers* (16 vols, 1748–52), ed. Sir Walter Scott (London, 1809–15), vol. 1, pp. 251–82; William Camden did likewise in his history of Elizabeth's reign, which was published in Latin in 1615 and translated into English as *Annales: The True and Royall History of Elizabeth, Queen of England* (London, 1625; STC 4497). Camden's commonplace book is also revealing for the politics of courtiership. See Bodleian Library, Smith MS 17, ff. 37–49. The classic modern study of the subject is Wallace MacCaffrey's 'Place and Patronage in Elizabethan Politics,' in *English Government and Society*, ed. S.T. Bindoff, et al. (Lon-

don, 1961), pp. 95–126, which he has revisited in 'The Court: The Revival of Faction,' Part 4 of his *Elizabeth I: War and Politics 1588–1603* (Princeton, 1992).

6 Ralegh's accusation was centred on the Bye Plot, but the prosecution did its best to implicate him in the Main. See David Jardine, *Criminal Trials* (London, 1832–5), I, pp. 404–7. The prosecution papers in Ralegh's trial, long considered lost, have recently been discovered (in October 1995, by Cambridge University archivist Mark Nicholls), sparking renewed debate over Ralegh's actual complicity in treason. Although too late to be properly taken into account here, this evidence in no way impinges on the following discussion of Ralegh's political views, which I intend to revisit in light of those papers, in a forthcoming paper.

7 Nov. [?] 1603; in Edwards, *Letters*, II, p. 278.

8 Edwards, *Life*, I, pp. 383–439, gives a full account of Ralegh's self-defence; the opinion of the Scotsman, who reported the trial to the King, is quoted by Stephen J. Greenblatt, *Sir Walter Ralegh: The Renaissance Man and His Roles* (New Haven, 1973), p. 1; for Carleton's remark, see *Dudley Carleton to John Chamberlain 1603–1624: Jacobean Letters*, ed. Maurice Lee, Jr. (New Brunswick, N.J., 1972), p. 39.

9 Most historians argue that *Sejanus* refers to the trial of Essex, in 1601. The Ralegh parallel, however, is more likely, as this trial was in progress as Jonson was composing the play (which was not a hit with audiences). See *Sejanus His Fall*, ed. Philip J. Ayres, The Revels Plays Series (Manchester and New York, 1990), p. 17.

10 See Joel Hurstfield, 'The Succession Struggle in Late Elizabethan England,' in his *Freedom, Corruption and Government in Elizabethan England* (London, 1973), pp. 104–34, and Haigh, *Elizabeth I*, pp. 17–19 and 115–17.

11 Ralegh was approached by the Scots in 1602. He refused to participate in a furtive correspondence with the mediators for James, confiding in Cecil that an approach had been made that he turned down. Thompson, *The Last of the Elizabethans*, pp. 164–5.

12 Quoted in Greenblatt, *The Renaissance Man*, pp. 113–14.

13 Thompson, *The Last of the Elizabethans*, p. 177. Cf. the argument of Natalie Mears, '*Regnum Cecilianum*? A Cecilian Perspective of the Court,' in *The Reign of Elizabeth I: Court and Culture in the Last Decade*, ed. John Guy (Cambridge, 1995), pp. 46–64.

14 Thompson, *The Last of the Elizabethans*, p. 167; for a full-length study of Howard, see Linda Levy Peck, *Northampton: Patronage and Policy at the Court of James I* (London, 1982). Professor Peck has carried on the study of courtiership into the Jacobean period in *Court Patronage and Corruption in Early Stuart*

*England* (Boston, 1990), as well as contributing to and editing *The Mental World of the Jacobean Court* (Cambridge, 1991).
15 A copy of the original draft of this letter, dated 1602 and in the hand of Robert Cotton, is reprinted in Edwards, *Letters*, II, pp. 436–44.
16 *Aubrey's Brief Lives*, ed. Dick, p. 254.
17 Steven W. May, *Sir Walter Ralegh* (Boston, 1989), p. 9.
18 Sir Anthony Bagot, cited in Walter B. Devereux, *Lives and Letters of the Devereux, Earls of Essex, in the Reigns of Elizabeth, James I and Charles I, 1540–1656* (London, 1853), p. 186.
19 *Sir Walter Ralegh's Instructions to His Son and Posterity*, in *Advice to a Son*, ed. Louis B. Wright (New York, 1962), p. 20 (emphasis added). For the epigraph at the chapter opening, see ibid.
20 See his 1603 letter of farewell and consolation to his wife, in Edwards, *Letters*, II, p. 385.
21 See Peck, *Northampton*, p. 14.
22 Ibid., p. 17: Rowland White to Sidney (1599).
23 See Thompson, *The Last of the Elizabethans*, p. 148.
24 See Edwards, *Letters*, II, p. 385.
25 *Letters of James VI & I*, ed. G.P.V. Akrigg (Berkeley, 1984), p. 179.
26 The Ralegh–Sidney friendship is discussed in May, *Sir Walter Ralegh*, p. 31, and P.G. Croft (ed.), *The Poems of Robert Sidney* (Oxford, 1984), p. 70 ff; for Sidney's political views, see Blair Worden, 'Classical Republicanism and the Puritan Revolution,' *History and Imagination: Essays in Honour of H.R. Trevor-Roper*, ed. H. Lloyd-Jones, V. Pearl, and B. Worden (London, 1981), pp. 185–7, and Jonathan Scott, *Algernon Sidney and the English Republic, 1623–1677* (Cambridge, 1988), chap. 1–4. Kevin Sharpe, *Sir Robert Cotton, 1586–1631: History and Politics in Early Modern England* (Oxford, 1979), demonstrates both the personal and professional ties that existed between Ralegh and Cotton. Ralegh's friendship with Jonson included entrusting him as tutor to young Wat on a European tour in 1612. See Jonson's comments on Ralegh in 'Conversations with William Drummond' (1619), in *Ben Jonson: The Complete Poems*, ed. George Parfitt (Harmondsworth, 1988), pp. 459–80.
27 James's remark is recorded in *The Letters of John Chamberlain*, ed. N.E. McClure (Philadelphia, 1939), I, p. 568.
28 See Edwards, *Letters*, II, pp. 278–305, 333–41, 389–94.
29 See J.W. Williamson, *The Myth of the Conqueror. Prince Henry Stuart: A Study of 17th-Century Personation* (New York, 1978); Roy Strong, *Henry, Prince of Wales and England's Lost Renaissance* (New York, 1986).
30 *The Cabinet-Council* (London, 1658; STC [ed. Wing] R 156), p. 104: a strong echo of Ralegh's views as stated in his *History* and elsewhere.

31 Ralegh's death coincided with the outbreak of the Thirty Years War in Europe. Polemicists in favour of English intervention often invoked Ralegh's name and fate to argue their point. *Sir Walter Rawleighs Ghost* (1626) was only one of four 'Ralegh's Ghosts' to appear in the decade or so following his death. See Christopher Hill, *Intellectual Origins of the English Revolution* (Oxford, 1965), p. 206.

32 Hill, *Intellectual Origins*, pp. 131–224; see also his 'Parliament and People in 17th-Century England,' *The Collected Essays of Christopher Hill* (Amherst, 1986), III, pp. 30, 41; cf., too, Richard Helgerson, *Forms of Nationhood: The Elizabethan Writing of England* (Chicago and London, 1992), p. 181.

33 Richard Tuck, *Philosophy and Government 1572–1651* (Cambridge, 1993), pp. 116–17.

34 *The Cabinet-Council* was first published by Milton in 1658, and *The Maxims of State* in 1642 with at least three more editions appearing in the seventeenth century. For Lefranc's objections to ascribing these to Ralegh, see his *Sir Walter Ralegh Écrivain: l'Oeuvre et les Idées* (Paris, 1968), pp. 64–70; see also Strathmann, 'A Note on the Ralegh Canon,' *Times Literary Supplement*, 13 April 1956, p. 228.

35 Quoted in Roger Coke, *A Detection of the Court and State of England*, 3rd ed. (London, 1697; *STC* [ed. Wing] C 4975), p. 66.

36 *The Chamberlain Letters: A Selection of the Letters of John Chamberlain Concerning Life in England from 1597 to 1626*, ed. Elizabeth McClure Thomson (New York, 1965), p. 195.

37 See Sir Walter Ralegh, *History of the World* (London, 1614; *STC* 20637), Preface. References to the *History* are to this edition.

38 Quoted in V.T. Harlow, *Ralegh's Last Voyage* (London, 1932), p. 304.

39 Thomas Overbury, *The Arraignment and Conviction of Sr Walter Rawleigh* (London, 1648; *STC* [ed. Wing] A 3744), p. 34.

40 The most comprehensive study of Ralegh is that of Lefranc, *Sir Walter Ralegh Écrivain*, but see also, Felix Raab, *The English Face of Machiavelli* (London, 1964), pp. 70–3; N. Kempner, *Raleghs Staatstheoretische Schriften* (Leipzig, 1928); Greenblatt, *Renaissance Man*; Ernest A. Strathmann, *Sir Walter Ralegh: A Study in Elizabethan Skepticism* (New York, 1973); John Racin, *Sir Walter Ralegh as Historian: An Analysis of 'The History of the World'* (Salzburg, 1974); and J.G.A. Pocock, *The Machiavellian Moment: Florentine Political Thought and the Atlantic Republican Tradition* (Princeton, 1975), pp. 355–7.

41 See *History*, III, xii, 7 p. 153; IV, ii, 17 p. 201.

42 Seneca, *Epistles*, 70 and 26, in *The Workes of Lvcivs Annaevs Seneca*, trans. Thomas Lodge (London, 1614; *STC* 22213), pp. 286, 210.

43 'Of Death,' in *Francis Bacon: The Essays*, ed. John Pitcher (Harmondsworth, 1985), p. 65.

44 Hall, *Heaven Upon Earth and Characters of Vertues and Vices*, ed. Rudolph Kirk (New Brunswick, N.J., 1948), p. 88.
45 Ralegh's own attempted suicide, during the early days of his imprisonment in the Tower, might have been considered as no more than a theatrical gesture by contemporaries, but if so, critics failed to see how far the stoic concept of life as a role selected by destiny seems to have guided him, even when he came to rethink the virtues of stoic suicide, preferring incarceration to the freedom of suicide. And until his execution, when his stoical approach to death emerged in all its splendour, he lived by something akin to the Lipsian idea of constancy, adapting himself to the flux of the mundane experience of being once an Elizabethan courtier, next a Jacobean prisoner, all the while attempting to serve the king, and, failing him, the prince for whom he compiled so many writings.
46 See *History*, Preface, sig. A1, sig. E2; see also IV, ii, 9 p. 187, and IV, ii, 23 p. 211 and passim.
47 Ibid., I, i, 12 p. 17; I, ix, 4, p. 184; V, ii, 4, p. 384. Cf. the interesting remarks on Ralegh's scepticism in Katharine Eisaman Maus, *Inwardness and Theater in the English Renaissance* (Chicago and London, 1995), pp. 4–8 and passim.
48 J.W. Allen, *English Political Thought, 1603–1660* (London, 1938), I, p. 67. Other studies which conclude with Ralegh as traditionalist include F. Smith Fussner, *The Historical Revolution: English Historical Writing and Thought, 1580–1640* (London, 1962), pp. 191–210; Herschel Baker, *The Race of Time: Three Lectures on Renaissance Historiography* (Toronto, 1967), pp. 37–41; and C.A. Patrides, *The Grand Design of God: The Literary Form of the Christian View of God* (London, 1972).
49 Lily B. Campbell, *Shakespeare's Histories: Mirrors of Elizabethan Policy* (San Marino, 1947), and Allen, *English Political Thought*, I, p. 67.
50 This point can be gleaned from Ralegh's book collection while a prisoner in the Tower. His commonplace book, which lists classical and modern authors, is held by the British Library, Add. MS 57555; see also Walter Oakeshott, 'Sir Walter Ralegh's Library,' *The Library*, 5th ser., 23.4 (Dec. 1968), pp. 285–327.
51 Subsequent editions of Samson's translation, *Of Wisdome. Three Bookes, Written in French* were dedicated to others, but the first was dedicated to Henry (see *STC* 5051); for Prince Henry's library and education, see T.A. Birrell, *English Monarchs and Their Books: From Henry VII to Charles II* (London, 1987), pp. 30–40.
52 Ralegh's collection in the Tower included 'Cornelius Tacitus eng' (see Oakeshott, 'Ralegh's Library,' p. 315, no. 311). Sidney's Tacitism is discernable from the annotations in his copy of the 1585 Lipsian edition of Tacitus's *Opera* (held at the British Library). His greatest interest lay in maxims on power and wisdom in the *Annals*, and in both contrasting imperial Rome to the contem-

porary state of England and remarking upon distinguishing idiosyncracies of personality, again in relation to the *Annals*. His Tacitism is considered further, below, chap. 4, pp. 156–9 and 163.

53 Edwards, *Letters*, II, p. 169.
54 Quoted in Thompson, *The Last of the Elizabethans*, p. 122.
55 Edwards, *Letters*, II, p. 217.
56 Ibid., p. 222.
57 Ralegh, *Prerogative of Parliaments* (London, 1628; *STC* 20649), p. 43.
58 Ralegh's verse and the queen's response are quoted in May, *Sir Walter Ralegh*, p. 32.
59 See Leonard Tennenhouse, 'Sir Walter Ralegh and the Literature of Clientage,' in *Patronage in the Renaissance*, ed. Guy Fitch Lytle and Stephen Orgel (Princeton, 1981), p. 247.
60 Chamberlain recorded that through the *History*, Ralegh 'thought he had won his spurres and pleased the king extraordinarilie.' *Letters of John Chamberlain*, ed. McClure, I, p. 568.
61 'Literature of Clientage,' p. 247.
62 Ralegh, *History*, I, xi, 1, pp. 201–11. Ralegh also praised James for banning duelling, the subject of a long digression in the work. Cf. Racin, *Ralegh as Historian*, pp. 105–7.
63 Tennenhouse, 'Literature of Clientage,' p. 247.
64 See *Basilikon Doron: Devided into Three Bookes* (Edinburgh, 1599; *STC* 14348), p. 117, and the second edition of *Basilikon Doron*, which was published in London in 1603 (*STC* 14350) and is reprinted in *The Political Works of James I*, ed. Charles H. McIlwain (New York, 1965 [see pp. 9, 18, 40–2]). Here, the call against Lipsian 'constancy' was rendered less specific but still recognizable in its target, especially in its insistence against those professing 'Stoicke insensible stupiditie' and who, in fact, manifest 'inconstant behauiour in their owne liues' (*Works*, ed. McIlwaine, p. 41). James's thought is treated more fully below, pp. 55–7, 174–5, 193.
65 May, *Sir Walter Ralegh*, p. 99.
66 Sommerville, *Politics and Ideology*, p. 44.
67 Still, its first publication was not until 1628, in the wake of the parliamentary debates over the Petition of Right. Three editions appeared that year, though none admitted to an English publisher (the first announcing an origin at Middleburg). Sir John Eliot, a protagonist of the Petition of Right, owned and carefully annotated a manuscript copy of Ralegh's *Prerogative*. For Ralegh's effect on Eliot, see Hill, *Intellectual Origins*, pp. 204, 208–9; Sharpe, *Sir Robert Cotton*, p. 243, n. 123; and Harold Hulme, *The Life of Sir John Eliot* (London, 1957), p. 31.

68 Ralegh, *Prerogative*, sig. A3.
69 Ibid. sig. A3v.
70 Ibid., p. 26.
71 Ibid., p. 34.
72 This theme is treated at large in Peck, *Court Patronage and Corruption in Early Stuart England*.
73 James's letters of the period are full of this theme; see *The Letters of James VI & I*, ed. Akrigg, pp. 170–95.
74 F.J. Levy, 'Hayward, Daniel, and the Beginnings of Politic History in England,' *Huntington Library Quarterly*, 50 (1987), pp. 3–9, and J.H.M. Salmon, 'Stoicism and Roman Example: Seneca and Tacitus in Jacobean England,' *Journal of the History of Ideas*, 50 (1989), pp. 207–21.
75 Robert Dallington, *Aphorismes Civill and Militarie: Amplified with Authorities; and Exemplified with Historie, out of the first Quarterne of Fr. Guicciardine* (London, 1613; STC 6197), Bk. 5, Aphorisme 19, pp. 314–15. This edition was dedicated to Prince Charles; earlier Dallington had presented a MS copy to Henry.
76 See *Aphorismes*, passim, citing his sources in Latin and deriving many of them directly from Lipsius's own commentaries in the *Politica*; see also Salmon, 'Seneca and Tacitus in Jacobean England,' p. 216.
77 Quoted in Alan T. Bradford, 'Stuart Absolutism and the "Utility" of Tacitus,' *Huntington Library Quarterly*, 46 (1983), p. 138.
78 See Levy, 'Beginnings of Politic History,' pp. 13–14, 21–5, and Salmon, 'Seneca and Tacitus in Jacobean England,' pp. 219–20.
79 Quoted in Bradford, 'Stuart Absolutism and the "Utility" of Tacitus,' p. 139. Cf. James VI & I, *Trew Law of Free Monarchies*, in *Divine Right and Democracy*, ed. Wootton, p. 101.
80 See Ralegh, *Maxims of State* (London, 1650; STC [ed. Wing] R 174), p. 7; cf. *History*, I, ix, 1, p. 180. Cf., too, James VI & I, *Speech to the Lords and Commons* (1610) in *Divine Right and Democracy*, ed. Wootton, p. 107; and Lipsius, *Sixe Bookes of Politickes*, trans. William Jones (London, 1594; STC 15701), II, ii, p. 18.
81 For the pervasive 'monarchism' of the period, see Margaret Judson, *The Crisis of the Constitution* (New Brunswick, N.J., 1949), chap. 1; Sommerville, *Politics and Ideology*, pp. 9–56; *Divine Right and Democracy*, ed. Wootton, pp. 22–38.
82 See, for example, *History*, I, ix, 3, p. 183; V, ii, 4, p. 386; V, vi, 12, p. 774.
83 *Basilikon Doron* is full of moral admonitions like Ralegh's, but for the king's own taste in representing kingship, see Jonathan Goldberg, *James I and the Politics of Literature: Jonson, Shakespeare, Donne, and their Contemporaries* (Baltimore and London, 1983), and Graham Parry, *The Golden Age Restor'd: The Culture of the Stuart Court 1603–1642* (Manchester, 1981).

84 Dallington, *Aphorismes*, Bk. 3, Aphorisme 16, p. 176.
85 Ralegh, *Maxims of State*, p. 41.
86 Salmon, 'Seneca and Tacitus in Jacobean England,' pp. 207–9, and Michael Brennan, *Literary Patronage in the English Renaissance: The Pembroke Family* (London, 1988), p. 127.
87 Ralegh, *History*, II, xix, 1, p. 507.
88 For a catalogue of Ralegh's repudiations of Machiavelli, and for the areas in which Machiavellian wisdom were approved by him, see Lefranc, *Ralegh Écrivain*, pp. 614–32. Ralegh's attachment to a metaphysics of the text brings him closer to Lipsius than to Machiavelli. Cf., however, Victoria Kahn's argument about Ralegh condemning 'Machiavels' while admiring Machiavelli, the rhetorician; see Kahn, *Machiavellian Rhetoric, From the Counter-Reformation to Milton* (Princeton, 1994), pp. 106–13.
89 Ralegh, *History*, II, vi, 8, p. 328.
90 Ibid., III, x, 7, p. 118.
91 Ibid., I, ix, 3, p. 183; II, xix, 3, p. 552; II, xix, 1, p. 505; cf. *Maxims*, p. 30; *Cabinet-Council*, pp. 39–40.
92 *History*, Preface, sig. C2v.
93 See Greenblatt, *The Renaissance Man*, passim; stoic views on life as theatre are discussed by Giles Monsarrat, *Light From the Porch: Stoicism and English Renaissance Literature* (Paris, 1984), pp. 19, 29; see also Margarret E. Reesor, 'Necessity and Fate in Stoic Philosophy,' in *The Stoics*, ed. John M. Rist (Berkeley, Los Angeles and London, 1978), pp. 187–202.
94 Greenblatt, *The Renaissance Man*, Racin, *Ralegh as Historian*, and more recently Daniel R. Woolf, *The Idea of History in Early Stuart England: Erudition, Ideology and 'The Light of Truth' from the Accession of James I to the Civil War* (Toronto, 1990) conclude that the paradoxes in the *History* arise from the strong sceptical streak in Ralegh's thought and lead to a gloomy observation about 'man's tragic condition in history' (Racin, p. 208). Cf., however, Monsarrat on the acting metaphor among the stoics, *Light From the Porch*, p. 29, and G.B. Kerford, 'What Does the Wise Man Know?' and Charlotte Stough, 'Stoic Determinism and Moral Responsibility,' in *The Stoics*, ed. Rist.
95 In *Five Courtier Poets of the English Renaissance*, ed. Robert M. Bender (New York, 1967), pp. 621–3. Through this poem Ralegh rejects the practice of Elizabethan poetic play discussed by Daniel Javitch, *Poetry and Courtliness in Renaissance England* (Princeton, 1978).
96 See Worden, 'Classical Republicanism and the Puritan Revolution,' pp. 185–7.
97 This work was first published in 1632, and in 1636 it went through its fifth edition. See *Instructions*, in *Advice to a Son*, ed. Wright, pp. xix–xx.

98 Ibid., p. 20; see also the last epigraph at the opening of this chapter.
99 Strathmann, *Sir Walter Ralegh*, pp. 154–5.
100 Ralegh, *Instructions*, in *Advice to a Son*, ed. Wright, p. 25.
101 Ibid., p. 20.
102 Ibid., p. 25.
103 Ibid., p. 26.
104 Ibid., pp. 25–6.
105 *Tvvo Bookes of Constancie*, trans John Stradling (London, 1594; *STC* 15695), p. 122; this lesson became virtually *de rigueur* in later Stuart paternal admonitions. See, for example, the adaptation offered by Sir John Holles to his son in 1625 (replete with an example of Ralegh's folly towards kings) in *Letters of John Holles 1587–1637*, ed. P.R. Seddon (Nottingham, 1975–86), II, p. 314.
106 Ralegh, *Instructions*, in *Advice to a Son*, ed. Wright, p. 23.
107 As George Calvert complained in a letter of 1612 to Sir Thomas Edmondes. In Thomas Birch, *The Court and Times of James I; Ilustrated by Authentic and Confidential Letters from Various Public and Private Collections*, ed. R.F. Williams. (London, 1848), I, p. 191.
108 Milton 'thought it a kinde of injury to withold longer the work of so eminent an Author from the Publick; it being both answerable in Stile to other Works of his already Extant, as far as the subject will permit, and given [to Milton] for a true Copy by a Learned Man at his Death ...' *Cabinet-Council* (1658), Preface, sig. A2–A2v.
109 Austin Woolrych, 'Last Quests for a Settlement, 1657–1660,' *The Interregnum: The Quest for Settlement*, ed. G.E. Aylmer (London, 1972), pp. 183–204.
110 Ralegh, *History*, V, iii, 1, p. 422.
111 Ibid., V, vi, 7, p. 749; cf. Bacon, 'Of Cunning,' in *Essays*, ed. Pitcher, p. 126.
112 Ralegh, *History*, IV, vi, 5, p. 283; cf. Lipsius, *Sixe Bookes of Politickes*, trans. Jones, IV, xiiii, p. 120.
113 Ralegh, *History*, V, iii, 1, p. 426.
114 Ralegh, *Instructions*, in *Advice to a Son*, ed. Wright, p. 27.
115 Ralegh, *History*, V, vi, 12, p. 775.
116 Ibid.
117 Charron, *Of Wisdome*, trans. Lennard, p. 351. F.J. Levy, *Tudor Historical Thought* (San Marino, 1967), p. 291, argues that Ralegh's aim was 'to tame "politic" history.'
118 See *History*, I, vi, 9, p. 97.
119 Ibid., IV, ii, 3, p. 175; V, i, 1, pp. 311–13. Cf. Bacon's admiration of Caesar discussed below, chap. 3, pp. 80–4. The contrast is that between a thinker (Bacon) and a doer (Ralegh), although the humanism of Bacon – thinking

and writing as humanistic as the physical application of learning – was that which also informed Ralegh.
120 Ralegh, *History*, V, i, 1, p. 311.
121 Ibid., IV, ii, 4, p. 177.
122 Ibid., V, i, 1, p. 314.
123 Ibid., sig. E4v.
124 See figure 4; Jonson's verse was based on Cicero's *De oratore*, II, xxxvi: 'Historia vero testis temporum, lux veritatis, / vita memoriae, magister vitae, nuntia vetustatis.' For the changing appeal of Cicero in this period, see J.H.M. Salmon, 'Cicero and Tacitus in Sixteenth-Century France,' *American Historical Review*, 85 (1980), pp. 307–31; and for Cicero's ongoing appeal in England, see Peter N. Miller, *Defining the Common Good: Empire, Religion and Philosophy in Eighteenth-Century Britain* (Cambridge, 1994).
125 Ralegh, *History*, IV, ii, 3, p. 175.
126 *The Writings and Speeches of Oliver Cromwell*, ed. W.C. Abbot (Cambridge, MA, 1939), II, p. 236.
127 Ralegh, *History*, IV, ii, 4, p. 180.

## 2 Francis Bacon and the Advancement of Constancy

1 Bacon's writings are collected in *The Works of Francis Bacon*, ed. James Spedding, R.L. Ellis, and D.D. Heath, 7 vols. (London, 1858–61); hereafter abbreviated as Bacon, *Works*. James Spedding has also collected other writings in *The Letters and Life of Francis Bacon*, ed. Spedding, 7 vols. (London, 1862–74), hereafter referred to as Spedding, *Letters*.
2 *Aubrey's Brief Lives*, ed. Oliver Lawson Dick (London, 1949), p. 9. See also the editors' introductory remarks to Bacon's *Essays* in Bacon, *Works*, VI, p. 370, and to *De Sapientia Veterum*, in ibid., pp. 608–9; and see Richard Tuck, *Philosophy and Government 1572–1651* (Cambridge, 1993), pp. 108–15.
3 Anthony Quinton and others are correcting this perspective, arguing that Bacon's importance lies not in science proper but in the broad shifts taking place in social and intellectual assumptions during the early modern period. See Anthony Quinton, *Francis Bacon* (Oxford, 1980), Charles Whitney, *Francis Bacon and Modernity* (New Haven and London, 1986); cf. Lisa Jardine, *Francis Bacon: Discovery and the Art of Discourse* (Cambridge, 1974), esp. pp. 3, 133–49. Two recent studies explore the association been science and politics in Bacon: Julian Martin, *Francis Bacon, the State, and the Reform of Natural Philosophy* (Cambridge, 1992), and B.H.G. Wormald, *Francis Bacon: History, Politics and Science, 1561–1626* (Cambridge, 1993). For some distinct though standard approaches to Bacon and the relationship between science and society, see

Christopher Hill, *Intellectual Origins of the English Revolution* (Oxford, 1965); Hugh Kearney, *Science and Change 1500–1700* (New York, 1971); Barbara Shapiro, *Probability and Certainty in Seventeenth-Century England* (Princeton, 1982); and Mark H. Curtis, *Oxford and Cambridge in Transition 1558–1642* (Oxford, 1959).
4 Spedding, *Letters*, I, p. 109.
5 Coleridge as quoted by Anne Righter, 'Francis Bacon,' in *Essential Articles for the Study of Francis Bacon*, ed. Brian Vickers (Hamden, CT, 1968), pp. 303–4. The last epigraph above is from the *Advancement*, in Bacon, *Works*, III, p. 477.
6 Jonathan Marwil, *The Trials of Counsel: Francis Bacon in 1621* (Detroit, 1976).
7 Spedding, *Letters*, III, p. 86.
8 Ibid.
9 Bacon, *Works*, III, pp. 267–77.
10 Ibid., p. 268.
11 See Curtis, *Oxford and Cambridge in Transition 1558–1642* pp. 129–47. Cf. Margo Todd, *Christian Humanism and the Puritan Social Order* (Cambridge, 1987), chaps. 3–5. Also useful on this question is Geoffrey Bullough, 'Bacon and the Defence of Learning,' in *Essential Articles*, ed. Vickers, pp. 93–113.
12 See Anthony Grafton and Lisa Jardine, *From Humanism to the Humanities: Education and the Liberal Arts in Fifteenth- and Sixteenth-Century Europe* (Cambridge, MA, 1986), pp. 161–200, quotations at pp. 170, 189. For Ramus, see Walter J. Ong, *Ramus, Method, and the Decay of Dialogue: From the Art of Discourse to the Art of Reason* (Cambridge, MA, 1958); for Ramus's influence in England, see W.S. Howell, *Logic and Rhetoric in England, 1500–1700* (Princeton, 1956); and Lisa Jardine, *Discovery and the Art of Discourse*, pp. 17–65; and for Harvey, see especially Anthony Grafton and Lisa Jardine, '"Studied for Action": How Gabriel Harvey Read His Livy,' *Past & Present*, 129 (Nov. 1990), pp. 30–78. For a critique of the Grafton–Jardine thesis, see John Charles Adams, 'Gabriel Harvey's *Ciceronianus* and the Place of Peter Ramus' *Dialecticae libro duo* in the Curriculum,' *Renaissance Quarterly*, 43 (1990), pp. 551–69.
13 Bacon, *Works*, III, pp. 294, 295.
14 Spedding, *Letters*, III, p. 85; for Levy's discussion of the tenets of 'political humanism,' which he distinguishes from Italian 'courtier humanism,' see Francis Bacon, *The History of the Reign of King Henry the Seventh*, ed. F.J. Levy (Indianapolis, 1972), p. 2, n. 1; and Levy, 'Francis Bacon and the Style of Politics,' *English Literary Renaissance*, 16 (1986), pp. 101–22. An implicit critique of Levy's approach to Bacon is offered in Victoria Kahn, *Machiavellian Rhetoric. From the Counter-Reformation to Milton* (Princeton, 1994), pp. 113–19; and in John Michael Archer, *Sovereignty and Intelligence: Spying and Court Culture in the English Renaissance* (Stanford, 1993), especially, pp. 131–3.

15 Spedding, *Letters*, I, p. 223.
16 Ibid., pp. 254–55.
17 These were words that he advised Essex to abide by; see ibid., III, p. 144.
18 See Spedding, *Letters*, II, pp. 162, 173 ff., 247–74; cf. pp. 148, 158, where Bacon relates that the task of prosecuting Essex, and then of compiling the official account of it, was 'laid upon' him.
19 Ibid., III, pp. 139–62, p. 158.
20 Francis Bacon, *Of the Interpretation of Nature* (c. 1603), Proem, in ibid., III, p. 85.
21 See Ronald Rebholz, *The Life of Fulke Greville, First Lord Brooke* (Oxford, 1971), pp. 124–31.
22 For the reciprocity implicit in the politics of courtiership and patronage, see Wallace T. MacCaffrey, 'Place and Patronage in Elizabethan Politics,' in *Elizabethan Government and Society: Essays Presented to Sir John Neale*, ed. S.T. Bindoff et al. (London, 1961), pp. 95–126; A.J. Fletcher, 'Honour, Reputation and Local Officeholding in Elizabethan and Stuart England,' in *Order and Disorder in Early Modern England*, ed. Anthony Fletcher and John Stevenson (Cambridge, 1985), pp. 92–115; and Mark Kishlansky, *Parliamentary Selection: Social and Political Choice in Early Modern England* (Cambridge, 1986).
23 The words are those of Thomas Fuller, in his *History of the Worthies of England* (London 1662; *STC* [ed. Wing] F 2440), p. 242; Pope's judgment was expressed in his 'Essay on Man,' and is quoted in Quinton, *Francis Bacon*, p. 7.
24 *Aubrey's Brief Lives*, ed. Dick, pp. 12, 8.
25 *The Chamberlain Letters: A Selection of the Letters of John Chamberlain Concerning Life in England from 1597 to 1626*, ed. Elizabeth McClure Thomson (New York, 1965), pp. 253–4.
26 See W.J. Jones, *Politics and the Bench: The Judges and the Origins of the English Civil War* (London and New York, 1971), pp. 27–43, and 57–69; Catherine Drinker Bowen, *The Lion and the Throne* (Boston, 1957); Louis A. Knafla, *Law and Politics in Jacobean England: The Tracts of Lord Chancellor Ellesmere* (Cambridge, 1977); Stephen D. White, *Sir Edward Coke and the 'grievances of the commonwealth,' 1621–1628* (Chapel Hill, N.C., 1979); J.G.A. Pocock, *The Ancient Constitution and the Feudal Law: A Study of English Historical Thought in the Seventeenth Century. A Reissue with a Retrospect* (Cambridge, 1987); Glenn Burgess, *The Politics of the Ancient Constitution: An Introduction to English Political Thought 1603–1642* (University Park, PA., 1992); J.P. Sommerville, *Politics and Ideology in England 1603–1640* (London, 1986); Colin C.G. Tite, *Impeachment and Parliamentary Judicature in Early Stuart England* (London, 1974); and the brilliant exposition by Richard Helgerson, 'Writing the Law,' chap. 2 of *Forms of Nationhood: The Elizabethan Writing of England* (Chicago and London, 1992).

27 For Bacon's enemies in Parliament and the Council, and for his disgrace, see *Debates in the House of Lords in 1621*, ed. S.R. Gardiner (London, 1870); Elizabeth Read Foster, *The House of Lords, 1603–1649* (Chapel Hill, 1983), pp. 155–6; and Robert Zaller, *The Parliament of 1621* (Berkeley, 1971), p. 84. See also Conrad Russell, *Parliaments and English Politics 1621–1629* (Oxford, 1979); and for the rivalry between Bacon and Cranfield (who would succumb, *à la* Bacon, in 1624), see Menna Prestwich, *Cranfield: Politics and Profits Under The Early Stuarts* (Oxford, 1966), pp. 286–302.

28 An account of Bacon's abandonment of Essex is to be found in Robert Lacey, *Robert, Earl of Essex: An Elizabethan Icarus* (London, 1971), pp. 170–6, and p. 244; see also, pp. 311–18. For a strong critique of Essex's activities and the view that it was Essex who betrayed his clients, and not vice versa, see Mervyn James, 'The Essex Revolt, 1601,' in his *Society, Politics and Culture: Studies in Early Modern England* (Cambridge, 1986), p. 458; cf. however, Paul E.J. Hammer, 'Patronage at Court, Faction and the Earl of Essex,' in *The Reign of Elizabeth I: Court and Culture in the Last Decade*, ed. John Guy (Cambridge, 1995), pp. 65–86.

29 See Bacon's letter to Essex in Spedding, *Letters*, II, p. 191.

30 For Bacon's consistency in this attitude see the treatment of his essay, 'On Friendship,' below, pp. 98–9. And for a brief discussion of Ciceronian concepts of friendship and citizenship in early modern Europe, see Peter N. Miller, *Defining the Common Good: Empire, Religion and Philosophy in Eighteenth-Century Britain* (Cambridge, 1994), pp. 37–8.

31 For the association between Bacon and Hobbes, see *Aubrey's Brief Lives*, ed. Dick, p. 9: 'Mr. Thomas Hobbes was beloved by his Lordship [Bacon], who was wont to have him walke with him in his delicate groves where he did meditate: and when a notion darted into his minde, Mr. Hobbs [sic] was presently to write it downe, and his Lordship was wont to say that he did it better then any one els about him; for that many times, when he read their notes he scarce understood what they writt, because they understood it not clearly themselves.' See also, Tuck, *Philosophy and Government*, pp. 108–14, discussing Bacon as an exponent of what Tuck calls 'the new humanism,' and pp. 279–345, discussing Hobbes's engagement with, and transformation of, this movement. Cf. Quentin Skinner's focus on the importance of rhetoric, 'Thomas Hobbes and the Construction of Morality,' *Proceedings of the British Academy*, 76 (1990), pp. 27–56; and his, '"Scientia civilis" in Classical Rhetoric and in the Early Hobbes,' in *Political Discourse in Early Modern Britain*, ed. Nicholas Phillipson and Quentin Skinner (Cambridge, 1993), pp. 67–93.

32 Levy, 'Francis Bacon and the Style of Politics'; see also, Levy, 'Hayward, Daniel, and the Beginnings of Politic History in England,' *Huntington Library Quarterly*, 50 (1987), pp. 11–15.

33 James's distrust of Tacitism is discussed by Alan T. Bradford, 'Stuart Absolutism and the "Utility" of Tacitus,' *Huntington Library Quarterly*, 46 (1983), pp. 127–55; cf. Malcom Smuts, 'Court-Centred Politics and the Uses of Roman Historians, c. 1590–1630' and Kevin Sharpe, 'The King's Writ: Royal Authors and Royal Authority in Early Modern England,' both in Kevin Sharpe and Peter Lake (eds.), *Culture and Politics in Early Stuart England* (London, 1994).
34 See Grafton and Jardine, 'How Gabriel Harvey Read His Livy,' p. 75 and ibid., n. 144.
35 See Mark Morford, *Stoics and Neostoics: Rubens and the Circle of Lipsius* (Princeton, 1991), p. 112.
36 Bullough, 'Bacon and the Defence of Learning,' p. 112.
37 See the last epigraph at the beginning of this chapter, in Bacon, *Works*, III, p. 477.
38 Ibid., pp. 270–1.
39 Ibid., p. 271.
40 Ibid., p. 306.
41 Ibid., p. 307.
42 Ibid., p. 316.
43 Bacon's address to the king was much more prominent in the Latin translation of the *Advancement*, *De Augmentis* (1623). Not only is the authorial presence stronger there, but the urgency of instituting his program is more pronounced. (In view of his disgrace, the appeal is perhaps not surprising.) See Bacon, *Works*, IV and V.
44 Bacon, *Works*, III, p. 311.
45 Ibid., p. 308.
46 See J.W. Williamson, *The Myth of the Conqueror. Prince Henry Stuart: A Study of 17th Century Personation* (New York, 1978), and Roy Strong, *Henry, Prince of Wales and England's Lost Renaissance* (New York, 1986). Bacon's praise of these warrior figures might well have attracted the attention of the prince, into whose household he eventually gained entry. As for James and the image of Nero, it was not one to be embraced but could be pointed to in order to demonstrate that even under tyrants, governance (and good governance, at that) carried on. For James and tyranny, see *Trew Law of Free Monarchies*, in *Divine Right and Democracy: An Anthology of Political Writing in Stuart England*, ed. David Wootton (Harmondsworth, 1986), p. 102; and for James on Caesar, *Basilikon Doron*, in *The Political Works*, ed. C.H. McIlwain (Cambridge, MA, 1918), p. 40.
47 Bacon, *Works*, III, p. 308.
48 See Grafton and Jardine, *From Humanism to the Humanities*, pp. 197–9.
49 Tuck, *Philosophy and Government*, p. 108.

50 See Spedding, *Letters*, II, pp. 21–6 (quotation at p. 22); see also Vernon F. Snow, 'Francis Bacon's Advice to Fulke Greville on Research Techniques,' *Huntington Library Quarterly*, 23 (1960), pp. 369–78.
51 See the first epigraph of this chapter, in Bacon, *Works*, III, p. 421.
52 See, for instance, *Works*, III, pp. 408–10 (*Advancement*), and V, p. 4 (*De Augmentis*, VII).
53 See Margo Todd, 'Seneca and the Protestant Mind: The Influence of Stoicism on Puritan Ethics,' *Archiv für Reformationsgeschichte*, 74 (1983), pp. 182–99.
54 Lipsius's edition of Seneca's *oeuvre* appeared in 1605, the same year as Bacon's *Advancement*. For more on the dispute over the authoritative interpretation of Seneca, see below, chap. 5, especially the section entitled, 'The Making of "our English Seneca,"' pp. 172–84. The role of Seneca in neo-stoicism is overlooked by J.H.M. Salmon, 'Cicero and Tacitus in Sixteenth-Century France,' *American Historical Review*, 85 (1980), pp. 307–31, and is seen to have operated differently than I portray here in both Salmon, 'Stoicism and Roman Example: Seneca and Tacitus in Jacobean England,' *Journal of the History of Ideas*, 50 (1989), pp. 199–225, and Tuck *Philososphy and Government*, passim.
55 Kenneth C. Schellhase, *Tacitus in Renaissance Political Thought* (Chicago, 1976), pp. 157–63, quotation at p. 160; see also Salmon, 'Seneca and Tacitus in Jacobean England,' pp. 212–13; and Edwin B. Benjamin, 'Bacon and Tacitus,' *Classical Philology*, 60 (1965), pp. 102–10.
56 See *Works*, III, pp. 338, 436, 453, and *Works*, V, pp. 21–2. See also below, chap. 5, pp. 184–95.
57 Bacon, *Works*, III, p. 438.
58 Ibid., pp. 333, 311. For the subsequent quotations here, see pp. 311–13.
59 Bacon, *Works*, VII, p. 113. This is Spedding's translation of Bacon's Latin rendition in praise of apophthegms in *De Augmentis*, II, 12. (It is rendered somewhat differently in *Works*, IV, p. 314.) See also Bacon's less fulsome remarks in the *Advancement* (*Works*, III, p. 342), and his prefacing words in the published collection of *Apophthegms* (*Works*, VII, p. 123).
60 *Advancement*, *Works*, III, p. 344. Cf. the similar comments made by Bacon in his prefatory remarks to *De Sapientia Veterum* (*Of the Wisdom of the Ancients*), in *Works*, IV, p. 314; and see also the third epigraph at the introduction of this chapter (from *Works*, VI, p. 762). For a recent assessment of Bacon's parabolic predilections, see Lisa Jardine, *Discovery and the Art of Discourse*, pp. 179–93, who argues an essential contradiction posed by Bacon's claims; on the one hand he called for the use of his techniques as a means of uncovering new knowledge and on the other, as he practised those techniques, he seemed to aver that his was the last word in that area of knowledge. Thus there was

more of the 'art of discourse' than of 'discovery' and the quest for new knowledge in his writings.
61 For example, Charles Webster, *The Great Instauration: Science, Medicine and Reform, 1626–1660* (London, 1975); Jerry Weinberger, 'Science and Rule in Bacon's Utopia: An Introduction to the Reading of the *New Atlantis*,' *American Political Science Review*, 70 (1976), pp. 865–85; and the same author's *Science, Faith and Politics: Francis Bacon and the Utopian Roots of the Modern Age* (Ithaca, 1985). Bacon's *New Atlantis* is also popular among writers of fiction, science fiction, and 'philosophical fiction.' See Umberto Eco, *Foucault's Pendulum*, trans. William Weaver (New York, 1990), where Bacon is far from virtuous in the mythical extravaganza experienced by a modern Casaubon (still a nemesis).
62 See epigraph 3, above (*Works*, VI, p. 762).
63 Bacon, *Works*, VI, pp. 705–6. Baconian fables are discussed by Jardine, *Discovery and the Art of Discourse*, pp. 179–93.
64 *Essayes By Sir William Cornwallis the Younger*, ed. Don Cameron Allen (Baltimore, 1946), pp. 201 ('Of Essaies and Bookes'), 63 ('Of Imitation'), 234 ('Of Fortune and her Children').
65 Salmon, 'Seneca and Tacitus in Jacobean England,' p. 215.
66 See the introductory table compiled by William Jones in his translation, *Sixe Bookes of Politickes* (London, 1594; STC 15701)
67 Bacon, *Works*, III, pp. 329 ff., 366 ff.
68 See Paolo Rossi, *Francis Bacon: From Magic to Science*, trans. Sacha Rabinovitch (London, 1968); and Shapiro, *Probability and Certainty in Seventeenth-Century England*; cf. Kearney, *Science and Change, 1500–1700*.
69 Bacon's quotations are taken from *Works*, III, p. 387, but see also his remarks at p. 352. For this as an essentially Ramist position, see Ong, *Ramus, Method, and the Decay of Dialogue*, pp. 36, 171–95, 245–54, and passim; see also Grafton and Jardine, *From Humanism to the Humanities*, pp. 162–70; and Lisa Jardine, *Discovery and the Art of Discourse*, pp. 41–7. In this last named work, Jardine notes that Bacon probably came across Ramus at second-hand. See, however, her remarks, at pp. 66–75. A caveat against taking Bacon's criticisms at face value is offered by Mark Curtis, *Oxford and Cambridge in Transition*, pp. 227–60 (see especially pp. 251–6).
70 Bacon, *Works*, III, pp. 421, 439, 412.
71 Some suggestive remarks are found in Daniel Woolf, 'Conscience, Constancy, and Ambition in the Career and Writings of James Howell,' in *Public Duty and Private Conscience in Seventeenth-Century England: Essays Presented to G.E. Aylmer*, ed. John Morrill, Paul Slack, and Daniel Woolf (Oxford, 1993).
72 For Lipsius on Epictetus, see *Ivsti Lipsi De Constantia Libri Dvo* (London, 1592;

STC 15694.3), Sig. A3v ('Ad Lectorum') and passim. See also, Bacon, *Works*, III, p. 423. For Epictetus, I have relied on 'The *Discourses* of Epictetus,' trans. P.E. Matheson, in *The Stoic and Epicurean Philosopher*, ed. Whitney J. Oates (New York, 1940), pp. 223–487.
73 Bacon, *Works*, III, p. 387.
74 Ibid., p. 470.
75 See ibid., pp. 445, 423, and below, pp. 90–6.
76 Ibid., p. 409. Emphasis in original.
77 Ibid., p. 410 (emphasis added), and pp. 409–10.
78 Ibid., pp. 425–7.
79 Ibid., p. 422.
80 Ibid., pp. 423, 421.
81 See Levy, 'Bacon and the Style of Politics,' who bases this view on Bacon's evident Machiavellianism; cf. Tuck, *Philosophy and Government*, pp. 110–13.
82 See Jardine, *Discovery and the Art of Discourse*, p. 173, and, more generally, pp. 150–73; and cf. Kahn, *Machiavellian Rhetoric*, pp. 114–17.
83 Lipsius had been content, in the first two books of the *Politica*, merely to state the ethical basis of political behaviour; Bacon argued it in Ramist terms. Oddly enough (or perhaps not, in view of the nature of intellectual rivalry at the time), despite the fact that he virtually replicated in political philosophy what Ramism was about in moral philosophy, Lipsius wrote to a correspondent: 'Young man, listen to me: You will never be a great man if you think that Ramus was a great man.' *Miscellaneous Letters*, no. 89, as quoted and cited by Ong, *Ramus, Method, and the Decay of Dialogue*, title page. Harvey, too, distinguished between a good and a great man; see Grafton and Jardine, *From Humanism to the Humanities*, p. 189.
84 The *Advancement* included an analysis of the state of 'divinity,' addressed by Bacon much later in the work (see *Works*, III, pp. 477–91).
85 Bacon, *Works*, III, p. 350. Cf. the efforts of a contemporary in Italy like Scipione Ammirato, or those in Spain, like Juan Antonio de Vera y Zúñiga and Baltasar Gracián, who were attempting much the same as Bacon. See Eric Cochrane, *Florence in the Forgotten Centuries 1527–1800* (Chicago and London, 1973), pp. 95–161 (for Ammirato); and J.A. Fernandez-Santamaria, *Reason of State and Statecraft in Spanish Political Thought, 1595–1640* (Lanham, N.Y., and London, 1983), chaps. 6 and 7 (for the Spaniards).
86 Bacon, *Works*, III, p. 433.
87 Ibid., p. 435.
88 Ibid., p. 437.
89 Ibid., pp. 443–4 (emphasis in original).
90 Ibid., p. 435. Cf. epigraph 2 at the beginning of the chapter, a quotation from

Bacon, *Interpretatione Naturae*, trans. James Spedding, in Spedding, *Letters*, III, p. 84.
91  Bacon, *Works*, III, pp. 446–77. Of these pages, pp. 447–73 are devoted to discussing the art of negotiating.
92  See Grafton and Jardine, *From Humanism to the Humanities*, pp. 186–98; also see, Grafton and Jardine, 'How Gabriel Harvey Read His Livy,' where the authors demonstrate how Harvey (and his contemporaries) overcame the physical obstacle of comparing and ransacking a large number of books by recourse to a giant reading wheel.
93  See Snow, 'Bacon's Advice to Fulke Greville on Research Techniques.'
94  Bacon, *Works*, III, p. 445.
95  Levy, 'Francis Bacon and the Style of Politics,' p. 113.
96  The name most closely associated with this view was, of course, Machiavelli, whose influence was very apparent in Bacon's thought here, but whom contemporaries preferred to denote as a 'politique atheiste' (as a tract by the divine John Hull indicated). For the critique of Machiavelli at this time, which largely attributed religious attrocities, or the manoeuvres of the Jesuits, to his doctrines, see Innocent Gentillet, *Antimachiavel*, ed. C.E. Rathé (Geneva 1968; first published 1576), which appeared in English as *A Discourse upon the Meanes of Wel governing a Kingdome. Divided into Three Parts. Against N. Machiavell*, trans. S. Patericke (London, 1602; *STC* 11743); and for an English critique, see John Hull, *The Unmasking of the Politique Atheiste* (1602; *STC* 13934). See also, Felix Raab, *The English Face of Machiavelli* (London, 1964), pp. 73–6; G.N.G. Orsini, *Bacone e Machiavelli* (Genoa, 1936); and Jardine, *Discovery and the Art of Discourse*, pp. 163–8. Bacon's views are an obvious exception to those analysed in Katharine Eisaman Maus, *Inwardness and Theater in the English Renaissance* (Chicago and London, 1995).
97  See Bacon, *Works*, III, pp. 422–3, 430–1, 445, 446.
98  Ibid., pp. 431, 430.
99  Ibid., p. 432: another call for a rendering unto Caesar that which is Caesar's.
100 Ibid., pp. 434, 468–9. See Rexmond C. Cochrane, 'Francis Bacon and the Architect of Fortune,' *Studies in the Renaissance*, 5 (1958), pp. 176–95.
101 Bacon, *Works*, III, p. 461.
102 Ibid., pp. 457–66.
103 This also characterized his method of persuasion: see Brian Vickers, *Francis Bacon and Renaissance Prose* (Cambridge, 1968), p. 199; cf. Jardine, *Discovery and the Art of Discourse*, pp. 169–78; cf. also motion as the starting point of Hobbes's political philosophy in *Leviathan*.
104 See Epictetus, *Discourses*, 'On Things in Our Power and Things Not in Our Power,' 'How a Careful Life is Compatible with a Noble Spirit,' and 'On

What is Meant by "Indifferent" Things,' in *The Stoic and Epicurean Philosopher*, ed. Oates, pp. 224–6, 288–92.
105 Bacon, *Works*, III, p. 457.
106 Ibid., p. 471.
107 Ibid., p. 468.
108 Ibid.
109 See Whitney, *Francis Bacon and Modernity*, and his 'Francis Bacon's *Instauratio*: Dominion Of and Over Humanity,' *Journal of the History of Ideas*, 50 (1989), pp. 371–90.
110 See *Works*, III, p. 477.
111 Bacon was not alone in this view; see Brian Vickers, 'Leisure and Idleness in the Renaissance: The Ambivalence of *Otium*,' *Renaissance Studies*, 4 (1990), pp. 1–37 and 107–54.
112 Spedding, *Letters*, I, p. 291.
113 Bacon, *Works*, V, p. 79.
114 *Aubrey's Brief Lives*, ed. Dick, p. 16.
115 The connection between these two goals is explored in Martin, *Francis Bacon, the State, and the Reform of Natural Philosophy*, and Wormald, *Francis Bacon: History, Politics, and Science*.
116 See Bacon, *Works*, VII, p. 133 ff.
117 See Ian Box, 'Bacon's *Essays*: From Political Science to Political Prudence,' *History of Political Thought*, 3 (1982), pp. 31–49. Cf. the remarks in *Sir Francis Bacon: The Essayes*, ed. Michael Kiernan (Cambridge, MA, 1985), pp. xxiv–xxx.
118 Bacon, *Works*, VI, p. 386.
119 Ibid., p. 373. Cf. Lipsius, who believed that his *De constantia* would last as long as Latin letters.
120 Bacon, *Works*, VI, pp. 485–92.
121 *Aubrey's Brief Lives*, ed. Dick, pp. 12–15.
122 Ibid., p. 145.
123 Bacon, *Works*, VI, pp. 406–12; 444–52; 437–43.
124 'Of Friendship,' in *Works*, VI, p. 438.
125 Spedding, *Letters*, VI, p. 252.
126 In the *Advancement* he noted that he was 'studious to keep the ancient terms,' which implied that he hoped to revive their classical meanings. See *Works*, III, p. 352. Cf. Lipsius's motto of 'moribus antiquis.'
127 Bacon, *Works*, VI, p. 442.
128 Ibid., p. 485.
129 The Lipsian influence in this essay has been remarked upon by few, but cf. Leonard Forster, 'Lipsius and Renaissance Neostoicism,' *Festschrift for Ralph Farrell*, ed. Anthony Stephens et al (Bern, 1977), p. 211.

130 *Epistle*, 19; in *The Workes of Lvcivs Annaevs Seneca*, trans. Thomas Lodge (London, 1614; STC 22213), p. 194.
131 Spedding, *Letters*, VII, p. 297.
132 Ibid., p. 372.
133 Ibid., p. 538.

## 3 The Constant Friend: Fulke Greville's Life after Sidney

1 Fulke Greville, *A Treatise of Religion* is reprinted in *Fulke Greville: The Remains. Being Poems of Monarchy and Religion*, ed. G.A. Wilkes (Oxford, 1965), excerpt at p. 227; his Senecan play, *Mustapha*, is reprinted in full in *Selected Writings of Fulke Greville*, ed. Joan Rees (London, 1973), excerpt at p. 138; finally, Fulke Greville, *Life of Sidney*, or, 'A Dedication to Sir Philip Sidney,' is reprinted in *The Prose Works of Fulke Greville, Lord Brooke*, ed. John Gouws (Oxford, 1986), quotation at pp. 24–5.
2 This tendency is facilitated by the modern editions which perpetuate the separation of Greville's writings. The most authoritative text to date is *Prose Works*, ed. Gouws; Geoffrey Bullough's edition of the *Poems and Dramas of Fulke Greville, First Lord Brooke*, 2 vols. (London, 1939), does not have the benefit of reference to other MSS editions of those works, while Wilkes's edition of *Remains* contains only those last treatises published in the seventeenth century.
3 Morris W. Croll, *The Works of Fulke Greville: A Thesis* (Philadelphia, 1903).
4 See *Poems and Dramas*, ed. Bullough, I, pp. 1–23. A similar sort of inquiry dominates the scholarship on Milton; see Nancy Armstrong and Leonard Tennenhouse, *The Imaginary Puritan: Literature, Intellectual Labor, and the Origins of Personal Life* (Berkeley, Los Angeles, and Oxford, 1992), pp. 9–11.
5 Ronald Rebholz, *The Life of Fulke Greville, First Lord Brooke* (Oxford, 1971).
6 See Christopher Hill, *Intellectual Origins of the English Revolution* (Oxford, 1965), passim.
7 *Poems and Dramas*, ed. Bullough, p. 56; no one to date seems to have considered that Greville might have been indulging in the humanist rhetorical tradition of arguing *in utramque partem*. Cf. Victoria Kahn's remarks on Machiavelli, in *Machiavellian Rhetoric, From the Counter-Reformation to Milton* (Princeton, 1994), p. 237 and passim.
8 See, for example, Una Ellis-Fermor's chapter on Greville in, *The Jacobean Drama* (London, 1936); Ivor Morris, 'The Tragic Vision of Fulke Greville,' *Shakespeare Studies*, 14 (1961), pp. 66–75; Yvor Winters, *Forms of Discovery: Critical & Historical Essays on the Forms of the Short Poem in English* (Chicago, 1967), pp. 48–52; Jean Jacquot, 'Religion et Raison d'État dans l'Oeuvre de

Fulke Greville,' *Études Anglaises*, 5 (1952), pp. 211–22; and Rebholz, *Life of Greville*. Cf. Joan Rees, *Fulke Greville, Lord Brooke, 1554–1628: A Critical Biography* (Berkeley and Los Angeles, 1971).

9 F.J. Levy, 'Fulke Greville: The Courtier as Philosophic Poet,' *Modern Language Quarterly*, 33 (1972), pp. 433–48.

10 David Norbrook, 'Voluntary Servitude: Fulke Greville and the Arts of Power,' in his *Poetry and Politics in the English Renaissance* (London, 1984), pp. 157–74; and Jonathan Dollimore, '*Mustapha* (c. 1594–6): Ruined Aesthetic, Ruined Theology,' in his *Radical Tragedy; Religion, Ideology and Power in the Drama of Shakespeare and his Contemporaries* (Chicago, 1984), pp. 120–33.

11 Joan Rees, *Fulke Greville*, p. 206.

12 See Thomas Kranidas, 'Style and Rectitude in Seventeenth-Century Prose: Hall, Smectymnuus, and Milton,' *Huntington Library Quarterly*, 46 (1983), pp. 237–69, which, although referring to a much later date, addresses what might be termed the climax of this debate over authoritative voices.

13 For Daniel, see Joan Rees, *Samuel Daniel: A Critical and Biographical Study* (Liverpool, 1964); for Ralegh, Leonard Tennenhouse, 'Sir Walter Ralegh and the Literature of Clientage,' in *Patronage in the Renaissance*, ed. Guy Fitch Lytle and Steven Orgel (Princeton, 1981), pp. 235–58, and see also above, chap. 1, pp. 51–3.

14 See 'A Dedication,' in *Prose Works*, ed. Gouws, pp. 87–9.

15 Cf. Anthony Esler, *The Aspiring Mind of the Elizabethan Younger Generation* (Durham, N.C., 1966).

16 Norbrook, *Poetry and Politics*, p. 157. A fuller account of Greville's life than can be afforded here is to be found in Rebholz, *Life of Greville*.

17 See 'A Dedication,' in *Prose Works*, ed. Gouws, passim.

18 Greville to Archibald Douglas, 1586, as quoted in Rebholz, *Life of Greville*, p. 68.

19 See, for example, *Aubrey's Brief Lives*, ed. Oliver Lawson Dick (London, 1949), p. 86; Sir Robert Naunton, *Fragmenta Regalia* (London, 1641), in *Somers Tracts: Collection of Scarce and Valuable Tracts ... of the late Lord Somers*, ed. Sir Walter Scott (London, 1809) vol. 1, p. 266. For a compilation of contemporary estimations of Greville, see *The Works in Verse and Prose of the Lord Brooke* ed. A.B. Grosart (London, 1870), I, pp. lxix ff.

20 Rebholz, *Life of Greville*, pp. 74–5; see also below, pp. 110–12.

21 'A Dedication,' *Prose Works*, ed. Gouws, p. 89.

22 Ibid.

23 See Rebholz, *Life Of Greville*, p. 99; Henry Wotton noted that Greville 'was a man intrensical with [Essex], or at least admitted to his Melancholly houres.' In *A Parallel Between Robert Late Earle of Essex and George Late Duke of Bucking-*

ham, in *Reliquiae Wottonianae: Or a Collection of Lives, Letters, Poems, with Characters of Sundry Personages*, 2nd ed. (London, 1654; STC [ed. Wing] W 3649), p. 9.

24 See Greville's veiled comments about Cecil in his 'Dedication,' *Prose Works*, ed. Gouws, pp. 131–2; and for Cecil's distrust of Greville, see D.R. Woolf, 'Two Elizabeths? James I and the Late Queen's Famous Memory,' *Canadian Journal of History*, 20 (1985), p. 188. Cf. however, Natalie Mears, 'Regnum Cecilianum? A Cecilian Perspective of the Court,' in *The Reign of Elizabeth I: Court and Culture in the Last Decade*, ed. John Guy (Cambridge, 1995), pp. 46–64, which examines the rhetorical aspect of such political rivalries. For Howard, see Linda Levy Peck, *Northampton: Patronage and Policy at the Court of James I* (London, 1982).

25 See Rebholz, *Life of Greville*, pp. 235–9. Menna Prestwich describes Greville as the adaptable courtier he undoubtedly was in *Cranfield: Politics and Profits under the Early Stuarts* (Oxford, 1966), p. 156; cf. Christopher Hill's estimation, *Intellectual Origins*, passim, where Greville is portrayed as a providential Calvinist who consistently favoured an English challenge to Spain's imperial hegemony over the Americas.

26 Rebholz, *Life of Greville*, p. 245; cf. the tenor of Greville's letters in the period 1613–25, many of which are transcribed by Rebholz, ibid., chaps. 14–17.

27 As attested by Sir William Davenent; see *Aubrey's Brief Lives*, ed. Dick, p. 86.

28 Historical Manuscripts Commission, Portand MSS, vol. 9 (London, 1923), p. 39, as quoted and cited in Rebholz, *Life of Greville*, p. 235. When, two years later, Greville gained high office at the Exchequer, John Chamberlain remarked to a correspondant: 'Many marvel that a man of his years, wealth, and retired life, should affect such a place; but everybody hath a doting time, and ambition is blind.' Chamberlain to Isaac Wake, 12 October 1614, in Thomas Birch, *The Court and Times of James I; Illustrated by Authentic and Confidential Letters, from Various Public and Private Collections*, ed. R.F. Williams (London, 1848), I, p. 349.

29 See Perez Zagorin, *Ways of Lying: Dissimulation, Persecution, and Conformity in Early Modern Europe* (Cambridge, MA, and London, 1990). In his review of this work, Thomas F. Mayer has noted the political parallel (*Sixteenth Century Journal*, 22 [1991], pp. 585–6), and some time ago the association between religious and political nicodemism was suggested by Delio Cantimore, in 'Submission and Conformity: "Nicodemism" and the Expectations of a Conciliar Solution to the Religious Question,' trans. and ed. Eric Cochrane, *The Late Italian Renaissance, 1525–1630* (New York and London, 1970), pp. 244–65.

30 See James E. Phillips, 'George Buchanan and the Sidney Circle,' *Huntington Library Quarterly*, 12 (1948–9), pp. 23–55; for these 'Calvinist' theorists of revo-

lution, see J.H.M. Salmon, *The French Religious Wars in English Political Thought* (Oxford, 1959); for what was particularly Calvinist about them, see Quentin Skinner, 'The Origins of the Calvinist Theory of Revolution,' in *After the Reformation: Essays in Honor of J.H. Hexter*, ed. Barbara C. Malament (Philadelphia, 1980), pp. 309–30.
31 See Michael G. Brennan, *Literary Patronage in the English Renaissance: The Pembroke Family* (London and New York, 1988), p. 59.
32 Roger Howell, *Sir Philip Sidney: The Shepherd Knight* (London, 1968), p. 116.
33 See Norman Farmer, Jr., 'Fulke Greville and Sir John Coke: An Exchange of Letters on a History Lecture and Certain Latin Verses on Sir Philip Sidney,' *Huntington Library Quarterly*, 33 (1969–70), pp. 217–36. For a different view on Greville's reasons for composing his *Inquisition Upon Fame and Honour*, see Rebholz, *Life of Greville*, pp. 229–32.
34 *Caelica*, 84, in *Poems and Dramas*, ed. Bullough, I, p. 134; cf. Catherine Bates, *The Rhetoric of Courtship in Elizabethan Language and Literature* (Cambridge, 1992), pp. 144–5.
35 See Joel Hurstfield, 'The Succession Struggle in Late Elizabethan England,' in his *Freedom, Corruption and Government in Elizabethan England* (London, 1973), pp. 103–34. It is to be wondered, as well, whether Sidney, had he lived, would have remained as attached to the Protestant cause. See the remarks made by Levy, 'Fulke Greville,' p. 446, and Jan van Dorsten, 'The Final Year,' in *Sir Philip Sidney: 1586 and the Creation of a Legend*, ed. van Dorsten et al. (Leiden, 1986) pp. 16–24.
36 See Rebholz, *Life of Greville*, pp. 75–7.
37 'A Dedication,' *Prose Works*, ed. Gouws, p. 11.
38 Ibid.
39 For an incisive discussion of the importance of Greville's decision here, see Norbrook, *Poetry and Politics*, pp. 170–1.
40 These remarks were included in the Preface, addressed 'To the Reader.' See *The Complete Works of Sir Philip Sidney*, ed. A. Feuillerat (Cambridge, 1922), I, p. 524.
41 Rees, *Fulke Greville*, p. 55; see also Victor Skretkowicz, 'Building Sidney's Reputation: Texts and Editors of the *Arcadia*,' in *Sir Philip Sidney: 1586 and the Creation of a Legend*, ed. van Dorsten et al., pp. 111–24.
42 Brennan, *Literary Patronage*, p. 59. Of course, the countess did have good reason to seek solace in this way. Not only did she lose her brother in 1586, but her parents, as well.
43 Greville to Walsingham, 1586, as quoted by Rebholz, *Life of Greville*, p. 76.
44 'A Dedication,' *Prose Works*, ed. Gouws, p. 12.
45 *Letter to an Honourable Lady*, in *Prose Works*, ed. Gouws, p. 138.

46 Ibid., pp. 139, 165, 156.
47 Ibid., pp. 138, 141.
48 Ibid., pp. 156–60.
49 Ibid., p. 158.
50 Ibid., p. 150.
51 Ibid., p. 160.
52 Ibid., p. 165.
53 Ibid., pp. 154, 150, 156, 170.
54 For a discussion on the actuality of an addressee, and the tenor of Greville's *Letter*, see Gouws's 'General Introduction,' *Prose Works*, pp. xxv–xxix.
55 The differences between a language and the 'speech acts performed within and upon it' are discussed by J.G.A. Pocock, 'The Concept of a Language and the *Métier d'Historien*: Some Considerations on Practice,' in *The Languages of Political Theory in Early-Modern Europe*, ed. Anthony Pagden (Cambridge, 1987), pp. 19–38 (quotation at p. 29). Greville frequently uses Calvinist language; the speech acts he performs within this language, however, beg to be considered in a broader humanist context. In this case, the Lipsian paradigm provides a relevant model. For more on his uses of Calvinist 'speech acts,' see below, pp. 124–8, 134.
56 *Letter*, in *Prose Works*, ed. Gouws, p. 163. In 1615 Joseph Hall was to denounce the popularity of the maxim *qui nescit dissimulare, nescit vivere*. See below, chap. 5, p. 180 and n. 40, and cf. Epilogue and figure 10.
57 See Norbrook, *Poetry and Politics*, pp. 163–7.
58 Ibid., p. 161. Cf. Daniel Javitch, *Poetry and Courtliness in Renaissance England* (Princeton, 1978), whose thesis of courtly artfulness, *sprezzatura*, can hardly be extended to include the poetry of Greville.
59 *Mustapha*, V, iii, ll. 90–111, in Rees, *Selected Writings*, p. 133.
60 I have applied insights derived from Jonathan Dollimore, 'Mustapha,' in *Radical Tragedy*, pp. 120–33.
61 Cf. John Michael Archer, *Sovereignty and Intelligence: Spying and Court Culture in the English Renaissance* (Stanford, 1993), pp. 17–40 and 51.
62 For Montaigne, see Introduction above, pp. 12–13.
63 Rebholz and others make much of Greville's abstract approach to life. Cf., however, Greville's own concern with passion, expressed in many places, for example, *Treatise of Humane Learning*, stanzas 113–14, in *Poems and Dramas*, ed. Bullough, I, p. 182.
64 I have explored these issues further in 'Whose Life Is It, Anyway? Subject and Subjection in Fulke Greville's *Life of Sidney*,' in *The Rhetorics of Life-Writing in Early Modern Europe: Forms of Biography from Cassandra Fedele to Louis XIV*, ed. Thomas F. Mayer and D.R. Woolf (Ann Arbor, 1995), pp. 299–320.

65 In *Poems and Dramas*, ed. Bullough, I, p. 160, stanza 26.
66 *Remains*, ed. Wilkes, p. 211, stanza 36.
67 For contrasting views on the reach of the council see Kevin Sharpe, 'Introduction,' *Faction and Parliament*, ed. Sharpe (Oxford, 1978) and F.J. Levy, 'Hayward, Daniel, and the Beginnings of Politic History in England,' *Huntington Library Quarterly*, 50 (1987), pp. 1–34. Cf. D.H. Willson, *James VI & I* (London, 1956); D.R. Woolf, 'Two Elizabeths?'; and for a conservative estimate of the Crown's intervention in the production and dissemination of literature (Tacitist or otherwise), see A.B. Worden, 'Literature and Censorship in Early Modern England,' *Too Mighty to be Free: Censorship and the Press in Britain and the Netherlands*, ed. A.C. Duke and C.A. Tamse (Zutphen, 1987), pp. 45–62.
68 See Alan T. Bradford, 'Stuart Absolutism and the "Utility" of Tacitus,' *Huntington Library Quarterly*, 46 (1983), pp. 127–55; cf. Jonathan Goldberg, *James I and the Politics of Literature: Jonson, Shakespeare, Donne, and Their Contemporaries* (Baltimore, 1983), chap. 2.
69 See Levy, 'Beginnings of Politic History,' p. 27; D.R. Woolf, *The Idea of History in Early Stuart England: Erudition, Ideology, and 'The Light of Truth' from the Accession of James I to the Civil War* (Toronto, 1990), pp. 119–21; and for Camden's proud independence and autonomy, Richard Helgerson, *Forms of Nationhood: The Elizabethan Writing of England* (Chicago and London, 1992), p. 127.
70 See Farmer, 'Fulke Greville and Sir John Coke'; also see Kevin Sharpe, 'The Foundation of the Chairs of History at Oxford and Cambridge: An Episode in Jacobean Politics,' *History of Universities*, vol. 2 (1982), pp. 127–52, reprinted in his *Politics and Ideas in Early Stuart England* (London and New York, 1989), pp. 207–29.
71 Public Records Office, London, *State Papers, Domestic*, 16/86–7 (Wren to Laud, Dec. 1627); see also the good account of the entire letter in Rebholz, *Life of Greville*, pp. 298–9.
72 See Bullough's discussion of the context of the poem in *Poems and Dramas*, I, pp. 52–62.
73 See Grafton and Jardine, '"Studied for Action": How Gabriel Harvey Read His Livy,' *Past & Present*, 129 (Nov., 1990), p. 75.
74 This description is Bullough's, *Poems and Dramas*, I, p. 52; for Daniel's poem, see *Samuel Daniel's Musophilus*, ed. Raymond Himelick (West Lafayette, 1965).
75 D.R. Woolf, 'Community, Law and State: Samuel Daniel's Historical Thought Revisited,' *Journal of the History of Ideas*, 49 (1988), p. 63.
76 See Mark Curtis, *Oxford and Cambridge in Transition 1558–1642* (Oxford, 1959), especially pp. 128–48.

77 Bacon seems to have hoped to engage Greville in the type of research he promoted in his *Advancement*. See Vernon F. Snow, 'Francis Bacon's Advice to Fulke Greville on Research Techniques,' *Huntington Library Quarterly*, 23 (1960), pp. 369–78. The dating of the letter on which Snow bases his article is questionable.
78 See Brennan, *Literary Patronage*, pp. 78–82.
79 See Woolf, 'Daniel's Historical Thought,' pp. 73–5; and see also *Musophilus*, ed. Himelick, pp. 30–6.
80 *Musophilus*, l. 189 in Himelick (ed.), p. 67. Still, Daniel may have remained as concerned as ever with politics; see Richard Helgerson, 'Barbarous Tongues: The Ideology of Poetic Form in Renaissance England,' in *The Historical Renaissance: New Essays on Tudor and Stuart Literature and Culture*, ed. Heather Dubrow and Richard Strier (Chicago, 1988), pp. 286–9.
81 J.H.M. Salmon, 'Stoicism and Roman Example: Seneca and Tacitus in Jacobean England,' *Journal of the History of Ideas*, 50 (1989), pp. 213–15.
82 *Poems and Dramas*, ed. Bullough, I, pp. 170, 154, stanzas 67, 1.
83 Ibid., pp. 169 ff, stanzas 61 ff.
84 Ibid., p. 182, stanza 115.
85 See Bullough's dicussion of Greville and Calvin in *Poems and Dramas*, I, pp. 9–14; cf. Rebholz's view as stated throughout his *Life of Greville*; and for a discussion of Greville that stresses his Calvinism, see Richard Waswo, *The Fatal Mirror: Themes and Techniques in the Poetry of Fulke Greville* (Charlottesville, VA, 1972).
86 See Waswo, *The Fatal Mirror*, p. 21.
87 *Poems and Dramas*, ed. Bullough, I, pp. 175–6, stanzas 87–8.
88 For Greville and Preston, see Hill, *Intellectual Origins*, p. 24; for Andrewes, see Trevor A. Owen, *Lancelot Andrewes* (Boston, 1981).
89 *Humane Learning*, stanza 113, in *Poems and Dramas*, ed. Bullough, I, p. 182. For Greville as a religious 'utilitarian,' see Hill, *Intellectual Origins*, p. 94, n. 3.
90 The role of such 'seeming' in Bacon's philosophy is discussed above, chap. 2, pp. 92–6; cf. F.J. Levy, 'Francis Bacon and the Style of Politics,' *English Literary Renaissance*, 16 (1986), pp. 101–22.
91 Robert Dallington, *Aphorismes Civill and Militarie: Amplified with Authorities; and exemplified with Historie, out of the first Quarterne of Fr. Guicciardine* (London, 1613, STC 6197), Aphorisme 12, p. 15.
92 Cf. Rebholz, *Life of Greville*, passim.
93 See Quentin Skinner, 'Conquest and Consent: Thomas Hobbes and the Engagement Controversy,' in *The Interregnum: The Quest for Settlement 1646–1660*, ed. G.E. Aylmer (London, 1972), pp. 79–98. Greville's adherence to the *de facto* state was not complete, but it was strong, and it would be evoked by

a later generation that was confronted by the introduction of a new form of government in the wake of the execution of King Charles in 1649. See the Epilogue below, pp. 208–11.
94 'A Dedication,' *Prose Works*, ed. Gouws, p. 7.
95 Ibid., pp. 68, 24, 75; I have discussed the implications of the tensions in Greville's portrait of Sidney in 'Whose Life Is It, Anyway?', cited in full at n. 64 above.
96 Jonson's *Conversations with Drummond*, in *Ben Jonson: The Complete Poems*, ed. George Parfitt (Harmondsworth, 1988), p. 466.
97 'A Dedication,' *Prose Works*, ed. Gouws, p. 18.
98 Sir Walter Ralegh, 'An Epitaph,' in *Five Courtier Poets of the English Renaissance*, ed. Robert M. Bender (New York, 1967), pp. 606–7.
99 Greville, 'A Dedication,' *Prose Works*, ed. Gouws, p. 76.
100 See the editor's discussion of the dating hints in the 'Dedication.' *Prose Works*, ed. Gouws, pp. xxi–xxiv.
101 See Woolf, 'Two Elizabeths?' pp. 188–9; cf. Blair Worden's discussion of Greville's political inclinations in his review of Gouws, *Prose Works*, in *London Review of Books*, 3 July 1986, pp. 19–22.
102 See 'A Dedication,' *Prose Works*, ed. Gouws pp. 131–2.
103 See Rees, *Fulke Greville*, p. 124; Woolf, *The Idea of History*, pp. 175–8.
104 See Rebholz, *Life of Greville*, chaps. 11–13.
105 Hall, *Epistles* (1611; STC 12662), III, vi, 2, pp. 13–19. For a discussion of the friendship between Greville and Hall, see Richard A. McCabe, 'Fulke Greville and Joseph Hall,' *Notes and Queries* 226 (new series, vol. 28, no. 1) (Feb. 1981), pp. 45–6.
106 See Davenant's judgment recorded in *Aubrey's Brief Lives*, ed. Dick, p. 86.
107 G.A. Wilkes describes his view of the development of the *Treatise of Monarchy* and also notes the consistency of Greville's argument in *Remains*, ed. Wilkes, pp. 6–15.
108 See Greville, *Treatise of Monarchy*, stanzas 153, 164–75, 360, in *Remains*, ed. Wilkes, pp. 73, 76–9, 125. For an interpretation quite different from mine, see Hugh N. Maclean, 'Fulke Greville: Kingship and Sovereignty,' *Huntington Library Quarterly*, 16 (1952–3), pp. 237–71.
109 Greville, *Treatise of Monarchy*, stanzas 467, 535, 575, in *Remains*, ed. Wilkes, pp. 152, 169, 179.
110 Dallington, *Aphorismes Civill and Militarie*, pp. 314–15. See above, chap. 1, pp. 55–8, where Ralegh's repudiation of Dallington is discussed; and see also, Salmon, 'Seneca and Tacitus in Jacobean England,' pp. 215–17. For 'reason of state,' the essays in *Staatsrason: Studien zur Geschichte eines politischen Begriffs*, ed. Roman Schnur (Berlin, 1975) remain useful. In the same general

context, although concerned less with 'reason of state' than with the emergence of the abstract concept of the state, see Quentin Skinner, 'The State,' in *Political Innovation and Conceptual Change*, ed. Terence Ball, James Farr, and Russell L. Hanson (Cambridge, 1989), pp. 90–131.
111 See *Treatise of Monarchy*, stanzas 114, 238, in *Remains*, ed. Wilkes, pp. 63, 94.
112 Cf. Rebholz, *Life of Greville*, pp. 200–15.
113 Ten years later, a military theorist considered Greville the appropriate addressee in discussing the qualities of a lieutenant general, writing: 'The most materiall parts of his Office consisteth in Counsells, and the debatements of all serious designs.' See Francis Markham, *Five Decades of Epistles of Warre* (London, 1622; *STC* 17332), V, no. 9, p. 194. For the changed context of the 1620s, see Thomas Cogswell, *The Blessed Revolution: English Politics and the Coming of War* (Cambridge, 1990).
114 'A Dedication,' *Prose Works*, ed. Gouws, p. 3.
115 Greville probably did not idle away these two intervening years. Ever able to contemplate the same problem from various perspectives, he rethought some of his categories pertaining to war and, in his *Treatie of Warre*, came up with some far different conclusions than those that had been intended for a martial prince. For differing views on the dating of *Warres*, see Rebholz, *Life of Greville*, p. 337; Bullough, *Poems and Dramas*, I, pp. 67–72; and Hugh N. Maclean, 'Fulke Greville on War,' *Huntington Library Quarterly* 21 (1957–8), pp. 95–109.
116 This argument is succinctly made by Norbrook in *Poetry and Politics*, pp. 170–4; cf. J.W. Allen, *English Political Thought, 1603–1660* (London, 1938), I, pp. 68–72.
117 Cf. Achmat's position in *Mustapha*, and *A Treatise of Monarchy*, stanzas 1–4, and 9, in *Remains*, ed. Wilkes, pp. 35–6.
118 Cf. Rees, *Fulke Greville, Lord Brooke, 1554–1628: A Critical Biography*, pp. 124–5.
119 See 'A Dedication,' *Prose Works*, ed. Gouws, p. 32.
120 In *Remains*, ed. Wilkes, p. 41, stanza 26.
121 See Norbrook, *Poetry and Politics*, pp. 164–7.
122 See Peter Burke, 'Tacitism,' in *Tacitus*, ed. T.A. Dorey (New York, 1969), pp. 163–7, discussing the two types of Tacitism described by G. Toffanin in *Machiavelli e il tacitismo* (Padua, 1921).
123 Greville, as recorded by Simonds D'Ewes (*The Journals of All the Parliaments during the Reign of Queen Elizabeth, Both of House of Lords and House of Commons* [London, 1682], p. 490), and as quoted (and cited) by Rebholz, *Life of Greville*, p. 92.
124 Norbrook, *Poetry and Politics*, pp. 169–70.

125 In *Remains*, ed. Wilkes, p. 80, stanza 182.
126 Dorislaus was the second choice for the position since Gerhard Vossius, whom Greville's friend Coke recommended be offered the post, was unavailable. For the troubles Greville underwent trying to find a suitable candidate for the position, see Farmer, 'Fulke Greville and Sir John Coke,' and Sharpe, 'Foundations of the Chairs of History.' For more on Dorislaus, see below, 'Epilogue,' pp. 206–7.
127 'A Dedication,' *Prose Works*, ed. Gouws, p. 245.
128 See W.A. Ringler, Jr., 'Sir Philip Sidney: The Myth and the Man,' in *1586 and the Creation of a Legend*, ed. van Dorsten et al, pp. 3–15.
129 See van Dorsten, 'The Final Year,' in ibid., pp. 22–3.
130 Greville, quoted by Bacon, *Apophthegms*, no. 202, in *The Works of Francis Bacon*, ed. James Spedding et al (London 1858–61), VII, p. 153.

## 4 A Neostoic Scout: Ben Jonson and the Poetics of Constancy

1 For a sampling of the literature that examines the Stuart court according to Stephen Greenblatt's concept of 'self-fashioning,' see Jonathan Goldberg, *James I and the Politics of Literature: Jonson, Shakespeare, Donne, and their Contemporaries* (Baltimore and London, 1983); Graham Parry, *The Golden Age Restor'd: The Culture of the Stuart Court, 1603–1642* (Manchester, 1981); and R. Malcolm Smuts, *Court Culture and the Origins of a Royalist Tradition in Early Stuart England* (Philadelphia, 1987).
2 *Ben Jonson: The Man and his Works*, ed. C.H. Herford and P. and E. Simpson, 11 vols. (Oxford, 1925–52), VIII, pp. 561–649; the epigraph is on p. 563. Hereafter, reference to Jonson's writings will be mainly to this edition and will use the abbreviation, *Works*, ed. Herford and Simpson. Jonson's commonplace book was named *Timber, or Discoveries* and will hereafter be referred to as *Discoveries*.
3 Jonson's life has been the subject of two recent studies: Rosalind Miles, *Ben Jonson: His Life and Works* (London, 1986), and David Riggs, *Ben Jonson: A Life* (Cambridge, MA, 1989); other full-length studies which interpret his work in light of his life include, Anne Barton, *Ben Jonson, Dramatist* (Cambridge, 1984), and Robert C. Evans, *Ben Jonson and the Poetics of Patronage* (London, 1989). Jonson himself divulged aspects of his life to William Drummond of Hawthornden, recorded in his *Conversations with Drummond of Hawthornden*, *Works*, ed. Herford and Simpson, I, pp. 132–51 (hereafter referred to as *Conversations*). For his record of the soldiering experience, see *Conversations*, p. 139.
4 The Privy Council suspected it for 'very seditious and sclandrous matter,'

and prosecuted the actors for 'their Leude and mutynous behavior.' *Works*, ed. Herford and Simpson, I, p. 217, and Riggs, *Jonson: A Life*, p. 32. Jonson would probably be much amused at the new-found popularity of the Isle of Dogs among young Thatcherites in London.

5. Riggs, *Jonson: A Life*, pp. 49–53, 122–30; *Conversations*, in *Works*, ed. Herford and Simpson, I, p. 141. For Jonson's religion, see below, pp. 149–55.

6. Jonson's antipathy for Northampton was recorded by Drummond in 1618–19: see, *Conversations*, in *Works*, ed. Herford and Simpson, I, p. 141, and see also, for his career, Linda Levy Peck, *Northampton: Patronage and Policy at the Court of James I* (London, 1982). Jonson's animosity towards Buckingham developed, it seems, after the accession of Charles. For Buckingham's career, see Roger Lockyer, *Buckingham* (London, 1981). For the Daniel and Jones rivalries, see Riggs, *Jonson: A Life*, passim.

7. *Discoveries*, in *Works*, ed. Herford & Simpson, VIII, pp. 578–9.

8. Published in Latin in 1586 (*STC* 4503), the English translation of *Britannia*, by P. Holland, came out in 1610 (*STC* 4509). In 1605, Camden published his *Remaines of a Greater Worke Concerning Britaine* (*STC* 4521). For studies which treat Camden's historical technique, see F. Smith Fussner, *The Historical Revolution: English Historical Writing and Thought 1580–1640* (London, 1962); F.J. Levy, *Tudor Historical Thought* (San Marino, 1967); Arthur B. Ferguson, *Clio Unbound: Perception of the Social and Cultural Past in Renaissance England* (Durham, N.C., 1979); and Kevin Sharpe, *Sir Robert Cotton, 1586–1631: History and Politics in Early Modern England* (Oxford, 1979).

9. Studies which examine this topic include the sources mentioned at n. 1, above; see also, Stephen Orgel, *The Illusion of Power: Political Theater in the English Renaissance* (Berkeley, 1975); Stephen Orgel and Roy Strong, *Inigo Jones: The Theatre of the Stuart Court*, 2 vols. (Berkeley, 1973); and for a broader perspective, see *Rites of Power: Symbolism, Ritual & Politics Since the Middle Ages*, ed. Sean Wilentz (Philadelphia, 1985).

10. Sharpe, *Sir Robert Cotton*, p. 11.

11. *Epigrammes*, 14, in *Works*, ed. Herford and Simpson, VIII, p. 31; for the Lipsian example of the 'contubernium,' see Mark Morford, *Stoics and Neostoics: Rubens and the Circle of Lipsius* (Princeton, 1991), pp. 14–30. I have examined this concept in relation to Fulke Greville's *Life of Sidney*: see Adriana McCrea, 'Whose Life Is It, Anyway? Subject and Subjection in Fulke Greville's *Life of Sidney*,' in Thomas F. Mayer & D. R. Woolf (eds.), *The Rhetorics of Life-Writing in Early Modern Europe: Forms of Biography from Cassandra Fedele to Louis XIV* (Ann Arbor, MI, 1995), pp. 299–320.

12. *Works*, ed. Herford and Simpson, I, p. 250.

13. *Works*, ed. Herford and Simpson, VIII, p. 159. This Epistle to Selden was one

of eighty-nine previously unpublished verses collected and arranged into 'The Under Wood' by Sir Kenelm Digby for a two-volume edition of Jonson's works, published posthumously in 1640. The Epistle became *Underwoods*, 14, (in *Works*, ed. Herford and Simpson, VIII, pp. 158–61).
14 Leon Voet, *The Golden Compasses: A History and Evaluation of the Printing and Publishing of the Officina Plantiniana at Antwerp*, 2 vols. (Amsterdam, London, and New York, 1972); see figure 5, which is the emblem of the Officiana Plantiniana, appearing in all works published by the Plantin Press.
15 *Conversations*, *Works*, ed. Herford and Simpson, I, p. 148; the 'cover-ornament' on each volume of Jonson's *Works* edited by Herford and Simpson reproduces this *impresa*.
16 Riggs, *Jonson: A Life*, p. 205.
17 *Epigrammes*, 43, in *Works*, ed. Herford and Simpson, VIII, p. 40.
18 Francis Bacon, 'Of Praise,' in *Francis Bacon: The Essays*, ed. John Pitcher (Harmondsworth, 1985), p. 215.
19 *Epigrammes*, 65, in *Works*, ed. Herford and Simpson, VIII, p. 48. This poem of self-censure follows two epigrams addressed to Salisbury. For some pertinent remarks on Jonson's own ordering of his verses, see Annabel Patterson, *Censorship and Interpretation: The Conditions of Writing and Reading in Early Modern England* (Madison, WI, 1984), pp. 132–44; and for an insightful discussion of Jonson's theory of praise, see Blair Worden, 'Ben Jonson among the Historians,' in Kevin Sharpe and Peter Lake (eds.), *Culture and Politics in Early Stuart England* (London, 1994), pp. 67–89.
20 See Sharpe, *Sir Robert Cotton*, passim, and p. 210, n. 39.
21 See Conrad Russell, *Parliaments and English Politics 1621–1629* (Oxford, 1979) and *Faction and Parliament: Essays in Early Stuart History*, ed. K. Sharpe (Oxford, 1978), 'Introduction.'
22 Sharpe, *Sir Robert Cotton*, pp. 208–10. For Selden's politics, see David Berkowitz, *John Selden's Formative Years: Politics and Society in Early Seventeenth-Century England* (Washington, 1988), and Paul Christianson, *Discourse on History, Law, and Governance in the Public Career of John Selden, 1610–1635* (Toronto, 1996).
23 Sharpe, *Sir Robert Cotton*, p. 214.
24 *Works*, ed. Herford and Simpson, I, pp. 242–4.
25 *Stuart Royal Proclamations*, ed. James F. Larkin and Paul L. Hughes (Oxford, 1973), I, p. 324.
26 An annual pension was granted to Jonson for life; see 'Patent for Jonson's Pension of 1616,' in *Works*, ed. Herford and Simpson, I, pp. 231–2.
27 Cf. David Norbrook, 'Jonson and the Jacobean Peace,' in *Poetry and Politics in the English Renaissance*, (London, 1984), chap. 7.

28 *Discoveries, Works*, ed. Herford and Simpson, VIII, pp. 643, 595. For Jonson's masques, see Norbrook, *Poetry and Politics*, pp. 175–94; Stephen Orgel, *The Jonsonian Masque* (Cambridge, MA, 1965); Goldberg, *James I and the Politics of Literature*; and Parry, *The Golden Age Restor'd*.
29 Nathaniel Brent to a correspondent, quoted in *Works*, ed. Herford and Simpson, X, p. 576.
30 *Conversations, Works*, ed. Herford and Simpson, I, p. 141.
31 Parry, *Golden Age Restor'd*, p. 181.
32 See Jason L. Saunders, *Justus Lipsius: The Philosophy of Renaissance Stoicism* (New York, 1955), pp. 15–18; Morford, *Stoics and Neostoics*, p. 33 and passim.
33 *Discoveries, Works*, ed. Herford and Simpson, VIII, p. 565. Jonson entered this in Latin; the translation here is from *Ben Jonson: The Complete Poems*, ed. George Parfitt (London, 1988), p. 585.
34 See Dewey D. Wallace, *Puritans and Predestination: Grace in English Protestant Theology, 1525–1695* (Chapel Hill, N.C., 1982); Nicholas Tyacke, *Anti-Calvinists: The Rise of English Arminianism* (Oxford, 1987), and John Guy, 'The Elizabethan Establishment and the Ecclesiastical Policy,' in *The Reign of Elizabeth I: Court and Culture in the Last Decade*, ed. John Guy (Cambridge, 1995), pp. 126–49. For the argument that the English church was characterized by a broad consensus during this period, see Patrick Collinson, *The Religion of Protestants* (Oxford, 1982) and Kenneth L. Parker, *The English Sabbath: A Study of Doctrine and Discipline from the Reformation to the Civil War* (Cambridge, 1988); and for its collapse, see Margo Todd, *Christian Humanism and the Puritan Social Order* (Cambridge, 1987), chaps. 6–7. The origin of the 'Stage Puritan,' located in the 'nasty nineties' context of the Marprelate Tracts, is explored by Patrick Collinson, 'Ecclesiastical Vitriol: Religious Satire in the 1590s and the Invention of Puritanism,' in *The Reign of Elizabeth I: Court and Culture in the Last Decade*, ed. Guy, pp. 150–70.
35 *Works*, ed. Herford and Simpson, X, p. 213.
36 *Discoveries, Works*, ed. Herford and Simpson, VIII, pp. 595–6, 579–80. Emphasis added.
37 See figure 6, p. 156 below, illustrating Jonson's Senecan motto inscribed on his copy of Lipsius, *De Militia Romana* (1602 [first published Antwerp, 1595]), now held at the Houghton Library, Harvard University. Jonson's 'dialogue' with Lipsius, based on the marginalia in his copy of the 1623 edition of the *Politica* (held at the Library of Emmanuel College, Cambridge), is studied by Robert C. Evans, *Jonson, Lipsius and the Politics of Renaissance Stoicism* (Wakefield, N. H., 1992). The question of Renaissance stoicism and the nature of English Renaissance dramatists' engagement with it has been explored by Giles D. Monsarrat, *Light From the Porch: Stoicism and English Renaissance Lit-*

*erature* (Paris, 1984), and, more recently, by A.A. Bromham, '"Have You Read Lipsius?": Thomas Middleton and Stoicism,' *English Studies*, 77, 5 (Sept., 1996) pp. 401–21.

38 *Works*, ed. Herford and Simpson, VIII, p. 580. Cf. Lipsius, *Sixe Bookes of Politickes*, trans. William Jones (London, 1594; *STC* 15701), I.i, pp. 1–2, for this latter quotation, and I.ii, pp. 3–4, for the one above, whose original source is Tacitus in the *Germania* (n.p.). Notably, contemporaries continued to study and extract notes from the *Politica* throughout the seventeenth century. See, for example, British Library, London, Sloane MS 848, f. 27, where the author notes from Lipsius that 'it is more Reuerend to beleeue ye wonderfull workes of God, then to enquire why hee hath donne them'; and Sloane MS 1983B, ff. 86–88b, where the marginalia indicates that Lipsius was still studied in 1699.

39 'An Epistle to Master John Selden,' *Underwoods*, 14, in *Works*, ed. Herford and Simpson, VIII, pp. 158–61, quotations at ll. 39–46, l.14 and l.16. Selden's scholarship could profitably be examined against that of Lipsius, who also 'searched antiquity' (to adapt Jonson's words on Selden) to counter politico-religious claims to certainty; Selden's manuscript copy of Stradling's translation of *De constantia* is held at Gloucester Cathedral. *De constantia* continued to go through translations in the seventeenth century, for example, that by 'R.G.' in 1654 (*STC* [ed. Wing] L2359) and by Nathanial Wanley in 1670 (*STC* [ed. Wing] L2360).

40 *Underwoods*, 43, in *Works*, ed. Herford and Simpson, VIII, p. 207.

41 Wallace, *Puritans and Predestination*, pp. 71–2, 218, n. 241.

42 Ibid., p. 69.

43 Ibid., p. 72.

44 Todd, *Christian Humanism and the Puritan Social Order*, passim.

45 For proponents of the authority of the spirit, see Christopher Hill's essays on 'Heresy and Radical Politics,' in *The Collected Essays of Christopher Hill* (Amherst, 1986) vol. II, and also his *Antichrist in Seventeenth-Century England* (Oxford, 1971), see also *Radical Religion in the English Revolution*, ed. J.F. McGregor and B. Reay (Oxford, 1984), passim.

46 *Bartholomew Fair*, I, iii, 143–4, *Works*, ed. Herford and Simpson, VI, p. 27; cf. Anne Barton, *Ben Jonson, Dramatist*, pp. 210–18. Other targets in this play may have included pious divines of the ilk of Joseph Hall, whose Senecan strain was strong in his moral teachings. See Geoffrey Aggeler, 'Ben Jonson's Justice Overdo and Joseph Hall's Good Magistrate,' *English Studies*, 76. 5 (Sept., 1995), pp. 434–42. And for an examination of Hall's thought and teachings, see below, chap. 5.

47 *Conversations*, *Works*, ed. Herford and Simpson, I, p. 151.

48 Ibid., p. 139.

49 See Riggs, *Jonson: A Life*, pp. 51–2.
50 Norbrook, *Poetry and Politics*, p. 176.
51 See Richard Tuck, *Philosophy and Government, 1572–1651* (Cambridge, 1993), p. 60. I plan to examine the details of Lipsius's repair from Leiden in 1591 in a forthcoming study.
52 *An Humble Supplication to Her Majestie*, ed. R.C. Bald (Cambridge, 1953). For a discussion of the Catholics' dilemma during this period, see Elliot Rose, *Cases of Conscience: Alternatives Open to Recusants and Puritans under Elizabeth I and James I* (Cambridge, 1975), Perez Zagorin, *Ways of Lying: Dissimulation, Persecution, and Conformity in Early Modern Europe* (Cambridge, MA, and London, 1990), pp. 131–52, and Thomas M. McCoog, '"The Flower of Oxford": The Role of Edmund Campion in Early Recusant Polemics,' *Sixteenth Century Journal* 24, 4 (1993) pp. 899–913, and for a more general treatment of English Catholicism, John Bossy, *The English Catholic Community 1570–1850* (London, 1975), and Arnold O. Meyer, *England and the Catholic Church under Queen Elizabeth* (New York, 1967).
53 *The Political Works of James I*, ed. C.H. McIlwain (Cambridge, MA, 1918), p. 285.
54 *Works*, ed. Herford and Simpson, I, pp. 202–3.
55 *Conversations*, in ibid., p. 137,
56 *Underwoods*, I, 3; in *Works*, ed. Herford and Simpson, VIII, pp. 130.
57 *An Humble Supplication*, ed. Bald, pp. 35–42.
58 See *Works*, ed. Herford and Simpson, I, p. 198; and *Conversations*, in ibid., p. 140.
59 Ibid., p. 141.
60 See Riggs, *Jonson: A Life*, pp. 193–4.
61 See Quentin Skinner, *The Foundations of Modern Political Thought* (Cambridge, 1978), II, chaps. 5 and 6; and G. Lewy, *Constitutionalism and Statescraft During the Golden Age of Spain: A Study of the Political Philosophy of Juan de Mariana* (Geneva, 1960).
62 *Political Works of James I*, ed. McIlwain, p. 126. James, with much acumen but from a very different point of view, thus isolated the basic similarity in the resistance theories promoted by contending Christian factions in the late sixteenth century that are examined by Q. Skinner, 'The Origins of the Calvinist Theory of Revolution,' in *After the Reformation: Essays in Honor of J.H. Hexter*, ed. Barbara C. Malament (Philadelphia, 1980), pp. 309–30; cf. J.P. Sommerville, 'From Suarez to Filmer: A Reappraisal,' *Historical Journal*, 25 (1982), pp. 525–40, and his *Politics and Ideology in England 1603–1640* (London, 1986), chaps. 1 and 2.
63 *Political Works of James I*, ed. McIlwain, p. 153.

64 See Hugh Trevor-Roper, *Catholics, Anglicans and Puritans: Seventeenth Century Essays* (London, 1987), pp. 166–230.
65 *Aubrey's Brief Lives*, ed. Oliver Lawson Dick (London, 1949), p. 56; Francis Cheynell, *The Rise, Growthe, and Danger of Socinianisme* (1643; *STC* [ed. Wing] C 3815); and *Chillingworthi Novissima: Or, the Sicknesse, Heresy, Death, and Buriall of William Chillingworth* (1644; *STC* [ed. Wing] 3810). Lord Dacre describes Cheynell as 'a nasty Presbyterian' in the Index to his book; see Trevor-Roper, *Catholics, Anglicans and Puritans*, p. 303.
66 Wallace, *Puritans and Predestination*, pp. 109, 145–6.
67 Ibid., p. 144.
68 *Epigrammes*, 98, in *Works*, ed. Herford and Simpson, VIII, p. 63.
69 See Horace, *Satires*, II, vii (Loeb edition: Cambridge, MA, 1978; pp. 230–3). For more on the Horatian influence in Jonson's verse, see below, p. 161.
70 Katharine Eisaman Maus, *Ben Jonson and the Roman Frame of Mind* (Princeton, 1985), p. 44.
71 *Discoveries*, in *Works*, ed. Herford and Simpson, VIII, p. 568.
72 For the Sidney/Pembroke ties to the court during these years, see John Buxton, *Sir Philip Sidney and the English Renaissance*, 3rd ed. (London, 1987), Michael Brennan, *Literary Patronage in the English Renaissance: The Pembroke Family* (London, 1988); see also Blair Worden 'Classical Republicanism and the Puritan Revolution,' in *History and Imagination: Essays in Honour of H.R. Trevor-Roper*, ed. H. Lloyd-Jones, V. Pearl, and B. Worden (London, 1981), pp. 182–200; and Jonathan Scott, *Algernon Sidney and the English Republic, 1623–1677* (Cambridge, 1988), chaps. 2–4.
73 See J.C.A. Rathwell, 'Jonson, Lord Lisle and Penshurst,' *English Literary Review*, 6 (1971), pp. 250–60, Norbrook, *Poetry and Politics*, pp. 184, 190, and Don E. Wayne, *Penshurst: The Semiotics of Place and the Poetics of History* (Madison, WI 1984).
74 Thomas M. Greene, 'Ben Jonson and the Centered Self,' *Studies in English Literature*, 10 (1970), 325–48; see also Maus, *Jonson and the Roman Frame of Mind*, and Clarence B. Hilberry, *Ben Jonson's Ethics in Relation to Stoic and Humanist Thought* (Chicago, 1930).
75 See L.P. Wilkinson, *The Roman Experience* (New York, 1974), especially pp. 85–92.
76 *Underwoods*, 61, in *Works*, ed. Herford and Simpson, VIII, pp. 234–5. For more on this epigram, see Annabel Patterson, *Censorship and Interpretation*, pp. 134–44.
77 Todd, *Christian Humanism*, chap. 2; cf. the fine description of this transfer according to the rhetorical predilections of the day in Daniel Javitch, *Poetry and Courtliness in Renaissance England* (Princeton, 1978), pp. 18–49.

78 See Worden, 'Classical Republicanism,' J.G.A. Pocock, *The Machiavellian Moment: Florentine Political Thought and the Atlantic Republican Tradition* (Princeton, 1975), Sommerville, *Politics and Ideology,* chap. 2, and Zera Fink, *The Classical Republicans: An Essay in the Recovery of a Pattern of Thought in 17th-Century England,* 2nd ed. (Evanston, 1962).
79 Cf. Todd, *Christian Humanism*, chap. 6. This same criticism was a frequent plague to Tudor monarchs; for an incisive study of an earlier champion of such ideas, see Thomas F. Mayer, *Thomas Starkey and the Commonweal: Humanist Politics and Religion in the Reign of Henry VIII* (Cambridge, 1989).
80 Scott, *Algernon Sidney and the English Republic*, pp. 43–50, 67–8; cf. Fink, *Classical Republicans*, pp. 158–67.
81 For the preponderance of this attitude among intellectuals, see David Wootton, *Paolo Sarpi: Between Renaissance and Enlightenment* (Cambridge, 1983), p. 76; Carlo Ginzburg, 'High and Low: The Theme of Forbidden Knowledge in the Sixteenth and Seventeenth Centuries,' *Past & Present*, 73 (1976), pp. 28–41.
82 See Norbrook, *Poetry and Politics*, chap. 4; F.J. Levy, 'Philip Sidney Reconsidered,' *English Literary Renaissance*, 2 (1972), pp. 5–18; W.A. Ringler, Jr., 'Sir Philip Sidney: The Myth and the Man,' *Sir Philip Sidney. 1586 and the Creation of a Legend*, ed. Jan van Dorsten et al (Leiden, 1986), pp. 3–15.
83 *Conversations, Works*, ed. Herford and Simpson, I, p. 138.
84 *Epigrammes*, 5, in *Works*, ed. Herford and Simpson, VIII, pp. 128–9. For the question of the union, see D.H. Willson, 'King James I and Anglo-Scottish Unity,' in *Conflict in Stuart England*, ed. W. Aiken and B. Henning (London, 1960); Bruce Galloway, *The Union of England and Scotland, 1603–1608* (Edinburgh, 1986); and Brian P. Levack, *The Formation of the British State: England, Scotland, and the Union, 1603–1707* (London, 1987). Shakespeare's engagement with this issue is explored by Christopher Wortham, 'Shakespeare, James I and the Matter of Britain,' *English*, 45. 182 (Summer, 1996), pp. 97–122.
85 See Norbrook, *Poetry and Politics*, p. 225.
86 See Don E. Wayne, 'Jonson's Sidney: Legacy and Legitimation in *The Forrest*,' in *Sir Philip Sidney's Achievements*, ed. M.J.B. Allen et al (New York, 1990), pp. 227–50.
87 *Discoveries, Works*, ed. Herford and Simpson, I, p. 636.
88 Ibid., p. 595. In his preface to *Volpone,* Jonson wrote of the impossibility of being a 'good Poet, without first being a good man.' See *Works*, ed. Herford and Simpson, V, p. 17.
89 *Cynthia's Revels*, III, iv, 20–1; II, ii, 77–8; V, xi, 96–7, in *Works*, ed. Herford and Simpson, IV, pp. 89, 68, 178.
90 *Discoveries, Works*, ed. Herford and Simpson, VIII, p. 642. Notably, both

*Cynthia's Revels* (1600) and *Poetaster* (1601) are also taken to refer to Essex's cause, juxtaposing virtuous advice and flattery as the dominant pattern at court; see *Poetaster*, ed. Tom Cain, The Revel Plays Series (Manchester and New York, 1995), pp. 40–4.

91 Howard Erskine-Hill, *The Augustan Idea in English Literature* (London, 1983), p. 122; Graham Parry, 'Britain's Roman Poet,' *Seventeenth-Century Poetry: The Social Context* (London, 1985), p. 20. Chettle's Horatian ascription, it might be noted, came by way of a reproach; any Horace worth his salt would have written a lamentation on the death of his ruler, whereas Jonson wrote none after Elizabeth died. See *Ben Jonson: The Critical Heritage 1599–1798*, ed. D.H. Craig (London and New York, 1990), pp. 88–9. An astute study of Jonson's claim to be the English Horace is Richard Helgerson, *Self-Crowned Laureates: Spencer, Jonson, Milton and the Literary System* (Berkeley, Los Angeles, and London, 1983).

92 *Conversations, Works*, ed. Herford and Simpson, I, p. 142.

93 Ibid., pp. 138–9. Sidney's portrait in the National Gallery is very flattering, and John Aubrey recorded that Sidney 'was not only an excellent witt, but extremely beautifull: he much resembled his sister, but his Haire was not red, but a little inclining, viz. a darke amber colour.' Aubrey suggested that Sidney's main fault was that he was 'not masculine enough' in appearance. See *Aubrey's Brief Lives*, ed. Dick, p. 278. See also Roy Strong, 'Sidney's Appearance Reconsidered,' in *Sir Philip Sidney's Achievements*, ed. M.J.B. Allen et al, pp. 3–31.

94 *Conversations, Works*, ed. Herford and Simpson, I, p. 132.

95 The first quotation is from *Discoveries, Works*, ed. Herford and Simpson, VIII, p. 601, and derives from Lipsius's *Politica, Prefatio*. The second quotation is from Jonson's preface to *Volpone*, in *Works*, ed. Herford and Simpson, V, p. 17.

96 *Epigrammes*, 92, *Works*, ed. Herford and Simpson, VIII, pp. 58–9.

97 *Epigrammes*, 95, ibid., pp. 61–2.

98 Patterson, *Censorship and Interpretation*, p. 56; the suggestion that *Sejanus* referred to the Ralegh trial of 1601 is treated below p. 164 and n. 108. For the use of Tacitus, cf. Malcolm Smuts, 'Court-Centred Politics and the Uses of Roman Historians, c. 1590–1630,' in *Culture and Politics in Early Stuart England*, ed. Sharpe and Lake, pp. 21–43.

99 See Goldberg, *The Politics of Literature*, pp. 69–84.

100 Patterson, *Censorship and Interpretation*, p. 55; *Conversations, Works*, ed. Herford and Simpson, I, p. 136.

101 See Peter Burke, 'Tacitism,' in *Tacitus*, ed. T.A. Dorey (New York, 1969), pp. 149–71, who discusses the 'red' and 'black' version of Tacitism as defined by G. Toffanin in his *Machiavelli e il Tacitismo* (Padua, 1921).

102 *Works*, ed. Herford and Simpson, I, p. 46; Anne Barton, *Ben Jonson, Dramatist*, pp. 92–4.
103 *Epigrammes*, 1, in *Works*, ed. Herford and Simpson, VIII, p. 27; on Jonson's style, see Wesley Trimpi, *Ben Jonson's Poems: A Study in the Plain Style* (Stanford, 1962).
104 See *Conversations*, *Works*, ed. Herford and Simpson, I, pp. 149, 251–2.
105 In *Discoveries*, Jonson cites Machiavelli in several places with respect, yet his teachings are always tempered by Senecan and Lipsian qualifications; see *Works*, ed. Herford and Simpson, VIII, pp. 599–601. For Machiavelli's interpretation of Cicero, see Q. Skinner, *Machiavelli* (Oxford, 1981), pp. 3–4, 43–7. For studies that examine Jonson's sources for *Sejanus* and *Catiline*, see Daniel C. Boughner, 'Jonson's Use of Lipsius in *Sejanus*,' *Modern Language Notes*, 73 (1958), pp. 247–55 and his *The Devil's Disciple: Ben Jonson's Debt to Machiavelli* (New York, 1968); Barbara N. DeLuna, *Jonson's Romish Plot: A Study of 'Catiline' in its Historical Context* (Oxford, 1967); and Howard Norlund, 'The Design of Ben Jonson's *Catiline*,' *Sixteenth Century Journal*, 9 (1978), pp. 67–89. For Lipsius's use of Cicero, see J.H.M. Salmon, 'Cicero and Tacitus in Sixteenth-Century France,' *American Historical Review*, 85 (1980), pp. 323–4.
106 *Catiline*, I, 541–4, *Works*, ed. Herford and Simpson, V, p. 452.
107 Jonson wrote two prefacing statements for *Catiline*. One addressed the 'reader in ordinarie'; the other 'the reader extraordinary.' See *Works*, ed. Herford and Simpson, V, p. 432. See also, Miles, *Jonson: His Life and Works*, pp. 142–4; and on Jonson's themes in both *Sejanus* and *Catiline*, John Michael Archer, 'Light of Base Stuff: Jonson's Roman Plays,' chap. 4 of his *Sovereignty and Intelligence: Spying and Court Culture in the English Renaissance* (Stanford, 1993), pp. 95–120.
108 J.H.M. Salmon, 'Stoicism and Roman Example: Seneca and Tacitus in Jacobean England,' *Journal of the History of Ideas*, 50 (1989), pp. 219–20; for the farcical nature of Ralegh's trial, which was taking place as Jonson composed *Sejanus*, see above, chap. 1. While most historians have considered the play as a commentary on Essex's trial in 1601, the case for the Ralegh 'parallel' has been stated by Philip J. Ayres in his edition of *Sejanus His Fall*, The Revel Plays Series (Manchester and New York, 1990), p. 17. See also Fritz Levy's recent analysis of the play: 'The Theatre and the Court in the 1590s,' in *The Reign of Elizabeth I: Court and Culture in the Last Decade*, ed. Guy, pp. 274–300.
109 *Catiline*, V, 694–702, *Works*, ed. Herford and Simpson, V, p. 549.
110 *Discoveries*, *Works*, ed. Herford and Simpson, VIII, p. 636.
111 For Jonson and the Tribe of Ben, see Katherine A. McEuen, *The Classical Influence upon the Tribe of Ben: A Study of Classical Elements in the Non-Dramatic*

*Poetry of Ben Jonson and His Circle* (Cedar Rapids, IA, 1939); Earl Miner, *The Cavalier Mode from Jonson to Cotton* (Princeton, 1971); A.C. Partridge, ed., *The Tribe of Ben: Pre-Augustan Classical Verse in England* (London, 1966).

112 See Morford, *Stoics and Neostoics*, pp. 30–51.
113 *Works*, ed. Herford and Simpson, V, p. 431.
114 See DeLuna, *Jonson's Romish Plot*, pp. 288–90.
115 Jean Bodin's influential *Six Lives de la République* (1576) was translated and published in English by R. Knolles in 1606 (see *STC* 3193). For Bodin, see Julian H. Franklin, 'Sovereignty and the Mixed Constitution: Bodin and his Critics,' and J.P. Sommerville, 'Absolutism and Royalism,' both in *The Cambridge History of Political Thought, 1450–1700*, ed. J.H. Burns with Mark Goldie (Cambridge, 1991) pp. 298–328 and 347–73. See also Johann P. Sommerville, 'English and European Political Ideas in the Early Seventeenth Century: Revisionism and the Case of Absolutism,' *Journal of British Studies*, 35 (April, 1996), pp. 168–94.
116 *Discoveries*, *Works*, ed. Herford and Simpson, VIII, p. 565.
117 Ibid., p. 594.
118 Ibid., p. 602.
119 Ibid., p. 592.
120 *Underwoods*, ibid., pp. 175–6; see chap. 1 pp. 66–70 above, and figure 4; and see also Patterson, *Censorship and Interpretation*, pp. 127–31.
121 *Discoveries*, *Works*, ed. Herford and Simpson, VIII, p. 591.
122 Ibid.
123 For Cotton's history, see Sharpe, *Sir Robert Cotton*, pp. 232–42; see also Salmon, 'Seneca and Tacitus in Jacobean England,' p. 213.
124 Quoted in Sharpe, *Sir Robert Cotton*, p. 238, n. 89 (emphasis added).
125 See British Library, Cottonian MSS, Julius F.IV, ff. 75b–76 (Tacitean excerpts); Harleian MS 6018 ff. 174–5 (Cotton's book-lending list).
126 Sharpe, *Sir Robert Cotton*, p. 106 and n. 115.
127 For Eliot, see Harold Hulme, *The Life of Sir John Eliot* (London, 1957), pp. 339–81 and J.N. Ball, 'Sir John Eliot and Parliament, 1624–1629,' in *Faction and Parliament*, ed. Sharpe, pp. 173–208.
128 See Martin Butler, 'Ben Jonson and the Limits of Courtly Panegyric,' in *Culture and Politics in Early Stuart England*, ed. Sharpe and Lake, pp. 91–115.
129 *Underwoods*, 79, *Works*, ed. Herford and Simpson, VIII, p. 265.
130 See Derek Hirst, *Authority and Conflict: England 1603–1658* (Cambridge, MA, 1986), pp. 160–87; Esther S. Cope, *Politics Without Parliaments, 1629–1640* (London, 1987); Thomas Cogswell, 'The Politics of Propaganda: Charles I and the People in the 1620s,' *Journal of British Studies*, 29 (1990), pp. 187–215.
131 See Norbrook, *Poetry and Politics*, chaps. 7–9.

## 5 Joseph Hall and 'That Proud Inconstant Lipsius'

1 The French soubriquet was conferred by Loiseau de Torval, translator of Hall's *Characters*, for which see *Heaven Upon Earth and Characters of Vertues and Vices*, ed. Rudolph Kirk (New Brunswick, N.J., 1948), pp. 53–6. Thomas Fuller, *The History of the Worthies of England* (London, 1662; STC [ed. Wing] F2440), p. 130.
2 Hall's writings have been collected and edited by Philip Wynter in *The Works of the Right Reverend Joseph Hall, D.D.*, 10 vols. (Oxford, 1863; repr. New York, 1969). Throughout this chapter, however, I rely mainly, though not exclusively, on the original publications. For a measure of Hall's numerous mentions in commonplace books, see below, nn. 46 and 123.
3 For Hall as a Christian-stoic, see *Heaven Upon Earth and Characters of Vertues and Vices*, ed. Kirk, Introduction, and cf. Giles D. Monsarrat, *Light From the Porch: Stoicism and English Renaissance Literature* (Paris, 1984), pp. 98–105. Hall's ideas are treated by F.L. Huntley, *Bishop Joseph Hall, 1574–1656: A Biographical and Critical Study* (Cambridge, 1979) and Leonard D. Tourney, *Joseph Hall* (Boston, 1979). The 'intrinsic excellence' of his work is argued by Richard A. McCabe, *Joseph Hall: A Study in Satire and Meditation* (Oxford, 1982); quotation at pp. x–xi.
4 In the words of Fuller, *The Worthies of England*, p. 130.
5 This latter was an account of, or rather, 'Observations of Some Specialties of Divine Providence in His life Noted by His Own Hand,' as Hall called the account in 1653. For Hall's life I have relied upon the posthumous edition of the 'Observations,' in *The Shaking of the Olive-Tree* (London, 1660; STC [ed. Wing] H416) as well as Huntley, *Bishop Joseph Hall*, and T.F. Kinloch, *The Life and Works of Joseph Hall, 1574–1656* (London, 1951).
6 He attended Emmanuel College and was later proud to recall that for two consecutive years he was 'chosen to the Rhetorick Lecture in the publick School.' See 'Observations,' *The Shaking of the Olive-Tree*, pp. 10–11. And for the emergence of professional clergymen in this period, see Rosemary O'Day, *The English Clergy: The Emergence and Consolidation of a Profession 1558–1642* (Leicester, 1979).
7 Reprinted in *The Poems of Joseph Hall*, ed. Arnold Davenport (Liverpool, 1969), pp. 5–99. A good discussion of Hall's role in the satire controversy of the late 1590s is contained in McCabe, *Joseph Hall*, pp. 53–72; and for the nature of the prohibition of satires, see McCabe's, 'Elizabethan Satire and the Bishop's Ban of 1599,' *Yearbook of English Studies*, 11 (1981), pp. 188–93. On this question, see also Patrick Collinson, 'Ecclesiastical Vitriol: Religious Satire in the 1590s and the Invention of Puritanism,' and Jenny Wormald, 'Eccle-

siastical Vitriol: The Kirk, the Puritans and the Future King,' both in *The Reign of Elizabeth I: Court and Culture in the Last Decade*, ed. John Guy (Cambridge, 1995), pp. 150–70 and 171–91.

8 See Claire Cross, *The Puritan Earl: The Life of Henry Hastings, Third Earl of Huntingdon, 1536–1595* (London, 1966) and Paul Slack, 'Poverty and Social Regulation in Elizabethan England,' in *The Reign of Elizabeth I*, ed. Christopher Haigh (London, 1984), p. 223.

9 On the nature of the divisions in the English church, see Peter Lake, *Anglicans and Puritans? Presbyterianism and English Conformist Thought from Whitgift to Hooker* (London, 1988); cf. Nicholas Tyacke, *Anti-Calvinists: The Rise of English Arminianism* (Oxford, 1987). In many orthodox religious histories, Hall is portrayed as falling into the Anglican Puritan divide of the period. See, for example, J. Sears McGee, *The Godly Man in Stuart England: Anglicans, Puritans, and the Two Tables, 1620–1670* (New Haven and London, 1976), passim, and John Spurr, *The Restoration Church of England, 1646–1689* (New Haven and London, 1991), passim.

10 Hall, 'Observations,' *The Shaking of the Olive-Tree*, p. 12; see also R.C. Bald, *Donne and the Drurys* (Cambridge, 1959), pp. 50–3, 62–4.

11 Hall, 'Observations,' p. 24.

12 *Poems of Joseph Hall*, ed. Davenant, p. 112.

13 Ibid.

14 Howard Erskine-Hill, *The Augustan Idea in English Literature* (London, 1983), p. 104.

15 See ibid., p. 107, n. 31. Applying the Augustus image to Elizabeth was also a very prudent and politic gesture on James's part; in 1599, the year of the appearance of *Basilikon Doron*, his own negotiations for the English crown were starting to bear fruit.

16 Kinloch tends to take this position in *The Life and Works of Joseph Hall, 1574–1656*, although the entire tenor of McCabe's *Joseph Hall* is to give Hall his proper due. Cf., however, Thomas Kranidas, 'Style and Rectitude in Seventeenth-Century Prose: Hall, Smectymnuus, and Milton,' *Huntington Library Quarterly*, 46 (1983), pp. 237–69.

17 Tourney, *Joseph Hall*, p. 65.

18 John N. King, *Royal Tudor Iconography: Literature and Art in an Age of Religious Crisis* (Princeton, 1989), p. 8.

19 On the tenth anniversary of James's accession in 1613, Hall delivered 'An Holy Panegyrick' in which he reminded his listeners 'that the tenth compleat year of our Constantine deserves to be solemne and Iubular.' Solomon was Hall's image for James in a 1624 sermon, 'The True Peace-Maker.' For discussions of Hall's sermons, see McCabe, *Joseph Hall*, pp. 257–305, Tourney, *Joseph*

280   Notes to pages 174–6

*Hall*, pp. 106–19, and Graham Parry, *The Golden Age Restor'd: The Culture of the Stuart Court, 1603–1642* (Manchester, 1981), pp. 232–5. Christopher Wortham has recently discussed Shakespeare's participation in the rhetoric of Jacobean mythology and cosmology in 'Shakespeare, James I and the Matter of Britain,' *English*, 45. 182 (summer, 1996), pp. 97–122.

20 Huntley, *Bishop Joseph Hall*, p. 53.
21 *The Political Works of James I*, ed. Charles H. McIlwain (New York, 1965), pp. 18, 41–2.
22 See ibid., pp. 9, 40, and *Basilikon Doron* (Edinburgh, 1599; STC 14348), p. 117. The last quotation, naming Lipsius, was expunged from the second edition of *Basilikon Doron*, which was published in London in 1603. Here, the call against Lipsian 'constancy' was rendered less specific but still recognizable in its target, especially against those professing 'Stoicke insensible stupiditie,' who, in fact, manifest 'inconstant behauiour in their owne liues' (*Works*, ed. McIlwaine, p. 41).
23 See *Another World and Yet the Same: Bishop Hall's Mundus Alter et Idem*, trans. John Millar Wands (New Haven and London, 1981). Wands's introduction and editorial comments have been most useful for the analysis which follows. The very seventeenth-century genre of travel satire has recently acquired 'novel' application at the hands of Umberto Eco; see his *Island of the Day Before*, trans. William Weaver (New York, San Diego, and London, 1995).
24 *Another World*, p. 73. The original in *Mundus Alter et Idem* reads thus: 'dextra catelli venustioris capiti innixa, sinistra librum semiapertum gerebat; pars altera chamaeleontem colorib. suis variegatum; et superne scriptum erat CONST. LIP.' See *Mundus Alter et Idem* (1605; STC 12685), p. 129. See figure 7; as Richard McCabe, *Joseph Hall*, p. 371, n. 76, notes: 'Lipsius may be seen in the pose the *Mundus* illustrates in the engraved portrait opposite the title-page of *L. Annaei Senecae Philosophi Opera ... a Iusto Lipsio emendata* (Antwerp, 1605).' Although McCabe does not go into it, this may well have some implications for the accurate dating of the *Mundus*, a subject of certain disagreement among scholars. Notice that the illustrations do not accurately reflect the text, though an earlier, famous portrait of Lipsius indeed portrayed him with right hand resting on his dog's head and left hand holding a half-opened book. That portrait, dated 1587, when Lipsius was at the height of his fame (and nearly middle-aged), is reproduced in Jan van Dorstem, *Poets, Patrons, and Professors: Sir Philip Sidney, Daniel Rogers, and the Leiden Humanists* (Leiden and London, 1962), facing p. 117. Comparing that portrait with the frontispiece in Lipsius's 1605 edition of Seneca's *Opera* (shown in figure 8), what we see is an older Lipsius in a mirror-image pose of the 1587 portrait. Cf. figure 2, above, p. 25, the frontispiece of the 1675 edition of Lipsius's

own *Opera Omnia*. This is a rougher version – and a mirror image – of the famous Rubens design for the frontispiece of the original (1637) edition of Lipsius's *Opera*, for which see Mark Morford, *Stoics and Neo-stoics: Rubens and the Circle of Lipsius* (Princeton, 1991), illustration no. 17. Alternatively, see *Tacitus and the Tacitean Tradition*, ed. T.J. Luce and A.J. Woodman (Princeton, 1993), frontispiece.

25 For example, in Crapula, an oblique reference is made when Mercurius encounters gardens that outdo that of Langius – Lipsius's host in *De constantia* (see Wands, trans., *Another World*, p. 28); in Moronia Pia, one of the 'best' villages is 'Lipsanium,' and Lipsius is made to be the authority on inns (p. 101).

26 For Lipsius's love of dogs, see Charles Nisard, *Le Triumverat Littéraire au xvi Siècle: Juste Lipse, Joseph Scaliger et Isaac Casaubon* (Paris, 1852, repr. Geneva, 1970), pp. 137–9. For criticism of Lipsius's flexibility of religion, see the sources at n. 31, below.

27 See Jason L. Saunders, *Justus Lipsius: The Philosophy of Renaissance Stoicism* (New York, 1955), pp. 51–2. For the implications of Lipsius's left-handedness cf. Hall's own portraits, where he always holds his book in the right hand. See figure 9, below, p. 181.

28 McCabe, *Joseph Hall*, p. 105.

29 Tourney, *Joseph Hall*, p. 38.

30 The popularity of the *Mundus* can be gauged from the publication data accrued by Wands, trans. *Another World*, pp. lii–liv. For an analysis of shifts and adaptations of style following the success of a parody, see Margaret Anne Doody, *The Daring Muse: Augustan Poetry Reconsidered* (Oxford, 1985).

31 Lipsius was still alive and busy refuting critics in 1605. He died the next year, aged fifty-nine. See Saunders, *Justus Lipsius: The Philosophy of Renaissance Stoicism*, pp. 51–8; Morford, *Stoics and Neostoics*, pp. 96–138.

32 An oblique acknowledgment was made in his 'Epistle to William Bedell,' in Hall's first volume of *Epistles* (London, 1608; STC 12662), pp. 75–6. As Richard McCabe has noted, however, 'that reference occurs *only* in the 1608 edition of *Epistles*. In Hall, *Recollection of such Treatises as have beene severally published* (1615), it is completely deleted and does not reappear in any of the other collected editions.' See McCabe, *Joseph Hall*, pp. 332–3 (emphasis on 'only' is McCabe's). In this chapter I refer to and cite the contemporary editions of Hall's *Epistles*. He published three volumes in all, each volume consisting of twenty epistles, divided into two 'decades' each, with the decades numbered consecutively through the three volumes. Henceforth, reference will include year of publication, volume, decade, and epistle number. Thus the 'Epistle to William Bedell' appears as: *Epistles* (1608) I, i, vii.

33 See Anthony Grafton and Lisa Jardine, *From Humanism to the Humanities: Education and the Liberal Arts in Fifteenth- and Sixteenth-Century Europe* (Cambridge, MA, 1986), pp. 184–96, and their, '"Studied for Action": How Gabriel Harvey Read His Livy,' *Past & Present*, 129 (Nov. 1990), pp. 30–78. Despite some real problems in establishing the addressee of Bacon's letter, see also Vernon F. Snow, 'Francis Bacon's Advice to Fulke Greville on Research Techniques,' *Huntington Library Quarterly*, 23 (1960), pp. 369–78.

34 Hall's account of the trip, together with his reasons for taking it, are recorded in two places. The more contemporary one is given in his 'Epistle to Sir Tho[mas] Challoner: A report of some observations in my travel,' *Epistles* (1608) I, i, v, pp. 35–52. A later record is contained in Hall, 'Observations,' *The Shaking of the Olive-Tree*, pp. 15–22.

35 He went to hear Lipsius lecture in 1599; in 1605, he made Lipsius an honourary member of the state council of Brabant. See Saunders, *Justus Lipsius*, pp. 49, 65.

36 'Observations,' *The Shaking of the Olive-Tree*, p. 21.

37 See *Epistles* (1608), I, i, v, pp. 40–1 and 48–9. In 'To Sir David Murray, Concerning the miracles of our times,' Hall also disparaged Lipsius and his scholarship; see *Epistles* (1608) I, i, vi, pp. 54, 59.

38 *Tvvo Bookes of Constancie*, trans. John Stradling (London, 1595; STC 15695); see above, Introduction, p. 5 ff.

39 The first volume of *Epistles* opens with a letter to Jacob Wadsworth, 'lately revolted, in Spain,' which puts Wadsworth's conversion (his 'revolt') to Catholicism down to the bad foreign influences afforded by travel. Another in the same decade warns the young Earl of Essex about the perils of travelling. See, *Epistles* (1608), I, i, i, pp. 1–10, and I, i, viii pp. 79–90.

40 *Quo Vadis: A iust censure of trauell as it is commonly undertaken by gentlemen* (London, 1617; STC 12705b). At pp. 26–7 Hall states that far from perfecting the 'intellectiue powers of our Gentry,' travel 'rather robs them of the very desire of perfection.' Instead of picking up sound moral values, they were exposed, among other evils, to ideas such as the maxim *'Qui nescit dissimulare, nescit viuere*: and would this alone teach [future governors] to rule well?' This nice little axiom was an adaptation of the Tacitean tenet defended by Lipsius, *qui nescit dissimulare, nescit regnare* (see *Sixe Bookes of Politickes*, trans. William Jones [London, 1594; STC 15701], IV, xiiii, p. 117). Hall's critique had little effect on the popularity of the adapted maxim in contemporary parlance. See below, Epilogue, and figure 10 (p. 210).

41 'Observations,' *The Shaking of the Olive-Tree*, p. 12.

42 The quotation comes from the dedicatory epistle to *Meditations and Vowes* (London, 1605; STC 12679), sig. A3.

43 Hall, *Heaven Upon Earth* (London, 1606; *STC* 12666), p. 1
44 This central lesson was reaffirmed in the address to readers in *Characters of Vertues and Vices* (London, 1608; *STC* 12648), which also stressed, however, that it would not do to ignore the many good lessons taught by the heathens. The idea that English neostoicism revolved around this very issue has recently been restated by A.A. Bromham, '"Have Your Read Lipsius?": Thomas Middleton and Stoicism,' *English Studies*, 77. 5 (Sept., 1996), pp. 401–21.
45 Hall's epistolary style is explored in a number of Morris Croll's essays; see *Style, Rhetoric, and Rhythm*, ed. J. Max Patrick et al (Princeton, 1966); and by George Williamson, *The Senecan Amble* (Chicago, 1951).
46 Seneca's influence is traced by Ralph Graham Palmer, *Seneca's 'De Remediis Fortvitorum' and the Elizabethans* (Chicago, 1953); and more recently by Margo Todd, 'Seneca and the Protestant Mind: The Influence of Stoicism on Puritan Ethics,' *Archiv für Reformationsgeschichte*, 74 (1983), pp. 182–99, and in her *Christian Humanism and the Puritan Social Order* (Cambridge, 1987). Seventeenth-century students and readers frequently collapsed Seneca, Lipsius, Hall, Bacon, and others into one general (neostoic) framework. For example, one commonplace book compiled in the 1620s (St. John's Library, Cambridge, MS S. 34) recorded extracts from Charron and Hall, while a catalogue of books compiled in 1632 (St. John's Library, Cambridge, MS V.5) included titles by Bacon, Lipsius, Tacitus, Seneca, and Hall. Other seventeenth-century collections and compilations (e.g., British Library, Sloane MSS 836, 922, and 2521) reveal similar habits of reading and note-taking.
47 See 'Observations,' *The Shaking of the Olive-Tree*, p. 16, where Hall recalls his meeting with Thomas Lodge, a practicing Catholic then in exile in the Low Countries. Their conversation on recent miracles attested by 'Lipsius Apricollis' developed into a row which Bacon finally managed to quell. Lodge would return to England; in 1614 he published his English translation of Seneca's writings and included Lipsius's 'Life' of Seneca and Lipsian summaries of Seneca's ideas.
48 See *Epistles* (1608), I, i, v, pp. 40–9 (to Challoner).
49 *Characters of Vertues and Vices*, p. 72.
50 Ibid., p. 108.
51 It was in this edition that Lipsius's portrait, invoked by Hall in the *Mundus*, appeared, thereby suggesting that the Hall satire followed and did not precede his first journey to the Low Countries.
52 Lipsius's published epistles were intended for use in the classroom and for emulation. For his success here, see Saunders, *Justus Lipsius*, pp. 24–7, Morford, *Stoics and Neostoics*, pp. 76–7, and Wesley Trimpi, *Ben Jonson's Poems: A Study of the Plain Style* (Stanford, 1962), pp. 49–53 and 62–6. English students

did not have to depend on foreign editions of Lipsian letters, since two 'Centuries' of them were published in London in 1593. See *Iusti Lipsi Epistolarum Centuriae Duae* (London, 1593; STC 15699).
53 A point clearly made in many of his *Epistles*, particularly when he treated foreign travel and the contagion of Catholicism.
54 See F.J. Levy, 'Francis Bacon and the Style of Politics,' *English Literary Renaissance*, 16 (1986), pp. 101–22; chap. 2, above, pp. 87–96.
55 Prince Henry seemed disposed to favour him. See Jonathan Marwil, *The Trials of Counsel: Francis Bacon in 1621* (Detroit, 1976), pp. 131–2, and p. 220, n. 65; see also, *Sir Francis Bacon: The Essayes or Counsels, Civill and Morall*, ed. Michael Kiernan (Cambridge, 1985), pp. xxiii–xxiv.
56 *Epistles* (1608), I, i, iv, p. 33. In *Inwardness and Theater in the English Renaissance* (Chicago and London, 1995) Katharine Eisaman Maus analyses the extent of concern /discussion (albeit mainly through the drama of the period) over the gap between outward appearances and inward integrity and authenticity.
57 Ben Jonson, *The Forest*, 3, 'To Sir Robert Wroth'; *Epigrammes*, 98, 'To Sir Thomas Roe,' in *Ben Jonson: The Complete Poems*, ed. George Parfitt (Harmondsworth, 1988), pp. 100, 69.
58 Geoffrey Aggeler discerns an ongoing feud between Jonson and Hall over rival interpretations of ethics; see his 'Ben Jonson's Justice Overdo and Joseph Hall's Good Magistrate,' *English Studies*, 76. 5 (Sept., 1995) pp. 434–42.
59 Hall gradually came to stress this point, which is more pronounced in his later meditations. For example, the 1650 edition of Hall, *Holy Self-Conferences: Soliloquies*, nos. 1–7, 9, 18, 42, 51, in *Works*, ed. Wynter, VIII, pp. 24–8, 30, 37, 59, 65. Even here, the active life remains a vital part of his teachings. See the third epigraph at the opening of this chapter: *Soliloquies*, no. 42, 'Faith's Victory,' in ibid., p. 59.
60 For a summary and brief analysis of Bacon's *Religious Meditations*, see Marwil, *Trials of Counsel*, pp. 91–2.
61 The 1625 edition incorporated this description into the title as it simultaneously dropped the inclusion of *Religious Meditations*. See *Bacon: The Essayes*, ed. Kiernan, pp. lxiv–lxxxv.
62 *Meditations and Vowes* (1605), I, 83, pp. 97–9.
63 For Bacon's style and its relation to that of Lipsius, see the essays of Morris Croll, in *Style, Rhotoric, and Rhythms*, ed. Patrick et al. Milton described Hall's prose as 'hopping in the measure of convulsion fits' (Tourney, *Joseph Hall*, p. 62) and complained that he 'makes sentences by the Statute, as if all above three inches long were confiscat' (Huntley, *Bishop Joseph Hall*, p. 130).
64 Hall's repudiation of the stoics is taken at face value by a number of scholars, including Audrey Chew, 'Joseph Hall and Neo-Stoicism,' *Publications of the*

*Modern Language Association of America*, 65 (1950), pp. 1130–45, and Harold Fisch, 'The Limits of Hall's Senecanism,' *Proceedings of the Leeds Philosophical Society,* 6 (1950), 453–63.
65 Huntley, *Bishop Joseph Hall*, p. 71.
66 Ibid.
67 *Epistles* (1611), III, vi, ii, p. 16; useful on this point, although incorporating a different perspective, is Linda Levy Peck, *Court Patronage and Corruption in Early Stuart England* (Boston, 1990), especially pp. 168–72.
68 Hall, *The Arte of Diuine Meditation* (London, 1606, 1607; STC 12643), dedicatory epistle, sig. A3v–sig. A4 (misprinted as F4).
69 The charge of atheism was incurred by Ralegh; I am unaware of whether or not Bacon's writings, too, were construed as atheistic, but it would be surprising if they were not in some quarters. For the contemporary approach to atheism, see G.E. Aylmer, 'Unbelief in Seventeenth-Century England,' in *Puritans and Revolutionaries: Essays in Seventeenth-Century History Presented to Christopher Hill*, ed. Donald Pennington and Keith Thomas (Oxford, 1978), pp. 22–46.
70 *The Letters of Sir Francis Hastings*, ed. Claire Cross, Somerset Record Society, vol. 69 (1969), no. 55, pp. 76–7 (Hastings to Sir Robert Cecil, May, 1601).
71 Bald, *Donne and the Drurys*, pp. 36, 67.
72 Ibid., pp. 45, 110.
73 During the investigation into Drury's suspected complicity in Essex's rebellion, one witness reported that he had heard Sir Robert remark that 'some which shewed themselves the Earl of Essex's friends were his enemies, meaning Mr. Bacon, the lame man [i.e., Anthony].' (Bald, *Donne and the Drurys*, p. 45.) The remark suggests that Drury would have thought even less of the healthy Bacon, who, by command of the Crown, was 'conscientiously' prosecuting Essex. For later favours done by Bacon for his niece, see Bald, *Donne and the Drurys*, p. 140.
74 See Marwil, *Trials of Counsel*, pp. 63–72.
75 Interestingly, Hall recorded that during his Belgian expedition with Sir Edmund Bacon, it was Sir Nicholas Bacon, the elder, whose name was invoked for ease of passage, not Francis's, nor even that of Anthony, who was well known on the Continent. *Observations, The Shaking of the Olive-Tree,* p. 21.
76 See, for example, *Epistles* (1608; STC 12662), II, iii, x: 'A description of a good and faithful Courtier,' where Hall remarks that he is about to portray 'What you should be' (p. 99), and goes on to suggest that the good courtier is to be 'free, as of heart, so of tongue, to speak what he ought, not what he might' (p. 105). For Bacon's opposite view, see above, chap. 2, pp. 91–6.

77 In *The Works of Joseph Hall* (London, 1625; STC 12635), p. 482.
78 Bald, *Donne and the Drurys*, pp. 66–7.
79 Cf. Hall's *Epistles* (1608), I, i, ix, addressed 'To Sir Robert Drury and His Lady,' in which Hall made public his resignation from Hawstead and declared 'with how unwilling a heart' he left (p. 91).
80 'Observations,' *The Shaking of the Olive-Tree*, p. 26.
81 Cf. the complete title of the posthumous edition of those memoirs: 'Observations of Some Specialties of Divine Providence in the Life of Jos. Hall Bishop of Norwich Written with his own Hand', *The Shaking of the Olive-Tree*, p. 1.
82 *Epistles* (1608), II, iii, x, pp. 101–2.
83 For this aspect of Henry's court, see J.W. Williamson, *The Myth of the Conqueror. Prince Henry: A Study of 17th-Century Personation* (New York, 1978); Roy Strong, *Henry, Prince of Wales and England's Lost Renaissance* (New York, 1986); and Parry, *Golden Age Restor'd*, chap. 3.
84 Joseph Hall, *Characters of Vertues and Vices*; the description of 'vertues' comprises pp. 1–56. For the origin and development of 'characters' in England, see Benjamin Boyce, *The Theophrastan Character in England to 1642* (Cambridge, MA, 1947), chap. 3.
85 Hall, *Characters*, p. 62. Cf. Aggeler's discussion of Jonson's parody of such a magistrate in 'Ben Jonson's Justice Overdo and Joseph Hall's Good Magistrate' (see n. 58 above).
86 Boyce, *The Theophrastan Character*, pp. 124–5.
87 For a close analysis of the relationship between the works of James and Hall, see Huntley, *Bishop Joseph Hall*, pp. 49–56.
88 McCabe, *Joseph Hall*, p. 111. The popularity of Theophrastus in early modern Europe is charted in Charles B. Schmitt, 'Theophrastus,' *Catalogus Translationum et Commentarium: Medieval and Renaissance Latin Translations and Commentaries*, ed. Paul Oskar Kristeller (Washington, 1971), II, especially pp. 247, 260–5.
89 Quoted in Mark Pattison, *Isaac Casaubon, 1559–1614* (Oxford, 1892), p. 264.
90 Ibid., p. 272.
91 See Grafton and Jardine, '"Studied for Action,"' p. 75; and for a wider discussion of James and his tastes in scholarship, Malcolm Smuts, 'Court-Centred Politics and the Uses of Roman Historians, c. 1590–1630,' in *Culture and Politics in Early Stuart England*, ed. Kevin Sharpe and Peter Lake (London, 1994), pp. 21–43; see also above chap. 3, pp. 79–87.
92 This is not to say that Prince Henry's interests were narrowly focused on the same interests. For an inkling into the broad range of his readings and cultural predilections, see Strong, *Henry, Prince of Wales and England's Lost*

*Renaissance*, and T.A. Birrell, *English Monarchs and Their Books: From Henry VII to Charles II* (London, 1987), pp. 30–40.
93 See Michael G. Brennan, *Literary Patronage in the English Renaissance: The Pembroke Family* (London, 1988), pp. 108–9, 122–3.
94 See Karl Josef Holtgen, 'Sir Robert Dallington (1566–1637): Author, Traveler, and Pioneer of Taste,' *Huntington Library Quarterly*, 47 (1984), pp. 147–78.
95 Robert Dallington, *Aphorismes Civill and Militarie: Amplified with Authorities; and exemplified with Historie, out of the first Quarterne of Fr. Guicciardine* (London, 1613; STC 6197). Many of the aphorisms derived directly from Lipsius's *Politica* or the commentaries on Tacitus. Excerpts from Guicciardini's history provided illustrations, and thus validation, of the political maxims adumbrated by Dallington.
96 McCabe, *Joseph Hall*, Appendix A (pp. 321–30).
97 Discussions of the recognition of these initials by contemporaries are in McCabe, *Joseph Hall*, pp. 333–6, and Wands, ed. and trans., *Another World*, pp. xv–xx.
98 As quoted in McCabe, *Joseph Hall*, p. 324.
99 Translated as *The New-found Politicke* (London, 1626; STC 3185); for Boccalini, see Peter Burke, 'Tacitism, Scepticism, and Reason of State,' *The Cambridge History of Political Thought, 1450–1700*, ed. J.H. Burns with Mark Goldie (Cambridge, 1991), p. 490, and C. Varese, *Traiano Boccalini* (Padua, 1958). See also Frances Yates, *John Florio: The Life of an Italian in Shakespeare's England* (New York, 1968), pp. 301–9.
100 For Healey's works, see Brennan, *Literary Patronage*, pp. 121–2; for Lipsius's admiration of Epictetus, see *De Constantia Libri Duo* (London, 1592 [STC 15694.3]), sig. A3v and passim. Bacon's use of Epictetus is discussed above, chap. 2, pp. 88–95.
101 See McCabe, *Joseph Hall*, p. 321, n. 2; cf. J.H.M. Salmon, 'Stoicism and Roman Example: Seneca and Tacitus in Jacobean England,' *Journal of the History of Ideas*, 50 (1989), p. 207.
102 See Brennan, *Literary Patronage*, pp. 101–2, 123–8.
103 The idea permeates Hall's writings but may first have been expressed in his *Epistle* 'To Sir Edmund Bacon,' written perhaps shortly after the return from the 'secret' voyage undertaken by the two in 1605. See *Epistles* (1608), I, ii, ii, pp. 111–18, entitled, 'On the benefits of Retiredness and Secrecie.'
104 Ibid., p. 112.
105 For the correspondence between Hall and Laud over *Episcopacy by Divine Right*, see *Calendar of State Papers. Domestic Series, Charles I*, 1639/40, pp. 30–

1, 54–6, 87–8, 100, 186–7, 349–50, and 602. The idea for the pamphlet originated with Hall, whose confidence in the power of the written word, however, proved sadly misplaced. On this point, see Kranidas, 'Style and Rectitude in Seventeenth-Century Prose.'
106 *The Life and Letters of Sir Henry Wotton*, ed. L.P. Smith (Oxford, 1907), II, p. 370. Cf. also Kenneth Fincham and Peter Lake, 'Popularity, Prelacy and Puritanism in the 1630s: Joseph Hall Explains Himself,' *English Historical Review*, 111. 443 (Sept., 1996), pp. 856–81.
107 Hall's polemical tracts refuting Catholic attacks on the doctrine and practice of the English Church are treated in Huntley, *Bishop Joseph Hall*, passim.
108 Hall, *Contemplations upon the Principall Passages of the Holie Storie* (London, 1615) III, 10, in *The Works of Joseph Hall* (London, 1625; STC 12635), p. 928.
109 Cf. the recent study by Maurice Lee, Jr., *Great Britain's Solomon: James VI and I in His Three Kingdoms* (Urbana and Chicago, 1990).
110 McCabe, *Joseph Hall*, p. 247.
111 Hall, *Contemplations* (1622) VI, 17, in *Works* (1625), p. 1274.
112 *Contemplations* (1623) VII, 18, in *Works* (1625), p. 1316.
113 For a recent study that explores the similarities between Christian and stoical concepts of fortitude, and also draws attention to misunderstandings about the differences between them, see J. Douglas Stewart, '"Death Moved Not His Generous Mind": Allusions and Ideas, Mostly Classical, in Van Dyck's Work and Life,' *Anthony Van Dyck*, ed. Arthur K. Wheelock, Jr., Susan J. Barnes, and Julius S. Held (Washington, 1990), pp. 69–74.
114 *Works of Joseph Hall* (1625), p. 518.
115 Quoted in Erskine-Hill, *The Augustan Idea in English Literature*, p. 165. For the preceding quotation, see n. 104, above.
116 For the public outcry against James's pacific policy in face of the crisis in Europe, see Thomas Cogswell, *The Blessed Revolution: English Politics and the Coming of War* (Cambridge, 1990); see also Peter Lake, 'The Moderate and Irenic Case for Religious War: Joseph Hall's Via Media in Context,' in *Political Culture and Cultural Politics in Early Modern England*, ed. Susan Amussen and Mark Kishlansky (Manchester, 1995), pp. 55–83.
117 *Contemplations* (1620), V, 14, in *Works* (1625), p. 1121.
118 *Contemplations* (1618), IV, 12, in *Works* (1625), p. 1062.
119 See Hall, 'Character of the Good Magistrate,' *Characters of Vertues and Vices*, p. 61; and for Hall's relationship with Greville, Richard A. McCabe, 'Fulke Greville and Joseph Hall,' *Notes and Queries* 226 (new series 28, 1) (Feb. 1981), pp. 45–6.
120 For Hall's popularity see Kirk (ed.), *Heaven Upon Earth*, Introduction; see also n. 46, above.

121 Joseph Hall, *Resolutions and Decisions of Divers Practical Cases of Conscience In continuall Use amongst Men* (1649; 2nd ed. 1650; *STC* [ed. Wing] H407), pp. 235–6.
122 Margaret Sampson, 'Laxity and Liberty in Seventeenth-Century English Political Thought,' in *Conscience and Casuistry in Early Modern Europe*, ed. Edmund Leites (Cambridge, 1988), p. 117; cf. the more even-handed treatment of the casuistical tradition as given by Barbara Donagan in 'Godly Choice: Puritan Decision-Making in Seventeenth-Century England,' *Harvard Theological Review*, 76.3 (1983), pp. 307–34, and by Keith Thomas in 'Cases of Conscience in Seventeenth-Century England,' in *Public Duty and Private Conscience in Seventeenth-Century England: Essays Presented to G.E. Aylmer*, ed. John Morrill, Paul Slack and Daniel Woolf (Oxford, 1993), pp. 20–56.
123 John Whitefoot, preaching at Hall's funeral in 1656, as quoted by Huntley, *Bishop Joseph Hall*, p. 144. For Hall's influence, see Maren-Sophie Røstvig, *The Happy Man: Studies in the Metamorphoses of a Classical Ideal 1600–1700* (Oslo, 1954), especially pp. 51–2; see also, Huntley, *Bishop Joseph Hall*, and McCabe, *Joseph Hall*, passim. Though Margo Todd does not stress it, several seventeenth-century commonplace books in her bibliography reflect Senecan teachings and Seneca as distilled through Hall's writings. Those of Francis Russell, 4th Earl of Bedford, until his death in 1641 one of the prime voices for political reform under Charles I, are replete with notes on Hall's writings – as well as those of other neostoics. See Additional Papers, Bedford Estates, especially Box 2 (cards 43 and 44); for the earl's extracts of Hall's literary writings and 31, for extracts from Hall's sermons, Cornwallis's *Essayes*, and Charron's *Of Wisdome*. For access to these documents, I wish to thank Mrs M.G.P. Drapper, Archivist, and the Trustees of the Bedford Estates.
124 See Huntley, *Bishop Joseph Hall*, pp. 119–34.
125 Hall, *The Free Prisoner* was published along with *The Devout Soul* (1643; *STC*, [ed. Wing] H379). Lovelace's 'To Althea, from Prison,' is reprinted in *The New Oxford Book of Seventeenth-Century Verse*, ed. Alastair Fowler (Oxford and New York, 1992), p. 569. For Lovelace, see my 'Reason's Muse: Andrew Marvell, R. Fletcher, and the Politics of Poetry in the Engagement Debate,' *Albion*, 23 (1991), pp. 655–80.
126 Cf. Fuller's description of Hall, *The Worthies of England*, pp. 129–30. Hall continued to perform pastoral duties and to consecrate during his last years. In 1649, he wrote a justification of 'the institution of imposition of hands.' For a list of his writings in these latter years, see Huntley, *Bishop Joseph Hall*, pp. 140–1.

127 See Huntley, *Bishop Joseph Hall*, p. 118. Cf. Tourney's assessment of Hall in *Joseph Hall*, pp. 134–7; and see also, Kranidas, 'Style and Rectitude.'
128 See John Morrill, 'The Church in England, 1642–9,' in *Reactions to The English Civil War, 1642–1649*, ed. Morrill (London, 1982); cf. Claire Cross, 'The Church in England, 1646–1660,' in *The Interregnum: The Quest for Settlement*, ed. G.E. Aylmer (London, 1972); and see also, R.S. Bosher, *The Making of the Restoration Settlement: The Influence of the Laudians* (Westminster, 1951).
129 For example, Hall, *Great Mysterie of Godliness, laid forth by way of affectuous and feeling meditation* ... (1652; *STC* [ed. Wing] H383); and *Holy Raptures: or, Pathetical Meditations of the Love of Christ* ... (1652; *STC* [ed. Wing] H 285A). These same years also saw the appearance of Hall, *Soliloquies* (1651), which continue to promote the active life. See epigraph 3 at chapter opening (in *Works*, ed. Wynter, VIII, p. 59).
130 Hall's problem was that he tended to act the verbal bully to establish his point. See Kranidas, 'Style and Rectitude.' Cf. Huntley, *Bishop Joseph Hall*, pp. 111–14, where the author insists that Hall consistently stood for moderation although he inevitably provoked anger by being extreme himself.
131 Hall, *Cases of Conscience* pp. 71–160. The only other case that appears to have bearing on the times was 'Whether and how farre a man may take up armes in the publique quarrel of a warre' (pp. 143–9). Here, Hall argued that war was a necessary evil, and that the taking up of arms should always be conditional upon a call from the legitimate authority. For what constituted legitimate authority in Hall's view, see below.
132 Ibid., p. 78. On this point, see Sampson, 'Laxity and Liberty,' p. 94; and for Hall's place in the casuist tradition, ibid., and Camille Wells Slights, *The Casuistical Tradition in Shakespeare, Donne, Herbert and Milton* (Princton, 1981) as well as the studies of Donagan and Thomas (cited above, n. 122). While it has no explicit reference to Hall, see also, George L. Mosse, *The Holy Pretence: A Study of Christianity and Reason of State from William Perkins to John Winthrop* (Oxford, 1957).
133 Hall, *Certain Irrefragable Propositions Worthy of Serious Consideration* (1639; *STC* 12646b), p. 5. Emphasis in the original. Recent studies devoted to understanding the complexity of the 'origins' of the English Civil War, include Conrad Russell, *The Causes of the English Civil War* (Oxford, 1990) and his *The Fall of the British Monarchies, 1637–1642* (Oxford, 1991); see also the various essays in *The Scottish National Coverant in its British Context 1638–51*, ed. John Morrill (Edinburgh, 1991).
134 See epigraph 5 at chapter opening: Hall, Dedicatory epistle, *A Recollection of such treatises as haue bene heretofore seuerally published and are now reuised, corrected, augmented* (1615; *STC* 12706), sig. A3.

135 The problem was compounded by the Rump Parliament's decision to introduce the notorious 'Engagement' of loyalty. See John M. Wallace, 'The Engagement Controversy 1649–1652: An Annotated List of Pamphlets,' *Bulletin of the New York Public Library,* 68 (1964), pp. 384–405.

136 See the fourth epigraph at chapter opening from Hall, *Christian Moderation* (1640; STC 12648b), pp. 167–8.

**Epilogue**

1 I have treated this subject in greater detail in [Adriana Ferris] 'Politics and Poetry in the Engagement Debate: The Problem of Legitimacy in the English Revolution' (MA thesis, Dalhousie University, 1986); see also my 'Reason's Muse: Andrew Marvell, R. Fletcher, and the Politics of Poetry in the Engagement Debate,' *Albion,* 23 (1991), pp. 655–80.

2 See Blair Worden, 'Classical Republicanism and the Puritan Revolution,' in *History and Imagination: Essays in Honour of H.R. Trevor-Roper,* ed. H. Lloyd-Jones, V. Pearl, and B. Worden (London, 1981), pp. 186–7.

3 See Kevin Sharpe, 'The Foundations of the Chairs of History at Oxford and Cambridge: An Episode in Jacobean Politics,' in his *Politics and Ideas in Early Stuart England* (London and New York, 1989), pp. 221–3.

4 See J.H.M. Salmon, 'Stoicism and Roman Example: Seneca and Tacitus in Jacobean England,' *Journal of the History of Ideas,* 50 (1989), pp. 199–225.

5 In his *Criticism and Compliment: The Politics of Literature in the England of Charles I* (Cambridge, 1987), Kevin Sharpe explores the formal and dominant political culture under this doomed King, as does Malcolm R. Smuts in his *Court Culture and the Origins of a Royalist Tradition in Early Stuart England* (Philadelphia, 1987).

6 C.V. Wedgwood, *The Trial of Charles I* (Harmondsworth, 1983), pp. 104, 215.

7 See, for example, Howard D. Weinbrot, 'Politics, Taste, and National Identity: Some Uses of Tacitism in Eighteenth-Century Britain,' in *Tacitus and the Tacitean Tradition,* ed. T.J. Luce and A.J. Woodman (Princeton, 1993), pp. 168–84. See also the same author's *Augustus Caesar in 'Augustan' England: the Decline of a Classical Norm* (Princeton, 1978), and Steven N. Zwicker and David Bywaters, 'Politics and Translation: The English Tacitus of 1698,' *Huntington Library Quarterly,* 52 (1989), pp. 319–46.

8 Milton as quoted by Peter Burke in 'Tacitism,' in *Tacitus,* ed. T.A. Dorey (New York, 1969), p. 164. For Milton's growing republican militancy, see his *Readie and Easie Way to Establish a Free Commonwealth,* in *Revolutionary Prose of the English Civil War,* ed. Howard Erskine-Hill and Graham Storey (Cambridge, 1983), pp. 203–39. The 'mind' of Milton (as well as a number of other impor-

tant issues) has been freshly analysed by Nancy Armstrong and Leonard Tennenhouse in *The Imaginary Puritan: Literature, Intellectual Labor, and the Origins of Personal Life* (Berkeley, Los Angeles, and Oxford, 1992). Geoffrey Aggeler notes the neostoic strain in Milton's Civil War tracts in '"Sparkes of Holy Things": Neostoicism and the English Protestant Conscience,' *Renaissance and Reformation*, 26, 3 (1990), pp. 223–40; cf. Sharon Achinstein, 'Milton Catches the Conscience of the King: *Eikonoklastes* and the Engagement Controversy,' *Milton Studies*, vol. 29, ed. Albert C. Labrida (Pittsburgh and London, 1993), pp. 143–63. Blair Wordew briefly analyzes Milton's thought with an emphasis on his debt to Machiavelli in his 'Marchamont Nedham and the Beginnings of English Republicanism, 1649–1656,' in *Republicanism, Liberty, and Commercial Society, 1649–1776*, ed. David Wootton (Stanford, 1994), pp. 56–60. See also Barbara Riebling, 'Milton on Machiavelli: Representations of the State in *Paradise Lost*,' *Renaissance Quarterly*, 49 (1996), pp. 573–97.

9  See Jonathan Scott, *Algernon Sidney and the English Republic, 1623–1677* (Cambridge, 1988), especially chaps. 3, 4, 9; cf. Blair Worden, 'Republicanism and the Restoration, 1660–1683,' in *Republicanism, Liberty, and Commercial Society*, ed. Wootton, pp. 153–74.

10 Cf. Christopher Hill, 'The Norman Yoke,' in his *Puritanism and Revolution: Studies in Interpretation of the English Revolution of the 17th Century* (Harmondsworth, 1986), pp. 58–125. For the politics of 'republican England,' see Austin Woolrych, *Commonwealth to Protectorate* (Oxford, 1982), and for the republican tradition which emerged see Blair Worden, 'English Republicanism,' in *Cambridge History of Political Thought 1450–1700*, ed. J.H. Burns with Mark Goldie (Cambridge, 1991), pp. 443–75, as well as Worden's four chapters in *Republicanism, Liberty, and Commercial Society*, ed. Wootton. The impact of the 'republican' decade to subsequent English history has been strongly reaffirmed recently by Derek Hirst, 'Locating the 1650s in England's Seventeenth Century,' *History*, 81.263 (July, 1996), pp. 359–83.

11 See David Underdown, *Pride's Purge: Politics in the Puritan Revolution* (Oxford, 1971); and Blair Worden, *The Rump Parliament 1648–1653* (Cambridge, 1974).

12 For the issue of the war, see Philip Hunton's tract, *A Treatise of Monarchy* (1643), important excerpts of which are included in *Divine Right and Democracy: An Anthology of Political Writings in Stuart England*, ed. David Wootton (Harmondsworth, 1986), pp. 175–211; and for a transcript of the Engagement, see ibid., pp. 357–8. See also, John M. Wallace, 'The Engagement Controversy 1649–1652: An Annotated List of Pamphlets,' *Bulletin of the New York Public Library*, 68 (1964), pp. 384–405; the same author's *Destiny His Choice: The Loyalism of Andrew Marvell* (Cambridge, 1968), chaps. 1–3; and Keith Thomas,

'Cases of Conscience in Seventeenth-Century England,' in *Public Duty and Private Conscience in Seventeenth-Century England: Essays Presented to G.E. Aylmer*, ed. John Morrill, Paul Slack, and Daniel Woolf (Oxford, 1993) pp. 42–4.

13 Ascham, *Of the Confusions and Revolutions of Governments* (1649), excerpts of which are reprinted in *Divine Right and Democracy*, ed. Wootton, pp. 340–53. For Greville, see above chap. 3, especially pp. 128–37; and for de factoism in political debate, see Quentin Skinner, 'Conquest and Consent: Thomas Hobbes and the Engagement Controversy,' in *The Interregnum: The Quest for Settlement 1646–1660*, ed. G.E. Aylmer (London, 1972), pp. 79–98.

14 An overly critical analysis of Ascham's politics and political thinking is provided by Irene Coltman, *Private Men and Public Causes: Politics and Philosophy in the English Civil War* (London, 1962), pp. 197–239.

15 *The Case of the Commonwealth of England, Stated by Marchamont Nedham*, ed. Philip A. Knachel (Charlottesville, 1969); Blair Worden, 'Classical Republicanism and the Puritan Revolution,' pp. 192–4 (Worden asserts the raiding technique quoted in the text at p. 194); see also his 'Andrew Marvell, Oliver Cromwell, and the Horatian Ode,' in *Politics of Discourse: The Literature and History of Seventeenth-Century England*, ed. Kevin Sharpe and Steven Zwicker (Berkeley, 1987), pp. 147–80, and his 'Marchamont Nedham and the Beginnings of English Republicanism, 1649–1656,' in *Republicanism, Liberty, and Commercial Society*, ed. Wootton, pp. 60–81.

16 See Worden, 'Classical Republicanism and the Puritan Revolution,' pp. 192–4; and for the tag of 'politicke shuttle-cock,' see *Making the News: An Anthology of the Newbooks of Revolutionary England 1641–1600*, ed. Joad Raymond (Moreton-in-Marsh, Glouc., 1993), p. 332.

17 I argue this point in greater detail in my 'Reason's Muse,' cited n. 1, above; see also, Worden, 'Andrew Marvell ... and the Horatian Ode,' pp. 153–62.

18 R.F[letcher], *Mercurius Heliconicus. Or, A Short Reflection of Moderne Policy* (1650) (British Library, London, Thomason Collection, no. E623 [13]). For the title-page of this poem, see figure 10. This was one of three 'Heliconicus' poems composed by Fletcher, the third of which closely resembles the argument of Marvell's 'Horatian Ode.' This poem, as well as Fletcher's other two, are fully examined in my MA thesis, 'Politics and Poetry in the Engagement Debate.'

# Bibliography

**Manuscript Sources**

*London*

Public Record Office, Chancery Lane
 S.P. 9 (State Papers, Miscellaneous)
 S.P. 14 (State Papers, Domestic Series, James I)

British Library
 Additional Manuscripts
 20028   Virgilio Malvezzi, letters, life of King Numa (Tacitean History, published 1640s)
 36294   William Camden's letterbook
 57555   Sir Walter Ralegh's notebook

 Burney MSS
 370   Letter from Lipsius to Jan Dousa discussing the virtues of Sir Philip Sidney (f. 35)

 Cottonian MSS
 Julius F. IV   Tacitean excerpts (ff. 75b–76)
 Titus C.VI   Letters and papers of Northampton

 Harleian MSS
 182   Simonds D'Ewes commonplace book (neostoic headings to topics: ff. 23 ff.)
 192   D'Ewes historical collection

| | |
|---|---|
| 6018 | Cotton's book-lending list, 1621 |
| 6521 | Edmund Bolton's notes on Roman history |

Lansdowne MSS

| | |
|---|---|
| LXXXIX–XCI | Includes Greville correspondence |
| CIII | Sentences from Tacitus (f. 109) |

Sloane MSS

| | |
|---|---|
| 402 | Joseph Hall's refutation of Lipsius's sententia (1633 ?) (ff. 180–2). |
| 836 | Extracts from Bacon's *Essayes*; comments on Seneca; references to Lipsius. |
| 848 | 17th-century extracts from Lipsius, *Politica*. |
| 922 | Nehemiah Wallington's collection. Extracts from Seneca and Hall (ff. 34–51b). |
| 1048 | Edward Sherburne's notebook (late 1660s?). Translations of Tacitus (ff. 1–57). |
| 1775 | Letters and pamphlets by Bacon. |
| 1983b | List of Lipsius's works (ff. 86–88b). |
| 2521 | 17th-century notes on Roman Imperial history; Tacitean excerpts; notes on Seneca's Epistles. |
| 2764 | Lipsian letters (in Latin). |

Stowe MSS

| | |
|---|---|
| 1045 | Francis Tate's collections: references to Lipsius (ff. 69–70); to Tacitus (ff. 70 ff.). |

Bedford Settled Estates
  Additional Papers

| | |
|---|---|
| 10–43 | Commonplace books of Francis Russell, 4th Earl of Bedford: dotted with excerpts from Hall's writings. |

*Oxford*

Bodleian Library
  Rawlinson MSS

| | |
|---|---|
| D.360 | Stoic *sententiae* (compiled 1700s) |
| D.368 | Notes on classical and English histories. |
| D.1062 | Hayward's dedication of *Henry IIII* to Essex; political and Lipsian commonplaces. |

Sancroft MSS
87          William Sancroft's commonplace book (1630s?)

Smith MSS
17          William Camden's commonplace book.

*Cambridge*

St. John's Library
K.38        Henry Vaughn's commonplace book (1630s). Commendations of Lipsius's edition of Tacitus (f. 168).
O.64        Commonplace book [Wm Johnson]: neostoic extracts (ff. 51 ff.) (late 17th century).
S.34        Commonplace book (1620s ff.): references to Charron; extracts from Hall.
S.44        Notes on Roman histories: on stoics; (1635–6 ?).
U.5         Catalogue of books (1632): includes works by Bacon, Lipsius, Tacitus, Seneca, Hall.

*Chichester*

West Sussex Record Office
Lib. 5650   'Copies of Certain Letters in the Possession of Earl Winterton.' Vol. 1, pp. 1–7. Letters between the Earl of Essex and Sir Thomas Egerton, 1599.

*Aberystwyth*

National Library of Wales
MS 5666C    John Stradling's 'A Politicke Discourse' (1625).

## Printed Works

For ease of reference, I have not followed the usual practice of dividing 'primary' and 'secondary' works, but have instead integrated them into the following list of printed works. Place of publication of all items is London, except where otherwise specified. For books printed between 1500 and 1700 *STC* and Wing numbers are included following the date.

Achinstein, Sharon. 'Milton Catches the Conscience of the King: *Eikonoklastes*

and the Engagement Controversy.' *Milton Studies*, no. 29, ed. Albert C. Labrida. Pittsburg and London, 1993.
Adams, John Charles. 'Gabriel Harvey's *Ciceronianus* and the Place of Peter Ramus's *Dialecticae libro duo* in the Curriculum.' *Renaissance Quarterly*, 43 (1990), pp. 551–69.
Adams, Robert P. *The Better Part of Valor: More, Colet, and Vives, on Humanism, War, and Peace, 1496–1535*. Seattle, 1962.
Aggeler, Geoffrey. '"Sparkes of Holy Things": Neostoicism and the English Protestant Conscience.' *Renaissance and Reformation*, 26.3 (1990), pp. 223–40.
– 'Ben Jonson's Justice Overdo and Joseph Hall's Good Magistrate.' *English Studies*, 76.5 (Sept. 1995), pp. 434–42.
Aiken, W., and B. Henning, eds. *Conflict in Stuart England*. 1960.
Allen, John W. *English Political Thought, 1603–1660*. 2 vols. 1938.
Allen, M.J., Dominic Baker-Smith, Arthur F. Kinney, with Margaret M. Sullivan, eds. *Sir Philip Sidney's Achievements*. New York, 1990.
Anderson, Judith A. *Biographical Truth: The Representation of Persons in Tudor-Stuart Writing*. New Haven, 1984.
Archer, John Michael. *Sovereignty and Intelligence: Spying and Court Culture in the English Renaissance*. Princeton, 1993.
Armitage, Christopher M. *Sir Walter Ralegh: An Annotated Bibliography*. Chapel Hill and London, 1987.
Armstrong, C.J.R. 'The Dialectical Road to Truth: the Dialogue.' In *French Renaissance Studies*, ed. Peter Sharratt. Edinburgh, 1976.
Armstrong, Nancy, and Leonard Tennenhouse. *The Imaginary Puritan: Literature, Intellectual Labor, and the Origins of Personal Life*. Berkeley, Los Angeles, and Oxford, 1992.
Arnold, E. Vernon. *Roman Stoicism*. New York, 1958.
Ascham, Anthony. *Of the Confusions and Revolutions of Governments*. 1649. STC (ed. Wing) A 3922.
Ascoli, Albert Russell, and Victoria Kahn, eds. *Machiavelli and the Discourse of Literature*. Ithaca, N.Y., and London, 1993.
Ashton, Robert, ed. *James I by his Contemporaries: An Account of his Career and Character as seen by some of his Contemporaries*. 1969.
Aubrey, John. *Brief Lives*, ed. Oliver Lawson Dick. 1949.
Aylmer, G.E. *The King's Servants: The Civil Service of Charles I*. 1961.
– 'Unbelief in Seventeenth-Century England.' In *Puritans and Revolutionaries: Essays in Seventeenth-Century History Presented to Christopher Hill*, ed. Donald Pennington and Keith Thomas. Oxford, 1978.
Bacon, Francis. *The Works of Francis Bacon*, ed. J. Spedding, R.L. Ellis and D.D. Heath, 7 vols. 1858–61.
– *The Letters and Life of Francis Bacon*, ed. James Spedding, 7 vols. 1862–74.

- *Francis Bacon: Selections*, ed. P.E. Matheson and E.F. Matheson. Oxford, 1927.
- *The History of the Reign of Henry the Seventh*, ed. F.J. Levy. Indianapolis, 1972.
- *Sir Francis Bacon: The Essayes or Counsels, Civill and Morall*, ed. Michael Kiernan. Cambridge, MA.
- *Francis Bacon: Essays*, ed. John Pitcher. Harmondsworth, 1985.

Baker, Herschel. *The Race of Time: Three Lectures on Renaissance Historiography.* Toronto, 1967.

Bakos, Adrianna E. 'The Historical Reputation of Louis XI in Political Theory and Polemic During the French Religious Wars.' *Sixteenth Century Journal*, 21 (1990), pp. 3–32.
- '"Qui nescit dissimulare, nescit regnare": Louis XI and *Raison d'État* During the Reign of Louis XIII.' *Journal of the History of Ideas*, 52 (1991), pp. 399–416.

Bald, R.C. *Donne and the Drurys*. Cambridge, 1959.

Ball, J.N. 'Sir John Eliot and Parliament, 1624–1629.' In *Faction and Parliament: Essays in Early Stuart History*, ed. Kevin Sharpe. Oxford, 1978.

Barker, Thomas M. *The Military Intellectual and Battle: Raimondo Montecuccoli and the Thirty Years War*. Albany, 1975.

Baron, Hans. 'The Secularization of Wisdom and Political Humanism in the Renaissance.' *Journal of the History of Ideas*, 21 (1960), pp. 131–50.
- *The Crisis of the Early Italian Renaissance*, 2nd ed. Princeton, 1966.
- 'Leonardo Bruni: "Professional Rhetorician" or "Civic Humanist"?' *Past & Present*, 36 (1967), pp. 21–37.

Barton, Anne. *Ben Jonson, Dramatist*. Cambridge, 1984.

Bates, Catherine. *The Rhetoric of Courtship in Elizabethan Language and Literature*. Cambridge, 1992.

Bender, Robert M., ed. *Five Courtier Poets of the English Renaissance*. New York, 1967.

Benjamin, Edwin B. 'Bacon and Tacitus.' *Classical Philology*, 60 (1965), pp. 102–10.

Berkowitz, David. 'Reason of State in England and the Petition of Right, 1603–1629.' In *Staatsrason: Studien zur Geschichte eines politischen Begriffs*, ed. Roman Schnur. Berlin, 1975.
- *John Selden's Formative Years: Politics and Society in Early Seventeenth-Century England*. Washington, 1988.

Berry, Edward, I. 'History and Rhetoric in Bacon's *Henry VII*.' In *Seventeenth-Century Prose*, ed. Stanley E. Fish. New York, 1971.

Bertelli, Sergio. *Ribelli, Libertine e Ortodossi nella Storiografia Barocca*. Florence, 1973.

Birch, Thomas. *The Court and Times of James I; Illustrated by Authentic and Confidential Letters, From Various Public and Private Collections*, 2 vols., ed. R.F. Williams. 1848.

Bireley, Robert. *The Counter-Reformation Prince: Anti-Machiavellianism or Catholic Statecraft in Early Modern Europe*. Chapel Hill and London, 1990.

Birrell, T.A. *The Library of John Morris: The Reconstruction of a Seventeenth-Century Collection*. 1976.

– *English Monarchs and Their Books: From Henry VII to Charles II*. 1987.

Bloom, Harold, 'The Breaking of Form.' In *Deconstruction and Criticism*, ed. H. Bloom et al. 1979.

Boase, A.M. 'The Early History of the *Essai* Title in France and Britain.' In *Studies in French Literature Presented to H.W. Lawton*, ed. J.C. Ireson, I.D. McFarlane, and Garnet Rees. Manchester, 1968.

Bodin, Jean. *The Six Bookes of a Commonweale*, trans. R. Knolles. 1606. STC 3193.

Bosher, R.S. *The Making of the Restoration Settlement: The Influence of the Laudians*. Westminister, 1951.

Bossy, John. *The English Catholic Community 1570–1850*. 1975.

Botero, Giovanni. *Reason of State*, trans. P.J. and D.P. Waley. 1956.

Boughner, Daniel C. 'Jonson's Use of Lipsius in *Sejanus*.' *Modern Language Notes*, 73 (1958), pp. 247–55.

– *The Devil's Disciple: Ben Jonson's Debt to Machiavelli*. New York, 1968.

Bouwsma, William J. *The Interpretation of Renaissance Humanism*. Washington, 1966.

– *The Culture of Renaissance Humanism*. Washington, 1973.

– 'The Two Faces of Humanism: Stoicism and Augustinianism in Renaissance Thought.' In *Itinerarium Italicum: The Profile of the Italian Renaissance in the Mirror of Its European Transformations*, ed. Heiko A. Oberman with Thomas A. Brady. Leiden, 1975.

– *John Calvin: A Sixteenth-Century Portrait*. New York, 1988.

– 'The Spirituality of Renaissance Humanism.' In *Christian Spirituality*, vol. 2, ed. Jill Raitt. New York, 1988.

Bowen, Catherine Drinker. *The Lion and the Throne*. Boston, 1957.

Box, Ian. 'Bacon's *Essays*: From Political Science to Political Prudence.' *History of Political Thought*, 3 (1982), pp. 31–49.

Boyce, Benjamin. *The Theophrastan Character in England to 1642*. Cambridge, MA, 1947.

Boyle, Marjorie O'Rourke. *Rhetoric and Reform: Erasmus' Civil Dispute with Luther*. Cambridge, MA, 1983.

Bradford, Alan T. 'Stuart Absolutism and the "Utility" of Tacitus.' *Huntington Library Quarterly*, 46 (1983), pp. 127–55.

Brennan, Michael. *Literary Patronage in the English Renaissance: The Pembroke Family*. 1988.

Bromham, A.A. '"Have You Read Lipsius?": Thomas Middleton and Stoicism.' *English Studies*, 77.5 (Sept. 1996), pp. 401–21.
Brooks, Cleanth. *Historical Evidence and the Reading of Seventeenth-Century Poetry.* 1991.
Bullough, Geoffrey. 'Bacon and the Defence of Learning.' In *Essential Articles for the Study of Francis Bacon*, ed. Brian Vickers. Hamden, CT, 1968.
Burgess, Glenn. *The Politics of the Ancient Constitution: An Introduction to English Political Thought, 1603–1642*. University Park, PA, 1992.
Burke, Kenneth. *The Philosophy of Literary Form: Studies in Symbolic Action.* 3rd ed. Berkeley, 1973.
Burke, Peter. 'A Survey of the Popularity of Ancient Historians, 1450–1700.' *History and Theory*, 5 (1966), pp. 135–52.
- 'Tacitism.' In *Tacitus*, ed. T.A. Dorey. New York, 1969.
- 'Tacitus, Scepticism, and Reason of State.' In *Cambridge History of Political Thought 1450–1700*, ed. J.H. Burns with Mark Goldie. Cambridge, 1991.
Burns, J.H., with Mark Goldie, eds. *Cambridge History of Political Thought 1450–1700*. Cambridge, 1991.
Butler, Martin. 'Early Stuart Court Culture: Compliment or Criticism?' *Historical Journal*, 32 (1989), pp. 425–35.
- 'Politics and the Masque: *Salmacida Spolia*.' In *Literature and the English Civil War*, ed. Thomas Healey and Jonathan Sawday. Cambridge, 1990.
- 'Ben Jonson and the Limits of Courtly Panegyric.' In *Culture and Politics in Early Stuart England*, ed. Kevin Sharpe and Peter Lake. 1994.
Buxton, John. *Sir Philip Sidney and the English Renaissance.* 3rd ed. 1987.
*Cabala: Sive Scrinia Sacra. Secrets of Empire in Letters of Illustrious Persons.* 1654. STC (ed. Wing) C184.
Camden, William. *Britiannia siue florentissimorum regnorum Angliae, Scotiae, Hiberniae chorographica descriptio.* 1586. STC 4503.
- *Remaines of a Greater Worke, concerning Britaine, the Inhabitants thereof, [etc.].* 1605. STC 4521.
- *Britain, or a Chorographicall Description of England, Scotland, and Ireland, Beautified with Mappes*, trans. P. Holland. 1610. STC 4509.
- *Annales: The True and Royall, History of Elizabeth, Queene of England*, trans. A. Darcie 1625. STC 4497.
Cameron, James K. 'Humanism in the Low Countries.' In *The Impact of Humanism on Western Europe*, ed. Anthony Goodman and Angus Mackay. London and New York, 1990.
Campbell, Lily B. *Shakespeare's Histories: Mirrors of Elizabethan Policy.* San Marino, 1947.
Cantimore, Delio. 'Rhetoric and Politics in Italian Humanism,' trans. Frances

A. Yates. *Journal of the Warburg and Courtauld Institutes*, 1 (1937–8), pp. 83–102.
– 'Submission and Conformity: "Nicodemism" and the Expectations of a Conciliar Solution to the Religious Questions,' trans. and ed. Eric Cochrane. In *The Late Italian Renaissance, 1525–1630*, ed. Eric Cochrane. New York, Evanston, and London, 1970.
Carleton, Dudley. *Dudley Carleton to John Chamberlain 1603–1624: Jacobean Letters*, ed. Morris Lee, Jr. New Brunswick, N.J., 1972.
Chamberlain, John. *The Letters of John Chamberlain*, ed. N.E. McClure. 2 vols. Philadelphia, 1939.
– *The Chamberlain Letters: A Selection of the Letters of John Chamberlain Concerning Life in England from 1597 to 1626*, ed. Elizabeth McClure Thomson. New York, 1965.
Charron, Pierre. *Of Wisdome. Three Bookes*, trans. Samson Lennard. 1608. STC 5051.
Chew, Audrey. 'Joseph Hall and Neo-Stoicism.' *Publications of the Modern Language Association of America*, 65 (1950), pp. 1130–45.
Cheynell, Francis. *The Rise, Growthe, and Danger of Socinianisme*. 1643. STC (ed. Wing) C 3815.
– *Chillingworthi Novissima: Or, the Sicknesse, Heresy, Death, and Buriall of William Chillingworth*. 1644. STC (ed. Wing) C 3810.
Christianson, Paul. *Reformers and Babylon: English Apocalyptic Visions from the Reformation to the Eve of the Civil War*. Toronto, 1978.
– 'John Selden, the Five Knights' Case, and Discretionary Imprisonment in Early Stuart England.' *Criminal Justice History*, 6 (1985), pp. 65–87.
– *Discourse on History, Law, and Governance in the Public Career of John Selden, 1610–1635*. Toronto, 1996.
Church, William F. *Richelieu and Reason of State*. Princeton, 1972.
– 'France.' In *National Consciousness, History, and Political Culture in Early-Modern Europe*, ed. Orest Ranum, Baltimore, 1975.
Cibber, Theophilus. *The Lives of the Poets of Great Britain and Ireland*. 4 vols. 1753.
Clark, Peter, ed. *The European Crisis of the 1590s*. 1985.
Clarke, M.L. *The Roman Mind: Studies in the History of Thought from Cicero to Marcus Aurelius*. Cambridge, MA, 1956.
Cochrane, Eric. *Florence in the Forgotten Centuries 1527–1800*. Chicago, 1973.
Cochrane, Rexmond C. 'Francis Bacon and the Architect of Fortune.' *Studies in the Renaissance*, 5 (1958), pp. 176–95.
Cogswell, Thomas. *The Blessed Revolution: English Politics and the Coming of War*. Cambridge, 1990.

- 'The Politics of Propaganda: Charles I and the People in the 1620s.' *Journal of British Studies*, 29 (1990), pp. 187–215.
Coke, Roger. *A Detection of the Court and State of England*. 3rd ed. 1697. STC (ed. Wing) C 4975.
Collins, Stephen L. *From Divine Cosmos to Sovereign State: An Intellectual History of Consciousness and the Idea of the Order in Renaissance England*. Oxford, 1989.
Collinson, Patrick. *The Religion of Protestants*. Oxford, 1982.
- 'Ecclesiastical Vitriol: Religious Satire in the 1590s and the Invention of Puritanism.' In *The Reign of Elizabeth I: Court and Culture in the Last Decade*, ed. John Guy. Cambridge, 1995.
Coltman, Irene. *Private Men and Public Causes: Philosophy and Politics in the English Civil War*. 1962.
Condren, Conal. *The Status and Appraisal of Classic Texts: An Essay on Political Theory, Its Inheritance and the History of Ideas*. Princeton, 1985.
Coote, Stephen. *A Play of Passion: The Life of Sir Walter Ralegh*. 1993.
Cope, Esther S. *Politics Without Parliaments, 1629–1640*. 1987.
Corbett, Theodore G. 'The Cult of Lipsius: A Leading Source of Early Modern Spanish Statecraft,' *Journal of the History of Ideas*, 36 (1975), pp. 139–52.
Cornwallis, William. *The Essayes*, ed. Don Cameron Allen. Baltimore, 1946.
- *Discourses upon Seneca the Tragedian*, ed. Robin Hood Bowers. Gainesville, 1952.
Craig, D.H., ed. *Ben Jonson: The Critical Heritage 1599–1798*. London and New York, 1990.
Croll, Morris. *The Works of Fulke Greville*. Philadelphia, 1903.
- *'Attic' and Baroque Prose Style: The Anti-Ciceronian Movement, Essays by Morris Croll*, ed. J. Max Patrick and Robert O. Evans. Princeton, 1966.
- *Style, Rhetoric, and Rhythm*, ed. J. Max Patrick and Robert O. Evans. Princeton, 1966.
Cromwell, Oliver. *The Writings and Speeches of Oliver Cromwell*, ed. W.C. Abbott. Cambridge, MA, 1939.
Cross, Claire. *The Puritan Earl: The Life of Henry Hastings, Third Earl of Huntingdon, 1536–1595*. 1966.
- 'The Church in England, 1646–1600.' In *The Interregnum: The Quest for Settlement*, ed. G.E. Aylmer. 1972.
Curtis, Mark H. *Oxford and Cambridge in Transition 1558–1642*. Oxford, 1959.
- 'The Alienated Intellectuals of Early Stuart England.' *Past & Present*, 23 (1962), pp. 25–43.
Curtius, Ernst Robert. *European Literature and the Latin Middle Ages*, trans. W.R. Trask. New York, 1953.
Dallington, Robert. *Aphorismes Civill and Militarie: Amplified with Authorities; and*

*Exemplified with Historie, out of the first Quarterne of Fr. Guicciardine*. 1613. STC 6197.
Daly, J.W. 'The Idea of Absolute Monarchy in Seventeenth-Century England.' *Historical Journal*, 21 (1978), pp. 227–50.
Daniel, Samuel. *The Poeticall Essayes of Sam. Danyel. Newly Corrected and Augmented*. 1599. STC 6261.
– *Musophilus*, ed. Raymond Himelick. West Lafayette, 1965.
Davies, G.A. 'The Influence of Justus Lipsius on Juan de Vera y Figueroa's *Embaxador* (1620).' *Bulletin of Hispanic Studies*, 42 (1965), pp. 160–73.
DeLuna, Barbara N. *Jonson's Romish Plot: A Study of 'Catiline' in its Historical Context*. Oxford, 1967.
Devereux, Walter B. *Lives and Letters of the Devereux, Earls of Essex, in the Reigns of Elizabeth, James I and Charles I, 1540–1656*. 1853.
Dickerman, Edmund H., and Anita M. Walker. 'The Choice of Hercules: Henry IV as Hero.' *Historical Journal*, 39.2 (June, 1996), pp. 315–37.
Dollimore, Jonathan. *Radical Tragedy: Religion, Ideology and Power in the Drama of Shakespeare and his Contemporaries*. Chicago, 1984.
Donaldson, Peter S. *Machiavelli and Reason of State*. New York, 1988.
Doody, Margaret A. *The Daring Muse: Augustan Poetry Reconsidered*. Oxford, 1985.
van Dorsten, J.A. *Poets, Patrons, and Professors: Sir Philip Sidney, Daniel Rogers, and the Leiden Humanists*. Leiden and London, 1962.
– 'The Final Year.' In *Sir Philip Sidney. 1586 and the Creation of a Legend*, ed. Jan van Dorsten, Dominic Baker Smith, and Arthur Kinney. Leiden, 1986.
van Dorsten, J.A., Dominic Baker-Smith, and Arthur F. Kinney, eds. *Sir Philip Sidney. 1586 and the Creation of a Legend*. Leiden, 1986.
Duncan-Jones, Katherine. *Sir Philip Sidney. Courtier-Poet*. New Haven and London. 1991.
Eagleton, Terry. *Literary Theory: An Introduction*. Minneapolis, 1983.
Easthope, Anthony. *Literary into Cultural Studies*. 1991.
Eco, Umberto. *Foucault's Pendulum*, trans. William Weaver. New York, 1990.
– *The Island of the Day Before*, trans. William Weaver. New York, San Diego, and London, 1994.
Edmond, Mary. *Rare Sir William Davenant*. Manchester, 1987.
Edwards, Edward. *Life of Sir Walter Ralegh*. 2 vols. 1868.
Edwards, Philip. *Sir Walter Ralegh*. 1953.
Elliott, J.H. 'Quevedo and the Count-Duke of Olivares.' In *Quevedo in Perspective: Eleven Essays*, ed. James Iffland. Newark, 1980.
– *Richelieu and Olivares*. Cambridge, 1984.
– 'Yet Another Crisis?' In *The European Crisis of the 1590's*, ed. Peter Clark. 1985.
– *The Count-Duke of Olivares: The Statesman in an Age of Decline*. New Haven, 1986.

- 'A Europe of Composite Monarchies.' *Past & Present*, 137 (Nov. 1992), pp. 48–71.
Ellis-Fermor, Una. *The Jacobean Drama*. 1936.
Eliot, John. *De Iure Maiestatis*, ed. A.B. Grosart. 1882.
Epictetus. *Discourses; Manual*, trans. P.E. Matheson, in *The Stoic and Epicurean Philosopher*, ed. Whitney J. Oates. New York, 1940.
Epstein, Joel. *Francis Bacon: A Political Biography*. Athens, Ohio, 1977.
Erskine-Hill, Howard. *The Augustan Idea in English Literature*. 1983.
Erskine-Hill, Howard, and Graham Storey, eds. *Revolutionary Prose of the English Civil War*. Cambridge, 1983.
Esler, Anthony. *The Aspiring Mind of the Elizabethan Younger Generation*. Durham, N.C., 1966.
Ettinghausen, Henry. 'Neo-Stoicism in Pictures: Lipsius and the Engraved Title-Page and Portrait in Quevedo's "Epicteto y Phocilides".' *Modern Language Review*, 46 (1971), pp. 94–100.
- *Francisco de Quevedo and the Neostoic Movement*. Oxford, 1972.
Eusden, John Dykstra. *Puritans, Lawyers, and Politics in Early Seventeenth-Century England*. New Haven, 1958.
Evans, Robert C. *Ben Jonson and the Poetics of Patronage*. 1989.
- *Jonson, Lipsius and the Politics of Renaissance Stoicism*. Wakefield, N.H., 1992.
Evans, R.J.W. *Rudolph II and his World: A Study in Intellectual History 1576–1612*. Oxford, 1973.
- *The Wechel Presses: Humanism and Calvinism in Central Europe 1572–1627. Past & Present*. Supplement 2 (1975).
- *The Making of the Hapsburg Monarchy 1550–1700: An Interpretation*. Oxford, 1979.
Farmer, Norman, Jr. 'Fulke Greville and Sir John Coke: An Exchange of Letters on a History Lecture and Certain Latin Verses on Sir Philip Sidney.' *Huntington Library Quarterly*, 33 (1969–70), pp. 217–36.
Ferguson, Arthur B. *The Articulate Citizen and the English Renaissance*. Durham, N.C., 1965.
- *Clio Unbound: Perception of the Social and Cultural Past in Renaissance England*. Durham, N.C., 1979.
Fernandez-Santamaria, Jose A. 'Reason of State and Statecraft in Spain (1595–1640).' *Journal of the History of Ideas*, 41 (1980), pp. 355–79.
- *Reason of State and Statecraft in Spanish Political Thought, 1595–1640*. Lanham, N.Y., and London, 1983.
Ferris, Adriana A.N. 'Politics and Poetry in the Engagement Debate: The Problem of Legitimacy in the English Revolution,' MA thesis. Dalhousie University, Halifax, N.S., 1986.

Fincham, Kenneth and Peter Lake. 'Popularity, Prelacy and Puritanism in the 1630s: Joseph Hall Explains Himself.' *English Historical Review*, 111. 443 (Sept. 1996), pp. 856–81.

Fink, Zera. *The Classical Republicans: An Essay in the Recovery of a Pattern of Thought in 17th-Century England*. 2nd ed. Evanston, 1962.

Fisch, Harold. 'The Limits of Hall's Senecanism.' *Proceedings of the Leeds Philosophical Society*, 6 (1950), pp. 453–63.

Fish, Stanley. *Self-Consuming Artifacts*. Berkeley, 1972.

– ed. *Seventeenth-Century Prose: Modern Essays in Criticism*. New York, 1971.

Fletcher, A.J. 'Honour, Reputation and Local Officeholding in Elizabethan and Stuart England.' In *Order and Disorder in Early Modern England*, ed. Anthony Fletcher and John Stevenson. Cambridge, 1985.

Fletcher, R. *Mercurius Heliconicus, No. 2*. 1652. (The British Library, Thomason Collection No. E623[13].)

Forster, Leonard. 'Lipsius and Renaissance Neostoicism.' In *Festschrift for Ralph Farrell*, ed. Anthony Stephens, H.L. Rogers, and Brian Cloghan. Bern, 1977.

Foster, Elizabeth Read. *The House of Lords, 1603–1649*. Chapel Hill, N.C., 1983.

Foster, Herbert D. 'Liberal Calvinism: The Remonstrants at the Synod of Dort.' *Harvard Theological Review*, 16 (1923), pp. 1–37.

Fowler, Alastair, ed. *The New Oxford Book of Seventeenth-Century Verse*. Oxford and New York, 1992.

Fox, Alistair, and John Guy, eds. *Reassessing the Henrician Age: Humanism, Politics and Reform 1500–1550*. Oxford, 1986.

Franklin, Julian H. 'Sovereignty and the Mixed Constitution: Bodin and his Critics.' In *Cambridge History of Political Thought, 1450–1700*, ed. J.H. Burns with Mark Goldie. Cambridge, 1991.

Fulbrook, Mary. *Piety and Politics: Religion and the Rise of Absolutism in England, Württemberg and Prussia*. Cambridge, 1983.

Fuller, Thomas. *The History of the Worthies of England*. 1662. STC (ed. Wing) F 2440.

Fussner, F. Smith. *The Historical Revolution: English Historical Writing and Thought, 1580–1640*. 1962.

Galloway, Bruce. *The Union of England and Scotland, 1603–1608*. Edinburgh, 1986.

Gardiner, S.R., ed. *Parliamentary Debates in 1610*. 1862.

– *Notes of the Debates in the House of Lords, 1621*. 1870.

Garver, Eugene. *Machiavelli and the History of Prudence*. Madison, 1987.

Gasquet, Emile. *Le Courant Machiavelien dans la Pensée et la Littérature Anglaises du XVIe Siècle*. Montreal, 1974.

van Gelderen, Martin. 'The Machiavellian Moment and the Dutch Revolt: the

Rise of Neostoicism and Dutch Republicanism.' In *Machiavelli and Republicanism*, ed. Gisela Bock, Quentin Skinner, and Maurizio Viroli. Cambridge, 1990.

Gentillet, Innocent. *A Discourse Upon the Means of Wel Governing a Kingdom. Divided into Three Parts. Against N. Machiavell*, trans. S. Patericke. 1602. STC 11743.

– *Antimachiavel*, ed. C.E. Rathé. Geneva, 1968.

Gerlo, A., and H.D.L. Vervliet. *Inventaire de la Correspondence de Juste Lipse*, 1564–1606. Antwerp, 1968.

Gilbert, Felix. *Machiavelli and Guicciardini: Politics and History in Sixteenth-Century Florence*. Princeton, 1965.

Gilson, Étienne. *Reason and Revelation in the Middle Ages*. New York, 1966.

Ginzburg, Carlo. 'High and Low: The Theme of Forbidden Knowledge in the Sixteenth and Seventeenth Centuries.' *Past & Present*, 73 (1976), pp. 28–41.

Goldberg, Jonathan. *James I and the Politics of Literature: Jonson, Shakespeare, Donne, and their Contemporaries*. Baltimore and London, 1983.

Goodman, Anthony, and Angus MacKay, eds. *The Impact of Humanism on Western Europe*. London and New York, 1990.

Grafton, Anthony. 'Portrait of Justus Lipsius.' *American Scholar*, 56 (1986–7), pp. 382–90.

– *Defenders of the Text: The Traditions of Scholarship in an Age of Science*. Cambridge, MA, and London, 1991.

– 'Humanism and Political Theory.' In *The Cambridge History of Political Thought, 1450–1700*, ed. J.H. Burns with Mark Goldie. Cambridge, 1991.

Grafton, Anthony, and Lisa Jardine. *From Humanism to the Humanities: Education and the Liberal Arts in Fifteenth- and Sixteenth-Century Europe*. Cambridge, MA, 1986.

– '"Studied For Action": How Gabriel Harvey Read His Livy.' *Past & Present*, 129 (Nov. 1990), pp. 30–78.

Graves, Michael A.R. *The Tudor Parliaments: Crown, Lords and Commons, 1485–1603*. 1985.

Gray, Hanna H. 'Renaissance Humanism: The Pursuit of Eloquence.' *Journal of the History of Ideas*, 24 (1963), pp. 497–514.

Greenblatt, Stephen. *Sir Walter Ralegh: The Renaissance Man and his Roles*. New Haven and London, 1973.

– *Renaissance Self-Fashioning: From More to Shakespeare*. Chicago, 1980.

Greene, Thomas M. 'Ben Jonson and the Centered Self.' *Studies in English Literature*, 10 (1970), pp. 325–48.

Grendler, Paul F. 'Pierre Charron: Precursor to Hobbes.' In his *Culture and Censorship in Late Renaissance Italy and France*. 1981.

Greville, Fulke. *The Works in Prose and Verse of the Lord Brooke*, ed. A.B. Grosart. 4 vols. 1868.
- *Poems and Dramas of Fulke Greville, First Lord Brooke*, ed. Geoffrey Bullough. 2 vols. 1939.
- *The Remains, Being Poems of Monarchy and Religion*, ed. G.A. Wilkes. Oxford, 1965.
- *Selected Writings of Fulke Greville*, ed. Joan Rees. 1973.
- *Prose Works of Fulke Greville, Lord Brooke*, ed. John Gouws. Oxford, 1986.

Güldner, G. *Das Toleranz-Problem in der Niederlanden in Ausgang des 16 Jahrhunderts*. Lubeck, 1968.

Guy, John. 'The Elizabethan Establishment and the Ecclesiastical Polity.' In *The Reign of Elizabeth I: Court and Culture in the Last Decade*, ed. John Guy. Cambridge, 1995.

Van der Haeghen, F. *Bibliographie Lipsienne*. 3 Vols. Ghent, 1886–8.

Haigh, Christopher, *Elizabeth I*. London and New York, 1988.
- , ed. *The Reign of Elizabeth I*. 1984.
- , ed. *The English Reformation Revised*. Cambridge, 1987.

Hale, J.R. *Renaissance War Studies*. Hambledon, 1983.
- *War and Society in Renaissance Europe 1450–1620*. 1985.

Hall, Joseph. *Meditations and Vowes*. 1605. STC 12679.
- *Mundus Alter et Idem*. 1605. STC 12685.
- *The Arte of Divine Mediation*. 1606. STC 12642.
- *Heaven Upon Earth*. 1606. STC 12666.
- *Characters of Vertues and Vices*. 1608. STC 12648.
- *Epistles*, 3 vols. 1611. STC 12662.
- *A Recollection of Such Treatises as have bene heretofore severally published and are now revised, corrected, augmented*. 1615. STC 12706.
- *Quo vadis? A Just Censure of Traveil as it is Commonly Undertaken by the Gentlemen of our Nation*. 1617. STC 12705.
- *The Works of Joseph Hall*. 1625. STC 12635.
- *Certaine Irrefragable Propositions*. 1639. STC 12646b.
- *An Humble Remonstrance to the Right Honourable, the Lords in the High Court of Parliament*. 1641. STC (ed. Wing) H 3627.
- *Resolutions and Decisions of Divers Practicall Cases Of Conscience*. 2nd ed. 1650. STC (ed. Wing) H 407.
- *The Shaking of the Olive-Tree*. 1660. STC (ed. Wing) H 416.
- *Heaven Upon Earth and Characters of Vertues and Vices by Joseph Hall*, ed. Rudolph Kirk. New Brunswick, N.J., 1948.
- *The Poems of Joseph Hall*, ed. Arnold Davenport. Liverpool, 1969.
- *The Works of the Right Reverend Joseph Hall, D.D.*, ed. Philip Wynter. 10 vols. New York, 1969.

- *Mundus Alter et Idem*, trans. John Millar Wands. New Haven and London, 1981.
Hamilton, Alistair. *The Family of Love*. Cambridge, 1981.
Hammer, Paul E.J. 'Patronage at Court, Faction and the Earl of Essex.' In *The Reign of Elizabeth I: Court and Culture in the Last Decade*, ed. John Guy. Cambridge, 1995.
Hampton, Timothy. *Writing From History: The Rhetoric of Exemplarity in Renaissance Literature*. Ithaca and London, 1990.
Hanson, Donald W. *From Kingdom to Commonwealth: The Development of Civic Consciousness in English Political Thought*. Cambridge, MA, 1970.
Hariman, Robert. 'Composing Modernity in Machiavelli's *Prince*.' *Journal of the History of Ideas*, 50 (1989), pp. 3–29.
Harlow, V.T. *Ralegh's Last Voyage*. 1932.
Hastings, Francis. *The Letters of Sir Francis Hastings, 1574–1609*, ed. Claire Cross, Frome, Somerset, 1969.
Hay, Millicent V. *The Life of Robert Sidney, Earl of Leicester, 1563–1626*. 1984.
Haydn, Hiram. *The Counter-Renaissance*. New York, 1950.
Hayward, John. *The History of the Life and Raigne of Henry IIII, King of England*. 1642. STC (ed. Wing) C 6494.
Held, Julius S. *Rubens and the Book: Title Pages by Peter Paul Rubens*. Williamstown, MA, 1977.
Helgerson, Richard. *Self-Crowned Laureates: Spenser, Jonson, Milton and the Literary System*. Berkeley, Los Angeles, and London, 1983.
- 'Barbarous Tongues: The Ideology of Poetic Form in Renaissance England.' In *The Historical Renaissance: New Essays on Tudor and Stuart Literature and Culture*, ed. Heather Dubrow and Richard Strier. Chicago, 1988.
- *Forms of Nationhood: The Elizabethan Writing of England*. Chicago and London, 1992.
Hexter, J.H. 'The Early Stuarts and Parliament: Old Hat and the Nouvelle Vague.' *Parliamentary History*, 1 (1982), pp. 181–214.
Hilberry, Clarence B. *Ben Jonson's Ethics in Relation to Stoic and Humanist Thought*. Chicago, 1930.
Hill, Christopher. *Intellectual Origins of the English Revolution*. Oxford, 1965.
- *Antichrist in Seventeenth-Century England*. Oxford, 1971.
- 'A Bourgeois Revolution?' In *Three British Revolutions: 1641, 1688, 1776*, ed. J.G.A. Pocock. Princeton, 1980.
- *Collected Essays*. 3 vols. Amherst, MA, 1985–6.
- *Puritanism and Revolution: Studies in Interpretation of the English Revolution of the Seventeenth Century*. Harmondsworth, 1986.
- *Society and Puritanism in Pre-Revolutionary England*. Harmondsworth, 1986.
Hirst, Derek. *Authority and Conflict: England, 1603–1658*. Cambridge, MA, 1986.

- 'Locating the 1650s in England's Seventeenth Century.' *History*, 81. 263 (July, 1996), pp. 359–83.
Hobbes, Thomas. *Leviathan*, ed. C.B. Macpherson. Harmondsworth, 1968.
Holles, John. *Letters of John Holles*, ed. Peter Seddon. 3 vols. Nottingham, 1975–86.
Holmes, Stephen. 'Political Psychology in Hobbes's *Behemoth*.' In *Thomas Hobbes and Political Theory*, ed. Mary Dietz. Kansas, 1990.
Holtgen, Karl Joseph. 'Sir Robert Dallington (1566–1637): Author, Traveler, and Pioneer of Taste.' *Huntington Library Quarterly*, 47 (1984), pp. 147–78.
Hoopes, Robert. *Right Reason in the English Renaissance*. Cambridge, MA, 1962.
Howell, Roger. *Sir Philip Sidney: The Shepherd Knight*. 1968.
Howell, W.S. *Logic and Rhetoric in England, 1500–1700*. Princeton, 1956.
Hull, John. *The Unmasking of the Politique Athieste*. 1602. STC 13934.
Hulme, Howard. *The Life of Sir John Eliot*. 1957.
Huntley, F.L. *Bishop Joseph Hall, 1574–1656: A Biographical and Critical Study*. Cambridge, 1979.
Hurstfield, Joel. 'The Succession Struggle in Late Elizabethan England.' In his *Freedom, Corruption and Government in Elizabethan England*. 1973.
Ijsewijn, Jozef. 'The Coming of Humanism to the Low Countries.' In *Itinerarium Italicum: The Profile of the Italian Renaissance in the Mirror of Its European Transformations*, ed. Heiko A. Oberman with Thomas A. Brady, Jr. Leiden, 1975.
Jacquot, Jean. 'Religion et Raison d'État dans l'Oeuvre de Fulke Greville.' *Études Anglaises*, 5 (1952), pp. 211–22.
James VI & I. *Basilikon Doron. Devided into Three Bookes*. Edinburgh, 1599. STC 14348.
- *Political Works*, ed. C.H. McIlwain. Cambridge, MA, 1918.
- *Letters*, ed. G.P.V. Akrigg. Berkeley, 1984.
James, Mervyn. *Society, Politics and Culture: Studies in Early Modern England*. Cambridge, 1986.
Jardine, David. *Criminal Trials*. 2 vols. 1832–5.
Jardine, Lisa. *Francis Bacon: Discovery and the Art of Discourse*. Cambridge, 1974.
Javitch, Daniel. *Poetry and Courtliness in Renaissance England*. Princeton, 1978.
Jehasse, Jean. *La Renaissance de la Critique: L'Essor de l'Humanisme Érudit de 1560 à 1614*. Saint Étienne, 1976.
Johnson, William C. 'The Family of Love in Stuart Literature: A Chronology of Name-Crossed Lovers.' *Journal of Medieval and Renaissance Studies*, 7.1 (1977) pp. 95–112.
Jones, Rufus M. *Studies in Mystical Religion*. 1909.
- *Spiritual Reformers in the 16th and 17th centuries*. Boston, 1914.
Jones, W.J. *Politics and the Bench: The Judges and the Origins of the English Civil War*. London and New York 1971.

Jonson, Ben. *The Man and his Works*, ed. C.H. Herford and P. and E. Simpson. 11 vols. Oxford, 1925–52.
– *The Complete Poems*, ed. George Parfitt. 1988.
– *Sejanus His Fall*, ed. Philip J. Ayres. The Revels Plays Series. Manchester and New York, 1990.
– *Poetaster*, ed. Tom Cain. The Revels Plays Series. Manchester and New York, 1995.
Judson, Margaret. *The Crisis of the Constitution*. New Brunswick, N.J., 1949.
– *From Tradition to Political Reality*. Hamden, CT, 1980.
Kahn, Victoria. *Rhetoric, Prudence, and Skepticism in the Renaissance*. Ithaca and London, 1985.
– *Machiavellian Rhetoric. From the Counter-Reformation to Milton*. Princeton, 1994.
Kamen, Henry. *The Rise of Toleration*. 1967.
Kaplan, Benjamin J. 'Dutch Particularism and the Calvinist Quest for "Holy Uniformity".' *Archiv für Reformationsgeschichte*, 82 (1991), pp. 239–55.
– *Calvinists and Libertines: Confession and Community in Utrecht, 1578–1620*. New York, 1995.
Kearney, Hugh, *Science and Change 1500–1700*. New York, 1971.
Kelley, Donald R. *Foundations of Modern Historical Scholarship: Language, Law and History in the French Renaissance*. New York, 1970.
– 'Martyrs, Myths and the Massacre: The Background of St. Bartholomew.' *American Historical Review*, 77 (1972), pp. 1323–41.
– *The Beginning of Ideology: Consciousness and Society in the French Reformation*. Cambridge, 1981.
– 'Horizons of Intellectual History: Retrospect, Circumspect, Prospect.' *Journal of the History of Ideas*, 48 (1987), pp. 143–69.
– 'The Theory of History.' In *Cambridge History of Renaissance Philosophy*, ed. Charles B. Schmitt, Quentin Skinner et al., Cambridge, 1988.
– 'What is Happening to the History of Ideas?' *Journal of the History of Ideas*, 51 (1990), pp. 3–25.
– '*Tacitus Noster*: The *Germainia* in the Renaissance and Reformation.' In *Tacitus and the Tacitean Tradition*, ed. T.J. Luce and A.J. Woodman. Princeton, 1993.
Kelliher, W. Hilton. 'The Warwick Manuscripts of Fulke Greville.' *British Museum Quarterly*, 34 (1970), pp. 107–21.
Kempner, N. *Raleghs Staatstheoretische Schriften*. Leipzig, 1928.
Keohane, Nannerl. *Philosophy and the State in France: The Renaissance to the Enlightenment*. Princeton, 1980.
Kerford, G.B. 'What Does the Wise Man Know?' In *The Stoics*, ed. John M. Rist. Berkeley, Los Angeles, and London, 1978.
van Kessel, Peter J. 'The Denominational Pluriformity of the German Nations at

Padua and the Problem of Intolerance in the 16th Century.' *Archiv für Reformationsgeschichte*, 75 (1984), pp. 256–75.
King, John N. *Tudor Royal Iconography: Literature and Art in an Age of Religious Crisis*. Princeton, 1989.
Kinloch, T.F. *The Life and Works of Joseph Hall, 1574–1656*. 1951.
Kinney, Arthur F. *Continental Humanist Poetics: Studies in Erasmus, Castiglione, Marguerite de Navarre, Rabelais, and Cervantes*. Amherst, MA, 1989.
Kipling, Gordon. 'Henry VII and the Origins of Tudor Patronage.' In *Patronage in the Renaissance*, ed. Guy Fitch Lytle and Stephen Orgel. Princeton, 1981.
Kishlansky, Mark A. *Parliamentary Selection: Social and Political Choice in Early Modern England*. Cambridge, 1986.
Knafla, Louis A. *Law and Politics in Jacobean England: The Tracts of Lord Chancellor Ellesmere*. Cambridge, 1977.
Knecht, R.J. *The French Wars of Religion 1559–1598*. 1989.
Kranidas, Thomas. 'Style and Rectitude in Seventeenth-Century Prose: Hall, Smectymnuus, and Milton.' *Huntington Library Quarterly*, 46 (1983), pp. 237–69.
Kraye, Jill. 'Moral Philosophy.' In *The Cambridge History of Renaissance Philosophy*, ed. Charles B. Schmitt, Quentin Skinner et al. Cambridge, 1988.
Kristeller, Paul O. *Renaissance Thought: The Classic, Scholastic, and Humanist Strains*. New York, 1955.
– 'Humanism.' In *The Cambridge History of Renaissance Philosophy*, ed. Charles B. Schmitt, Quentin Skinner et al. Cambridge, 1988.
Kritzman, L.D. *Destruction/Découverte: Le Fonctionnement de la Rhétorique dans L'Éssais de Montaigue*. Lexington, 1980.
Kuhn, Thomas. *The Structure of Scientific Revolutions*. Chicago and London, 1962.
LaCapra, Dominick, and Steven Kaplan, eds. *Modern European Intellectual History: Reappraisals and New Perspectives*. Ithaca and London, 1982.
Lacey, Robert. *Robert, Earl of Essex: An Elizabethan Icarus*. 1971.
– *Sir Walter Ralegh*. 1973.
Lacey, W.K. *Cicero and the End of the Roman Republic*. 1978.
Lake, Peter. *Anglicans and Puritans? Presbyterianism and English Conformist Thought from Whitgift to Hooker*. 1988.
– 'The Moderate and Irenic Case for Religious War: Joseph Hall's *Via Media* in Context.' In *Political Culture and Cultural Politics in Early Modern England*, ed. Susan Amussen and Mark Kishlansky. Manchester, 1995.
Lamont, William. *Godly Rule: Politics and Religion, 1603–1660*. 1964.
Lapidge, Michael. 'Stoic Cosmology.' In *The Stoics*, ed. John M. Rist. Berkeley, Los Angeles, and London, 1928.
Larkin, James F., and Paul L. Hughes, eds. *Stuart Royal Proclamation*. 2 vols. Oxford, 1973.

Larson, C.H. *Fulke Greville*. Boston, 1980.
Laursen, John Christian. 'Michael de Montaigne and the Politics of Skepticism.' *Historical Reflections*, 16 (1989), pp. 99–133.
Lecler, J. 'Les Origines et le Sens de la Formule *Cujus Regio, Ejus Religio*.' *Recherches de Science Religieuse*, 38.1 (1951/2), pp. 119–31.
- *Toleration and the Reformation*, 2 vols. Trans. T.L. Weston. New York, 1960.
Leedham-Green, E.S. *Books in Cambridge Inventories: Booklists from the Vice-Chancellor's Court Probate Inventories in the Tudor and Stuart Periods*. 2 vols. Cambridge, 1984.
Lefranc, Pierre. *Sir Walter Ralegh Écrivain: l'Oeuvre et les Idées*. Paris, 1968.
Leites, Edmund, ed. *Conscience and Casuistry in Early Modern Europe*. Cambridge, 1988.
Lerer, Seth. *Boethius and Dialogue: Literary Method in The Consolation of Philosophy*. Princeton, 1985.
Levack, Brian P. *The Formation of the British State: England, Scotland, and the Union, 1603–1707*. 1987.
Levine, Joseph M. *Humanism and History: Origins of Modern English Historiography*. Ithaca and London, 1987.
Levy, F.J. *Tudor Historical Thought*. San Marino, 1967.
- 'Fulke Greville: The Courtier as Philosophic Poet.' *Modern Language Quarterly*, 33 (1972), pp. 433–48.
- 'Philip Sidney Reconsidered.' *English Literary Renaissance*, 2 (1972), pp. 5–18.
- 'How Information Spread Among the Gentry, 1550–1640.' *Journal of British Studies*, 21 (1982), pp. 11–34.
- 'Francis Bacon and the Style of Politics.' *English Literary Renaissance*, 16 (1986), pp. 101–22.
- 'Hayward, Daniel, and the Beginnings of Politic History in England.' *Huntington Library Quarterly*, 50 (1987), pp. 1–34.
- 'The Theatre and the Court in the 1590s.' In *The Reign of Elizabeth I: Court and Culture in the Last Decade*, ed. John Guy. Cambridge, 1995.
Lewy, G. *Constitutionalism and Statescraft During the Golden Age of Spain: A Study of the Political Philosophy of Juan de Mariana*. Geneva, 1960.
Lipsius, Justus. *Iusti Lipsi De Constantia Libri Duo, Qui Alloquium Praecipue Continent in Publicis Malis*. Antwerp and Leiden, 1584; London, 1592. STC 15694.3.
- *Iusti Lipsi Politicorum sive Civilis Doctrinae Libri Sex. Qui ad Principatum Maxime Spectant. Additae Notae Auctiores*. 1590. STC 15700.7.
- *A Direction for Travellers (Epistola de peregrinatione italica)*, trans. John Stradling. 1592. STC 15696.
- *Iusti Lipsi Epistolarum Centuriae Duae*. 1593. STC 15699.
- *Sixe Bookes of Politickes, or Civil Doctrine*, trans. William Jones. 1594. STC 15701.
- *Tvvo Bookes of Constancie*, trans. John Stradling. 1595. STC 15695.

- *Iusti Lipsi Monita et Exempla Politica Libri Duo. Qui Virtutes et Vitia Principum Spectant*. Antwerp, 1605.
- *A Discourse of Constancy*, trans. R.G. 1654. STC (ed. Wing) L 2359.
- *A Discourse of Constancy in Two Books*, trans. Nathaniel Wanley. 1670. STC (ed. Wing) L 2360.
- *Iusti Lipsi Opera Omnia*, 4 vols. Wesel, 1675.
- *Two Books of Constancie by Justus Lipsius*, trans. John Stradling and ed. by Rudolph Kirk. New Brunswick, N.J., 1939.
- *Epistolario de Justo Lipsio y los Espanoles (1577–1606)*, ed. Alejandro Ramirez. Madrid, 1966.

Lockyer, Andrew. '"Traditions" as Context in the History of Political Theory.' *Political Studies*, 27 (1979), pp. 201–17.

Lockyer, Roger. *Buckingham*. 1981.
- *The Early Stuarts: A Political History of England 1603–1642*. 1989.

Loe, William. *Vox Clamantis: A Stil Voice to the Three Thrice-Honourable Estates of Parliament*. 1621. STC 16691.

Lofstedt, Einar. 'On the Style of Tacitus.' *Journal of Roman Studies*, 38 (1948), pp. 1–8.

Logan, George M. 'Substance and Form in Renaissance Humanism.' *Journal of Medieval and Renaissance Studies*, 7 (1977), pp. 1–34.

Luce, T.J., and A.J. Woodman, eds. *Tacitus and the Tacitean Tradition*. Princeton, 1993.

MacCaffrey, Wallace T. 'Place and Patronage in Elizabethan Politics.' In *Elizabethan Government and Society*, ed. S.T. Bindoff, J. Hurstfield, and C.H. Williams. 1961.
- *Elizabeth I: War and Politics 1588–1603*. Princeton, 1992.

Maclean, Hugh N. 'Fulke Greville: Kingship and Sovereignty.' *Huntington Library Quarterly*, 16 (1952–3), pp. 237–71.
- 'Fulke Greville on War.' *Huntington Library Quarterly*, 21 (1957–8), pp. 95–109.

Mahoney, John L. 'Donne and Greville: Two Christian Attitudes Toward the Renaissance Idea of Mutability and Decay.' *College Language Association Journal*, 5 (1962), pp. 203–12.

Marsh, Christopher W. *The Family of Love in English Society, 1550–1630*. Cambridge, 1994.

Marshall, Sherrin. *The Dutch Gentry, 1500–1650: Family, Faith, and Fortune*. New York, Westport, and London, 1987.

Martin, Julian. *Francis Bacon, the State, and the Reform of Natural Philosophy*. Cambridge, 1992.

Martin, Ronald. *Tacitus*. Berkeley, 1981.

Marvell, Andrew. *Poems and Letters*, ed. H.M. Margoliouth. 3rd ed. 2 vols. Oxford, 1971.
Marwil, Jonathan. *The Trials of Counsel: Francis Bacon in 1621*. Detroit, 1976.
Maus, Katharine Eisaman. *Ben Jonson and the Roman Frame of Mind*. Princeton, 1985.
– *Inwardness and Theater in the English Renaissance*. Chicago and London, 1995.
May, Steven W. *Sir Walter Ralegh*. Boston, 1989.
Mayer, Thomas F. *Thomas Starkey and the Commonweal: Humanist Politics and Religion in the Reign of Henry VIII*. Cambridge, 1989.
– Review of Perez Zagorin, *Ways of Lying*, Sixteenth Century Journal, 22 (1991), pp. 585–6.
Mayer, Thomas F. and Daniel R. Woolf, eds. *The Rhetorics of Life-Writing in Early Modern Europe: Forms of Biography from Cassandra Fedele to Louis XIV*. Ann Arbor, MI, 1995.
McCabe, Richard A. 'Elizabethan Satire and the Bishop's Ban of 1599.' *The Yearbook of English Studies*, 11 (1981), pp. 188–93.
– 'Fulke Greville and Joseph Hall.' *Notes and Queries* 226 (new ser. vol. 28, no. 1) (Feb. 1981), pp. 45–6.
– *Joseph Hall: A Study in Satire and Meditation*. Oxford, 1982.
McCoog, Thomas M. '"The Flower of Oxford": The Role of Edmund Campion in Early Recusant Polemics.' *Sixteenth Century Journal*, 24.4 (1993), pp. 899–913.
McCoy, Richard C. *Sir Philip Sidney: Rebellion in Arcadia*. New Brunswick, N.J., 1987.
McCrea, Adriana. 'Reason's Muse: Andrew Marvell, R. Fletcher, and the Politics of Poetry in the Engagement Debate.' *Albion*, 23, (1991), pp. 655–80.
– 'Whose Life Is It, Anyway? Subject and Subjection in Fulke Greville's *Life of Sidney*.' In *The Rhetoric of Life-Writing in Early Modern Europe: Forms of Biography from Cassandra Fedele to Louis XIV*, ed. Thomas F. Mayer and D.R. Woolf. Ann Arbor, MI, 1995.
McEuen, Katherine A. *The Classical Influence Upon the Tribe of Ben: A Study of Classical Elements in the Non-Dramatic Poetry of Ben Jonson and his Circle*. Cedar Rapids, IA, 1939.
McGee, J. Sears. *The Godly Man in Stuart England: Anglicans, Puritans, and the Two Tables, 1620–1670*. New Haven and London, 1976.
McGregor, J.F., and B. Reay, eds. *Radical Religion in the English Revolution*. Oxford, 1984.
McPherson, David. 'Ben Jonson Meets Daniel Heinsius.' *English Language Notes*, 44 (1976), pp. 105–9.
Mears, Natalie. '*Regnum Cecilianum*? A Cecilian Perspective of the Court.' In *The

*Reign of Elizabeth I: Court and Culture in the Last Decade*, ed. John Guy, Cambridge, 1995.

Meinecke, F. *Machiavellism: The Doctrine of Raison d'État and its Place in Modern History*, trans. Douglas Scott. New Haven, 1957.

Mellor, Ronald. *Tacitus*. New York and London, 1993.

Merrill, Elizabeth. *The Dialogue in English Literature*. New Haven, 1969.

Meyer, Arnold O. *England and the Catholic Church under Queen Elizabeth*. New York, 1967.

Miles, Rosalind. *Ben Jonson: His Life and Works*. 1986.

Miller, Peter N. *Defining the Common Good: Empire, Religion and Philosophy in Eighteenth-Century Britain*. Cambridge, 1994.

Milton, John. *Complete Poems and Major Prose*, ed. Merrit Y. Hughes. Indianapolis, 1957.

Miner, Earl. *The Cavalier Mode from Jonson to Cotton*. Princeton, 1971.

de Molen, Richard L. *The Library of William Camden*. Philadelphia, 1984.

Momigliano, Arnaldo. 'The First Political Commentary on Tacitus.' *Journal of Roman Studies*, 37 (1947), pp. 91–101.

– *Essays in Ancient and Modern Historiography*. Middletown, CT, 1977.

Monsarrat, Giles D. *Light From the Porch: Stoicism and English Renaissance Literature*. Paris, 1984.

Montaigne, Michel de. *The Essayes or Morall, Politike and Militarie Discourses*, trans. J. Florio. 1603. STC 18041.

Morford, Mark. *Stoics and Neostoics: Rubens and the Circle of Lipsius*. Princeton, 1991.

– 'Tacitean *Prudentia* and the Doctrines of Justus Lipsius.' In *Tacitus and the Tacitean Tradition*, ed. T.J. Luce and A.J. Woodman. Princeton, 1993.

Morrill, John. 'The Church in England, 1642–9.' In *Reactions to the English Civil War, 1642–1649*, ed. John Morrill. 1982.

– ed. *The Scottish National Covenant in its British Context, 1638–51*. Edinburgh, 1991.

Morris, Ivor. 'The Tragic Vision of Fulke Greville.' *Shakespeare Studies*, 14 (1961), pp. 66–75.

Moss, Jean D. *'Godded with God': Hendrik Niclaes and His Family of Love*. Philadelphia, 1981.

Mosse, George L. 'The Influence of Jean Bodin's *Republique* on English Political Thought.' *Medievalia et Humanistica*, 5 (1948), pp. 73–83.

– *The Holy Pretence: A Study of Christianity and Reason of State from William Perkins to John Winthrop*. Oxford, 1957.

Mulier, Eco Haitsma. 'The Language of Seventeenth-Century Republicanism in the United Provinces: Dutch or European?' In *The Languages of Political Theory in Early-Modern Europe*, ed. Anthony Pagden. Cambridge, 1987.

Murphy, James J., ed. *Renaissance Eloquence: Studies in the Theory and Practice of Renaissance Rhetoric.* Berkeley, Los Angeles and London, 1983.

Naunton, Robert. *Fragmenta Regalia.* 1641. *STC* (ed. Wing) N 249.

De Nave, Francine, 'De Polemiek tussen Justus Lipsius en Dirck Volckerstyn Coornheert (1590).' *De Gulden Passer*, 48 (1970), pp. 1–40.

Nedham, Marchamont. *The Case of the Commonwealth of England, Stated*, ed. Philip A. Knachel. Charlottesville, 1969.

Nijenhuis, W. 'Variant Within Dutch Calvinism in the Sixteenth Century.' *The Low Countries History Yearbook*, 12 (1979), pp. 48–64.

Nisard, Charles. *Le Triumverat Littéraire au xvie Siècle: Juste Lipse, Joseph Scaliger et Isaac Casaubon.* Paris, 1852; repr. Geneva, 1970.

Norbrook, David. *Poetry and Politics in the English Renaissance.* 1984.

– 'Marvell's Horatian Ode and the Politics of Genre.' In *Literature and the English Civil War*, ed. Thomas Healey and Jonathan Sawday. Cambridge, 1990.

Norlund, Howard. 'The Design of Ben Jonson's *Catiline*,' *Sixteenth Century Journal*, 9 (1978), pp. 67–89.

Notestein, Wallace. *The House of Commons, 1604–1610.* New Haven, 1971.

Oakeshott, Walter. 'Sir Walter Ralegh's Library.' *The Library*, 5th ser. 23.4 (Dec. 1968), pp. 285–327.

Oates, Whitney J., ed. *The Stoic and Epicurean Philosopher.* New York, 1940.

Oberman, Heiko A., with Thomas A. Brady, eds. *Itinerarium Italicum: The Profile of the Italian Renaissance in the Mirror of Its European Transformations.* Leiden, 1975.

O'Day, Rosemary. *The English Clergy: The Emergence and Consolidation of a Profession 1558–1642.* Leicester, 1979.

Oestreich, Gerhard. *Neostoicism and the Early Modern State*, ed. Brigitta Oestreich and H.G. Koenigsberger, trans. David McLintock. Cambridge, 1982.

Ong, Walter J. *Ramus, Method, and the Decay of Dialogue: From the Art of Discourse to the Art of Reason.* Cambridge, MA, 1958.

Oosterhoff, F.G. *Leicester and the Netherlands 1586–1587.* Utrecht, 1988.

Orcibal, Jean. *Saint-Cyran et le Jansenisme.* Bourges, 1961.

Orgel, Stephen. *The Jonsonian Masque.* Cambridge, MA, 1965.

– *The Illusion of Power: Political Theater in the English Renaissance.* Berkeley, 1975.

Orgel, Stephen, and Roy Strong. *Inigo Jones: The Theatre of the Stuart Court.* 2 vols. Berkeley, 1973.

Orsini, G.N.G. *Bacone e Macchiavelli.* Genoa, 1936.

Osborn, James M. *Young Philip Sidney 1572–1577.* New Haven and London, 1972.

Overbury, Thomas. *The Arraignment and Conviction of Sir Walter Rawleigh.* 1648. *STC* (ed. Wing) A 3744.

Owen, Trevor A. *Lancelot Andrewes.* Boston, 1981.

Palmer, R.G. *Seneca's 'De Remediis Fortvitorum' and the Elizabethans.* Chicago, 1953.

Parker, Geoffrey. *The Dutch Revolt*. Ithaca, 1977.
– *Spain and the Netherlands, 1559–1659*. Glasgow, 1979; rev. ed. 1990.
– *The Military Revolution: Military Innovation and the Rise of the West, 1500–1800*. Cambridge, 1988.
Parker, Kenneth L. *The English Sabbath: A Study of Doctrine and Discipline from the Reformation to the Civil War*. Cambridge, 1988.
Parmelee, Lisa Ferraro. 'Neostoicism and Absolutism in Late Elizabeth England.' In *Politics, Ideology and the Law in Early Modern Europe*, ed. A.E. Bakos. Rochester, N.Y., 1994.
Parry, Graham. *The Golden Age Restor'd: The Culture of the Stuart Court, 1603–1642*. Manchester, 1981.
– *Seventeenth-Century Poetry: The Social Context*. 1985.
Partridge, A.C., ed. *The Tribe of Ben: Pre-Augustan Classical Verse in England*. 1966.
Patrides, C.A. *The Grand Design of God: The Literary Form of a Christian View of God*. 1972.
Patterson, Annabel. *Censorship and Interpretation: The Conditions of Writing and Reading in Early Modern England*. Madison, WI, 1984.
Peck, Linda Levy. *Northampton: Patronage and Policy at the Court of James I*. 1982.
– *Court Patronage and Corruption in Early Stuart England*. Boston, 1990.
– ed. *The Mental World of the Jacobean Court*. Cambridge, 1991.
Peltonen, Markku. *Classical Humanism and Republicanism in English Political Thought 1570–1640*. Cambridge, 1995.
Pennington, Donald and Keith Thomas, eds. *Puritans and Revolutionaries: Essays in Seventeenth-Century History Presented to Christopher Hill*. Oxford, 1978.
Phillips, James E. 'George Buchanan and the Sidney Circle.' *Huntington Library Quarterly*, 12 (1948–9), pp. 23–55.
Pigman, G.W., III. 'Imitation and the Renaissance Sense of the Past: The Reception of Erasmus' *Ciceronianus*.' *Journal of Medieval and Renaissance Studies*, 9 (1979), pp. 155–77.
Pocock, J.G.A. *The Machiavellian Moment: Florentine Political Thought and the Atlantic Republican Tradition*. Princeton, 1975.
– *The Ancient Constitution and the Feudal Law: A Study of English Historical Thought in the Seventeenth Century. A Reissue with a Retrospect*. Cambridge, 1987.
– 'The Concept of a Language and the *Métier d'Historien*: Some Considerations on Practice.' In *The Languages of Political Theory in Early-Modern Europe*, ed. Anthony Pagden. Cambridge, 1987.
– *Politics, Languages, and Time: Essays on Political Thought and History*. Chicago, 1989.
Poort, Marjon. 'The Desired and Destined Successor.' In *Sir Philip Sydney. 1586*

*and the Creation of a Legend*, ed. Jan van Dorsten, Dominic Baker-Smith and Arthur F. Kinney. Leiden, 1986.

Porter, Roy, and Mikulas Teich, eds. *The Renaissance in National Context*. Cambridge, 1992.

Prestwich, Menna. *Cranfield: Politics and Profits Under the Early Stuarts*. Oxford, 1966.

Quilligan, Maureen. 'Sidney and His Queen.' In *The Historical Renaissance: New Essay on Tudor and Stuart Literature and Culture*, ed. Heather Dubrow and Richard Strier. Chicago, 1988.

Quint, David. *Origin and Originality in Renaissance Literature: Versions of the Source*. New Haven and London, 1983.

– 'Humanism and Modernity: A Reconsideration of Bruni's *Dialogues*.' *Renaissance Quarterly*, 38 (1985), pp. 423–45.

Quinton, Anthony. *Francis Bacon*. Oxford, 1980.

Raab, Felix. *The English Face of Machiavelli*. 1964.

Racin, John. *Sir Walter Ralegh as Historian: An Analysis of 'The History of the World.'* Salzburg, 1974.

Ralegh, Walter. *A Report of the Truth of the Fight ... betwixt the Revenge ... and an Armada ...* 1591. STC 20651.

– *The Discoverie of the ... Empyre of Guiana*. 1596. STC 20634.

– *The History of the World*. 1614. STC 20637.

– *The Prerogative of Parliaments in England*. 1628. STC 20649.

– *Maxims of State*. 1650. STC (ed. Wing) R 174.

– *The Cabinet-Council*. 1658. STC (ed. Wing) R 156.

– *Instructions to his Son*, in *Advice to a Son*, ed. Louis B. Wright. New York, 1962.

Ranum, Orest. *Artisans of Glory: Writers and Historical Thought in Seventeenth-Century France*. Chapel Hill, N.C. 1980.

Rathwell, J.C.A. 'Jonson, Lord Lisle and Penshurst.' *English Literary Review*, 6 (1971), pp. 250–60.

Raymond, Joad, ed. *Making the News: An Anthology of the Newsbooks of Revolutionary England 1641–1660*. Moreton-in-Marsh, Glouc., 1993.

Rebholz, Ronald. *The Life of Fulke Greville, First Lord Brooke*. Oxford, 1971.

Rees, Joan. *Samuel Daniel: A Critical and Biographical Study*. Liverpool, 1964.

– *Fulke Greville, Lord Brooke, 1554–1628: A Critical Biography*. Berkeley and Los Angeles, 1971.

Reesor, Margaret E. 'Necessity and Fate in Stoic Philosophy.' In *The Stoics*, ed. John M. Rist. Berkeley, Los Angeles, and London, 1978.

Rekers, B. *Benito Arias Montano*. London and Leiden, 1972.

Riebling, Barbara. 'Milton on Machiavelli: Representations of the State in *Paradise Lost*.' *Renaissance Quarterly*, 49 (1996), pp. 573–97.

Riggs, David. *Ben Jonson: A Life*. Cambridge, MA, 1989.
Righter, Anne. 'Francis Bacon.' In *Essential Articles for the Study of Francis Bacon*, ed. Brian Vickers. Hamden, CT, 1968.
Ringler, W.A. 'The Myth and the Man.' In *Sir Philip Sidney. 1586 and the Creation of a Legend*, ed. Jan van Dorsten, Dominic Baker-Smith and Arthur F. Kinney. Leiden, 1986.
Rist, John, M. *Stoic Philosophy*. Cambridge, 1969.
– ed. *The Stoics*. Berkeley, Los Angeles, and London, 1978.
Roberts, Michael. *The Military Revolution, 1560–1660*. Belfast, 1956.
Rose, Elliot. *Cases of Conscience: Alternatives Open to Recusants and Puritans under Elizabeth I and James I*. Cambridge, 1975.
Rossi, Paolo. *Francis Bacon: From Magic to Science*, trans. Sacha Rabinovitch. 1968.
Røstvig, Maren-Sophie. *The Happy Man: Studies in the Metamorphoses of a Classical Ideal 1600–1700*. Oslo, 1954.
Rowen, Herbert H. 'The Dutch Revolt: What Kind of Revolution?' *Renaissance Quarterly*, 43 (1990), pp. 570–90.
– 'The Dutch Republic and the Idea of Freedom.' In *Republicanism, Liberty, and Commercial Society, 1649–1776*, ed. David Wootton. Stanford, CA, 1994.
Rowse, A.L. *Court and Country: Studies in Tudor Social History*. Brighton, 1987.
Ruch, Michel. *Le Préamble dans les Oeuvres Philosophiques de Ciceron: Essai sur la Genèse et l'Art du Dialogue*. Paris, 1958.
Russell, Conrad. 'Arguments for Religious Unity in England, 1530–1650.' *Journal of Ecclesiastical History*, 18 (1967), pp. 201–26.
– 'Parliamentary History in Perspective, 1604–1629.' *History*, 51 (1976), pp. 1–27.
– *Parliaments and English Politics 1621–1629*. Oxford, 1979.
– *The Causes of the English Civil War*. Oxford, 1990.
– *The Fall of the British Monarchies, 1637–1642*. Oxford, 1991.
– ed. *Origins of the English Civil War*. 1973.
Salmon, J.H.M. *The French Religious Wars in English Political Thought*. Oxford, 1959.
– 'Cicero and Tacitus in Sixteenth-Century France.' *American Historical Review*, 85 (1980), pp. 307–31.
– *Renaissance and Revolt: Essays in the Intellectual and Societal History of Early Modern France*. Cambridge, 1987.
– 'Stoicism and Roman Example: Seneca and Tacitus in Jacobean England.' *Journal of the History of Ideas*, 50 (1989), pp. 199–225.
Sampson, Margaret. 'Laxity and Liberty in Seventeenth-Century English Political Thought.' In *Conscience and Casuistry in Early Modern Europe*, ed. Edmund Leites. Cambridge, 1988.

Saunders, Jason L. *Justus Lipsius: The Philosophy of Renaissance Stoicism*. New York, 1955.

Saunders, J.W. 'The Stigma of Print: A Note on the Social Bases of Tudor Poetry.' *Essays in Criticism*, 1 (1951), pp. 139–64.

Savile, Henry. *A View of Certaine Militarie Matters, or Commentaries Concerning Roman Warefare*. In *The Ende of Nero and the Beginning of Galba, Fower Bookes of the Histories of Cornelius Tacitus, The Life of Agricola*, trans. and ed. H. Savile. Oxford, 1591. STC 23642.

– 'Report of the Wages Paid to the Ancient Roman Soldiers, Their Vitayling and Apparel, in a Letter to Lord Burghley.' 1595. In *Somers Tracts: Collection of Scarce and Valuable Tracts ... of the Late Lord Somers*, ed. Sir Walter Scott. vol. 1. 1809–15.

Schaefer, David Lewis. *The Political Philosophy of Montaigne*. Ithaca and London, 1990.

Schellhase, Kenneth C. *Tacitus in Renaissance Political Thought*. Chicago, 1976.

Schmitt, Charles B. 'Theophrastus.' In *Catalogus Translationum et Commentariorum: Medieval and Renaissance Latin Translations and Commentaries*, ed. Paul Oskar Kristeller. Vol. 2. Washington, 1971.

Schmitt, Charles B., Quentin Skinner, Eckhard Kessler, and Jill Kraye, eds. *The Cambridge History of Renaissance Philosophy*. Cambridge, 1988.

Schnur, Roman, ed. *Staatsrason: Studien zur Geschichte eines politischen Begrifts*. Berlin, 1975.

Schreiber, Roy E. *The Political Career of Sir Robert Nanton, 1589–1631*. 1981.

Scott, Jonathan. *Algernon Sidney and the English Republic 1623–1677*. Cambridge, 1988.

Seigel, Jerrold. '"Civic Humanism" or Ciceronian Rhetoric? The Culture of Petrarch and Bruni.' *Past & Present*, 34 (1966), pp. 3–48.

– *Rhetoric and Philosophy in Renaissance Humanism: The Union of Eloquence and Wisdom From Petrarch to Valla*. Princeton, 1968.

Sellin, Paul R. *Daniel Heinsius and Stuart England*. 1958.

Seneca, Lucius A. *The Workes of Lvcivs Annaevs Seneca*, trans. Thomas Lodge. 1614. STC 22213.

Shapiro, Barbara. *Probability and Certainty in Seventeenth-Century England*. Princeton, 1982.

Sharpe, Andrew, ed. *Political Ideas of the English Civil Wars 1641–1649*. 1983.

Sharpe, Kevin. *Sir Robert Cotton, 1586–1631: History and Politics in Early Modern England*. Oxford, 1979.

– 'The Foundation of the Chairs of History at Oxford and Cambridge: An Episode in Jacobean Politics.' *History of Universities*, 2 (1982), pp. 127–52. Reprinted in Kevin Sharpe, *Politics and Ideas in Early Stuart England*. 1989.

- *Criticism and Compliment: The Politics of Literature in the England of Charles I.* Cambridge, 1987.
- ed. *Faction and Parliament: Essays in Early Stuart History.* Oxford, 1978.

Sharpe, Kevin, and Steven Zwicker, eds. *Politics of Discourse: The Literature and History of Seventeenth-Century England.* Berkeley, 1987.

Sharpe, Kevin, and Peter Lake, eds. *Culture and Politics in Early Stuart England.* 1994.

Sidney, Philip. *Complete Works*, ed. A. Feuillerat. 3 vols. Cambridge, 1922.

- *Miscellaneous Prose of Sir Philip Sidney*, ed. Katherine Duncan-Jones and Jan van Dorsten. Oxford. 1973.

Sidney, Philip, and Hubert Languet. *The Correspondence of Sir Philip Sidney and Hubert Languet*, trans. and ed. Steuart A. Pears. 1845.

Sidney, Robert. *The Poems*, ed. P.J. Croft. Oxford. 1984.

Skinner, Quentin. 'Conquest and Consent: Thomas Hobbes and the Engagement Controversy.' In *The Interregnum: The Quest for Settlement 1646–1660*, ed. G.E. Aylmer. 1972.

- *The Foundation of Modern Political Thought.* 2 vols. Cambridge, 1979.
- 'The Origins of the Calvinist Theory of Revolution.' In *After the Reformation: Essays in Honor of J.H. Hexter*, ed. Barbara C. Malament. Philadelphia, 1980.
- *Machiavelli.* Oxford, 1981.
- 'The State.' In *Political Innovation and Conceptual Change*, ed. Terence Ball, James Farr, and Russell L. Hanson. Cambridge, 1989.
- 'Machiavelli's *Discoursi* and the Pre-Humanist Origins of Republican Ideas.' In *Machiavelli and Republicanism*, ed. Gisela Bock, Quentin Skinner, and Maurizio Viroli. Cambridge, 1990.
- 'Thomas Hobbes: Rhetoric and the Construction of Morality.' *Proceedings of the British Academy*, 76 (1990), pp. 1–61.
- '"*Scientia Civilis*" in Classical Rhetoric and in the Early Hobbes.' In *Political Discourse in Early Modern Britain*, ed. Nicholas Phillipson and Quentin Skinner. Cambridge, 1993.

Skretkowicz, Victor. 'Building Sidney's Reputation: Texts and Editions of the *Arcadia.*' In *Sir Philip Sidney: 1586 and the Creation of a Legend*, ed. Jan van Dorsten et al. Leiden, 1986.

Slack, Paul. 'Poverty and Social Regulation in Elizabethan England.' In *The Reign of Elizabeth I*, ed. Christopher Haigh. 1984.

Slights, Camille. *The Casuistical Tradition in Shakespeare, Donne, Herbert and Milton.* Princeton, 1981.

Smith, Philip A. 'Bishop Hall, "Our English Seneca."' *Publications of the Modern Language Association of America*, 63 (1948), pp. 1191–1204.

Smither, James R. 'The St. Bartholomew's Day Massacre and Images of Kingship in France: 1572–1574.' *Sixteenth Century Journal*, 22 (1991), pp. 27–46.
Smuts, R. Malcolm. *Court Culture and the Origins of a Royalist Tradition in Early Stuart England*. Philadelphia, 1987.
– 'Court-Centered Politics and the Uses of Roman Historians, c. 1590–1630.' In *Culture and Politics in Early Stuart England*, ed. Kevin Sharpe and Peter Lake. 1994.
Snow, Vernon F. 'Francis Bacon's Advice to Fulke Greville on Research Techniques.' *Huntington Library Quarterly*, 23 (1960), pp. 369–78.
*Somers Tracts: Collection of Scarce and Valuable Tracts ... of the late Lord Somers*. 16 vols. (1748–52). Ed. Sir Walter Scott. 1809–15.
Sommerville, J.P. 'From Suarez to Filmer: A Reappraisal.' *Historical Journal*, 25 (1982), pp. 525–40.
– *Politics and Ideology in England 1603–1640*. 1986.
– 'Absolutism and Royalism.' In *Cambridge History of Political Thought 1450–1700*, ed. J.H. Burns with Mark Goldie. Cambridge, 1991.
– 'English and European Political Ideas in the Early Seventeenth Century: Revisionism and the Case of Absolutism.' *Journal of British Studies*, 35 (April 1996), pp. 168–94.
Southwell, Robert. *An Humble Supplication to Her Majestie*, ed. R.C. Bald. Cambridge, 1953.
Spurr, John. *The Restoration Church of England, 1646–1689*. New Haven and London, 1991.
Starkey, David. 'England.' In *The Renaissance in National Context*, ed. Roy Porter and Mikulas Teich. Cambridge, 1992.
Starkey, David et al, eds. *The English Court: From the War of the Roses to the Civil War*. London and New York, 1987.
Stewart, J. Douglas. '"Death Moved Not His Generous Mind": Allusions and Ideas, Mostly Classical, in Van Dyck's Work and Life.' In *Anthony Van Dyck*, ed. Arthur K. Wheelock, Jr., Susan J. Barnes, and Julius S. Held. Washington, 1990.
Stone, Lawrence. *The Family, Sex and Marriage in England, 1500–1800*. Abridged ed. Harmondsworth, 1979.
Stough, Charlotte. 'Stoic Determination and Moral Responsibility.' In *The Stoics*, ed. John M. Rist. Berkeley, Los Angeles, and London, 1978.
Strathmann, Ernest A. 'A Note on the Ralegh Canon.' *Times Literary Supplement*, 13 April 1956, p. 228.
– *Sir Walter Ralegh: A Study in Elizabethan Skepticism*. New York, 1973.
Strong, Roy. *Henry, Prince of Wales and England's Lost Renaissance*. New York, 1986.

- 'Sidney's Appearance Reconsidered.' In *Sir Philip Sidney's Achievements*, ed. M.J.B. Allen et al. New York, 1990.
Struever, Nancy S. *The Language of History in the Renaissance: Rhetoric and Historical Consciousness in Florentine Humanism*. Princeton, 1970.
Syme, Ronald. *Tacitus*. 2 vols. Oxford, 1958.
- *Ten Studies in Tacitus*. Oxford, 1970.
Tacitus, C. Cornelius. *Opera Omnia Quae Extant*, ed. Justus Lipsius. Antwerp, 1581, 1585.
- *The Ende of Nero and the Beginning of Galba, Fower Bookes of the Histories of Cornelius Tacitus, The Life of Agricola*, trans. and ed. H. Savile. Oxford, 1591. STC 23642.
- *The Agricola and Germany of Tacitus and The Dialogue on Oratory*, trans. A.J. Church and W.J. Brodribb. 1877.
- *Annals*, Book 1, ed. N.P. Miller. Oxford, 1959.
- *De Vita Agricolae*, ed. R.M. Ogilvie and Sir Ian Richmond. Oxford, 1967.
Tennenhouse, Leonard. 'Sir Walter Ralegh and the Literature of Clientage.' In *Patronage in the Renaissance*, ed. Guy Fitch Lytle and Stephen Orgel. Princeton, 1981.
Tenney, Mary. 'Tacitus in the Politics of Early Stuart England.' *The Classical Journal*, 37 (1941), pp. 151–63.
Thomas, Keith. 'Cases of Conscience in Seventeenth-Century England.' In *Public Duty and Private Conscience in Seventeenth-Century England: Essays Presented to G.E. Aylmer*, ed. John Morrill, Paul Slack, and Daniel Woolf. Oxford, 1993.
Thompson, Edward. *Sir Walter Ralegh: The Last of the Elizabethans*. 1935.
Thompson, I.A.A. 'The Impact of War.' In *The European Crisis of the 1950s*, ed. Peter Clark. 1985.
Tinkler, John F. 'The Rhetorical Method of Francis Bacon's *History of the Reign of Henry VII*.' *History and Theory*, 26 (1987), pp. 32–52.
Tite, Colin C.G. *Impeachment and Parliamentary Judicature in Early Stuart England*. 1974.
Todd, Margo. 'Seneca and the Protestant Mind: The Influence of Stoicism on Puritan Ethics.' *Archiv für Reformationsgeschichte*, 74 (1983), pp. 182–99.
- *Christian Humanism and the Puritan Social Order*. Cambridge, 1987.
Todd, Robert B. 'Monism and Immanence: The Foundations of Stoic Physics.' In *The Stoics*, ed. John M. Rist. Berkeley, Los Angeles, and London, 1978.
Toffanin, Guiseppe. *La Fine dell 'Umanismo*. Milan, Torino, and Rome, 1920.
- *Machiavelli e il Tacitismo*. Padua, 1921.
Tomlinson, Howard, ed. *Before the English Civil War: Essays on Early Stuart Politics and Government*. New York, 1984.
Tourney, Leonard D. *Joseph Hall*. Boston, 1979.

Tracy, James D. 'Humanism and the Reformation.' In *Reformation Europe: A Guide to Research*, ed. Steven Ozment. St. Louis, 1982.
- 'With and Without the Counter-Reformation: The Catholic Church in the Spanish Netherlands and the Dutch Republic, 1580–1650.' *Catholic Historical Review*, 71 (1985), pp. 547–75.
- 'Two Erasmuses, Two Luthers: Erasmus's Strategy in Defence of *De Libero Arbitrio*.' *Archiv für Reformationsgeschichte*, 78 (1987), pp. 37–59.

Trevelyan, G.M. *History of England*. 3rd ed. 1945.

Trevor-Roper, H.R. *Catholics, Anglicans and Puritans: Seventeen-Century Essays*. 1987.

Trimpi, Wesley. *Ben Jonson's Poems: A Study of the Plain Style*. Stanford, CA, 1962.

Trinkaus, Charles. *The Scope of Renaissance Humanism*. Ann Arbor, MI, 1983.
- '*Antiquitas* versus *Modernitas*: An Italian Humanist Polemic and Its Resonance.' *Journal of History of Ideas*, 48 (1987), pp. 11–21.
- 'Renaissance Ideas and the Idea of the Renaissance.' *Journal of the History of Ideas*, 51 (1990), pp. 667–84.

Trompf, G.W. *The Idea of Historical Recurrence in Western Thought*. Berkeley, 1979.

Tuck, Richard. *Natural Rights Theories*. Cambridge, 1979.
- 'The "Modern" Theory of Natural Law.' In *The Languages of Political Theory in Early-Modern Europe*, ed. Anthony Pagden. Cambridge, 1987.
- 'Optics and Sceptics: The Philosophical Foundations of Hobbes's Political Thought.' In *Conscience and Casuistry in Early Modern Europe*, ed. Edmund Leites. Cambridge, 1988.
- 'Scepticism and Toleration in the Seventeenth Century.' In *Justifying Toleration*, ed. Susan Mendus. Cambridge, 1988.
- *Hobbes*. Oxford, 1989.
- 'Humanism and Political Thought.' In *The Impact of Humanism on Western Europe*, ed. Anthony Goodman and Angus MacKay. London and New York, 1990.
- *Philosophy and Government 1572–1651*. Cambridge, 1993.

Tully, James. *Meaning and Context: Quentin Skinner and his Critics*. Princeton, 1988.

Turchetti, Mario. 'Religious Concord and Political Tolerance in Sixteenth- and Seventeenth-Century France.' *Sixteenth Century Journal*, 22 (1991), pp. 15–25.

Tyacke, Nicholas. *Anti-Calvinists: The Rise of English Arminianism*. Oxford, 1987.

Underdown, David. *Pride's Purge: Politics in the Puritan Revolution*. Oxford, 1971.

Ungerer, Gustav. *A Spaniard in Elizabethan England: The Correspondence of Antonio Perez's Exile*. 2 vols. 1974, 1976.

Du Vair, Guillaume. *A Buckler against Adversity; or a Treatise of Constancie*, trans. (*De la constance* [Paris, 1594]) A. Court. 1622. STC 7373.

- *The Moral Philosophie of the Stoicks*, trans. Thomas James (1598), ed. Rudolph Kirk. New Brunswick, N.J., 1951.
Varese, C. *Traiano Boccalini*. Padua, 1958.
Vasoli, Cesare. 'The Machiavellian Moment: A Grand Ideological Synthesis.' Review Article in *Journal of Modern History*, 49 (1977), pp. 661–70.
Vickers, Brian. *Francis Bacon and Renaissance Prose*. Cambridge, 1968.
– *In Defence of Rhetoric*. Oxford, 1988.
– 'Leisure and Idleness in the Renaissance: The Ambivalence of *Otium*.' *Renaissance Studies* 4.1 (1990), pp. 1–37, and 4.2 (1990), pp. 107–54.
–, ed. *Essential Articles for the Study of Francis Bacon*. Hamden, CT, 1978.
Viroli, Maurizio. 'Machiavelli and the Republican Idea of Politics.' In *Machiavelli and Republicanism*, ed. Gisela Bock, Quentin Skinner, and Maurizio Viroli. Cambridge, 1990.
– *From Politics to Reason of State: The Acquisition and Transformation of the Language of Politics 1250–1600*. Cambridge, 1992.
Voet, Leon. *The Golden Compasses: A History and Evaluation of the Printing and Publishing Activities of the Officina Plantiniana at Antwerp*. 2 vols. Amsterdam, London, and New York, 1972.
Walker, B. *The Annals of Tacitus: A Study in the Writing of History*. Manchester, 1952.
Walker, D.P. *The Decline of Hell*. 1964.
Wallace, Dewey D. *Puritans and Predestination: Grace in English Protestant Theology, 1525–1695*. Chapel Hill, N.C., 1982.
Wallace, John M. 'The Engagement Controversy 1649–1652: An Annotated List of Pamphlets.' *Bulletin of the New York Public Library*, 68 (1964), pp. 384–405.
– *Destiny His Choice: The Loyalism of Andrew Marvell*. Cambridge, 1968.
Waswo, Richard. *The Fatal Mirror: Themes and Techniques in the Poetry of Fulke Greville*. Charlottesville, VA, 1972.
Wayne, Don E. *Penshurst: The Semiotics of Place and the Poetics of History*. Madison, WI, 1984.
– 'Jonson's Sidney: Legacy and Legitimation in *The Forrest*.' In *Sir Philip Sidney's Achievements*, ed. M.J.B. Allen et al. New York, 1990.
Webster, Charles. *The Great Instauration: Science, Medicine and Reform, 1626–1660*. 1975.
Wedgwood, C.V. *The Trial of Charles I*. Harmondsworth, 1983.
Weinberger, Jerry. 'Science and Rule in Bacon's Utopia: An Introduction to the Reading of the *New Atlantis*.' *American Political Science Review*, 70 (1976), pp. 865–85.
– *Science, Faith and Politics: Francis Bacon and the Utopian Roots of the Modern Age*. Ithaca, N.Y., 1985.

Weinbrot, Howard D. *Augustus Caesar in 'Augustan' England: The Decline of a Classical Norm.* Princeton, 1978.
- 'Politics, Taste, and National Identity: Some Uses of Tacitism in Eighteenth-Century Britain.' In *Tacitus and the Tacitean Tradition*, ed. T.J. Luce and A.J. Woodman. Princeton, 1993.
Weiner, Andrew D. *Sir Philip Sidney and the Poetics of Protestantism: A Study of Contexts.* Minneapolis, MN, 1978.
White, Stephen D. *Sir Edward Coke and the 'grievances of the commonwealth,' 1621–1628.* Chapel Hill, N.C., 1979.
Whitney, Charles. *Francis Bacon and Modernity.* New Haven and London, 1986.
- 'Francis Bacon's *Instauratio*: Dominion Of and Over Humanity.' *Journal of the History of Ideas*, 50 (1989), pp. 371–90.
Wilentz, Sean, ed. *Rites of Power: Symbolism, Ritual & Politics Since the Middle Ages.* Philadelphia, 1985.
Wilkinson, L.P. *The Roman Experience.* New York, 1974.
Williams, George H. *The Radical Reformation.* Philadelphia, 1962.
Williamson, George. *The Senecan Amble.* Chicago, 1951.
- 'Senecan Style in the Seventeenth Century.' In *Seventeenth-Century Prose: Modern Essays in Criticism*, ed. Stanley Fish. New York, 1971.
Williamson, J.W. *The Myth of the Conqueror. Prince Henry Stuart: A Study of 17th-Century Personation.* New York, 1978.
Willson, D.H. *James VI & I.* 1956.
- 'King James I and Anglo-Scottish Unity.' In *Conflict in Stuart England*, ed. W. Aiken and B. Henning. 1960.'
Wilson, E.K. *Prince Henry and English Literature.* Ithaca, N.Y., 1946.
Winters, Yvor. *Forms of Discovery: Critical & Historical Essays on the Forms of the Short Poem in English.* Chicago, 1967.
Wiseman, Susan J. 'History Digested: Opera and Colonialism in the 1650s'. In *Literature and the English Civil War*, ed. Thomas Healey and Jonathan Sawday. Cambridge, 1990.
Wolin, Sheldon S. 'Hobbes and the Culture of Despotism.' In *Thomas Hobbes and Political Theory*, ed. Mary G. Dietz. Kansas, 1990.
Woolf, Daniel R. 'Two Elizabeths? James I and the Late Queen's Famous Memory.' *Canadian Journal of History*, 20 (1985), pp. 167–91.
- 'Community, Law and State: Samuel Daniel's Historical Thought Revisited.' *Journal of the History of Ideas*, 49 (1988), pp. 61–83.
- *The Idea of History in Early Stuart England: Erudition, Ideology and 'The Light of Truth' from the Accession of James I to the Civil War.* Toronto, 1990.
- 'Conscience, Constancy, and Ambition in the Career and Writings of James Howell.' In *Public Duty and Private Conscience in Seventeenth-Century England:*

*Essays Presented to G.E. Aylmer*, ed. John Morrill, Paul Slack, and Daniel Woolf. Oxford, 1993.

Woolrych, Austin. 'Last Quests for a Settlement, 1657–1660.' In *The Interregnum: The Quest for Settlement*, ed. G.E. Aylmer. 1972.

– *Commonwealth to Protectorate*. Oxford, 1982.

Wootton, David. *Paolo Sarpi: Between Renaissance and Enlightenment*. Cambridge, 1983.

–, ed. *Divine Right and Democracy: An Anthology of Political Writing in Stuart England*, Harmondsworth, 1986.

– 'From Rebellion to Revolution: The Crisis of the Winter of 1642/3 and the Origins of Civil War Radicalism.' *English Historical Review*, 105 (1990), pp. 654–69.

Wotton, Henry. *Reliquiae Wottonianae: Or a Collection of Lives, Letters, Poems, with Characters of Sundry Personages*. 2nd ed., 1654. STC (ed. Wing) W 3649.

– *Life and Letters*. 2 vols., ed. Logan Pearsall Smith. Oxford, 1907.

Worden, Blair. *The Rump Parliament, 1648–1653*. Cambridge, 1974.

– 'Classical Republicanism and the Puritan Revolution.' In *History and Imagination: Essays in Honour of H.R. Trevor-Roper*, ed. H. Lloyd-Jones, V. Pearl, and B. Worden. 1981.

– 'Constancy.' *London Review of Books*, 20 January – 2 February 1983, pp. 13–14.

– 'Friend to Sir Philip Sidney.' *London Review of Books*, 3 July 1986, pp. 19–22.

– 'Andrew Marvell, Oliver Cromwell, and the Horatian Ode.' In *Politics of Discourse: The Literature and History of Seventeenth-Century England*, ed. Kevin Sharpe and Steven Zwicker. Berkeley, 1987.

– 'Literature and Political Censorship in Early Modern England.' In *Too Mighty to be Free: Censorship and the Press in Britain and the Netherlands*, ed. A.C. Duke and C.A. Tamse. Zutphen, 1987.

– 'English Republicanism.' In *The Cambridge History of Political Thought 1450–1700*, ed. J.H. Burns with Mark Goldie. Cambridge, 1991.

– 'Marchamont Nedham and the Beginnings of English Republicanism, 1649–1656.' In *Republicanism, Liberty, and Commercial Society, 1649–1776*, ed. David Wootton. Stanford, CA, 1994.

– 'Republicanism and Restoration, 1660–1683.' In *Republicanism, Liberty, and Commercial Society, 1649–1776*, ed. David Wootton. Stanford, CA, 1994.

– 'Ben Jonson among the Historians.' In *Culture and Politics in Early Stuart England*, ed. Kevin Sharpe and Peter Lake, 1994.

Wormald, B.H.G. *Francis Bacon: History, Politics and Science, 1561–1626*. Cambridge, 1993.

Wormald, Jenny. 'James VI and I: Two Kings or One?' *History*, 68 (1983), pp. 187–207.

– 'Ecclesiastical Vitriol: The Kirk, the Puritans and the Future King of England.'

In *The Reign of Elizabeth I: Court and Culture in the Last Decade*, ed. John Guy. Cambridge, 1995.
Wortham, Christopher. 'Shakespeare, James I and the Matter of Britain.' *English*, 45. 182 (Summer, 1996), pp. 97–122.
Yates, Frances. *John Florio: The Life of an Italian in Shakespeare's England*. New York, 1968.
Young, Michael B. *Servility and Service: The Life and Work of Sir John Coke*. 1986.
– 'Charles I and the Erosion of Trust, 1625–1628.' *Albion*, 22 (1990), pp. 217–35.
Zagorin, Perez. *A History of Political Thought in the English Revolution*. 1966.
– *Ways of Lying: Dissimulation, Persecution, and Conformity in Early Modern Europe*. Cambridge, MA, and London, 1990.
Zaller, Robert. *The Parliament of 1621*. Berkeley, 1971.
Zanta, L. *La Renaissance du Stoïcisme au XVIe Siècle*. Paris, 1914.
Zapalac, Kristin. *'In His Image and Likeness': Political Iconography and Religious Change in Regensburg, 1500–1600*. Ithaca and London, 1990.
Zeitlin, Jacob. 'The Development of Bacon's Essays – with Special Reference to the Question of Montaigne's Influence upon them.' *Journal of English and German Philology*, 27 (1928), pp. 496–519.
Zwicker, Steven N., and David Bywaters. 'Politics and Translation: The English Tacitus of 1698.' *Huntington Library Quarterly*, 52 (1989), pp. 319–46.

# Index

absolutism, neostoicism and 31, 211; England and 42, 53, 135, 167. *See also* divine right theories; reason of state; state, the, ideas of
Addled Parliament. *See* Parliaments
Albert, archduke, Lipsius and 179
Alençon, François, duke of, suitor of Elizabeth I 32
Alexander the Great, Bacon's use of 80, 82
Alba, duke of 22, 150
Ammirato, Scipione 47
ancient constitution 77
Andrewes, Lancelot, bishop of Winchester 100, 126, 174
Anne of Denmark, Queen of England 46, 194
Antiquaries, Society of 141
Antwerp, emblem of 141; sack of 22
Aristotelianism 11, 27, 105, 135; anti- 74, 87–8
Aristotle, as authority 12, 80, 82, 144, 165
Arminianism 126. *See also* Laud, William
Ascham, Anthony 208–9

Aubrey, John 35, 44, 77, 78, 98, 153, 251n31, 275n93
Augustan age, parallel of 138, 174, 199, 279n15

Bacon, Anthony 35, 189, 285n73, 285n75
Bacon, Sir Edmund, Joseph Hall and 179, 189, 196
Bacon, Francis, Viscount St Albans xix, xxvi, xxvii, xxx, 11, 49, 55, 64, 66, 71–101, 103, 105, 106, 122, 134, 163, 167, 169, 184–5, 188–9, 192, 195; attitudes of 71, 72, 75–7, 78; Caesar and 80, 81, 84, 86, 97; death 97; Essex and xxx, 37, 75–6; Harvey and 74, 83; Lipsius and 83, 97–100, 257n126; Machiavelli and 93; reputation xxx, 72, 76–8, 122, 168, 188–9; rivalry with Coke 77–8, 185; Seneca and 100; 1621 disgrace 77; stoicism and 88–9, 94–5. Works: *Advancement of Learning* 71, 72–5, 78, 79–96, 97, 122; dedicated to James I 81, 185; *Apology* 76, 78, 79; *Apophthegms* 84, 97; *De Augmentis Scientarum* 84, 96, 97; *De Sapientia Veterum* 71, 85;

## Index

*Essayes* 72, 78, 83, 86, 97–101, 124, 126, 131, 141, 184–5, 186; *Henry VII* 97; *New Atlantis* 85, 254n61. *See also* constancy; essay; garden setting; history; humanism; knowledge; language; Lipsian paradigm; metaphor; stoics; Tacitism; virtue; *vita contemplativa*
Bacon, Nicholas, Lord Keeper 72, 189, 285n75
Bancroft, Richard, archbishop of Canterbury 173
Baron, Hans xxv
du Bartas, Guillaume Salluste 112
Bedingfield, Thomas 47, 64
Bellarmine, Robert, Cardinal 153
Bireley, Robert xxiii, 17
Bloom, Harold xxix
Bodin, Jean 23, 27, 31, 167, 277n115
Boethius 3, 41, 49, 52
la Boëtie, Étienne de 116
Bolton, Edmund 56
Botero, Giovanni 47, 58, 81
Bouwsma, William J. xxv
Boyce, Benjamin 192
Bradford, Alan T. 56
Brennan, Michael 112
brevity, technique of 11–12, 15. *See also* language; Senecanism
Buchanan, George 153
Buckingham, George Villiers, duke of 37, 77, 97–100, 108, 139, 143–4, 160, 199, 207. *See also* favourites; Spanish match
Bullough, Geoffrey 79, 104
Burghley, Lord. *See* Cecil, William
Burke, Kenneth xxviii
Burke, Peter 14

Caesar, Julius, Bacon and 80, 81, 84, 86, 97; Ralegh and 66–7

Calvin, John, attitude to the past 23; Seneca and 7, 125
Calvinism xxx, 115, 150; rhetoric of 124–7, 134; stoicism and 7. *See also* language
Camden, William 121, 140
Cameron, James K. xxvi
Carleton, Sir Dudley, 47
Carr, Robert, earl of Somerset 63, 143
Casaubon, Isaac 193; on Tacitus and politic knowledge 56, 79, 80, 87, 122, 193
Cavaliers, 169, 172. *See also* Lovelace, Richard
Cavendish, William, Lord, 145
Cecil, Robert, earl of Salisbury, Essex and 35, 37; Greville and 108, 130, 133; Jonson and 166; Prince Henry's court and 191, 194; Ralegh and 43–6, 48, 50, 51; the Sidneys and 156, 157
Cecil, William, Lord Burghley 35, 50, 72
Chamberlain, John 47, 77, 260n28
Chapman, George 152
Charles I, King 42, 70, 101, 137, 140, 160, 173, 197, 207; Jonson and 169–70
Charron, Pierre xxvii, 49, 52, 57, 62, 66, 87, 92, 123, 125, 132, 283n46. Works: *De la sagesse* 27–31, 159; English translation 50; frontispiece 28. *See also* history; obedience; virtue
Chettle, Henry 161, 275n91
Cheynell, Francis 154
Chillingworth, William 154
Christianity, neostoicism and 4, 6, 109, 126, 154, 172, 180, 182, 186, 192. *See also* providence

Index  333

Church, William 31
Cicero, neostoicism and 12, 15, 18–21, 70, 78, 89, 95, 100, 159, 164
Ciceronians, anti- 11, 19–20, 73
Civil War, English 173, 202–4, 206
Cobham, Henry Brooke, Lord 44
Coke, Sir Edward, attorney-general, later chief justice, Bacon and 77–8, 185; Ralegh and 42–3
Coke, Sir John, 110
Coleridge, Samuel Taylor, on Bacon 72
Commonwealth, English 121, 206–11
constancy, Bacon and 91, 95–6; Greville and 114, 115–17; Jonson and 158–60; Lipsius and xxii, xxv, 3, 8–10, 19, 30, 141, 183; other uses of 41, 52, 175, 195, 196, 208; symbol of 141; du Vair and 47
Constantine, emperor, James I as 174, 279n19
Coornhert, Dirck 15
Cornwallis, William. *See* essay; humanism, English
Cotton, Sir Robert, Sir John Eliot and 207; Jonson and 141, 144; library of 143; Ralegh and 46; Tacitism and 168–9. *See also* Lipsian paradigm
counsel, crisis of xxviii. *See also* humanism, English; *vita activa*
Croll, Morris 11, 12, 21, 104
Cromwell, Oliver, Ralegh and 42, 70
Cuffe, Henry 35, 38

Dallington, Sir Robert 55, 93, 132, 196. Works: *Aphorismes Civill and Militarie* 55–6, 126, 245n76, 287n95; presented to Prince Henry 194, 245n75. *See also prudentia mixta*

Daniel, Samuel 56, 63, 105, 139. Works: *Musophilus* 122; *Philotas* 56, 121, 123. *See also* humanism, English
Davenant, Sir William 131
deceit, Lipsius's three categories of 17, 29
decorum, Jonson and 162
defactoism 127, 208. *See also* state, idea of
Denny, Edward, earl of Norwich 190
dialogue, the, function of 5, 13, 53–4, 222n20; techniques of 21–2, 52–3
Digby, Sir Kenelm 268–9n13
discourse. *See* language
dissimulation, Bacon on 92–5; Greville and 125–7; Hall on 196; King James on 52, 175; Lipsius on 17–20; Nicodemism and 108–9; Ralegh on 64–5. See also *prudentia mixta*; virtue
divine right theories, Greville and 134–5; Hall and 201; John Selden and 148; King James and 56; Ralegh and 56
*doctrina*. *See* learning; Lipsian paradigm
Dollimore, Jonathan 105
Donne, John, Hall's sermons and 174
Dorislaus, Isaac 122, 137, 206, 267n126. *See also* History chair, Cambridge; Tacitism
Drake, Sir Francis 110
Drummond of Hawthornden, William 11, 129, 152, 160, 161
Drury, Lady Anne 173, 189
Drury, Sir Robert 173, 188–90
duty of kings, Jonson on 167–70; Ralegh on 54, 64, 70

duty of subjects. *See* obedience

Earle, John, on Lipsius 13
Egerton, Sir Thomas, lord keeper, later Baron Ellesmere and lord chancellor xxx, 37
Eliot, Sir John, Charles I's policies and 42, 169, 207, 244n67
Elizabeth I, Queen 37, 41–3, 45, 47, 51–2, 63, 107, 108; as Cynthia 38, 51, 161; policies of 32–3, 75, 128–30
Elliott, J.H. xxiii, 17, 31
Elyot, Sir Thomas 174
engagement, oath of 208, 211
Epictetus, Bacon and 88, 94–5, 96; John Healey and 195
Erasmianism 4, 23, 149, 159
Erasmus, Desiderius 4, 11; Luther and 7; Seneca and 7
Erskine-Hill, Howard 172
essay, the function of, Bacon and 72, 78, 83, 86, 98–100, 124; Cornwallis and 86, 124; Hall and 185–6; Montaigne and 13, 24
Essex, Robert Devereau, earl of xxx, 34–9, 62, 76, 78, 96, 107, 123, 130, 163, 168, 237n153, 259n23; circle 35, 43, 45, 75, 80, 109, 131, 134, 237n154, 285n73; personality 37, 259n23; rebellion 38, 45, 77, 107, 120, 188; rivalry with Ralegh 35–40, 50–1, 53–5, 62–3; trial 45, 76, 240n9. *See also* humanism, English; Tacitism
evil, role of in neostoicism 18–19, 93, 126

Falkland, Lucius Cary, 2nd Viscount, 145, 153
family of love 8, 10, 33
favourites, the politics of, 35, 37–8, 41–7, 51–2, 60, 63, 139, 239n5; Bacon on 98–100; Ralegh on 54, 62–4; Sir Robert Cotton and 169. *See also* flattery
Fawkes, Guy 139
flattery, Hall on 185–6; Jonson on 141
Fletcher, R., author of the neostoic verse pamphlet *Mercurius Heliconicus No 2* (1650) 209–11
forest laws 169
fortune, as a force in human affairs, Bacon and 90, 91, 94; Essex and 37; Jonson's use of 138; as literary trope, Ralegh and 51
free will, doctrine of, humanism and 7, 9
Fuller, Thomas 172

garden setting in neostoicism, Bacon and 98–100; Lipsius and 20, 222n20
Garnier, Robert 112
Garver, Eugene 20
Godolphin, Sidney 161
Golding, Sir Arthur 109
Gondomar, Count 197
Grafton, Anthony 24; and Lisa Jardine 74, 82
Great Contract (1610) 168
Great Tew Circle 145, 153
Greville, Fulke, Lord Brooke xix, xxvii, 102–37, 158, 188, 200, 206, 208; death 108; Essex and 35, 39, 76, 107, 130, 134; Montaigne and 116–18; personality 109–11; problem of closure in 118; reputation 76–7, 104–5, 108, 120, 260n28; Sidney and xxx–xxxi, 33, 35, 77, 105–7, 110–11, 116; Sidney's *Arcadia* and 33, 111–12; use of verse 43, 135–6. Works: *Alaham* 116; *Caelica* 110, 116, 125;

Index 335

*Fame and Honour* 104; *Humane Learning* 119, 122–8; *Letter to an Honourable Lady* 110, 112–16, 118, 119, 125, 208; *Life of Sidney* 103, 105, 111–12, 127, 128–32; *Monarchy* 103, 127, 132–3, 135–6; *Mustapha* 102, 116–18, 134, 136; *Of Religion* 102, 104, 119, 120; *Of Warres* 104, 266n115. *See also* constancy; history; humanism, English; language; Lipsian paradigm; metaphor; Tacitism; virtue
Grotius, Hugo xxii
Guicciardini, Francesco 55–6, 194; Tacitus and 14
Gunpowder Plot 151, 152, 196

Hall, Joseph, bishop of Norwich xix, xxiv, xxvii, xxxi, 49, 131, 171–205, 206, 271n46; ambition 173–4, 179, 184, 187, 192–3; Bacon and 184–9, 285n76; education 173; Lipsius and xxxi, 174–84, 201, 202–5; portrait of 181; reputation 171–2, 178, 182, 197, 201; Seneca and 172, 182; sobriquets xxiv, 172, 197; Tacitism and 194–6; Theophrastus and 192–3. Works: *The Arte of Divine Meditation* 180, 182, 188; *Cases of Conscience* 200, 203, 290n131; *Certain Irrefragable Propositions* 204; *Characters of Vertues and Vices* 180, 183–4, 192, 200; *Epistles* 180, 183–5, 190–1, 198–9, 200, 202, 282n39, 285n76; *Heaven Upon Earth* 171–2, 180, 182; *The King's Prophecie* 171, 173; *Meditations and Vowes* 171–2, 180, 182, 186–7, 198, 200; *Mundus Alter et Idem* 175–80, 194; *Quo Vadis* 180, 282n40; *Sermons* 199; *The Shaking of the Olive-Tree* 181; *Virgidimiae* 173. *See also* humanism, English; Lipsian paradigm; obedience
Hammond, Henry 154
Hampton Court conference 196
Hariman, Robert 17
Harington, Sir John, on Essex 51
Harvey, Gabriel 74; Bacon and 82, 83, 92
Hastings, Sir Francis 188
Hastings, Henry, 3rd earl of Huntington 173, 188
Hayward, Sir John 38, 120–1
Healey, John 194–6. *See also* humanism, English
Heath, Sir Robert, attorney-general, later chief justice 143
Henry III, King of France 27
Henry IV, King of France 26, 30, 31, 107, 130, 153, 164
Henry Stuart, prince of Wales xxx, 46–8, 50, 52, 57, 66, 82, 131–3, 136, 156, 174–5, 184–5, 190–1, 194–5, 199
Herbert, Mary, countess of Pembroke. *See* humanism, English
Herbert, William, earl of Pembroke 143–4, 145, 156–7, 194, 196, 199; Jonson's *Catiline* dedicated to 166
Hill, Christopher 46
history, lessons of xx, xxv; Bacon and 91; Charron and 27; Greville and 137; Lipsius and 9–10, 13, 20, 22, 31; Ralegh and 49, 53–5, 65–7; Tacitean 14, 35, 168–9. *See also* similitudo temporum
History chair, Cambridge 121–2, 137, 207, 267n126. *See also* Dorislaus, Isaac
Hobbes, Thomas xxii, 78, 145, 251n31
Holles, Sir John 108, 109

336  Index

Horace, as model for Jonson 138, 154–5, 161, 275n91
Howard, Catherine, countess of Suffolk 108
Howard, Henry, earl of Northampton, Grenville and 108; Jonson and 139, 164; Prince Henry's court and 191, 194; Ralegh and 43, 44–6, 48; Sir Robert Cotton and 141
humanism, English 31–9, 206, 247n119; Bacon and 79–87; Essex and 35–9; Greville and 120–8; Hall and 173, 182–4, 185–96; John Healey and 195; Jonson and 146–9, 160–9; Mary Herbert and 111, 121, 123, 128; Samuel Daniel and 122–4; William Cornwallis and 86, 90, 93, 124, 132. *See also* learning; Lipsian paradigm; neostoicism; virtue; *vita activa*
humanism, modern debate over xxii, xxv–xxvii, 18, 23–4, 47, 74, 75, 104, 216n17, 219n39, 220n8, 231n97, 258n7
Huntington, earl of. *See* Hastings, Henry
Huntley, F.L. 174, 187

idols of learning 78
Interregnum xxi, 204, 205. *See also* Commonwealth, English; republicanism, classical

James VI and I, King 37, 41–6, 56, 79, 100, 108, 134, 153, 160, 166, 168, 172, 173, 193, 272n62; Essex and 55, 76; Lipsius and xxx, 24, 52, 175; motto 82; policy towards Spain 42, 143, 156–7, 199; politic learning and 121, 130; Ralegh's *History of the World* and 46; Tacitus and 56. Works: *Basilikon Doron* 52, 174–5, 192; *Trew Law of Free Monarchies* 52
Javitch, Daniel xxv
Jesuits, English attitudes towards 128, 151, 153, 175, 179, 187, 272n62
Jones, Inigo 139
Jonson, Ben xix, xxvii, 11, 35, 43, 46, 67–70, 106, 129, 138–70, 186; classicism and xxxi, 145–6, 155, 160–1; impresa 141; Lipsius and 138, 155; motto 155–6; personality 139–40, 160; religion and 149–55; Sir Philip Sidney and xxxi, 160–2. Works: *The Alchemist* 146, 152; *Bartholomew Fair* 146, 271n46; *Catiline* 121, 144, 163–6; *Cynthia's Revels* 161; *Discoveries* 138, 146, 168; *Eastward Ho* 139, 141, 152; 'Epistle to Master John Selden' 140, 147–8, 268n13; 'Epistle to the Countess of Rutland' 157; 'Execration upon Vulcan' 148; *Golden Age Restor'd* 143; *Isle of Dogs* 139; 'A New Year's Gift' 169–70; 'On the Union' 160; *Pleasure Reconciled to Virtue* 144; *Poetaster* 161; *Sejanus* 43, 56, 121, 139, 163–4, 240n9; 'To my Muse' 141; 'To Penshurst' 157–8, 163; 'To Sir Robert Wroth' 157–8. *See also* constancy; decorum; humanism, English; language; Lipsian paradigm; Tacitism
Juvenal, as model for Jonson 138, 145

Kahn, Victoria xxvi
Keohane, Nannerl O. 29
knowledge, as scientia 72; Bacon's category of civil 88, 90–1, 95–6; debate on extent of 119–20, 122–8; need for reform of 73–5, 87. *See also*

humanism, English; learning; reason
Kristeller, Paul O. xxv
Kuhn, Thomas xx, 213n2

Lambarde, William 38
Lambeth Articles (1595) 148, 152
language, Baconian 84, 93–6, 98–100, 188; Greville's Calvinist 103, 124–7, 133–4, 135, 158, 208, 262n55; Jonsonian 158, 160–3; Lipsian 106, 116, 178, 182, 187, 224n35; neostoicism and xxvii–xxx, 15–16, 19, 24, 30, 117, 135, 165; Senecan 11–12, 15, 178; Tacitean 10–11, 13–15, 36, 86, 105, 184, 195, 197; virtue and 61–4, 135, 158, 165. *See also* metaphor; rhetoric; virtue
Languet, Hubert 32
Latin, use of xx, 20, 97, 179, 213n5; Lipsius and 13, 23–4; translations from xx, 15, 18, 26, 195, 271n39; translations to 97, 195
Laud, William, archbishop of Canterbury 122, 197, 201
*laudando praecipere*, humanist principle of 141
learning, debate over role of in society 21–4, 30–2, 39, 72–90, 96, 121–8, 133, 146–9, 155; as *doctrina* 21–4, 31, 34, 36, 66, 112, 231n91; politic 76, 121–2, 186. *See also* humanism, English; Lipsian paradigm
Lefranc, Pierre 47
Leicester, Robert Dudley, earl of 16, 32, 34–5, 37, 106, 110, 130, 150
Lennard, Samson 159, 194
Levy, F.J. xxv, 35, 38, 75, 79, 89, 92
Lipsian paradigm xix–xxvii, 3–24, 31; Bacon and 72, 86; Greville and 106,

112; Hall and 182, 191, 196, 205; Interregnum England and 211; Jonson and 138, 147, 149, 155, 156; Ralegh and 62, 66; Sidney and 32, 34, 112; Sir Robert Cotton and 168–9. *See also* neostoicism
Lipsius, Justus xix–xxi, 3–34, 36–7, 46–7, 56–8, 82, 88, 91, 94, 103, 109, 134, 140, 149, 155, 166, 167, 169, 175, 176, 195, 209; Calvin and 7; criticisms of xxx, 24, 31, 52, 79, 175–84, 281n31; cult of (in Spain) 26; Epictetus and 254n72; family of love and 8, 10, 33; humanism and xxvi, 22–4; Machiavelli and xxiii, 17–21, 215n10; Montaigne and 12–13; motto 24, 170, 214n6, 257n126; parodies of 176, 178, 280n24; Philip Sidney and 32–4, 36, 112; portrait of xxi, 177, 214n6, 280n24; Ramus and 255n83; religious peregrinations of xxv, 24, 149–50, 175; self-portrait xix; Seneca and 4, 21–4; Tacitus and 4, 9, 10–11, 16, 18, 20–4, 32, 137, 164, 227n53; textualism of 20–1. Works: *Antiquae Lectiones* 145; *De constantia* xx, xxii, 3, 5–15, 20–4, 26, 33–4, 49, 61, 115, 169, 175; *De Militia Romana* xxiii, 79, 156, 233n113; *Diva Virgo Hallensis* 179; *Epistolae* 184, 283n52; *Opera Omnia*, 1675 frontispiece of 24–5; *Politica* xx, xxii, 3, 5–6, 16–21, 26, 31, 67, 86, 131, 147, 207, 271n39; translations of 18, 26, 271n39. *See also* dialogue; history; language; Latin; Lipsian paradigm; metaphor; providence; prudence; *prudentia mixta*; rhetoric; stoicism
Lockyer, Andrew xxvii, 23
Lodge, Thomas 15, 283n47

Loe, William 31
Lofstedt, Einar 14
Lovelace, Richard 201–2. *See also* Cavaliers
Luther, Martin 6, 7

Machiavelli, Nicolo xxiii, 11, 134, 164, 167, 189, 209; humanism and 17–18; Lipsius and 17, 18–21, 215n10; republicanism and xxix; *virtù* and xxiii, 17. Works: *Discourses* xxix, 189; *History of Florence* 47; *The Prince* 31
Machiavellism 16–17, 26, 92, 136, 246n88, 256n96; anti- xxiii, 31, 58
Malvezzi, Virgilio 9
Mariana, Juan de 153
Martial, as model for Jonson 138, 145
Marvell, Andrew 209, 211
Marwil, Jonathan 72
Mary, Queen of Scots 45, 153
Maus, Katharine E. 155
May, Steven 44, 53
McCabe, Richard A. 178, 198
Melanchthon, Philip 21, 231n91
*mens adepta* (stoic 'right reason'), debated 5, 114–15, 119, 129. *See also* reason
metaphor, uses of, Bacon and 84, 87 (medical); Greville and 133–4 (*melancholia*); Lipsius and 8, 15–16, 222n23, 228n64, 228n65 (medical), 19, 230n77 (nautical), 22 (*theatrum mundi*); neostoicism and 16; Ralegh and 58–9, 243n45 (*theatrum mundi*). *See also* language
Montaigne, Michel de xxii, xxv, 11–12, 23, 26–7, 35, 62, 116, 123; irenicism of 13; Lipsius and 12–13; reason and 12, 118. Works: *Essais* 13. *See also* essay
Nantes, Edict of 153
Narcissus, fable of, Bacon and 85
natural rights theories xxii, 203
Navarre, Henry of. *See* Henry IV, King of France
Nedham, Marchamont 208–9
neostoicism, as discipline 12; France and 26–31; gardens and 20, 98–100, 222n20; as a language and method xx, 5, 15, 21–4, 106, 116, 126, 145, 158, 186, 192, 211, 283n46; as political engagement xx, 4–5, 10, 22–3, 34, 67, 131, 206–7
Nero, as historical *exemplum* 36, 56, 80, 252n46
Niclaes, Hendrik, of Westphalia 8. *See also* family of love
Nicodemism 108. *See also* dissimulation
Niethammer, F.J. xxv
Norbrook, David 105–6, 116, 150, 170
Northumberland, Henry Percy, earl of 44

obedience, the politics of xxii; Bacon and 75–8, 89, 92–3, 100–1; Charron and 29; Duvergier and 30; Greville and 108, 114–15, 118, 134; Hall and 200–5; Interregnum England and 208–11; Jonson and 155, 157–60; Lipsius and 12–13, 24, 150; Ralegh and 54, 60. *See also* language; virtue
*obscura brevitas*, technique of 15. *See also* brevity; language; Senecanism; Tacitism
Oestreich, Gerhard xxiii, 12
Overbury, Sir Thomas 63

Index  339

*paradiastole*, rhetorical figure of, Lipsius and 20
Parliaments: of 1593 75, 136–7; of 1614 (Addled) 52; of 1628 143
Parma, duke of 150
Parry, Graham 145
Patterson, Annabel 168
patriotism, as an issue in neostoicism 6, 13, 20, 27
Pembroke, earl of. *See* Herbert, William
Perez, Antonio 35
Petition of Right 121, 244n67
Pius V, Pope, admired by Bacon 80
Plantin Press, 232n108, 268n14; impresa of 141
Plato's Commonwealth (Ciceronian trope) 21, 24, 120
du Plessis-Mornay, Philippe 109, 112
Pocock, J.G.A. xxvii, 217n28, 262n55
*politiques*, French 26; Bacon's category of 73, 80
Polybius xxiii, xxix
Pope, Alexander 76
precedents, role of. *See* history, lessons of
Presbyterians, the Civil War and 201, 204; Hall and 196–7. *See also* Puritans
Preston, John, Greville and 126
prophecy 33. *See also* family of love
providence, doctrine of, Bacon and 90, 93; Greville and 129; Hall and 180; Lipsius and 6–9; Ralegh and 49, 70
prudence, discussion of xxii, xxxi, 3, 16, 20; as wisdom 21, 27, 29, 60–2, 95. *See also* language; *prudentia mixta*; virtue
*prudentia mixta* xxiii, xxv; Commonwealth apologists and 209; constancy and 19; dissimulation and 17; Greville and 120–1, 125–8, 131; Jonson and 165; Lipsius and 3, 16–21, 94–5; Machiavellian *virtù* and 17; Ralegh and 56–65; Robert Dallington and 55–7, 92, 126. *See also* dissimulation; language; virtue
Puritanism xxiv
Puritans, satirized by Jonson 145–6, 149; Archbishop Bancroft's policy towards 173; James I on 153, 272n62. *See also* Presbyterians

*qui nescit dissimulare, nescit regnare* (Tacitean aphorism) 16, 115, 209–10, 282n40. *See also* dissimulation
Quint, David xxvi

Raab, Felix 17
Ralegh, Sir Walter xix, xxvii, 35, 39, 40–70, 103, 105–6, 129, 132, 134–5, 143, 169; attitude towards death 48–9; career 41–8; Charron and 66; death 48, 242n31; on dissimulation 64–5; Essex and xxx, 40, 50–1, 53–5, 62–3; Prince Henry and xxx, 46–8, 57; on relationship between virtue and language 61–4, 66; reputation 40–1, 44, 46–7, 242n31; on Spain 65; trial 42–3, 163–4. Works: *Cabinet-Council* 47, 64, 207, 247n108; *History of the World* 40, 46–7, 49, 52, 56, 64–7, 129, 168; banned by James I 46, 121; frontispiece 68–9; *Instructions to his Son* 40, 46, 60–2; *Maxims of State* 47, 57; Poems 51, 59, 62; *Prerogative of Parliaments* 46, 51, 52–4, 63. *See also* language; Lipsian paradigm; *prudentia mixta*; stoics; Tacitism; tyranny; virtue

Ralegh, Young Wat 60, 144
Ramus, Peter 74, 255n83; Bacon and 83, 87, 89, 95
Ravaillac, François 153
reason, debate over, Bacon and 87–98; Charron and 29, 234n122; Greville and 116–19, 125–8; Hall and 172, 182; Lipsius and 5, 6, 9; Montaigne and 12, 23. See also *mens adepta*; stoics
reason of state 17–18, 26, 29, 31, 58, 132, 164
Rebholz, Ronald 104, 108, 130
Rees, Joan 105, 111
republicanism, classical xxix, 33, 159, 211
rhetoric, debate between philosophy and 21–4, 87–90, 135; functions of 19–21, 23, 89–90, 186–8; techniques of xxv, 8, 13, 20, 133, 141, 190, 208. See also metaphor; virtue
Richard II, as conceit 53–5, 63; drama of 38, 40. See also favourites
Richelieu, Cardinal 31, 47, 72
Roe, Sir Thomas 154
Rome, as *exemplum* 26, 33–4, 37, 47, 66–7, 80, 138, 209, 233n113. See also republicanism, classical; virtue
Romulus, state of (Ciceronian trope) 21, 24, 57, 120
Root and Branch Campaign 201
Rubens, Peter Paul 24, 280–1n24
Rubens, Philip 24
Russell, Francis, 4th earl of Bedford 289n123

Sackville, Sir Edward, later earl of Dorset 157
sage, theories of the, 29–30, 111, 192
Saint Bartholomew's Day, 1572 massacre of, 17, 24

Salisbury, earl of. See Cecil, Robert
Salmon, J.H.M. xxiv, 164
Sampson, Margaret 200
Sanford, Hugh 111
Savile, Sir Henry 35, 38, 162, 168, 238n162; translator of Tacitus's *Histories* 36
Scaliger, Joseph xxvi, 79
Schellhase, Kenneth C. 14, 83
Scipio the Younger, as literary parallel 130
Scott, Jonathan xxix, 208
Sejanus, Aelius, as historical parallel 207. See also Jonson, Ben, Works
Selden, John 140, 143–4, 146, 148–9
self-censorship, Greville and 130; Ralegh and 52, 61
Seneca xx, 3, 7, 19, 24, 37, 41, 49, 52, 80, 82, 154, 159, 167; attitudes towards 7, 37, 49; as authority 49, 83, 86, 89, 155; Bacon and 100–1; Hall and 172, 182; Lipsius and 4, 21–4; studied in universities 4. Works: *Epistles* to Lucilius 100; *Opera*, ed Erasmus 4; ed Lipsius 24, 177, 178, 183. See also Senecanism
Senecan drama 103, 110, 112, 116, 123
Senecanism 11–20, 114
separatists, religious. See Puritans
Sextus V, Pope, admired by Bacon 80
Sharpe, Kevin 140, 143; and Peter Lake xxix
Sidney, Algernon xxix, 159, 208
Sidney family 144–5, 156–7
Sidney, Sir Philip xxx–xxxi, 32–4, 46, 77, 105–7, 116, 275n93; education and career 32; legacy of 34, 107–8, 112, 133, 137, 160–1, 196, 208; Lipsius and 15–16, 32–4, 36, 112, 137; as model of virtue 32, 34, 112, 128–9;

as stoic sage 111. Works: *Arcadia* 32–3, 110–12; *Defense of Poesie* 32, 160. *See also* Greville, Fulke; humanism, English; learning; Tacitism; virtue
Sidney, Sir Robert 32, 45, 60, 145, 156; Essex and 76; Lipsius and 46; Tacitus and 50. *See also* Tacitism
*similitudo temporum* (humanist trope) xxvii, 22–4, 33, 36, 38, 50, 128–9, 209. *See also* history; humanism; Lipsian paradigm; metaphor
Skinner, Quentin xxii, xxiv, xxviii, 20, 217n28
Smuts, R. Malcolm 36
Socinianism 153–4
Socrates, Duvergier and 30; Lipsius and 5; Ralegh and 61
Solomon, King, as authority 61; James I as 198, 279n19
Somerset, earl of. *See* Carr, Robert
Sommerville, J.P. 53
Southwell, Robert, SJ, admired by Jonson 151–2
Spanish match 197–200
Spedding, James 91
Spenser, Edmund 135
Spenser, Gabriel 150
Starkey, David xxvi
state, the, ideas of 12, 29–30, 47, 159, 208, 211
statism. *See* reason of state
stoicism, Christian 3–4, 49, 172, 186; classical xxiv, 7, 21–2, 109, 222n17, 230n89
stoics, the, Bacon and 88–9; criticisms of 10, 89, 119, 175, 187, 225n37; and death 48–9, 243n45; priority of reason for 6, 88, 116; Ralegh and 48, 67, 243n45; revival of ethics of xxiv, 158, 182; and suicide 30. *See also* Epictetus; *mens adepta*; Seneca
Strathmann, Ernest A. 47, 60, 64
Stuart, Lady Arabella 42
succession question 43, 46, 63
Syme, Sir Ronald 15

Tacitism xxii, 14, 26, 31, 55, 121–2, 206–8; anti- 56, 79, 130, 191–6; Bacon and 79–87; Dorislaus and 207; Essex and 35–7, 50; Greville and 136; Jonson and 162–5; Machiavelli and 17; Pembroke and 194; Ralegh and 63–5; Robert Sidney and 32, 163, 243n52. *See also* language; history
Tacitus, Cornelius xx, 7, 19, 37, 183; as authority 22, 37, 41, 56, 86, 163, 207–8. Works: *Agricola* 20, 31, 36; *Annals* 20–2, 164, 207, 243n52; *Histories* 20, 36; *Opera*, ed Lipsius 13–14, 24, 32, 142, 178, 243n52; translation of 36, 50, 162. *See also* Tacitism
Tennenhouse, Leonard 52
Theophrastus 191–2
Thirty Years War 199, 242n31
Thompson, I.A.A. xxiii
Tiberius, emperor, as historical parallel 16, 43, 99, 207
Todd, Margo 148
Toffanin, Guiseppe 23, 227n57
toleration, religious, question of 9, 15, 22, 152
Tourney, Leonard D. 178
Tracy, James D. xxvi
Thrasea, Clodius Paetus, stoic martyr 10
Trevelyan, G.M. 42
Tuck, Richard xxii, 26, 47, 82
tyranny, Charles I charged with com-

mitting 137, 207; Essex and 38; Greville and 113, 116–17, 135; King James and 56, 252n46; Ralegh and 54–5, value of Tacitus on 14

du Vair, Guillaume xxvii, 27
Villiers, George. *See* Buckingham, duke
virtue, problem of disjuncture between private and public xx, 20; Bacon and 89–93; Charron and 30; Greville and 114–16, 126–8, 129, 132–4; political 39, 41, 64, 72, 103, 118, 126–7, 131–4; as prudence 21, 26, 95, 165; public 10, 62, 89, 93, 158, 170, 205; Ralegh and 57–80, 62–6; Roman xxiii, 20, 33, 74, 100, 156, 159, 167; rhetoric of 17, 62, 89–90; Sidney as model of 32, 34, 112, 128–9. *See also* language, Lipsian paradigm, *prudentia mixta*
virtuoso, cult of the 73
*vita activa*, the, humanist principle of xxvii, 32, 39, 48, 72–3, 96, 124, 206, 211
*vita contemplativa*, the, Bacon and 96–101

Vives, Juan Luis 167

Walker, B. 15
Wallace, Dewey 148, 154
Walsingham, Sir Francis 34, 110
wars of religion, European, impact of on humanism xxii, xxiv, 6, 12, 13, 26, 33, 73, 110, 120, 128, 129, 160, 205, 206
Wechel Press, Frankfurt, Lipsius and 24
Wedgwood, C.V. 207
Whig historiography 201
Whitgift, John, archbishop of Canterbury 152
William, prince of Orange 32
Williams, John, bishop of Lincoln 158
Woolf, D.R. 122
Worden, Blair 209
Wotton, Sir Henry xxiv, 35, 37, 197, 237n153, 259n23
Woverius, Johannes 24

Zagorin, Perez 108
Zeno, as a literary convention 19, 23, 232n103; Bacon and 89

GENERAL THEOLOGICAL SEMINARY
NEW YORK